# WAR OF ATTRITION

ALSO BY WILLIAM PHILPOTT

*Three Armies on the Somme:*
*The First Battle of the Twentieth Century*

# WAR OF ATTRITION

## FIGHTING THE FIRST WORLD WAR

WILLIAM PHILPOTT

THE OVERLOOK PRESS
NEW YORK, NY

This edition first published in hardcover in the United States in 2014 by
The Overlook Press, Peter Mayer Publishers, Inc.

141 Wooster Street
New York, NY 10012
www.overlookpress.com
For bulk and special sales, please contact sales@overlookny.com,
or write us at the above address.

Cataloging-in-Publication Data is available from the Library of Congress

*Book design and typeformatting by Bernard Schleifer*
Manufactured in the United States of America
ISBN 978-1-4683-0268-4
FIRST EDITION
10  9  8  7  6  5  4  3  2

*This book is dedicated to the memory of my mother*
*Ruby May Philpott*
*1928–2009*

# CONTENTS

# LIST OF ABBREVIATIONS
## IN TEXT AND FOOTNOTES

| | |
|---|---|
| AAT | *Service historique de la défense, Archives de l'armée de terre* |
| BEF | British Expeditionary Force |
| CIGS | Chief of the Imperial General Staff |
| CA | *Corps d'armée* (French Army Corps) |
| DI | *Division d'infanterie* (French infantry division) |
| GHQ | British General Headquarters |
| GQG | *Grand quartier général* (French general headquarters) |
| NCO | Noncommissioned officer |
| OHL | Oberste Heeresleitung (German supreme army general headquarters) |
| SPD | German Social Democratic Party |
| SWC | Allied Supreme War Council |
| TNA | The National Archives, Kew |

# NOTE ON MILITARY ORGANISATION

European armies were able to field millions of men in the First World War. To command, control and administer them a rigid structure was needed, and each army was organised along similar lines. Subordinate to the commander in chief there were army groups, commanded by senior generals. Each army group comprised two or three armies, each commanded by a general (the British army did not have army groups, the British armies in France and Flanders formed after January 1915 effectively comprising a single army group). An army was composed of a number of army corps, typically three or four per army, each commanded by lieutenant-generals, with attached air, heavy artillery and later tank units. An army corps was made up of divisions commanded by major-generals. Early war army corps usually had two divisions, but from 1915 three or four divisions was the norm, with supporting units being attached as required. Divisions were all-arms units (with infantry, field artillery, cavalry, engineers and supporting services) organised to fight as independent units, and were the basic tactical building blocks of armies. Each division was divided into brigades, each commanded by a brigadier-general. Continental divisions typically had two brigades of infantry, each comprised of two regiments of three infantry battalions, plus an artillery brigade or regiment of field gun batteries. From 1915 continental armies reduced infantry battalions to nine per division, eliminating the brigade level of command in favour of the regiment commanded by a colonel. For much of the war British divisions were organised into three brigades, each with four battalions, with three supporting field artillery brigades. In 1918 British infantry brigades were reduced to a three-battalion strength. Infantry battalions commanded by lieutenant-colonels were around 1,000 men strong in 1914, and had four infantry companies commanded by majors or captains. All armies decreased battalion size as the war went on, with a machine-gun company often replacing one of the infantry companies.

# SEIZING THE HINDENBURG LINE

In late September 1918 Captain Alban Bacon of the Hampshire Regiment visited an artillery battery that was to support his battalion's next attack. 'I was greeted with great good will by the Gunner Officers,' he recollected:

> They had also heard that every infantry solider in France was going "over the top" on the following morning, and prayed that it might not rain too hard, for, if so, the guns would be mud-logged, and unable to move to support the infantry. Armageddon was evidently set. A last great push was about to be called for to free France from Hohenzollern shackles. In any case, I was given an excellent lunch, to an orchestra of their guns.[1]

The roar and whoosh of gunfire was nothing new. The First World War had recently entered its fifth year, and soldiers had grown used to bombardments. Still, the cacophony of thousands of guns launching hundreds of thousands of shells through the air never failed to surprise and shock, especially since it presaged another attack and close, bloody combat. The British, American, Australian and French soldiers who sheltered in their front trenches in Picardy were naturally apprehensive. Although many were veterans by now, accustomed to the sounds and actions of battle and trained to advance confidently across no man's land into the enemy's trenches, an attack still meant danger, wounds, and death. They knew that many of them would not survive it, although by autumn 1918 many had become inured and fatalistic. If their time had come, they appreciated that their personal sacrifice would help to seal the fate of the German army, which was on its last legs after four years of sustained attrition. At the same time, among the troops 'spirits were high for this must be the final goodbye to trench warfare at last'.[2] As always the coming attack would be a test of flesh and blood, but it would also be a vindication of fire and steel.

In late September 1918 battle was raging along the whole length of the western front in France and Belgium. Allied generalissimo Marshal Ferdinand Foch had just launched a carefully orchestrated offensive to break the German army once and for all and British, French, American, Belgian and Italian troops were striking at the German defences. An attack at first light on 29 September would be the culminating blow, against the centre of the Hindenburg Line that the German army had constructed over the winter of 1916 as a final line of defence. This was a formidable defensive system, comprising three successive defensive positions up to nine kilometres deep. Its trenches were sited so as to be hard to target with artillery fire and were heavily wired and reinforced with concrete strongpoints and antitank ditches. 'Such defences are valid against primitive opponents, but against the full mechanical resources of a well-equipped army seem to be, in the end, futile,' artillery officer Lieutenant Richard Dixon believed. 'And Germany was now up against a mighty concentration of power built up over four years by Britain and her Dominions. Masses of artillery and tanks were ready to go into action to smash through the famous Hindenburg Line and we in the 53rd Brigade were a small part of that huge and – as it proved – irresistible concentration.'[3] After four years of combat the Allied armies now had the means and skill to assault it, while the German army no longer possessed the manpower and resolve needed to hold it. 'Within the last four weeks we had captured 77,000 prisoners and nearly 800 guns!' Field Marshal Sir Douglas Haig noted proudly. 'There has never been such a victory in the annals of Britain . . . The discipline of the German army is quickly going, and the German officer is no longer what he was . . . The enemy's troops will not await our attacks even on the strongest positions.'[4]

Between 1914 and 1918 warfare had changed its nature. Attrition, the cumulative exhaustion of the enemy's fighting capacity, had done its work. When the attacking companies left their trenches, they followed a raging wall of artillery fire across no man's land that protected them until they were within the enemy's defences. The enemy soldiers they encountered there were still brave but outnumbered and exhausted. The raw American troops attacking on the northern end of British Fourth Army's front, across the Bellicourt tunnel that bridged the St Quentin Canal at this point, were engaged by machine-gun and artillery fire and the Australian battalions coming up in support found themselves sucked into the fight. There the attack seemed to be checked. But to the south British troops of the 46th Division supported by 'probably the heaviest weight of artillery fire ever to accompany the attack of a single British division' had crossed the St Quentin Canal under the cover of early morning fog and pushed on into the centre of the German defences.[5] Many dazed German soldiers were caught in their underground shelters by this dynamic attack and faced the choice of surrender or death in their holes. Those gaunt prisoners that emerged into the daylight were dressed in faded and patched uniforms. Over four years the Allied blockade had deprived Germany and her allies of food, industrial raw materials, and manufactured goods, and the sorry state of her army was a reflection of the parlous living standards which now afflicted Germany's home front. French troops attacking on either side of St Quentin extended the penetration further south, but their progress was slow as the enemy put up fierce resistance. German counterattacks were desperate but generally doomed to failure. With German divisions seriously undermanned and fresh reserves unobtainable, there were simply not enough men to defend such a position by autumn 1918, nor the necessary enthusiasm for the fight. 'Three quarters of the men here wish an end, no matter how. It is only discipline keeping them still together, no more if and buts of politics,' Heinrich Aufderstrasse wrote home: 'The enemy has given us "Republic" as a password for defection' and many men were taking advantage of the opportunity to desert the army and the kaiser's imperial regime which it represented.[6] It required only one week of intensive fighting for the Hindenburg Line to fall into Allied hands. A defensive position judged impregnable in 1916 was no match for the techniques and military technology that the Allies could now deploy against it. Behind the Hindenburg Line there were only partly constructed defences for the disintegrating German army to fall back on as the empire's leaders sought an armistice against a background of domestic political upheaval. Fighting was still fierce until Armistice Day, 11 November 1918, but the Allied war machine was now unstoppable and the German army more or less spent.

Since 1914 Germany had turned most of the world against her with her actions on land and at sea. At home her people had endured hunger and shortages while her civilian politicians had been largely silenced as her military leadership had staked the nation in an all-or-nothing struggle for supremacy in Europe. Her allies were near to collapse too: Bulgaria had sued for an armistice a few days earlier and Turkey and Austria-Hungary would soon do the same. The Great War had taken a great deal out of Germany's opponents too, but they had proved resilient, resolute, and well resourced – advantages which Germany could never match. While Germany had torn herself apart in waging an unwinnable war, her adversaries had come together, united in their shared sense of purpose, organised into a collaborative war effort and sustained through a popular consensus that the war was just. The only way to win a war that pitted coalitions of industrialised empires against each other was through a process of mass mobilisation and sustained attrition.

Although casualties mounted as the war went on, a collective sense of justice, personal engagement and cumulative military success sustained one side's will to victory. The First World War ended decisively on the battlefield, but the effort of waging it had shattered empires and challenged the values of the societies that fought. Rather than glorious victory followed by peace, its legacy would be a century of seemingly interminable conflict and upheaval.

# WAR OF ATTRITION

# INTRODUCTION
## 'THE WAR IS EVERYTHING'

'The war is everything: it is noble, filthy, great, petty, degrading, inspiring, ridiculous, glorious, mad, bad, hopeless yet full of hope. I don't know what to think about it.'

—BRUCE CUMMINGS, July 1916.[1]

BRUCE CUMMINGS, ZOOLOGIST AND DIARIST, STRUGGLED IN JULY 1916 to come to grips with the war of which he was a reluctant spectator: in November 1915 a medical board had passed him unfit to serve, and revealed to him that he was suffering from the multiple sclerosis that was to kill him shortly after the war's end. He could not join the war and seek a hero's death like so many of his contemporaries. Nor could he escape it: 'And the war? What may not have happened by this time next year?'[2]

By its mid point in 1916, the First World War had become all consuming, its beginning no longer remembered, its end impossible to foresee, its scale vast and growing and its course relentless, sucking in and spitting out humanity. Begrimed soldiers at the front, men and women working on home front production lines, home-sick sailors on the warships and merchantmen that kept the whole military machine running were all playing their small part; doing their bit. The statesmen and soldiers who claimed to control and direct the great military enterprise seemed to be floundering, pushing for victory yet unable to conceive the nature of peace, or how it might be achieved: if no longer at a reasonable cost, at least in a form that justified the sacrifice of millions of men and the disruption of everyone's life.

Although the Allies' victory medal would proclaim it 'the Great War for Civilization, 1914–1919', a century later one cannot but reflect on the irony in that statement; and perhaps that irony was not lost on those trying to make sense of a war more extensive, barbaric and devastating than any previous conflict. That the war was great no one could deny; that it was civilized none would argue; that it changed the world for the better few could see. Surveying the world made by war and knowing the devastating global ideological confrontations it spawned certainly does not give much credence to lingering claims of civilization. Appreciating how and why the great powers that dominated the globe before 1914 chose to make war among themselves and to fight on to a bitter, self-destructive end is nonetheless necessary: not least because their Great War determined the world's cleavages and conflicts thereafter.

The German military philosopher Carl von Clausewitz's famous dictum that war would be the pursuit of state policy by other means held sway in Europe's previous phase of great power conflict. In the mid-nineteenth century professional armies had been entrusted with conducting wars and statesmen with negotiating their outcomes. Yet the naïve perception that war might be limited by the objectives of statesmen was passing as a new century began. War was clearly changing its nature, if not its purpose. Society and economy had altered significantly in the past fifty years, locked in a tightening symbiosis with the state's capacity to make war. Moreover, the people and their passions, Clausewitz had warned, were the third volatile element which statesmen and soldiers would have to factor into any conflict. It was an age of mass education and literacy in which a growing print media preached issues and causes to ordinary men and women in strident, simplistic forms. Although the decisions of quasi-absolute monarchs still determined the fate of many Europeans, and ministers, diplomats and generals had a free hand almost everywhere, their actions were not immune from the approval or censure of public opinion, suggesting that the early twentieth-century world was modern and different. Armies had certainly changed from the professional forces of the previous century. Now continental states raised huge conscript forces that represented their societies, equipped with the best modern weaponry science and industry could invent and manufacture. In increasingly urbanised and industrialised empires, were the people now citizens with rights, or did they remain the subjects of emperors who expected steadfast loyalty to the nation's cause? They might be led to war, and sacrificed in battle; but in the new type of war would they be willing participants or demanding collaborators? Would the people finish a war which statesmen had started, and if so to what purpose? Those questions would be asked and answered once the transformative processes of warfare – Leon Trotsky's 'locomotive of history' – swept societies up in a frantic, bloody torrent in which all would be flotsam.

Peering back through the distorting lens of subsequent events, to its traumatised participants and their descendants the war became distant, obscured, unexplainable. To many survivors, such as the English writer J. B. Priestley, the world their war made seemed very different, its making hardly worth the sacrifice. Reflecting fifteen years afterwards on the Great War in which he had played his own small past he lamented his fallen friends:

> they were killed by greed and muddle and monstrous cross-purposes, by old men gobbling and roaring in clubs, by diplomats working underground like monocled moles, by journalists wanting a good story, by hysterical women waving flags, by grumbling debenture-holders, by strong silent be-ribboned asses, by fear or apathy or downright lack of imagination.[3]

Priestley and others recast their war as a crime against its combatants by its directors, a global trauma in which even the victors were losers, and the losers themselves 'hopeless yet full of hope' for a different world or a vengeful refight. Since the participants themselves so soon lost sight of the war they fought in, and of what they had fought for, it should come as no surprise that the First World War remains misunderstood one hundred years later: reduced all too often to the clichés which Priestley had already accepted and catalogued back in the 1930s. While societies passed through it, however, the issues of the war were genuine, the leadership was committed, the rank and file determined, the war effort Herculean. It was the very nature of the war that threatened to overwhelm all.

European empires were not entirely civilized before 1914, and their leaders had few qualms about unleashing a horrifying new type of conflict on their people, one that would seep into the furthest corners of society, suck up national resources and change the lives of all who participated. Once the shock of the ending of peace had been negotiated this was to prove a popular war: not just in the sense that peoples indoctrinated with nationalistic rhetoric for many decades rallied to the cause, but also in the fact that the people would be fighting it. Men in uniform, workers on production lines, emancipated women in new roles would all prove vital in this mass war, which pitched industries and empires as well as armies and navies into a struggle for survival. All this was yet to come as the bands played and the flags waved as men marched off to war in August 1914, in quaint uniforms and with outmoded ideas.

After 1914's dynamic yet indecisive military campaign came to an end the reality of twentieth-century conflict became manifest. Winston Churchill initially expected the quick, decisive manoeuvres of the turn-of-the-century wars he had reported on as a young journalist, only to be disabused by his own strategic misadventures as first lord of the Admiralty in the early months of the war. On resigning from the cabinet at the end of 1915 he admitted:

> In this war the tendencies are far more important than the episodes. Without winning any sensational victories we may win this war. We may win it even during a continuance of extremely disappointing and vexatious events. It is not necessary for us in order to win the war to push the German lines back over all the territory they have absorbed, or to pierce them . . . [Victory depends on] the capacity of the ancient and mighty nations, against whom Germany is warring, to endure adversity, to put up with disappointments and mismanagement, to recreate and renew their strength, and to pass on with boundless obstinacy through boundless sufferings to the achievement of their cause.[4]

This is a suitable epitaph for a war that is remembered for its strain, errors, misery and sacrifice. It was seemingly a war without object, one devoid of imagination. But it was one waged with systematic and decisive, if notorious, method. By the middle of 1915 both sides accepted that the only way to conduct and win such a war was by mobilising all society's resources and grinding down the enemy's capacity and will to fight in a sustained war of attrition. Such a strategy lacks much of the dynamism and drama of earlier wars: 'The term usually conjures up images of futile and bloody slogging matches, epitomised by the Western Front of the First World War.'[5] A perception of attrition as a cruel, simplistic military strategy predicated merely on killing men on account formed as the war prolonged, and became deeply entrenched thereafter. Yet the gradual, systematic destruction of the enemy's military capability proved both necessary and effective when huge armies backed by industrialised empires took the field. Ever since Sparta ground down Athens in the Peloponnese, and Fabius Maximus 'Cunctator' wore down Hannibal's invading army by refusing to fight it, attrition had been employed to great effect, not least when the enemy was strong enough to respond in kind, or was militarily effective enough to triumph repeatedly on the battlefield. Attrition really came into its own in the twentieth century, with its huge wars conducted by homogeneous, industrialised mass societies welded into multinational alliances. It differed from its classical progenitors because modern societies could not avoid fighting, but needed to engage in huge, grinding battles to break the military power of their enemies.

THE STALEMATED WAR THAT FACED THE BELLIGERENTS FROM THE END OF 1914 had to be fought and won on five distinct but interlinked fronts. Most important was the land front: the battlefields, on which armies fought for advantage, and on which the enemy's strength would be worn down to the point that he would collapse. The First World War is notorious for its 'fronts', the separate land campaigns that were engaged at its start and sustained throughout the war. These came about after Germany and Austria-Hungary launched offensives against the coalition of hostile power – France, Russia and the British Empire – that surrounded them and was perceived to be set on their destruction. As well as the most notorious, the western front in France and Flanders on which the French, British and German armies were principally engaged from 1914, Russia fought German and Austro-Hungarian armies on an eastern front in Poland and Galicia between 1914 and 1917. Once the war spread into the Middle East and the Mediterranean at the end of 1914, new land fronts were opened against the Ottoman Empire: in Mesopotamia, the Caucasus, Egypt and Palestine, and during 1915 at the Dardanelles. Italy's entry into the war in May 1915 opened a new, southern front against the Habsburg Empire along their shared frontier, and Bulgaria's entry in October 1915 inaugurated a further subsidiary front in the Balkans at Salonika. By then the structure of the land was had emerged. The Central powers were besieged by an Allied coalition of their prewar and new wartime enemies, determined to crush them with armed force.* The means to achieve this turned out to be through prolonged attritional battles, most notoriously around Ypres, at Verdun, on the Somme and along the River Isonzo along the Austro-Italian border, which killed and maimed men and consumed material in ever increasing quantities. The land fronts were the war's focal points, with both sides' military strategy predicated on allocating resources between them in the expectation that, singly or collectively, these military campaigns would determine the outcome of the war. Collectively they were the theatres of attrition, in which the armies of Germany and her allies were engaged and defeated.

These land fronts were dependent on the second front, the maritime front. The war at sea governed the deployment and supply of the Allied armies as well as sustaining the civilian war effort on both sides. Although navies might fight each other on occasion, the principal weapon on the maritime front was the economic blockade, a slow working attritional weapon of a different kind that sought to interrupt the flow of trade and to undermine financial solvency and popular morale. With

---

*The term 'Allies' will be used to denote the alliance against the Central powers of Germany, Austria-Hungary, Turkey (from November 1914) and Bulgaria (from September 1915). The alliance was founded on the three 'Entente' powers: the Entente Cordiale was signed between Britain and France in 1904 and supplemented by an Anglo-Russia Entente in 1907. Britain's ally Japan entered the war in late August 1914 and Italy joined the alliance in April 1915. Belgium and Serbia were aligned with the Entente from the outbreak of hostilities, with Portugal and Rumania joining in 1916 and Greece in 1917. The United States entered the war as an 'associated power' on the Allied side in 1917, followed by China and many smaller states.

three of the world's five largest navies at their disposal by summer 1915, and with a fourth, the United States Navy, joining them in spring 1917, the Allies began the war with, and always maintained, a substantial advantage on this front. But Germany's powerful Imperial High Seas Fleet, the world's second largest navy, and the significant Austrian and Turkish naval forces in the Mediterranean Sea and the Black Sea ensured that the Central powers would always be able to contest Allied control of the seas. While a standoff between the British and German battle fleets continued in the North Sea, the real war at sea was conducted against Allied trade in the first Battle of the Atlantic. It countered an increasingly tight Allied maritime blockade of the Central powers. The maritime war was to be one in which new underhand and undersea weapons, the submarine and the floating mine, came into their own. Begun by surface raiders in 1914, attacks on commercial shipping, the mainstay of the maritime front, were escalated with German declarations of unrestricted submarine warfare in 1915 and again from spring 1917. Defending seaborne commerce became the main objective of Allied maritime strategy in the second half of the war. By then their blockade was firmly in place and would gradually enhance the pressure exerted by Allied land forces. Sea power on its own, however, was not a decisive weapon in a war between a maritime and a land-based coalition.

The full mobilisation of the home front, the third of the war's five fronts, was crucial for the outcome of the war. In twentieth-century warfare a state's population, financial strength, raw material resources, industrial productivity and transport capacity, political cohesion and diplomatic reach, and public opinion sustained by mass communications media were all factors in the 'war effort' that supports the military conduct of war. Industry's productive capacity, the state's financial solvency, government leadership and the managerial ability of the civil service make the war work, which enhances military effectiveness on the fighting fronts. Sustaining the will of the people to victory, manifested in national unity, was a novel element in strategy that had to be addressed by both sides once initial popular acceptance of the justice of the war transmuted into war weariness as the land and naval campaigns ground on inconclusively. Although both coalitions had mobilised populations and industrial resources intensively by 1916, the Allies had more manpower, money and greater access to resources than their adversaries, and thereafter overtook Germany's early lead in mobilisation. Significantly, to their own superior industrial, commercial and financial capacity they could gear that of the large American economy, even before America became a belligerent, giving them an overwhelming advantage on this front. Moreover, greater democratisation among the Allies (with the notable exception of Russia) ensured that popular unity behind the war effort and their peoples' will to victory could be renewed within the Allied states in 1917, at a time when their enemies were dividing against themselves. In time, the home front became a legitimate military target. By the last years of the war small-scale strategic bombing against domestic resources, the scourge of the next world war, had commenced. Although not yet a war-winning weapon, air power had emerged as a factor in the struggle between mobilised economies and societies which characterised twentieth-century conflict.

Success on the fourth front, the diplomatic front, enhanced Allied advantages on land, sea and at home. Diplomacy too was a competitive arena, for hearts and minds and commercial opportunities in neutral countries, as well as to expand the war, to justify it, or to negotiate peace. In 1914 and 1915 both coalitions gained more members. Thereafter, only the Allies were able to expand their alliance, as widely reported German 'atrocities', imperial opportunities, as well as the shifting fortunes of war persuaded many nonaligned nations that the Allied coalition was both more just and more potent. After the war reached its full extent in 1917, war aims (and, potentially, peace terms) became the diplomatic battleground. America's president, Woodrow Wilson then introduced a new liberal agenda into Europe's war. Although this clashed with the imperial and security interests of the other great powers, it chimed with the emerging popular internationalist agenda, social democrats' call for a negotiated peace without territorial annexations or financial indemnities. On this front the Allies proved both more flexible and effective than the Central powers.

Diplomacy counted for much on the fifth front, the 'united front': the organisation and maintenance of a cohesive, effective alliance. In a war between two coalitions of great powers unity and collaboration took on increasing significance as the war went on. By pooling resources, coordinating military strategy and operations, and through shared diplomatic initiatives, joint war making would prove more potent than the loose alignment of separate national strategies, which characterised the first phase of the war on both sides. On this front too the Allies fared far better. Their enemies' early military successes, intended to sunder them, served to bring them closer together. Eventually a joint management structure, the Supreme War Council, and an Allied generalissimo emerged. This increasingly collaborative Entente alliance contrasted with the autocratic Central powers coalition in which the dominant partner, Germany, asserted her power and control over her increasingly unwilling allies as the war went on.

It was the complexity of this five-front war – land, sea, home, diplomatic and united – that made strategy and policy so problematic between 1914 and 1918. Victory ultimately depended on being successful on all five fronts. The Allies began with or secured advantages on them all as the war progressed, making their victory only a matter of time after the Central powers failed in their strategy to win a quick, decisive victory on the land front before Christmas in 1914. Demonstrating to a powerful coalition that they had lost the war, however, was to require intensive, prolonged and traumatic effort, endurance and sacrifice.

To make war effectively, the mobilisation of society must integrate with strategic policy and military operations. Strategic attrition involved mobilising and deploying an empire's resources to best engage the enemy on the battlefield, which would never be straightforward given the competing demands on finite assets. Creating, equipping, financing and utilising armed forces were the central elements of strategy; balancing the manpower and material needs of the domestic war effort with the demands of the fight and moving those forces and resources to where they might best secure the short- and long-term objectives of the war were ongoing challenges for soldiers and statesmen. Strategy also entailed interdicting or degrading the enemy's capacity to do the same. The better that generals and politicians understood these realities and worked together, the more effective the war effort would be. Yet strategic effectiveness would ultimately be measurable only in terms of success in combat – at sea and especially on land.

Military operations – committing forces against the enemy at the right place and time in the best way and sustaining them in the fight – formed the link between strategy and tactics. Battlefield attrition is probably the most misunderstood and controversial element of the conduct of the First World War, with attention drawn inevitably to the three-year standoff between France and Britain and Germany on the western front, and the huge casualty bill on all fronts. Of course for operations to succeed, tactics had to be appropriate and effective. Military commanders were not incompetent or lacking in professionalism, although as they struggled with the theory and practice of a novel type of warfare mistakes would be made. A tactical revolution was underway and it is in this context – one of armies adapting their structure, methods and armaments rapidly – that military events have to be judged. On the attritional battlefield errors were corrected faster, and methods perfected sooner, than generally supposed. Attritional battles such as Verdun and the Somme in 1916 were certainly long, horrendous and hugely costly in lives and resources. But since the premise of attrition was to grind down the enemy on the battlefield by killing or capturing his soldiers en masse and destroying his war material, hopefully at a faster rate than he could replace them, thereby undermining his morale, intangible yet vital – and ideally doing so at acceptable loss to one's own forces – such battles were inevitable. In truth it was the scale and parameters of the war that lengthened the casualty lists.

In 1915 the war of exhaustion developed as a pragmatic response to the circumstances and nature of great power confrontation. Once the war became everything, it was a rational, necessary strategy that would produce a victory of sorts and ensure national survival, the only acceptable outcome. Both sides accepted the parameters of this war of attrition, even if its practice proved controversial and its consequences catastrophic. Military commanders who developed and pursued strategies of attrition were later accused of lacking imagination (often by politicians who had challenged them at the time, although the alternatives they suggested, if potentially spectacular, were naïve or impracticable). Collective effort was, however, to prove more significant than individual achievements or mistakes in determining the course and outcome of hostilities. Politicians and generals had to work together and cooperate with the unsung heroes of the war effort – industrialists and trade union leaders; shipping magnates and transport managers; newspaper proprietors and journalists – whose efforts were as essential to success as those of commanders and controllers of strategy and policy. But ordinary men and women proved to be the foundation of the war efforts, active participants in a national endeavour who offered their time, strength, money and, when called for, their lives in the cause.

Attrition was not limited to the battlefield but operated behind the lines, on the home front and at sea. From 1915 war making escalated inexorably in order to avoid an indecisive 'peace of exhaustion' that would render all effort and sacrifice pointless. One side needed to outproduce, outfight and outlast the other, since the alternative outcomes had become victory or collapse. Whether it was worth it today is impossible to judge. Why it was so might yet be understood.

# ONE

# READY AND WILLING

O N 21 JULY 1914 TSAR NICHOLAS II OF RUSSIA HAD AN AUDIENCE with the president and premier of France. Russia and France had been allies since 1892 and Raymond Poincaré and René Viviani were on a long-planned state visit to the Russian court. The talk was of alliance politics and international affairs, including the volatile state of Balkan affairs following the assassination of Archduke Franz Ferdinand, heir to the Habsburg throne. It was not yet apparent that the shot that would ignite the most destructive war the world had yet seen had been fired, although rumours that Austria-Hungary would take a tough line with her smaller neighbour Serbia were circulating among the diplomatic corps in St Petersburg. The tsar was anxious because Austria was not showing her hand, although, Poincaré was happy to note, he did not fear an imminent European conflict.[1] Yet the military parades witnessed by the French statesmen over the following days, 'tens of thousands of men . . . all fine troops', would have reassured them that should events take such a turn Russia would prove a doughty ally.[2] The Frenchmen assured Sergei Sazonov, Russia's foreign minister, that they would support Russia in the line she took in response to the crisis: Poincaré had always advocated a firm line in international crises, and this advice the Russians followed. They believed it might avoid the escalation of the crisis. Indeed, it might have, had not Germany already given her Austrian allies an equally forthright promise of support, the infamous blank cheque. As Poincaré and Viviani sailed on to Scandinavia for the next stage of their state tour, the Foreign Ministry in Vienna sent Serbia an ultimatum (specifically timed to arrive while the Frenchmen were at sea).[3] This the Serbians could not accept without fatally compromising their sovereignty. By the time the French statesmen returned hurriedly to France on 29 July, war had been declared and Austria's troops were mobilising. All Poincaré could do was 'tell the Russian government that, in the interests of peace, France will second her action'.[4] Russia ordered mobilisation that evening.

In a world of imperial great powers, no one disputed the right of states to make war in their national interest. Alliances, state diplomacy and localised wars were the accepted methods of international relations and in his promise to Russia Poincaré was merely endorsing the course of French foreign policy set after France allied with Russia. Wars were commonplace, although in recent decades these had largely been conducted outside the continent of Europe with the objective of expanding and consolidating imperial power: France and Italy had recently been engaged in colonial campaigns in North Africa, and Great Britain had fought the Boer republics in South Africa at the turn of the century. But there were still European issues to fight for, and the most bellicose empires were in Eastern Europe. Here three powerful, nationalistic, militarized semi-autocracies – Russia, Austria-Hungary and above all Germany –appeared to be weakening as the new century developed. It was not so much their declining diplomatic weight (although Russia had been defeated by Japan in 1904–5 and Germany was feeling increasingly diplomatically hemmed in) but their domestic troubles that were increasingly cause for concern at the higher levels of government. It came as no surprise therefore when war broke out in Eastern Europe, where Russia and Austria-Hungary had been competing for influence as Turkish power declined over more than half a century, and where the lesser states created by the expulsion of Turkey from Europe had recently been sparring over the spoils in two Balkan Wars. Were it not for the alliance system, the clash between Austria-Hungary and Serbia might merely have been a third.

Although in principle the alliance between Europe's most politically progressive regime, the French Third Republic, and its most conservative and reactionary monarchy, Russia, seemed incongruous, it epitomised the complicated, pragmatic features of so-called 'great power' diplomacy. What brought France and Russia together was their shared fear of the new militarily and economically powerful German Empire that had sprung up between them in central Europe. That this had come about following the military defeat of France was a bitter remembrance west of the Rhine. This Dual Alliance between France and Russia was itself a response to 1882's Triple Alliance between Germany, Austria-Hungary and Italy, designed to keep France isolated and impotent following Prussia's victory in 1870–71. Thereafter the 'lost provinces' of Alsace and Lorraine, nominally German but culturally still very French following their annexation, sat, disputed, between them. This was an old wound, which, if it still smarted, was unlikely of itself to lead to war. But in the new century there were many issues that might, and states and mutual-security alliances were organised on the assumption that sooner or later one would bring the continent to bayonet point.

Alliances such as that between France and Russia were the work of statesmen, and they would manipulate the levers of power which plunged Europe into war in 1914. It had been Europe's dominant statesman from the late nineteenth century, Germany's 'Iron Chancellor', Prince Otto von Bismarck, who had both orchestrated the defeat of France that established the Hohenzollern Empire in Germany, and thereafter inaugurated the system of great power alliances that kept a vengeful France in check. Although this security apparatus based on rival armed camps still operated in 1914, the man who worked it so perspicaciously had long gone, and his successors lacked the shrewd, calculating realpolitik skills with which he held a fractious continent in peaceful balance for two decades. Kaiser William II's dismissal of Bismarck from the chancellorship had opened the way for the Franco-Russia alliance, an alignment strengthened in the new century by the adhesion of the British Empire. Ententes were signed with France in 1904 and Russia in 1907, ostensibly to settle extra-European colonial differences, but encouraged by a growing global rivalry between Britain and Germany catalysed by the rapid expansion of the German navy and the kaiser's increasingly belligerent diplomacy.[5] For his part, the kaiser held the Triple Alliance together. But Austria-Hungary was decadent and dividing against itself, while Italy was a great power in ambition only, yet sly and covetous, and quite prepared to put self-interest ahead of treaty obligations. The balance that Bismarck had maintained in Germany's favour was shifting against her.

The essential theme of European affairs in the years immediately preceding the outbreak of war was the revival of France and Russia, with the concomitant isolation of Germany. It was poor recompense for two decades of active diplomacy designed to win Germany a place in the world commensurate with her strength. On coming to the throne the kaiser had chosen to pursue an active *weltpolitik* (global policy) in place of Bismarck's cautious diplomatic balancing act. This had brought Germany firm rivals without bringing her much power and glory. In conference with his war minister and leading generals and admirals on 8 December 1912 the kaiser had outlined Germany's increasing international isolation. The Balkan situation looked menacing, and Austria-Hungary's security appeared threatened by Serbia, backed by the Russians.[6] Undoubtedly the Dual Alliance was drawing more closely together: Poincaré had made his first state visit to Russia that summer. Moreover, perfidious yet usually aloof Albion, of which the half-English kaiser might have expected better, had placed herself more firmly in the rival camp. That summer Britain had agreed with France to a naval redistribution that allowed the Royal Navy to concentrate its warships in the North Sea against the Imperial High Seas Fleet, leaving France to contain Italy and Austria-Hungary in the Mediterranean. The December meeting was triggered by a report from the German ambassador in London that 'if we attacked France, [England] would unconditionally spring to France's aid, for England could not allow the balance of power in Europe to be disturbed'.[7] This conference may not have set Europe inevitably on the road for war as some have suggested. But the events of 1912, coming as they did after a series of diplomatic checks for Germany, were not propitious. War had broken out among the small Balkans states too, and that would distract, but also concern, Europe's leaders.

It remained the right – perhaps even the responsibility – of early twentieth-century statesmen to make war, and certainly to threaten to do so, as a means to appear strong abroad and popular at home. Memories of the mid-nineteenth century's successful war-makers and empire-builders, Bismarck foremost amongst them, remained fresh. While the kaiser's diplomacy in this vein was inept and antagonistic, Germany's sustained bluster and regular diplomatic bombshells had not so far brought the great powers to blows. Yet there were many other statesmen who felt that they held the destiny of nations in their hands, who felt obliged to stand up to Germany, and who might therefore take a share of responsibility for escalating great power tensions before 1914. Poincaré for one was enthusiastic and adept at the cut and thrust of international diplomacy, as well as a skilled manipulator of the public opinion on which it depended. Poincaré had first encountered German soldiers as a child, during the four-year occupation of his home town of Bar-le-Duc in the Meuse *département* after 1870. The experience instilled the future politician with a deep patriotism, but also wariness about war and its consequences. The mature national leader would not leave France unprepared, but nor would he seek a showdown with the old enemy without good cause and strong support.[8] By the time he was elected president of France by his peers in the French National Assembly in January 1913, however, France was being washed by a nationalist swell, stirred up by the passage of the German gunboat *Panther* to Morocco in 1911. Poincaré was quite prepared to ride its breakers, which had brought him the offices of premier and foreign minister a year earlier. A middle-class lawyer by background, to the left of centre politically, Poincaré typified the values and virtues of France, or at least of 'political' republican France, although there were many conservatives and socialists who championed different values. He was also firm in his advocacy of France's alliance with Russia and entente with Great Britain (that he hoped could be turned into a formal alliance), in which lay France's real strength and security; and also he believed the guarantee of European peace. If ultimately disappointed, when war broke out Poincaré readily accepted his destiny. As he pronounced to the National Assembly on 4 August, he intended to lead his country through the traumas of war to victory and to hold its rival political factions together in a *union sacrée* (sacred union) until the invader was vanquished.[9] A strong leader was needed, since although very progressive for its time the Third Republican political system had no tradition of political stability, and its politicians no experience of war management. Presidents of the Council of Ministers, as the premiers were formally titled, had to build and hold together ministries from members of the various factions in the French Chamber of Deputies and Senate, while facing off the challenges from more organised political parties that were starting to contest the four-yearly elections, and antirepublicans who wished to put an end to the game of political musical chairs for good. Having been in politics since the 1880s, Poincaré himself understood and could work the system. The man who held the premiership in July 1914, however, had weaker credentials to lead France in time of emergency. René Viviani also held the post of foreign minister during the July Crisis. He had assumed that portfolio somewhat reluctantly since he could find no suitable alternative candidate when he had built the latest French ministry. The state visit to Russia had shown that he had little interest in or aptitude for diplomacy: he was a left wing social reformer rather than a nationalist, although he shared the deep-seated patriotism of a true Frenchman, especially when menaced by Germany. But in the diplomatic maelstrom that swept Europe in the final days of July 1914 better men than Viviani were floundering. Poincaré, to whom Viviani entrusted France's brinkmanship on their return from Russia, could not prevent Europe from slipping over the edge.

The quarrel that started the First World War was a Balkan one and, as befits a powerful empire, France was not without interests there. Like Europe's other great powers, for nearly a century as the Ottoman Empire's power declined France had been active in trying to answer the intractable 'eastern question' in a way favourable to her own interests. In the new century this had been a growing element in her diplomacy with Germany, which was financing a Berlin to Baghdad railway to push her own influence in the Middle East, and training the Turkish army. In her turn France's war industries had armed and her soldiers had trained the forces of the Balkan states that had recently driven Turkey from Europe. This diplomatic game with complex and changing rules had altered in recent years. Crises and now wars in the Balkans, and successive crises over Morocco culminating in 1911 with a standoff between France and Germany after the kaiser sent the *Panther* to Agadir, convinced many that it was a potentially dangerous game to play. In recent years there had been moves by France and Britain for rapprochement with Germany, although they had only got so far. But France had signed an agreement with Germany over the partition of Asia Minor as recently as February 1914.[10] Europe's great powers were not at the brink in the summer of 1914. What brought them there was the aggressive diplomacy of the Habsburg Empire.

The polyglot Central and Southern European Empire ruled over by Emperor Francis Joseph was something of an anachronism in twentieth-century Europe, 'a dysfunctional political system which both exacerbated national conflicts and started a European, eventually world-wide war'.[11] Certainly all nations had their national minorities and linguistic and ethnic sub regions, but only Francis Joseph wore two crowns. That he had been emperor of Austria and king of Hungary since the *Ausgleich* of 1867 (the 'Habsburg compromise', itself the consequence of defeat by Bismarck's Prussia and the loss of territory in Italy) was indicative of the nationalist forces that were pulling the empire apart. The ageing emperor – he turned eighty-four in August 1914 – had come to the throne in a different era. But even in the year of his ascension, 1848, the empire had been torn asunder by civil war as Hungarians, Italians and Czechs took up arms against their German overlords (in the capital Vienna too German liberals had taken to the streets in protest against Habsburg autocracy). That threat had been mastered on the battlefield, and thereafter Francis Joseph had held his empire together, more or less; but the essential conservatism of the emperor and his ministers kept it largely unmodernised too. Such reluctant liberalising tendencies as he had shown as a younger monarch had largely been exhausted in the middle of the previous century. As he pronounced to his mother in 1860, 'Now we are going to have a little parliamentarianism, but all power stays in my hands, and the general effect will suit Austrian circumstances very well indeed.'[12] Above all he championed traditional dynastic principles over progressive political reforms. He could rule all his subjects as king or emperor, and this personal sovereignty would bind the empire together whatever the cultural difference of its peoples or the political aspirations of his subjects. But many realised that political and social forces that could not be contained forever were at work: the evidence was near at hand. Francis Joseph had watched the Turkish Empire in Europe, Austria-Hungary's southern neighbour, break up since he had come to the throne, and similar forces were gnawing away within his own dominions. In annexing Bosnia-Herzegovina, part of that crumbling empire, in 1908 he had sown the seeds of the empire's ultimate demise: his son Crown Prince Rudolph's percipient warning, 'You have put one foot forward in the Balkans; that is putting one foot in the grave', went unheeded.[13] In an attempted show of strength designed to impress dissidents at home as well as ward off the growing South Slav militancy on the empire's southern flank, foreign minister Baron Lexa von Aehrenthal provoked a crisis 'disastrous for not only the monarchy, but also the European balance of power'.[14] Thereafter, the Balkan situation remained menacing, and Austria's position delicate. The crisis set Russia, which had been on a course towards rapprochement with the empire, against Austria because on this occasion Russia was humiliated, while stirring the resentment of Serbia that had its own expansionist ambitions in the region.[15] The assassination on 28 June 1914 of Francis Joseph's nephew and heir, the Archduke Franz Ferdinand, by the Bosnian Serb separatist Gavrilo Princip backed by his compatriots in Serbia, could therefore not go unpunished.

The decision to despatch an ultimatum to Serbia some weeks after the assassination was perhaps a natural development of Francis Joseph and Aehrenthal's forceful foreign policy. Like so many pre-1914 statesmen, they judged a firm hand to be the best recourse, especially against a weak adversary. Field Marshal Franz Conrad von Hötzendorf, chief of staff of the Austrian army, who would be tasked with punishing the empire's upstart neighbour, certainly thought so. He pressed the emperor for war with one or other of Austria's encircling enemies year after year. A reckoning with Serbia had long been in his thoughts and this was reflected in Austria's war planning, his brinkmanship during the July Crisis, and the aggressive strategy adopted when Serbia refused to compromise her sovereignty for the bully across her northern border. Yet this was a stance borne out of desperation rather than optimism. It was death or glory for the fragile Dual Monarchy, Conrad understood, and, as he confided to his mistress Gina von Reininghaus, it would most likely be the former: 'It will be a hopeless struggle, but nevertheless it must be because such an ancient monarchy and such an ancient army cannot perish ingloriously.'[16] There was a certain degree of fatalism therefore about the plunge that Austria-Hungary took in July 1914. Francis Joseph himself had asserted in 1912, 'I don't want war. I have always been unlucky in wars. We would win, but lose provinces.'[17] This was a very old-fashioned way of thinking about wars. By the time he died in November 1916, it was clear that the stakes of war had become much higher.

EUROPE HAD NOT ENGAGED IN A GENERAL WAR FOR A LONG TIME, ALTHOUGH it had not forgotten how to make war. After Napoleon Bonaparte's ambition to dominate Europe had finally been thwarted on the field of Waterloo in 1815, the European continent had been relatively free of conflict. The nationalism and militarism that France's populist revolution had unleashed in a quarter-century cycle of devastating wars remained, however, powerful forces. War had also become a civil matter: the conflicts of the first half of the nineteenth century in Spain, Italy and central Europe were fought over rights and liberties at home more than state ambitions abroad. Nationalism had resurfaced in the middle of the century, in the series of localised wars associated with German and Italian unification. Thereafter the main arena for warfare had been beyond Europe as the established and rising great powers spread their influence worldwide in an era of active imperialism. The conquest of Asia and Africa, and the repression of local uprisings, had kept Europe's colonial armies busy for decades. As a new century started Europe remained warlike, even if it seemed less prone to wars within its boundaries. Yet the Balkans still simmered with pent-up nationalism as Turkey's grip weakened, and the great powers had inevitably been drawn in. The Bosnian crisis had not brought them to blows, but the two Balkan Wars that followed in 1912–13 hinted that there was still much to fight for in the region. Expansionist Serbia, which had done well out of the two previous conflicts and sought further territory, was certainly not blameless in the events of 1914. That Nikola Pašić, Serbia's nationalist and generally uncompromising prime minister, chose to accede to all but one of the demands of the Austrian ultimatum suggests that he was not yet prepared to take on Serbia's powerful neighbour unaided. But the fact that he did not concede on all points indicates that he knew that he had powerful friends to turn to.

Francis Joseph was not the only emperor who believed in dynastic rule and state power. Tsar Nicholas II inherited the Russian throne at a relatively young age, after the premature death of his father. Ever after he retained a degree of childlike naïvety when it came to affairs of state. Although born to rule, he had not received a particularly effective education in government and fell back on the traditional principle of Russian leadership, absolutist autocracy. Dynasty (Romanov), Orthodoxy (the church) and nationality (Russian) were the three central precepts of the last tsar's approach to ruling Russia. Extremely conservative himself, Nicholas remained out of touch with the popular currents of the age, retaining the belief that his benevolent relationship with the ordinary people – the tsar was always characterised as 'the little father' in Russia – transcended the liberal principles of constitutional government as well as the activities of the secret police designed to control such modernising tendencies and the intermittent pogroms and popular uprisings that left his subjects dead in the streets. The most widespread of these, a revolution in 1905 that followed defeat in the Russo-Japanese War, had forced liberalising reforms while the regime was weak. But the first national representative assembly that resulted, the Duma, had only very limited powers, its members were always suspect in the tsar's eyes, and it never had any authority over the ministers on whom the tsar relied for the management of public affairs. This would have mattered less if the tsar had not been so capricious in his dealings with the subordinates who ran the affairs of state on his behalf. He would work with them individually rather than collectively, and often replace them on an impulse. It was an exercise of the royal prerogative that ran counter to the principles of good government. It meant that in the years before the war Russia was an empire in which parliament and people exercised no restraint upon the whims of the monarch when it came to making foreign policy and war, and his responsible ministers exerted very little influence; although the intelligentsia and political progressives certainly had much to say on the matter, most of it critical of the regime's approach. Nicholas was a family man rather than a statesman, but his personal life was clouded with difficulties too. His empress who he loved, Alexandra, was not adored by the Russian people: her German ancestry became a liability after 1914, and the only son and heir that she bore him, Tsarevich Alexei, had inherited haemophilia from his great-grandmother, Queen Victoria. The tsar's obstinacy when it came to modernising the state and forcing Russia to face up to the challenges of war would lead ultimately to his forced abdication after a liberal revolution in March 1917, and to the whole family's execution at the hands of the most extreme of the many anti-tsarist revolutionary sects that were active during the last decades of his reign, Lenin's Bolsheviks.

Russia lay at one extreme of Europe, geographically and politically. In fact, a grand tourist of Europe in the first decade of the twentieth century would have travelled a continent of rich variety and stark contrasts: a volatile blend of modernity and tradition, of plutocrats and peasants, monarchs and democrats, reformers and revolutionaries had been brewing during the previous 'peaceful' century. Relative peace in Europe had allowed growing prosperity, although that brought domestic tensions and the potential for civil conflict over economic and social grievances. Private-enterprise capitalism had spread eastwards from Great Britain as the century progressed. In the Low Countries and Germany it had established firm roots; in France and Italy it was taking off, in the more prosperous northern regions at least; to the east, in the Habsburg Empire and Russia, the modern industrial economy and the social problems associated with it were less developed, concentrated in sprawling modern cities isolated in a vast, semifeudal agricultural hinterland. Europe therefore was far from homogeneous. Modern heavy industries – coal mining, iron and steel manufacturing, shipbuilding, railways and chemicals: the industries of war – were concentrated in larger cities or heavily urbanised manufacturing regions such as the Clyde, the Sambre-Meuse basin and the Ruhr. But with the exception of the maritime and manufacturing leviathan Britain, all states still had large agricultural sectors and a high proportion of the population remained dependent on the land: for example in East Prussia, the political if not the economic makeweight of the German Empire, Southern Italy and central France, where a pre-industrial semi-subsistence economy persisted.

The wealthy, whether well-established landowning aristocrats serving the crown in army or bureaucracy or nouveau riche factory owners from the growing middle class, still held political power, although their grip appeared less firm in the early years of a new century. As capitalism spread across Europe during the nineteenth century working men, and latterly women, started to organise and agitate for a fairer share of its profits and the political representation that might secure it; or in the most extreme manifestation of socialism, for the end of capitalism altogether. Although socialism had made only partial, and very variable, progress in the various European states before 1914, it was an ever-present threat. The rich certainly feared that if they did not hang together, they might hang separately.

In the kaiser's Germany, for example, the so-called 'alliance of iron and rye' (manufacturers and farmers) had been formed to contest the rise of social democracy. Since Bismarck's day socialists, along with Catholics, had been vilified as the enemy within the empire. By 1914 both appeared to be reconciled to the workings of imperial politics, although imperial politicians were yet to be reconciled to them. In a political system where factional interest-group politics prevailed, successive chancellors had manipulated the Reichstag parliamentary majority to ensure that the Social Democratic Party (SPD), despite being the largest political party in terms of votes and seats by 1912, would never share power. Ominously, that system was fracturing on the eve of war. Germany passed a new army service law in 1913, with socialists' votes. The workers' representatives favoured the land tax levied to pay for army expansion, while the landowners objected. Some judged this as modern representative democracy in action, but others saw it as a sign that the political system no longer equated to the true power structure of imperial Germany. Theobald von Bethmann Hollweg, the chancellor who with difficulty manufactured the parliamentary majority on this occasion, certainly felt that the imperial political system was on its last legs and needed reforming.

The German example is typical of the domestic uncertainties of Europe; and significant because Germany was both the most modern and powerful state on the continent, and its most troubled. Its political institutions, created by Bismarck in 1870 to sustain the power of Prussia in the new German Empire, and the political dominance of the landed interest in Prussia, no longer equated with its social structure. In the empire Kaiser William II reigned supreme, although he was not all-powerful. His ministers, particularly the Reich chancellor, managed the domestic affairs of the empire, while foreign policy and war making, if nominally controlled by the Prussian foreign and war ministries, were reserved to the emperor, who was advised by an inner cabinet dominated by his close military advisers. But William was a volatile man on whom it was dangerous to rest the destiny of Europe. A personality that was both 'brilliant and bizarre, aggressive and insecure'[18] controlling the continent's most powerful army and its second largest navy gave cause for concern, and not just in Germany. The kaiser certainly saw himself as a powerful ruler, although many who had to work with him saw him as a loose cannon and a liability; he was unguarded in the often extreme views he conveyed to intimates and prone to rash, provocative, policy-compromising outbursts to foreign representatives or journalists. Many suspected that he was slightly unbalanced. An accident at birth had starved him of oxygen: this had left him with a withered left arm, of which he was always self-conscious, but what invisible damage it had done to his brain was never ascertained. He was certainty immature and childish, had notoriously poor judgement and seemed never to learn from experience. Inevitably, as the successor of powerful Prussian warrior-kings, William II was a militarist who loved his army (and its uniforms, which he studied in detail and on occasion designed himself) and the company of officers. Nothing pleased him more than the title of 'supreme warlord', which he assumed when Germany went to war: although sensibly while dwelling near the Oberste Heeresleitung (OHL – German supreme army general headquarters) throughout the war he largely followed his commanders' advice on its conduct. As the son of an English mother, one of Queen Victoria's daughters, his education instilled an alternative liberal navalist perspective to conservative Prussian militarism. But while William admired and wished to replicate the Royal Navy, he had no time for Britain's parliamentary institutions or representative government.

Although the kaiser felt that he was a democrat (in that he treated all patriotic Germans equally, although like many of his compatriots he despised Jews, Catholics and social democrats whose racial, religious and political beliefs he saw as a cancers undermining Germany from within), he behaved like an autocrat and governed like a dilettante. It was at court and in the corridors of power that policy was made and actions determined: like his Austrian and Russian counterparts the kaiser was not responsible to parliament. Yet the imperial parliament (Reichstag) did have some power, particularly over the purse strings, as the crisis over the 1913 army service law demonstrated. Whether traditional elites were losing their grip on the levers of power, or whether the decision for war in 1914 represented powerful economic and political factions reasserting and exercising their authority in a new ultranationalist form,[19] it was evident that by 1914 Germany was difficult to govern, and therefore dangerous: 'The question of civil war and foreign war had indeed become the two sides of the same coin in the minds of the kaiser and his advisers, and it is virtually impossible to decide which issue obsessed them more.'[20] Germany's belligerent foreign policy under the kaiser's mercurial direction ensured that in the lead-up to war international relations increasingly focused on restraining or deterring German global ambitions.[21] The kaiser justified ratcheting up international tensions and raising the stakes to his own people as essential measures to ensure security, but these forays into foreign lands and waters were also closely linked to the ambitious naval and military expansion promoted by manufacturers and nationalists.

Armaments manufacturers stood supreme among capitalism's elite. By the twentieth century partnerships between the state and private enterprise (that would later be identified as 'military-industrial complexes') existed to meet the needs of the armed forces, the state's largest consumer of revenue and resources in the era before universal social welfare. Each state had long-established government-owned arsenals and dockyards, but as industrial processes became more sophisticated, and manufacture more complicated and expensive, state assets had to be increasingly supplemented or supplanted by the skills and resources of private manufacture. As well as new types of weaponry that needed expert design and precision engineering, armaments in much greater quantities were needed for Europe's large conscript armies. This was beyond the capacity of state-owned production, but perfect for the mass-production techniques of the metallurgical and light-engineering industries. Heavier weapons and weapons systems such as the huge *Dreadnought*-type battleships deployed by Europe's navies required an infrastructure of gun factories, engine shops, armour-plate works and assembly yards. All this sustained the heavy industries – coal, steel, shipbuilding and railways – which had powered the first phase of Europe's industrial revolution. A second phase of industrial development had commenced in the late nineteenth century: lighter industries mass producing consumer goods; electricity, oil and gas utilities as demand for energy grew; telecommunications; motor vehicles and more recently aircraft; and most significant for war making, modern scientific chemical industries, developing explosives, gases, early plastics, synthetics and medicines.

Krupp of Essen was Germany's largest private arms manufacturer, employing eighty-one thousand people in that city alone in Germany's largest industrial works. Krupp nurtured a close relationship with the imperial government, evidence of the complicated links that sustained the German military-industrial complex while encouraging the regime in its belligerent militarism. Friedrich Alfred Krupp had been a sponsor of the press agitation that accompanied Admiral Alfred von Tirpitz's turn-of-the-century plan to build a world-class German fleet. Wholly owned subsidiaries of the Krupp conglomerate then benefited from the award of contracts to build and armour-plate ships. Such a relationship gave Krupp strong political leverage and a clear commercial advantage over its domestic rivals. Army contracts were more fairly distributed. The state arsenal at Spandau dominated artillery production, but the demand it could not meet was put out to competitive tender. Krupp and its main rival Rheinmetall of Düsseldorf competed aggressively for the surplus, not without resort to the courts or underhand expedients. A major scandal broke in 1913 when a socialist deputy, Karl Liebknecht, exposed a Krupp employee who had bribed war ministry officials to furnish information about the firm's competitors.[22] This was a notorious, if not untypical, example of the all-pervading influence of industrial capitalism in high political circles. If it was at its most extreme in Germany, other leading European armaments firms – such as Vickers and Armstrong in Great Britain and Schneider and Saint-Chamond in France – also benefited from close personal links between their directors and leading political and military figures. Nonexecutive directorships were proffered to leading political figures, parliamentary seats and peerages to successful businessmen; the rich invested in armaments companies and in turn manufacturers funded political parties and the press that proselytised on their behalf.

Expenditure on armaments increased in all states in the decade before the war. It was an era of arms races: among the Balkan states; between the British and German navies; between the Italian and Austrian navies; between the Russian and Turkish navies; between the German, French and Russian armies. Although arms races alone do not cause wars, they certainly allow intensive, bloody campaigns to be fought once they break out. The war effort engaged from August 1914 rested on peacetime military organisation – the manning, equipment and training of the field army and navy – and deeper economic and strategic preparations for war. By the early years of the twentieth century the states of continental Europe had adopted a military system founded on the conscription of annual contingents of young men into the ranks of a citizen army. If the precise details differed from country to country, the guiding principles were the same. A proportion of the adult male population would serve a number of years in the active army before passing into the reserve. A reservist was liable to be called up if war broke out: when younger into the active reserve to serve with the field army; when older as a territorial soldier for home defence or to serve in rear-area administration. This system enabled a rapid expansion of the field army on the outbreak of war for those early battles which were expected to be decisive. If they were not, the gaps in the ranks occasioned by those battles could be filled from the reservists waiting in home depots. With such a system mass armies could be sustained in the field for many months and, if future annual contingents and untrained manpower was called up, potentially for years. Yet that presented other difficulties, not least the daunting cost. 'A strategy of attrition will not do, if the maintenance of millions costs billions,' General Alfred von Schlieffen, who planned Germany's prewar strategy, had identified.[23]

Before the war, nonetheless, millions were being spent as arms races intensified. All Europe's field armies had been expanding in the years before 1914. France had most recently increased the number of men she conscripted in 1913, in response to Germany's simultaneous army expansion that, ironically, was actually precipitated by fears of Russian revival and French aggressiveness.[24] France's new three-year military service law potentially allowed France to maintain an active field army of 910,000 men in peacetime, and to mobilise 1,865,000 men when war broke out.[25] Unfortunately for France, with war breaking out in 1914 her army, although enlarged by the 1913 law, was momentarily weaker. Adjusting her active army to the recruitment timetable introduced by the new law, two new classes had entered French depots in late 1913 and these half-trained men formed two-thirds of the active army deployed in August 1914.[26]

Germany had a significant advantage, in that with a population of almost 67,000,000 she could recruit a smaller percentage of her male population and still maintain parity with France, with a metropolitan population of 40,000,000. Many of those who did not do army service in Germany were nevertheless obliged to do partial military training in a militia-style ersatz reserve which could be brought up to full proficiency after the outbreak of war.[27] This enabled her to mobilise 2,147,000 men in August 1914, and to fill her empty home depots with a levy of partly trained conscripts and patriotic volunteers (*Freiwilliger*).

France's makeweight to Germany's numbers lay in the potentially inexhaustible manpower reserves of her Russian ally. It is not surprising that in patriotic prewar cartoons and for some time after hostilities broke out, in her allies' assessments Russia was characterised as a steamroller which would squash all in its path. On paper Russia appeared formidable, with a population of 175,000,000. Her military system enabled her to mobilise a 3,400,000-man field army in 1914, with potentially a vast, untapped reserve of manpower.[28] Yet such an industrial analogy, if not entirely wide of the mark, was deceptive. Russia had been industrialising faster than any other great power in the years before the war. Although relative to her huge population her industrial base appeared small, in her major cities a growing urban workforce predominated. Twenty million Russians now worked in factories, more industrial workers than in France, and Russia was ranked third in Europe in terms of manufacturing capacity (behind Britain and Germany) and rising fast as foreign capital was invested in her businesses and infrastructure. Her armaments industry was impressive, growing and relatively modern: the vast Putilov works in St Petersburg manufactured ships, guns and shells to supplement state small arms and artillery production, and was entering a phase of rapid expansion on the eve of war. Yet Russia's apparently overwhelming superiority masked other weaknesses. Her industrial base was inefficient compared to those of her allies and Germany, reliant on state contracts and old-fashioned management and production techniques, undercapitalized and riddled with corruption. It meant that Russia was at a distinct disadvantage when it came to fighting a modern war. Equipping, transporting and controlling such a huge force would prove problematic; although in a few years many of these deficiencies were expected to have been addressed by Russia's own army and infrastructure expansion, the so-called Great Plan of 1913, designed, in the words of its architect war minister Vladimir Sukhomlinov, to create 'a Russian army equal to the German army'.[29] There was some substance in German statesmen's fears that in a few years time Russia would be too powerful to fight with any hope of victory.

Germany's only reliable support against the Russian giant was the relatively unmodernised, heterogeneous Dual Monarchy. On paper the Habsburg forces were formidable – with a population of 52,000,000, she maintained a 440,000 man active army, expandable to 1,338,000 in wartime – although, reflecting the nature of the empire, Austria's forces too lacked homogeneity. An 'imperial and royal' army recruited 100,000 men per year from throughout the empire. To support this professional field army Austria and Hungary raised separate second-line forces, the Landwehr and the Honvéd respectively, their recruits supposedly serving for two years but in practice spending only about eight weeks a year in barracks and training. Similar reserve forces were raised in the other ethnic regions, creating a polyglot, semi-trained militia: three-quarters of the men mobilised in July 1914 were of this type.[30] The ethnic cleavages in the empire made the army's practical deployment problematic. The troops of the many disparate and often disloyal nationalities that lived under the imperial crowns had on mobilisation to crisscross the Habsburg lands to get to their war stations: since internal security was a significant military function it was judged dangerous to use troops in their home regions. Austria, which spent relatively little of her national budget on defence, was at a considerable disadvantage against the power that would come to Serbia's aid, Russia, with her huge population advantage and bigger armaments industry. Austria's armaments industry had its modern factories, notably those of the Czech conglomerate Škoda, which produced guns and armour for the navy and gun carriages for the army, as well as super-heavy artillery for smashing modern fortifications. The state-owned arsenals produced small arms, munitions and artillery barrels (still made of a steel-bronze alloy before 1914), but were not competitive in the international arms market and struggled to survive on government contracts alone. The state machine-gun works at Steyr had been bought out by the private sector in 1912.[31] The armaments industry reflected Austria-Hungary's relatively weak industrial base as a whole. Concentrated around the capital city of Vienna and in the Czech lands (then part of Hungary), it could not produce weapons and munitions on the same scale as the more industrialised economies of Northern and Western Europe. Consequently, Austrian divisions had fewer field guns than other armies when deployed in 1914, and a smaller reserve of shells to fire from them. Modern weapons were also in relatively short supply. Heavier artillery pieces were generally obsolescent nineteenth-century guns, there were few aircraft in service and machine guns were relatively few in number.

Relative to Austria, Russia's armaments industry looked impressive. Thanks in part to heavy French financial investment in her ally's military modernisation, considerable progress had been made in building production capacity. The factories concentrated in Russia's two principal cities, Petrograd* and Moscow, were relatively modern and could potentially produce guns and shells in large numbers. But getting Russian industry to produce sufficiently for the needs of Russia's vast army in a highly industrialised war would turn out to be a continual problem for the Allies. An imbalance between supply and demand, coupled with a railway network which was inadequate for transporting munitions from the factories to the distant front promptly and in bulk and excessive bureaucracy and corruption all along the production-supply chain, made it difficult to realise Russia's industrial potential. That Russia could at the start of a war put many millions of men into the field and keep the army's ranks filled

---

*St Petersburg's German sounding name was changed in August 1914.

with an apparently inexhaustible supply of reserves thereafter was comforting to her allies. That she could not equip or manoeuvre these masses effectively gave a real advantage to her enemies. Nevertheless, in a war between Austria-Hungary and Russia alone the latter would doubtless have prevailed.

EUROPE WAS CERTAINLY READY FOR WAR IN 1914. THE QUESTION REMAINED whether the people were willing. Pacifists rejected war altogether, but there were relatively few of them. Socialists contested the rights of the capitalists who made war. Many on the left accepted war as a means of pursuing state policy – a just, defensive war at least – but profiting from it was anathema. The socialists' vilification of 'merchants of death' was strong, even while these 'merchants of death' employed many hundreds of thousands of socialism's political supporters, just one of the many contradictions in Europe's prewar labour movement. In 1912, at their international congress in Basel, Europe's socialist party leaders had condemned war between states as inimical to workers' cross-border solidarity and voted that any outbreak of hostilities would be thwarted by a continent-wide general strike. French socialist leader Albert Thomas, who was in wartime to manage the production of armaments, had as recently as 1913 called upon French and German socialists to 'close ranks more firmly than ever before to fight jointly against these mad machinations of the ruling classes.'[32] Yet if in principle the workers should unite against war and the capitalists who manufactured for it and sustained the imperialist quasi-democracies that were prepared to wage it, in practice their choices were not so clear-cut. Nation offered an alternative allegiance to class, and cooperation with and support for the elites and their wars proffered political and social opportunities which outright hostility did not. Therefore, despite general anxiety about what the left would do if war broke out – France, for example, drew up a list of socialists, leaders and other antiwar agitators who were to be arrested on the outbreak of hostilities, the notorious Carnet B – rulers' fears generally proved unfounded. Although socialist-led or pacifist-inspired marches against war took place in July and early August 1914 in many towns and cities, these were generally before war had been declared.[33] They should be seen as pro-peace rather than antiwar demonstrations. Once the dogs of war had been unleashed, the mass of the population answered the call to arms and accepted the necessity for and justice of their country's war, with determination if not necessarily the enthusiasm of legend. In France the socialist party's leaders rallied their supporters to a war of national defence. Workers were patriots first, and they, their parents or grandparents still remembered the last German invasion. Ironically Jean Jaurès, the leader of the *Parti socialiste français*, was assassinated on 31 July by a right wing extremist fearful that he would actively oppose the war.[34] This was a rare act of partisan political violence. What was noticeable (and perhaps surprising at the time) was the unanimity of support for the war. Across Europe in the nation's hour of need political rivals and social adversaries suppressed their long-standing differences 'for the duration'. Poincaré's *union sacrée* was to manifest itself in temporary domestic harmony and a parliamentary truce between the factions in the Chamber of Deputies and Senate. Viviani broadened his government with the inclusion of socialist ministers. The kaiser declared 'social peace' (*Burgfrieden*) in Germany, while in Britain the opposition Conservative and Unionist Party pledged to cooperate with the governing Liberal Party's war effort. These were expressions of liberal Europe's fundamentally patriotic solidarity, although all such pronouncements were made on the assumption that war would be short and postwar political advantages would result from wartime cooperation. Sustaining such national unity and cross-party pacts would, however, prove challenging as the war was prolonged and the state's power expanded.

In the early twentieth century socialists (of many persuasions) were identified as the enemy within. Their credo, if ill-defined, sought to appeal to the expanding workforce of Europe's industrial cities; or in countries with relatively limited industrial development such as Russia and Italy, to the landless rural population, the peasantry. Their rivals would offer alternatives to class identity in the social competition for men's (and, increasingly, women's) loyalty. The very diversity of Europe at this time might paradoxically explain its coming together for war. Religion and race offered other identities and allegiances: Catholicism, Protestantism or Orthodoxy divided the Christian community of Europe. Most European states had Jewish communities, and Muslims were widespread in the Ottoman Empire and the Balkans, as well as in extra-European colonial territories. Modern societies increasingly privileged status and function over creed or race. Some such identities were highly traditional, such as the army, the navy or the state's bureaucracy, burgeoning as capitalist society took off. Capitalism itself gave different identities of trade or profession to those who functioned in the modern economy: miner, railwayman, engineer, teacher, white-collar clerical worker, lawyer, journalist and artist. With shared status came common interests, manifested in the spread of trade unionism among the workforce and the parallel growth of trade and professional associations among their employers. Life beyond the workplace was also becoming collaborative, an element of a growing leisure and consumer economy that saw the appearance of sports and social clubs. Even children did not escape the early twentieth-century tendency to organise and club together. The Boy Scout movement was founded in England in 1907 by Robert Baden-Powell, a lieutenant-general disgruntled at his country's poor state of military preparedness for the South African War, and the idea was quickly copied across the continent. Girl Guides followed in 1910.

There were clearly many distinctive and individualistic identities and roles that would define a person's place in prewar European society. One dogma, however, prevailed above all: nationalism – inclusive, patriotic, self- and society-affirming, yet strident and all-pervading in its message of the rights of nations, the legitimacy of empire, the inevitability of contests between races and the need to be armed and prepared to fight for all of these. Nationalism's images were martial and ubiquitous, ranging from the carefully stage-managed displays of sovereigns' annual birthday parades and fleet reviews showing off armed might to the jolly sailors and proud soldiers who advertised tea, cigarettes and other day-to-day commodities in newspapers and on street-corner hoardings. They were also inherently jingoistic and antagonistic, for the essence of nationalism was rivalry with other nations, and its practitioners were monarchs and statesmen.[35] Nationalism's heroes were soldiers, the popular celebrities of their times. In Britain Field Marshal Lord Horatio Kitchener and Field Marshal Sir John French, who would respectively manage Britain's early war effort and lead her expeditionary force in France, were men who had won or defended Britain's empire; Admirals Sir John Fisher, Sir John Jellicoe and Sir David Beatty, Britain's preeminent naval leaders, ensured that Britannia would forever rule the waves. During the war personality cults would grow up around military leaders everywhere: Kitchener in Britain and the early victors in the West and the East, France's 'miraculous' General Joseph Joffre and Germany's 'wooden titan' Field Marshal Paul von Hindenburg, would receive almost godlike devotion on the home front. In popular weekly pictorials such as France's *l'Illustration* and *Le Petit journal* French and Allied commanders' portraits remained a staple of wartime news.

Nationalists were many and everywhere, even in the liberal states. President Poincaré did not so much promote a nationalist revival in France after 1912 as benefit from its resurgence.[36] Italy (or at least Italy's liberal political class) was in the grip of a particular sort of aggressive, expansionistic nationalism that would induce understandable but ill-considered diplomatic decisions after July 1914. She had yet to finish the process of nation building begun in the 1860s, and irredentists of all political persuasions coveted provinces that remained under Habsburg rule. Britain had its doves, such as the 'little Englander' faction of the governing Liberal Party, whose members set themselves against expansive empire, armaments and secret diplomacy. Yet even they remained at heart patriotic. Although after the outbreak of war they would rally together with the antiwar wing of the Labour Party to become the Union of Democratic Control, committed to resisting warmongering and the increase of state power in wartime, they were not against just, defensive war. England counted for much, and even if it was morally questionable to export its values abroad at the point of a gun – or more accurately the prow of a gunboat – then the values it represented, the leafy lanes of England which nurtured it, were worth defending. This was an ideal, and perhaps a myth, but an outpouring of affirmative literature in the new century, such as Erskine Childers's bestselling 1903 novel *The Riddle of the Sands* whose premise was a secret German invasion plot, suggested that it was under threat. While England prided itself on the fact that it had never resorted to military conscription like its continental neighbours, British militarism took a distinct form: navalism. Britannia ruled the waves and her warships kept the seas around the British Isles and controlled the sealanes that tied her far-flung empire together. But in the new century, old, isolationist, ways were becoming redundant. Alliances and ententes became cornerstones of British diplomacy. Her home army and imperial forces were reorganised for defence and, in the form of her regular army British Expeditionary Force (BEF), for possible intervention in continental quarrels. Her warships were concentrated in home waters to confront the growing menace of the kaiser's High Seas Fleet, coupled with anxieties about invasion that were not confined to populist literature. A home defence army, the Territorial Force, was organised in 1908, and the National Service League, a pressure group calling for the introduction of military conscription on continental lines, emerged after the South African War.

Even though it was the country with the most developed socialism, Germany also had the strongest nationalism, which many saw as an antidote to domestic divisions. Difference of class, creed, birth, race, status or function could be subsumed into a greater German identity. The primary state institution that facilitated this was the army. National service could take a man and make him a German. Two years in uniform would not only teach a man how to use weapons, march and manoeuvre tactically in the field – it would also allow his officers and noncommissioned officers (NCO) to teach him about the army as a national institution and about the country that it was designed to defend. The glorious traditions of past wars and the threat posed by present enemies would be drilled into young recruits at an age at which this might leave a lasting impression. Thereafter, annual reserve training periods offered the opportunity to refresh martial skill and reinforce national identity. This was the way that European states fashioned citizen armies wedded to the nation and primed to defend it when the need arose. It should come as no surprise that, as the twentieth century developed, this militaristic nationalism threatened to absorb and corrupt the ideals of socialism just as it had those of liberalism in the previous century. Before 1914 'national socialism' was an unidentified societal malady. Nevertheless contrary, amorphous socialism was vulnerable to such infection; soldiers would be its pathogens and war would be its growth medium.

The process worked in France too.[37] Every year a homogenous, republican, democratic 'annual class' was fashioned from the myriad local contingents – Norman and Breton peasants, Parisian shop workers and factory hands, Lyonnais weavers and farmworkers from the Île-de-France – men who, when the mobilization decree was issued, would rally to the colours to avenge France's 1871 defeat with all the traditional *furia francese* they could muster. It was therefore no real surprise that when the call to arms was issued the trained men of Europe mustered at their war stations and passed without demur through the slightly surreal transition from civilian to soldier. Edouard Cœurdevey, an elementary school teacher in peacetime, recorded that when he departed from his local railway station 'calm reigned among all the men who had left their wives, their children, their harvest, their house, with the feeling that the war would cut them all down'. At his barracks in Besançon there was an unwelcome period of boring, listless waiting, still in the grip of recollections of painful farewells. Only once on the train to the front did the martial mood start to take the soldiers, now uniformed and armed. The men from the Midi were on their way to war: caricatures of the kaiser, a pig's head in a helmet, were passed around with much ribaldry. Patriotic songs were sung as soldiers bonded into military units in their last few days of calm. News of the progress of the war was sought at every halt. After detraining at Lure in the Vosges, they took trucks through villages peopled only by playful children and grim-faced women. Eventually signs of conflict appeared: columns of German prisoners and battle-weary men resting by the side of the road – men with lurid tales of combat. 'One fellow saw his pal cut in two. All laughed at the inaccuracy of the Germans' artillery fire and spoke with glee of the devastation by our 75s. They say that the Germans finish off the wounded.' Eventually they crossed the frontier into Germany (Alsace in fact, which was rightfully part of France). 'On the 13th I was woken by far-off gunfire. We were gripped with combat fever. The war will go well for us this time.'[38] Cœurdevey's picaresque journey was typical of the many millions made that autumn from quiet homes to thundering battlefields as prewar plans were put, it appeared seamlessly, into action.

EUROPE MAY HAVE BEEN SURPRISED BY THE WAR WHICH FOLLOWED FROM the assassination in Sarajevo – like Poincaré, many of Europe's crowned heads and diplomats were on state visits or holidaying in foreign resorts when it happened – but the continent was not unprepared for it. Since Europe was an armed camp of two rival alliances by 1914, many judged that it was not a case of would there be war, but when would that war be? Elaborate mobilisation plans existed for that eventuality. The alliance system did not actually cause the war (if anything it had averted it for several decades) but it certainly allowed it to spread rapidly from Europe's southeastern corner north, east and then west, as diplomatic obligations, national interest, military sabre-rattling and popular endorsement meshed together. As the July Crisis unfolded after the Austrians issued their ultimatum to Serbia Europe poised on tenterhooks. Europe's monarchs exchanged frantic telegrams, although these were designed more to limit the war to Eastern Europe than to reverse the fateful steps already taken by Austria, Germany and Russia. An appalled realisation that this might be the crisis that brought war swept the continent as events escalated, with crowds taking to the streets in vociferous, if essentially impotent, pro-peace demonstrations: they had abrogated the right to make war to their leaders. But once the declarations of war and orders for mobilisation started to buzz along Europe's telegraph wires, hardly any demurred. There followed a few weeks of suspended disbelief – although a general European war was something many had talked about, that the press had long speculated upon, few relished it. 'The keynote of popular feeling was quiet dignity, joined by determination, with an undercurrent of solemn gravity and responsibility,' Austrian reservist Fritz Kreisler noted as he passed through Vienna on his way to the front.[39] Dutifully the soldiers were cheered off to their war stations, with their bands playing and old men, women and children waving flags. Tears were shed too, but often in private: not perhaps because war was welcomed, but because this was the right thing to do now that war had taken hold of the nation. Children even played at war on France's beaches: 'The little girls insisted on being nurses, while the nervous little boys played the part of wounded.'[40]

Experiencing a different kind of nervousness, their fathers and elder brothers were already on their way to their war stations. 'Some of us will get killed,' one French major remarked to his hostess as he departed an overnight billet to lead his battalion back into battle. He had had four close shaves already, and the war was barely a month old. 'I wanted this war. I prayed for it. I should have been sad enough if I had died before it came. I have left a wife and children who I adore, but I am ready to lay down my life cheerfully for the victory of which I am so sure.' Such sentiments were commonplace.

The military system itself has frequently been blamed for the war. Such a rationale is too simplistic. If Europe's great powers were ready and willing to unleash their carefully prepared war machines in August 1914, these were much more than the armed forces themselves. It is states and societies, governments and peoples that make war. Armed forces are merely their instrument: the muscle power which links the actions of the ruling political brain and the passionate popular heart in Clausewitz's famous trinity of war making. Clearly, Europe was a volatile, fractious and militant continent, with governments spoiling for a fight and peoples willing and able to participate, collectively bellicose if privately apprehensive as to the personal consequences. The nineteenth century's relatively benign age of progress had, ironically, prepared and steeled soldiers and their societies for longer and bloodier wars. It was within this social, cultural and economic framework that the armies of 1914 went to war. The first clashes, defining events of the war that followed, would be on land. Behind these huge armies navies were deploying, states were organising, diplomats were plotting and statesmen were wondering, apprehensively, if they could actually control the tumult that had been released on the world. This was war, in all its horror, for all or nothing. It was everyone's war, and it would become everything.

# TWO

# INTO BATTLE

FROM THE GARDEN OF HER COTTAGE ON A HILL OVERLOOKING THE valley of the River Marne, Mildred Aldrich, an American expatriate, watched the decisive battle of the 1914 campaign, perhaps of the war, unfold.

This was Saturday morning, September 5, and one of the loveliest days I ever saw. The air was clear. The sun was shining. The birds were singing. But otherwise it was very still. It was a good day for battle. German cavalry patrols rode back and forth, in a cat-and-mouse hunt with English scouts mounted on bicycles as the armies searched for each other. The guns started firing mid-morning, rising to a crescendo in the early afternoon.

The battle had advanced right over the crest of the hill . . . From the eastern and western extremities of the plain we could see the artillery fire, but owing to the smoke hanging over the crest of the hill on the horizon, it was impossible to get an idea of the positions of the armies . . . When I first took this place on the hill, I had looked off at the plain and thought, "What a battlefield" . . . But when I thought that I had visions very different from what I was seeing. I had imagined long lines of marching soldiers, detachments of flying cavalry, like the war pictures at Versailles and Fontainebleau. Now I was actually seeing a battle, and it was nothing like that. There was only noise, belching smoke, and long drifts of white clouds concealing the hill . . . I could not but remember that we were only seeing the action on the extreme west of a battle-line which probably extended hundreds of miles. I had been told that Joffre had made a frontier of the Marne.[1]

The Battle of the Marne, Joffre's 'miracle' as it was soon to be eulogised in the Allied press, had begun.

Joffre's victory on the River Marne in September 1914 was far from miraculous: it represented the calm, pragmatic utilisation of France's railways by a man who understood the principles of strategic manoeuvre. An engineer and logistician before he had become France's prewar chief of staff, Joffre skilfully redeployed French forces from east to west in anticipation of the moment he would strike back. His own reserves could move more quickly on the railway than the Germans who were proceeding southwards at marching pace, and he was able to reinforce his centre, disengage his left wing and muster a new army on his left flank in the fortnight that it took the German armies to advance into France. Turning his retreating armies to counterattack the pursuing mass of German forces, he struck simultaneously with the newly formed Sixth Army out of Paris at the exposed German right wing. After five days of hard fighting along a 220-kilometre front stretching from the outskirts of Paris to the fortress of Verdun, the invader started to retire. But the German army, like the French, was far from beaten: mass armies were resilient things. In saving Paris, Joffre had condemned France to over four years of war on her own soil before the decisiveness of the counterattack on the Marne was finally demonstrated.

As the battle raged about them peasants stoically harvested the ripe wheat in the field below Aldrich's cottage: the soil was sacred to the French and the rhythms of rural life carried on in the face of adversity. Old men could remember the Germans trampling the ripening grain as they passed that way in 1870, and that catastrophe would not be repeated.[2] This time around, however, the earth was to be ravaged by far worse than marching feet:

> It was just about six o'clock when the first bomb that we could really see came over the hill. The sun was setting. For two hours we saw them rise, descend, explode. Then a little smoke would rise from one hamlet, then from another; then a tiny flame – hardly more than a spark – would be visible; and by dark the whole plain was on fire . . . There were long lines of grain-stacks and mills stretching across the plain. One by one they took fire, until, by ten o'clock, they stood like a procession of huge torches across my beloved panorama . . . and oh! The odour of it! I hope you will never know what it is like.[3]

The battle endured for several days, although the sound of cannon fire receding into the distance indicated how the fortunes of war had unfolded: the French centre had held against all the German army could throw at it. 'Be glad that you saw the turning of the tide in the noblest war fought for civilization,' a passing French officer remarked. 'I wonder', Aldrich noted, rhetorically: whether at the turning of the war, or of civilization, she did not specify.[4]

As the French army advanced again one medical orderly described to Aldrich the onrush of the enemy, with gusto and hyperbole perhaps, but identifying the essential nature of the war in which France was embroiled:

> We could only have stopped them [crossing the River Meuse], if at all, by an awful sacrifice of life. Joffre is not doing that. If the Germans want to fling away their men by the tens of thousands – let them. In the end we gain by it. We can rebuild a country; we cannot so easily rebuild a race. We mowed them down like a field of wheat, by the tens of thousands, and tens of thousands sprang into the gaps. They advanced shoulder to shoulder. Our guns could not miss them, but they were too many for us . . . We are bold enough, but we are not so foolhardy as to throw men away like that. They will be more useful to Joffre later.[5]

But, Aldrich attested, 'there was no sign on the fresh young face before me that the horror had left a mark' on the ambulance man. 'Perhaps it is lucky, since war is, that men can be like that. When they cannot, what then?'[6]

THE ARMIES THAT RANGED ACROSS NORTHERN FRANCE AND BELGIUM IN August and September 1914 were enormous, destructive and difficult to control. Already the stakes were high – the future of the country and the nation were in play – and if Germany and France had already sacrificed tens of thousands of lives to reach this point, there were millions more who could still be armed, trained and deployed to take up the fight. Prewar plans had existed to mobilise hundreds of thousands of men, to deploy multiple armies in a meticulously prepared plan of campaign and to engage the enemy in the hope that he could be overthrown in a huge, decisive encounter battle. Already these plans, and any such hopes, were in tatters. The German commander in chief, General Helmuth von Moltke, who had always doubted his ability to control the German military machine once it was unleashed, had suffered a nervous collapse.[7] While it was at least hoped that Joffre had learned one lesson from the costly early encounter battles on the frontiers, the manifest parameters of modern warfare entailed that the further sacrifice of Frenchmen's lives could not be avoided if France was to be liberated. In the short term it demanded a culling of France's high command, of those older generals who had a weak grasp on the precepts of modern warfare. In August and

September Joffre sacked two Army, ten army corps and thirty-eight divisional commanders. Men who better grasped the nature of the task that faced *la patrie* would take their place as armies began the halting and often painful process of adapting to attritional warfare.

General Joseph Joffre, who would dominate Entente strategy making in the first twenty-nine months of the war to an extent that was unprecedented and that today is unappreciated, did grasp the fundamental nature of the war. But he struggled to wage it effectively nonetheless. Born in 1852 in the Pyrenees, and the son of a cooper, he had first donned a uniform in 1870, one of many young Frenchmen hastily mobilised to meet the previous German invasion. Resuming his studies thereafter he graduated from France's prestigious École Polytechnique and joined the army, a respectable profession for a tradesman's son from the provinces. A military engineer by training, he was attuned to the needs of campaigning in modern conditions. He had made his command reputation leading a flying column in the capture of Timbuktu in 1894, but before then he had been a fortress and railway builder in France and the colonies. In a period of tense civil-military relations in turn-of-the-century France, his sound republican views brought him rapid promotion. Eventually he reached the top of the military hierarchy, appointed in 1911 as chief of the General Staff and tasked with preparing the army for war. Previously he had held the post of director of supply and communications, in which role he grasped the significance of railways and resources for warfare. As a man 'Papa' Joffre was popular with his troops if less so with politicians, who lived in constant fear of the return of a 'Napoleon' to French political life. Joffre himself was hardly cut out for the role: Britain's Prime Minister Herbert Asquith records meeting 'a big heavy man, stooping at the shoulders, with a shock of hay-coloured hair, eyebrows and moustache, bluish grey eyes, a broad hollow jowl and a soft low voice'. Yet his lack of military bearing and stout peasant figure belied a sharp, shrewd mind and determined will: 'I thought him more intelligent and impressive than the lean-faced more comical Foch,' Asquith noted, and he was struck by his 'resolute, confident, imperturbable optimism'.[8] His victory on the Marne in September 1914 when all seemed lost won him a popular reputation and for a time at least the freedom to direct French strategy unhindered by political interference. But he faced a tough challenge to master the battlefield as well as the broader strategic and political parameters of the people's war that was developing. No wonder then that he often felt out of his depth and beset with adversaries behind as well as in front. 'Poor Joffre', he was wont to exclaim in times of difficulty, with good reason.

\* \* \*

THERE HAD NOT BEEN A MAJOR WAR BETWEEN IMPERIAL POWERS FOR A century, and then industrialisation had been in its infancy. Certain recent conflicts had hinted at what modern war was like, the American Civil War for its longevity, and the Russo-Japanese War of 1904–5 for its intensity. But those wars were isolated and limited, both in the nations involved and the battle-space. Nevertheless, their nature was apparent to those who studied them closely. There would potentially be rather more to a future war than mobilisation and deployment plans and giant annihilating battles, Spenser Wilkinson, professor of the history of war at Oxford University, suggested. With the American Civil War as his template, in his 1910 study *War and Policy* he elaborated the 'elemental powers' that operated in conflicts between vast and complex industrial empires. Wars fought by modern states would 'sooner or later bring into action . . . the whole of the resources over which that nation has control', he believed. Once huge force met solid resistance 'a kind of inevitability [would pervade] them from beginning to end, and [give] to their results something of the character which in superstitious ages was assigned to the decrees of fate'.[9] A quick, smashing victory seemed to offer the only possible way of avoiding just such a protracted, fateful struggle.

The war that Europe remembered and that her military planners studied was that between France and Prussia from 1870–1. Perhaps, however, the wrong things were remembered for the wrong reasons. The defeat of France's field armies near her eastern frontiers was studied in Europe's military academies. The war's second phase of popular mobilisation which drew on the principles of the revolutionary *levée en masse* of 1793, when France had summoned her whole population to meet an earlier Prussian invasion, was less remarked, as was the breakdown of social order in France and the bloody repression of the 1871 Paris Commune as Frenchman fought Frenchman after peace with Germany had been agreed. This meant that those who theorized and prepared for a future war were more ready to fight great battles than a great war. Following Prussia's rapid defeat of Napoleon III's armies, Europe was gripped by an audacious new way of making war: prepare thoroughly, mobilise rapidly en masse, concentrate quickly using strategic railways, march fast and hit hard backed by powerful artillery, encircle and smash the enemy's armed forces with what the Prussian General Staff termed a strategy of annihilation (overlooking expediently that both French field armies had been besieged in fortresses before they capitulated, not smashed on the battlefield). Mass armies raised by universal conscription, elaborate planning for the first clash of battle which was expected to prove decisive and a general staff system to plan and manage it all were the fundamentals of early twentieth-century military method. This was, it was hoped, the way to make war swift, decisive and relatively cheap in lives and money. Even the British Empire had belatedly adopted the general staff system and planning as part of a more centralised system of imperial defence after the long and nearly humiliating encounter with the South African Boer republics.

War planning and strategic doctrine have ever since been condemned as detached from the reality of modern war. Generals on both sides were, nonetheless, quite aware of the sort of war that would develop should the enemy not be annihilated in the first great battles. There were ongoing and often bitter debates in military circles everywhere about the future of warfare. In Germany opinion was divided between those such as the author of the influential work *The Nation in Arms*, General Colmar von der Goltz, who accepted the inevitability of a mass war – a *Volkskrieg* or people's war – and argued that Germany should fashion her military institutions and plans accordingly, and others who believed effective planning and preparation could avoid such a worrying scenario.[10]

The operational plans drawn up before the war by Germany's General Staff (the elite army administration responsible for military planning) were realistic in this respect. A short war might secure Germany, while a long one would inevitably ruin her, whatever its outcome. Moreover, Germany faced an age-old strategic fear of war on two fronts at once. If one opponent could be annihilated – as France had been in 1870 – it offered a hope that the other might then be worn down in a longer struggle. When Helmuth von Moltke assumed the post of chief of the General Staff in 1905 the broad parameters of Germany's strategy had already been decided. Although he was the nephew of the elder Helmuth von Moltke who had masterminded the victory over France in 1871, he was far less capable of handling the responsibility of leading Germany's armies in 1914. Gottlieb von Jagow, Germany's foreign minister in 1914, later recollected that 'Moltke was a man who took his responsibilities very seriously but who rather suffered from the feeling that he was not quite up to the job – he was lacking in strategical genius'.[11] Moltke's predecessor, Schlieffen, had determined that France should be attacked first, with a powerful, sweeping 'right-hook' by four German armies through neutral Belgium. Russia, which would mobilise more slowly, and which at that time was temporarily weakened after her defeat by the Japanese and the ensuing political revolution, could wait: there would be time to rail Germany's victorious forces eastwards before Russia presented a credible threat. Although he tinkered with the details of the precise deployment of German armies in the West, Moltke did not feel competent enough to change the broad parameters of Germany's two-front strategy before 1914. In the interim, however, the window of opportunity that had existed in 1905 was closing. Although the principle of 'France first' still held sway, the practicalities had significantly changed, and not in Germany's favour. France would now be harder to beat. After the new 1913 army service law her army was increasing in size. French strategy, formulated in Joffre's so-called 'Plan XVII', was predicated on disrupting any German invasion with a violent counterattack and encouraging an early Russia offensive in the East to draw off German strength. Moltke therefore chose to strengthen the German defensive covering forces in Alsace and Lorraine at the expense of the strong right-flank manoeuvre that was the cornerstone of Schlieffen's strategy. More worrying were developments in the East. By 1914 Russia had more or less recovered her military strength, and was now expanding her army alarmingly under the Great Plan of 1913 initiated by war minister Sukhomlinov. Railway expansion in Poland (encouraged and partly paid for by the French) was accelerating Russian mobilisation such that Germany would no longer have the time to beat France before she had to face Russia.[12] This, it has been argued, was a significant factor in Germany's decision to go to war in 1914, when she felt she still had a chance.[13] This made it virtually impossible for Germany to limit herself to war with Russia only in 1914. Leaving aside the chaos that would have ensued in mobilisation if intricately timetabled railway movements had to be improvised from scratch, Russia's ally would not sit idly by if Germany went eastwards. In that case the French would have invaded, occupied the Rhineland and Ruhr industrial districts and immediately crippled Germany's war effort. If Germany was to be invaded, she could better afford to lose rural East Prussia than Krupp's industrial empire. Moltke would still have to gamble greatly in August 1914 that he could delay the Russians with a defensive covering force in East Prussia long enough to defeat France. He certainly appreciated that sooner or later he would have to redeploy substantial forces from West to East and that, however the first campaign developed, Germany faced 'a *Volkskrieg* that will not be settled by the means of one decisive battle . . . rather it will be a long, difficult struggle with a nation that will not give in before the entire strength of its people is broken and until our nation, even if we are victorious, is almost completely exhausted'.[14] German industry would decide such a war as much as her army and therefore to attack in the west was the best form of defence. Hardly surprising then, as Jagow remembered, that once war broke out Moltke was 'very nervous and obviously suffering from strong depression'.[15]

Germany's plan made strategic sense, but it was losing touch with military reality. General Ernst Köpke, Schlieffen's quartermaster general, had warned: 'We cannot expect quick, decisive victories. Army and nation will slowly have to get used to these unpleasant perspectives . . . the most offensive spirit [will only result in] a tedious and bloody crawling forwards step-by-step [in] siege-style [warfare].'[16] Communications and logistics would govern the tempo of operations. After detraining, the armies would only move at walking pace, and the side which could use the railways to redeploy reserves against marching columns would retain the initiative, as Joffre demonstrated so skilfully in redistributing his forces before the Battle of the Marne.

Strategy would take a back seat once battle was joined, as firepower and tactics were matched to determine who won on the battlefield. Weapons technology had made substantial advances since the late nineteenth century. Steel, rifled-barrelled, quick-firing artillery that could control the ground with firepower alone was the norm. The most famous and effective of the First World War's field guns, the French 75mm, could fire fifteen accurately aimed rounds per minute, and a four-gun battery could saturate an area of ground four hundred metres square with seventeen thousand shrapnel bullets in that time. More powerful explosives increased the range of projectiles, while specialised shells and fuses were developed for particular tasks. In particular, the high-explosive shell, which burst into jagged, lethal fragments when it hit the ground, could be fired with such intensity as to make the crossing of open ground all but impossible. The infantryman who had to attempt this dangerous mission was himself better equipped than ever before, with a breech-loading magazine rifle which in skilled hands could fire up to fifteen aimed shots a minute, a bayonet for hand to hand combat should the open killing ground be successfully crossed, and a personal entrenching tool, a recent but essential innovation. Also available, although in relatively small numbers when the war began, was the weapon that would become ubiquitous and synonymous with the industrial battlefield, the machine gun, generally deployed two per infantry battalion in 1914. All this new, efficient killing machinery was the product of a developing scientific-technological base geared to the needs of the state war machine. Novel technologies were to be incorporated into the mechanisms of battle too: the internal combustion engine; aircraft; electrical communications, both the fixed-line telephone and wireless telegraphy; barbed wire, the delineator of the trench lines, prosaic yet ubiquitous and a challenging tactical obstacle; and from early 1915 poison gas, the most appalling weapon of industrialised warfare. More mundane instrument of war – prefabricated buildings, electricity generators, medical supplies, typewriters, preserved food – sustained the bureaucracy and support services of Europe's huge armed forces and the men themselves. The coming war would be one of systems, into which men would have to be integrated, and which leaders would have to understand and manage.[17]

While the offensive spirit that animated the German and other European armies before 1914 cannot be denied – moral and psychological factors were understandably paramount when faced with the potential horrors of the technical battlefield – the practical limitations on making war did not go unnoticed and were evident when the armies clashed in August 1914. Tactics proved murderous when formations clashed frontally and deployed their full firepower: quick-firing artillery, machine guns and magazine rifles produced horrendous rates of casualties, while absolute numbers were astronomical given the scale of the early fighting. Some 210,000 French casualties on the frontiers were matched by a similar number of Germans. These numbers doubled by the end of the Battle of the Marne, after which, as Köpke predicted, siege-style warfare commenced.

Trenches, ubiquitous and synonymous with the First World War, appeared quickly. They were essential and practical, and as such would contribute to the prolongation of the war as well as determine the nature of the fighting. On the battlefield they offered shelter from the shells and bullets that controlled the ground. Even the most rudimentary excavation would protect a man from enemy fire; the deeper, reinforced dugouts that were rapidly engineered offered protection from all but the heaviest shells. In a war notorious for the number of men killed or wounded, there is a certain irony in the fact that the trench systems that evolved were created to protect human flesh and economise on manpower. Systems of field fortification could be held with fewer men than open ground: artillery and machine guns became the means for controlling the killing zone between the armies, which would be labelled 'no man's land', while barbed-wire entanglements restricted access to it. In the short term, therefore, defensive positions seemed to offer operational flexibility. The opposing trench lines that coagulated along the line of the River Aisne, to which the Germans had retreated after the Battle of the Marne, could be held with fewer men, and so army corps could be redeployed north and westwards in an attempt to turn the enemy's open flank. Late September and early October were spent in this so-called 'race to the sea', but neither side could force a decision. Come mid-October, when the opposing lines rested on the Belgian Channel coast, warfare had assumed a different form.

IN JOCKEYING FOR ADVANTAGE IN THE WESTERN THEATRE, TOO MANY MEN were crammed into too small a space, a problem exacerbated by the fact that military depots could quickly fill up the depleted ranks with reservists. In the East there was much more room to manoeuvre: perhaps too much, for there, in contrast, whole armies could be surrounded and broken without breaking the enemy's resistance completely. Here too, offensive plans were put into action in August 1914, with mixed results. After an early shock, Germany staved off the Russian invasion of East Prussia through a mixture of old-fashioned operational skill and Russian mistakes.

Austria rushed headlong at her enemies and came off worse everywhere. Conrad faced his own two-front war. He wished to punish the upstart Serbia – that was, after all, the reason why the empire had gone to war – but he also had to fend off Serbia's powerful Russian ally. Italy, a putative ally in 1914, was also a worry. Although the Italians chose to remain neutral in August 1914, reasoning that the actual circumstances of war did not oblige them to honour their Triple Alliance treaty obligations, they remained a potential threat to Austria's rear if, in time, they chose to intervene on the side of the other liberal states. Conrad certainly suspected them of duplicity, and on this occasion he turned out to be correct. Austria's chief of staff had a difficult personality: a workaholic obsessed with detail and a tough political operator, he was at times scheming and mistrustful, argumentative and vain. Such characteristics did not endear him to those he had to work with and on occasion they got him into trouble. In 1911 the emperor had temporarily relieved him from his post after a clash with the foreign minister over his demand for a preventive war against Italy. But Conrad was also a highly professional soldier who had risen by dint of talent and hard work. He was a thinker, an author on infantry tactics and a former staff college instructor, rather than a leader of men. Like so many of Europe's senior generals in 1914 he had not seen combat, and so while he encouraged active training in the army he thought in terms of strategic map manoeuvres rather than close-range battlefield encounters. His fertile, businesslike but detail-loving mind planned and replanned the campaigns that he would fight when the opportunity came.[18]

For Conrad Austria's German ally was her best security guarantee and shield against Russia. His forces would cooperate with Moltke's on the eastern front, but he expected his allies to blunt the main Russian advance into East Prussia and, given the lack of effective coordinated planning with his allies before the war, he had no reason to doubt their solid support.[19] He was well aware, however, that France would have to be defeated first and that his army would have to contain Russia's offensive in the short term. While Austria would deploy thirty-eight divisions northwards to defend the Hungarian frontier by advancing against Russia's southern flank, eight divisions would be concentrated against Serbia at the start of hostilities to settle that account once and for all. A third force, of thirteen divisions, would be held as a central reserve.

In the first weeks of the war Serbia seemed on the verge of collapse. Her capital, Belgrade, very close to her border with Austria-Hungary, had had to be abandoned by the field army that retreated into the interior. Conrad optimistically sent his strategic reserve southwards to finish things off. Before it reached Serbia, that order had to be countermanded because Russia had concentrated the bulk of her forces (four armies out of six) against Austria. The Russians met the Habsburg armies in a series of confused battles around the fortress of Lemberg. Initially checked by the Austrians' premature mid-August attacks, the weight of numbers began to tell as Russian forces concentrated, and by the end of the first week of September Conrad's forces were in retreat. Lemburg fell and the Russians besieged the empire's other frontier fortresses, Krakow and Przemyśl.

Like those in the West, the early battles in Galicia were huge and costly. 420,000 Austrians were killed, wounded or captured, around one-third of the army's effective field strength. Russian losses were comparable: the Russian army suffered 530,000 casualties in total by the end of 1914.[20] Evidently, as the Austro-Prussian war veteran and head of the emperor's military chancery General Alfred von Bolfras suggested to Conrad, 'Mars seems to have become very voracious . . . If war was once a chivalrous duel, it is now a dastardly slaughter.'[21] It had proved the same in the Balkans where General Radomir Putnik's Serbian army had struck back decisively, driving the Austro-Hungarian forces from Serbia by mid-September and invading Bosnia-Herzegovina themselves. That campaign went back and forth until December, with two more Austrian invasions being repulsed. By the time the Serbs recaptured their capital and drove the Austrians back across the River Danube once more the two sides had fought themselves to a standstill. The Balkan campaign cost the Habsburg army 150,000 and the Serbians 132,000 casualties, yet that front too was now stalemated.[22] It was becoming evident that the war would last years rather than months, and many hundreds of thousands of men would die. It was clear too that Conrad, who had lost the favourite of his three sons in Galicia, had lost heart. He was already counselling a separate peace with Russia, and blaming the Germans' failure to defeat France quickly and come to his aid for Austria's misfortunes.[23] The Germans for their part were worried about the fighting capacity and staying power of their ally. General Erich von Falkenhayn, Moltke's replacement, created a new Ninth Army in late September to support Austria's attempts to counterattack the Russians. A series of violent offensives and counteroffensives in Russian Poland and Galicia during the autumn proved indecisive. The Ninth Army was checked in its advance on Warsaw, although the siege of Przemyśl was lifted, at least temporarily.[24] Because she had not beaten France quickly, Germany could not come to her ally's aid in greater force, and in the East decisive victory would ultimately prove as chimerical as in the West.

Indeed if such a victory was possible, only the Russians could win it. Germany had her own Russian invasion to contend with, which she did with much more success than Conrad. Two Russian armies threatened East Prussia, but fortuitously they were ill-coordinated and separated by an impassable area of lakes and marshland. The German Eighth Army that opposed them was able to manoeuvre using East Prussia's railway infrastructure to engage them separately. In the sprawling Battles of Tannenberg (26–30 August) and the Masurian Lakes (8–11 September) the two Russian armies were broken. The East Prussian campaign represented the last hurrah of an old style of strategic manoeuvre warfare, but as in all the other battles of 1914 casualties were enormous: 203,000 Russians (with another 137,000 prisoners lost) and 52,000 Germans. At the same time these victories brought two previously unknown soldiers, General Paul von Hindenburg and his chief of staff Erich Ludendorff, to popular notice. Unfortunately for Germany, however, their crushing victory in East Prussia falsely suggested to them that annihilating battles remained a viable strategic alternative to attrition.

Breaking two Russian armies out of eight was no more going to end the multifront land war quickly than was Moltke's gamble on knocking out France, which merely hoped by eliminating one of Germany's adversaries to bring about a single-front war that might ultimately be winnable. Still, the two principal land fronts were interlinked, and Moltke had to pay sufficient attention to the eastern front as it was here that Germany might lose the war quickly herself. German's central strategic dilemma was immediately manifested. With the Eighth Army's situation precarious, Molke ordered the transfer of two army corps from east to west at the end of August, weakening the western attack at a crucial moment. The availability of interior lines – railways on which reserves could be moved to threatened points on the multiple fronts – would come to prove vital in Germany's long defensive war. This first use, however, showed that right from the start Germany was vulnerable.

By early September the truth of the elder Moltke's famous maxim, that no plan survives contact with the enemy, was manifest everywhere. After only six weeks of war, the fateful decision that would determine the war's course and nature was taken. Germany's armies had overstretched themselves on the battlefield just as the empire's leaders had done in taking on the combined might of Russia, France and the British Empire. A lieutenant-colonel of the General Staff, Richard Hentsch gained an infamous place in history on 9 September 1914, when acting on the authority vested in him by the OHL he ordered the right wing of the German armies to retreat from the Marne. The German armies merely retreated to a strong defensive line along the River Aisne, where they dug in to liberate their own reserves to strike elsewhere. There was insufficient space in which to manoeuvre vast armies and by mid-October improvised trench lines stretched all the way to the North Sea.

These manoeuvres demonstrated that the war on the land front was already slipping out of the grasp of its directors. In its early months war making had been left to generals who proffered plans which promised quick victory while privately believing that such a victory was unlikely and a lengthy attritional war too problematic to contemplate. Mass war was proving bigger than any commander, however bold or energetically executed his operations. As Ferdinand Foch, the French general who was to rise to supreme command of the Allied armies, had prophesied to the British secretary of state for war, John Seely, in 1912,

> the armies have outgrown the brains of the people who direct them. I do not believe that there is any man living big enough to control these millions. They will stumble about, and then sit down helplessly in front of each other thinking only of their means of communication to supply these vast hordes who must eat.[25]

The large armies deployed needed space and time in which to manoeuvre, and such ponderous formations were difficult to control, transport and supply. When they did engage, modern firepower made battles murderous, although the size of armies and the ability to replace casualties rapidly with trained reserves rendered them indecisive. Resilience was built into the military system, such that, although it was designed for short, decisive wars it proved ideally suited for protracted, attritional ones. The operational and tactical problems that emerged by the end of 1914 were unprecedented and would engage the brains of military professionals thereafter. They were not unsolvable, and many generals responded to the challenges presented by static, positional warfare. By 1918 Foch would be controlling these millions effectively once more. By then, warfare had changed fundamentally.

GERMANY'S PROBLEMS WERE NOT CONFINED TO THE BATTLEFIELD. ON THE other fighting front, at sea, Germany faced a further threat, since the might of the Royal Navy had been deployed to sink her ships and destroy her commerce. In speculating on a future world war in 1912, the Prussian general and military analyst Friedrich von Bernhardi had warned that the difficulty of fighting a land war against France and Russia would be exacerbated by the intervention of the world's leading naval power, Great Britain: 'It is in this double menace by sea and on the mainland of Europe that the grave danger of our political position lies, since all freedom of action is taken from us and all expansion barred.'[26] The truth of Bernhardi's contention would be tested in 1914. The British Admiralty at least thought that sea power was a quick-working, decisive weapon. But as it turned out, the Entente's navies, like their armies, were merely able to contain, but not defeat, the Central powers. By the end of the year Germany's global strategic options were certainly restricted, her surface fleet confined and her trade disrupted. But in the submarine Germany possessed the means to fight back: as on land, warfare at sea would present new challengers to the belligerents from 1915.

In their control of the sea the Entente had an immense advantage over the Central powers, one that would persist throughout the war but that would not prove rapidly decisive. The Allies possessed a vast superiority in warships, both in battleships and the smaller vessels (cruisers, destroyers, submarines and minesweepers) that were the workhorses of the fleet. In a competitive naval arms race before the war states had built huge, costly fleets that represented the height of military technology and embodied the pride and power of the nation. Germany in particular had built battleships to assert her global position, and Great Britain had built even more to assure hers, contributing to Great Britain's move firmly into the anti-German camp. In 1914 the kaiser's High Seas Fleet's twenty-two powerful, modern *Dreadnought*-style capital ships faced the thirty-two battleships and battle cruisers of Britain's Grand Fleet across the North Sea. In wartime it would be Britain and Germany that would contest control of the seas. But it turned out that war at sea would not be made with these battleships and their big guns but with the many smaller vessels that attacked and defended trade and also with modern industrial killing technologies: floating mines, torpedoes, hydrophone sound detectors and depth charges. The other great powers had followed suit. France had Europe's third largest navy with eleven dreadnoughts, although only four were fully commissioned in 1914; Austria-Hungary had four (with three in commission in August 1914); and Italy had four (by the time she went to war in May 1915), with two others being built.[27] Russia had eight on the stocks, and Turkey two, that were being completed in British shipyards. Their compulsory purchase by the Admiralty in August 1914 was one of the factors that pushed Turkey into the enemy camp.

The Entente dominated merchant shipping too. Almost 80 percent of the oceangoing merchant fleet – passenger liners and cargo vessels – was British, French, Japanese and Italian. Nearly two-thirds sailed under the red ensign of the British Empire, as well as more than half the world's smaller coastal trading vessels. British shipyards also built 60 percent of the world's merchant ships. German firms owned only 11 percent of oceangoing vessels, while neutrals had the remainder. Moreover, Germany's merchant ships were vulnerable when war broke out: they could either run for home and risk capture or take shelter in neutral ports. Either way, they would not be able to sustain Germany's overseas trade in the face of Allied naval power and immediately became a costly liability rather than an asset. Not surprisingly, German shipowners tried to sell their vessels en masse to neutral states (despite its questionable legality since the international Declaration of London in 1909 prohibited switching belligerents' vessels' flags in wartime) or allowed the navy to convert them to armed auxiliary merchant cruisers.[28] Thus, from the outbreak of hostilities it would be the Central powers' access to neutral shipping that would determine the viability of their import-export trade in wartime.

Commerce warfare, based on blockading enemy ports and interrupting overseas trade by taking prizes at sea, had been a weapon of war since ancient times and one that the British (and their enemies) had employed since Tudor times. The last time, in the wars against Napoleon a century earlier, maritime blockade had constrained the enemy but had not proved decisive. Whether in the era of modern capitalism things had changed or, as in 1814, a coup de grace on land would be needed to reap the rewards of slow economic strangulation remained to be tested. But the global economy seemed to offer another target, the financial and commercial viability of the enemy coalition. Economic chaos or bankruptcy had the potential to destroy a modern war effort more quickly and more decisively than military action, at least according to the predictions of Ivan Bloch, a Russian-Polish banker whose 1898 book *Is War Now Impossible?* was widely discussed.[29] Unfortunately, those who did study his theories took them as a template for how war might be brought to a swift, decisive conclusion in future and not, as Bloch had intended, as an argument against war.

One man who probably did read Bloch carefully (in an abridged English translation at least – the Russian edition of his book ran to over three thousand pages in six volumes) was Admiral Lord John Fisher, first sea lord (the professional head of the Royal Navy) from 1904–10.[30] 'Jacky' Fisher had a distinguished career at sea – and briefly on land when his construction of an armoured train during the Anglo-Egyptian War in 1882 brought him to public notice – that ended with him commanding the Mediterranean Fleet. But since he suffered from seasickness all his life, the desk jobs that he held at the Admiralty in the later stages of his career may have been more congenial. Although not a particularly tall man, with a fixed gaze and a forceful manner he cut a striking figure. He was a man of spirit and energy, which did not endear him to all those he met, and he had a number of long-running personality clashes with other admirals and senior politicians. But he also possessed considerable charm. He was an accomplished and enthusiastic dancer, which endeared him to the ladies, if perhaps less so to the junior officers who he insisted dance on board his ships. His complexion was rather jaundiced, a lasting effect of dysentery and malaria contracted when in Egypt, which gave him something of an Asian appearance. But he was an Englishman through and through, and in the first decade of the twentieth century that meant being hostile to Germany. As well as thoroughly modernising the British fleet and withdrawing it from its worldwide distribution to home waters to confront the Imperial High Seas Fleet, Fisher planned carefully how to wage war with Germany: how to defeat the German navy at sea of course, but also how to crush the German nation. Bloch's prediction that 'the future of war [is] not fighting but famine, not the slaying of men but the bankruptcy of nations and the break-up of the whole social organisation' was manna to the firebrand admiral who encouraged the Admiralty's planners to promote 'economic warfare' – a decisive attack on German economic solvency on the immediate outbreak of a war – as the way to do so.[31]

The prewar world economy had been integrated to an extent that was not replicated until the second half of the twentieth century, and the City of London was its hub. The world's financial and trading networks converged on the Square Mile. Dominating the maritime insurance market, the trade in international bills of exchange, and global gold holdings potentially gave Britain the whip hand in an economic war.[32] Yet the short-term financial expedients that had to be rushed through parliament by Chancellor of the Exchequer David Lloyd George to prevent the implosion of Britain's own economy in August 1914 indicated that perhaps the bigger and more developed economies were more vulnerable to economic warfare than the smaller. Britain went to war, fortuitously, on a bank holiday and the banks were to remain closed for three more days while the Treasury took steps, through the Bank of England, to adjust from a peacetime to a wartime economy. Lloyd George 'appealed to the public to refrain on patriotic grounds from attempting to hoard gold': new 'Treasury' banknotes were to be issued at the rate of five million pounds per day to prevent a run on the banks. To rescue the system of international commercial credit centred on the City of London a one-month moratorium on payments was arranged, while the Bank of England agreed to guarantee prewar bills of exchange and to underwrite the clearing houses' liabilities until one year after the war had ended: without a functional global trading system the Allied war machine could never get going.[33] These steps and other esoteric financial measures stopped the international financial economy from imploding. Every other belligerent took similar actions. Such government intervention in the financial sector was a harbinger of what was to follow in other sectors of the economy as war was prolonged. Bloch was wrong that war would break economies, although it would force considerable adaptation and far greater state involvement in and regulation of the private-enterprise economy, more so as the war stalemated from 1915. That Britain's own financial institutions proved shaky during the transition from war to peace suggested, however, that the German economy could be attacked with the expectation of substantial and rapid damage to the Central powers' financial stability.

This assumption proved false largely due to the fact that economic warfare would be fought as much on the diplomatic as the maritime front. A fortnight into the war the cabinet was starting to realise that 'the "strangulation" of Germany' was already being challenged: 'The Americans protest, in the interest of neutral shipping, against our following the German example and laying down mines in the North Sea . . . there was a lot of talk about international law and its niceties,' Asquith noted even before the armies had clashed.[34] Neutral opinion was the Scylla of economic warfare: the Charybdis was that government interference in international trade might prove potentially more harmful to Britain's global mercantile economy than to that of its enemies. Indeed from the war's early days the Foreign Office and the Board of Trade seemed to obstruct the Admiralty's conduct of commercial warfare more than the enemy.[35] Business confidence was and remained a pillar, if an obscure one, of the war effort. The Board of Trade put the case, often forcibly, for not taking measures that would harm Britain's own economic activity. As Walter Runciman, its ever-cautious president, acknowledged in May 1915, 'In so far as we had been able to conduct our great business concerns as though no war were interfering with them, we had added to our national strength and had been able to give material assistance to our Allies', valuable accomplishments in what was shaping up to be a long and costly war in which economic resilience was essential.[36]

In the first phase of the war an economic strategy of 'business as usual', which sustained Britain's own financial solvency (and therefore that of her allies, to whom in the early months of the war she acted as credit banker), was seen as vital to the war effort. This equated with the principles of British liberalism as well as following the well-worn ruts of British strategy, but its advocates had overlooked the fact that in the past 'the exercise of British sea power had not only annoyed its enemies but it had also upset its allies'.[37] To that list might be added neutrals. Military and diplomatic steps that threatened to harm Allied markets and credit would therefore not be taken lightly.

Certain financial weapons strengthened the Entente's economic arsenal. With government support the City of London, which controlled global credit and shipping finance, could potentially regulate the chartering of vessels, maritime insurance and bills of credit in their favour. In 1914 this was a step too far for state interference in the private-enterprise economy. In fact the British government stepped in to underwrite the maritime insurance market based on Lloyds of London which, like other elements of the global trading system, was close to collapse as the threat to merchant vessels sent premiums soaring. The truth was that any unilateral measures taken to restrict enemy economic activity by interfering in the working of the market were likely to rebound on the instigators who had a greater stake in keeping the system functioning than Germany, or on neutrals that might turn hostile.

'THE BRITISH ISLES LIE LIKE A BREAKWATER 600 MILES LONG ATHWART THE German trade stream,' the Admiralty noted in 1906, 'and nothing should elude our vigilance once "war on German trade" is established.'[38] This commanding position allowed a distant maritime blockade to be established by standing patrols operating across the Strait of Dover and the North Sea between Scotland and the Norwegian coast. Operating away from the enemy's defended coasts British warships would be less vulnerable to attrition by floating mines, submarine torpedoes and mechanical wear and tear. Merchant ships coming across the Atlantic would have to pass through these cordons on their way to Germany or the neutral countries through which she traded. If ships did not call at British ports for inspection they would be stopped and searched, and if contraband was found or the final destination of the cargo was uncertain the ship would be embargoed. In the Mediterranean too the French fleet (reinforced by a British battle cruiser squadron) possessed adequate superiority over the Austrian navy, and once Italy joined the war that fleet could be bottled up in the Adriatic with a blockade barrier established across the Strait of Otranto at its narrow mouth.

Clearing German trade from the high seas was relatively straightforward. By 19 August thirty-five German prizes had been taken as they tried to make it home. Many more enemy merchant ships were skulking in neutral ports, afraid to run the Royal Navy's gauntlet. Yet even while the seas were being cleared in August 1914, the limitations on controlling Germany's access to global trade were becoming evident. Enemy trade with Allied nations might be cut off (potentially, if not actually as it turned out), but the Central powers' trade with neutral countries – in particular the United States, Latin America and Scandinavia (and Italy until she joined the war) – could not easily be interfered with. Goods on a recognised list of commodities that were sustaining the war effort could legitimately be intercepted and confiscated as contraband. The list of goods actually designated as contraband was relatively short in 1914: essentially weapons, munitions and military equipment destined for a belligerent army. Enforcing a blockade was complicated by the concept of 'conditional contraband' – commodities such as foodstuffs, animal fodder and fuel, which had both civilian and military use – which legally could only be taken as a prize if it could be proved by documents of assignment that a cargo was destined for military use.

As well as the neutrals' direct seaborne trade with Germany and Austria-Hungary, overland trade through contiguous neutral states – Denmark, the Netherlands and Switzerland in particular – would ensure the Central powers' access to the global trading economy and financial system. Dutch neutrality had been respected in 1914, contrary to the wishes of the German General Staff, since Holland was identified as a vital commercial lifeline should the war not be won as quickly as the army expected. Holland was able to export Dutch produce to Germany at inflated prices, replacing it with imports, and also to import more Entente-produced commodities and reexport them to Germany at a profit, tearing a gaping hole in the Allied blockade. Understandably, many firms sought to divert their preexisting trade through neutral intermediaries. Before the war Britain in particular had a thriving commercial trade with Germany, which the outbreak of hostilities threatened to destroy, harming British firms' profitability, and in some cases threatening them with bankruptcy. In what was expected to be a short war decided by rapid military action, why should trade suffer and firms collapse? Why indeed should they not exploit this sudden short-term opportunity for greater profit? Trading with the enemy was therefore a concern for Allied governments. It led to some surprising anomalies, such as, for example, Germany importing large numbers of sausage skins from Britain via Holland, her own production being diverted to make the gasbags for zeppelin airships! Appeals to patriotic duty would only have limited impact when increased profits or a business's very viability were also factors. At the same time, it went against liberal economic principles for the state to intervene directly in private business affairs. The expanding war effort would test and erode such principles in time, but in its first phase the navy fought the economic war with one hand tied behind its back by political scruples, economic worries and diplomatic constraints. Britain and her allies needed to trade with, indeed to strengthen economic ties with, neutrals as their own war efforts took shape and therefore the Foreign Office became an important body for managing wartime economic regulations, often working at cross-purposes with the Admiralty. The navy might maintain the blockade physically, but the Foreign Office set the parameters of blockade, in terms of what was and was not contraband and how economic and commercial relations with allies and neutrals were managed.

GERMANY HAD MEANS TO CONTEST THE ALLIES' MASTERY OF THE SEAS. IN 1914 German surface raiders took the commerce war to the Allies, preying on merchant ships in the Atlantic, Pacific and Indian Oceans. The Admiralty sent bigger warships to hunt them down and destroy them. With one misfortune – the destruction of a British cruiser squadron by Vice-Admiral Maximilian Graf von Spee's Pacific squadron off Coronel in Chile on 1 November 1914 – that task was easily accomplished. Von Spee's five cruisers were caught by the British battle cruisers *Inflexible* and *Invincible* near the Falkland Islands on 8 December and all but one were sunk. Proving that some old-established martial traditions would persist despite the novelty of the war, the German admiral went down with his flagship. In 1914 German cruisers sank 423,600 tons of Allied shipping, but by the end of the year it looked as if the open oceans belonged to the Royal Navy.

The narrower seas might still be contested, at least while the High Seas Fleet remained afloat. But first blood was drawn by a new weapon, untested in war but destined to become the scourge of the seas in the twentieth century. Early in the morning on 22 September, three obsolescent British cruisers patrolling the North Sea – *HMS Aboukir, Hogue* and *Cressy* – were sunk by a single German submarine. While some cynical wits at the Admiralty had dubbed this patrol 'the live bait squadron' because its ships were no match for the fast, heavily armed battle cruisers that the German navy might have despatched into the North Sea to hunt them down, their sinking by the U-boat *U9* was an unpleasant surprise. After this early misfortune, 'periscopeitis' was to afflict the Royal Navy in the early months of the war, given the obvious vulnerability of capital ships. In the 'First Battle of Scapa Flow' a few weeks earlier the Grand Fleet had hastily put to sea as their escorting destroyers fired wildly at phantom submersibles – probably seals – that were invading the anchorage.[39]

All navies had been adding submarines to their fleets since submersible and diesel-electric turbine-engine technology became efficient around the turn of the century. Submarines' effectiveness had yet to be tested in wartime conditions, but Germany certainly planned that its growing U-boat fleet would have an important role in a naval war against Britain. At the war council on 8 December 1912 the kaiser had instructed Tirpitz specifically to build up the submarine fleet and to lay mines in the Thames estuary: then he suggested submarines might be used to disrupt British troop transports, but in the event the BEF was shipped to France without loss.[40] While the kaiser wanted a powerful battle fleet for reasons of prestige, he and his admirals appreciated that Germany possessed in the submarine a weapon that might help to even the odds against the Royal Navy as well as give her a fighting chance in the commerce war.

There was another naval weapon, the floating mine, which had the potential to take big prizes for small effort. In October the German auxiliary cruiser *Berlin* managed to evade the North Sea cordon and lay mines in the Irish Sea in the approaches to Liverpool. The intention was to catch merchantmen, but a bigger prize, the battleship *HMS Audacious*, hit one of these mines and sank.[41] Together, these balancing expedients seemed to put the Royal Navy's ascendancy in the narrow seas at risk. Rear-Admiral Sir David Beatty, who commanded the Grand Fleet's First Battle Cruiser Squadron, complained to Churchill: 'The menace of mines and submarines is proving larger every day, and adequate means to meet or combat them are not forthcoming, and we are gradually being pushed out of the North Sea and off our own particular perch.'[42] Following the occupation of the Belgian Channel ports Ostend and Zeebrugge in October 1914 the German naval threat came closer to home. Destroyers, submarines and minelayers based in those ports had the potential to challenge Allied naval control of the English Channel and menace the supply lines of the British army in France.

'Mines are a hellish device which every civilized nation except the Germans wanted to abolish at the Hague years ago,' Asquith opined.[43] Since they blew up ships indiscriminately their use was morally questionable, but they had not been banned by international law. After Germany deployed them in British coastal waters – the first Royal Navy ship sunk in the war, the cruiser *HMS Amphion*, hit a mine off Harwich on 6 August while returning from sinking the *Königin Louise* which had laid it – the Admiralty followed suit and started to lay its own mines in German coastal waters. This was the first blow in 'a war of sweeps, minelaying, sudden sharp clashes between relatively small numbers, and of course "ambushes" in the form of submarine attacks'.[44] Britain could and would resort to mining on a scale never imagined by Germany. After some debate and procrastination owing to a strong early war fear of antagonising neutrals, in November the Admiralty announced that the

Royal Navy would lay minefields in the North Sea, which was declared a 'military area'. This would force neutral vessels bound for Germany, Scandinavia or the Netherlands to sail via the English Channel, thereby obliging their captains to stop to receive instructions on the routes they might take to the continent and of course to have their cargoes inspected when they did so.[45]

The economic and maritime war was also to be one of challenges to the (somewhat vague, incomplete and contested) international laws of the sea, its weapons the exchange of diplomatic notes. The legitimacy of stopping and searching neutral vessels was the first belligerent right to be questioned. The United States, the greatest nonbelligerent commercial power and a long-term believer in the freedom of the seas, soon stood up as the champion of neutral rights in wartime. Following some desultory ambassadorial protests, on 26 December 1914 a formal diplomatic note denouncing British detention of neutral vessels in transit was submitted. '[It] is a nuisance, [although] long expected,' Asquith recorded. There was sharp practice on both sides.

> Their merchants and shipowners have behaved and are behaving as fraudulently as they can, knowing perfectly well that most of the copper etc which is shipped often under false papers for Holland and Denmark is really destined for Germany. But they have some technical points in their favour, and the President whose position becomes daily more precarious, dare not offend the powerful money interest. What a country![46]

Thereafter Britain's diplomats were obliged to negotiate the delicate way between maintaining and enhancing the Central powers' commercial isolation and mollifying neutral protest so as not to compromise the neutrals' willingness to trade with the Allies, whose war effort was much more dependent on non-European commodities than the Central powers'. In essence, early blockade policy became 'to impose the tightest controls that the Americans would tolerate'.[47] Keeping the neutrals sympathetic was probably more important diplomatically and commercially than undermining their relationship with the enemy. The better diplomacy was conducted, the more potent economic warfare would become.

In his prediction that the global capitalist economy could not withstand a lengthy conflict Bloch proved only half right: genuine bankruptcy and societal collapse would follow the fighting and slaughter, not substitute for it. Although there were financial ripples across Europe and the world in autumn 1914 as the global economy adjusted from peace to war, national economies proved as adaptable as societies to industrialised mass war, although the financial stability of states and the future of the global trading economy would also be staked on victory. Similarly, post-war economic and financial security was to become a key war aim of both sides as their vulnerability to economic pressure became apparent. Lord Selborne, president of Britain's Board of Agriculture, acknowledge the real role of 'economic and financial attrition' in a memorandum written for the prime minister in August 1915. Rather than starving the Central powers out, he suggested that 'the financial difficulties of both their government and of their commercial and industrial interests may bring them to their knees before their military force in exhausted.' To achieve such a victory, however, Britain had to conduct her own war effort with due economy and develop her domestic armaments industries, especially as her indebtedness to the United States was already growing alarmingly.[48]

IT TURNED OUT THAT NEITHER LAND POWER NOR SEA POWER, NOR ECONOMIC Armageddon, could bring the war to an end quickly. The land battles of 1914 may have been decisive in that they stopped the Germans getting to Paris and the Russians to Berlin, although they were not conclusive. Mass armies were resilient, especially when they had the people behind them. Moltke certainly identified the seed of defeat in Germany's failure to secure a quick victory on one front at least: 'Your Majesty, we have lost the war,' he pronounced to the kaiser shortly before being relieved of his command. Now, however, the war was stalemated. Germany accepted a state of siege, challenging the Entente to evict her armies from the ground they had occupied. The Entente on the other had faced the dilemma of whether and how to engage Germany in the continuing land war, or whether to exploit their advantages on the maritime and diplomatic fronts. For both sides, the home front would also start to become a preoccupation now that the war was deadlocked, as manpower and resources were organised for the long war that none had wanted, but all were resolved to continue. While this mobilisation was underway during 1915, armies and navies would continue to contest, and new land fronts would be opened, occasioned by Turkey's entry into the war in November.

As winter set in, both sides felt that they had secured an advantage over their adversaries: German troops were entrenching in French, Belgian and Russian-Polish territory; the Austrian fortress at Przemyśl, relieved in November, was besieged again. How to end the war without throwing away such advantages eluded both sides' leaders. In the meantime, hearts had been hardened behind the cause after the initial shock of war had morphed into the righteous indignation of conflict. A mounting hatred of the enemy, catalysed by his cruel actions on the battlefield and barbaric depredations on the civilian population as armies passed through, gripped combatants and people. They had good reasons to fight on now and no one yet wanted to end the war, even if they were already starting to hate its nature and consequences.[49] Military morale – whether that of the French *poilu* defending hearth and home, the British 'Tommy' sustaining 'brave little Belgium' or the German fighting for fatherland and honour – remained high.

In 1914 'Europeans experienced in full the ferocity of a war that combined industrial firepower and logistics with the fighting power and staying power that nationalism could generate'.[50] It had brought vast armies crashing against each other in France and Belgium, East Prussia, Poland, Hungary and Serbia, where they had locked in mortal combat. This was the ultimate legacy of the confrontational imperialistic politics of the great powers and the economic and social change brought about by the spread of capitalism. A war of unprecedented scale and impact came as no surprise. That the enemy's forces would have to be annihilated, or failing that ground into the mud, before such a war could end was fully realised. Yet in that short period of frantic fighting, war and the societies that fought it had changed irreversibly. Any war enthusiasm that had existed in July and August 1914 had been tempered by military reality. Yet as the fronts stalemated Europeans' sense of endeavour and purpose was just beginning in the face of the real challenge. 'The war is not actually between two armies, but between two nations. It will go on as long as they have resources,' French General Marie Émile Fayolle identified as the war entered its next phase.[51] In 1914 everything had been staked on the first clash of arms in the hope of forestalling just such a contest and the economic, social and political catastrophes that would result from prolonged war. It was a false, calamitous delusion – understandable, but unforgivable.

# THREE

# STALEMATE

O N A COLD NOVEMBER EVENING IN 1914 A COLUMN OF MUD-CAKED infantrymen marched out from improvised trench positions at Kleine Zillebeke, south of the Belgian town of Ypres. The survivors of the first battalion of the Irish Guards, 1,000 strong when it had departed with the British Expeditionary Force, trudged weary but unbowed towards Meteren, where a hot meal and a clean set of clothes awaited them.[1] Since August the guardsmen had marched back and forth across France, first retreating then pursuing the Germans between the huge battles that marked the collision of millions of armed men in autumn 1914. The route march to Meteren was the start of something different. A steady cycle of trench warfare was now setting in as the two sides which had locked across Belgium and northern France strove for a decision: into the line, out of the line; into rest areas, billets or training camps; now and then 'over the top' to death or glory. In the next four years notorious names – Loos, Somme, Arras, Cambrai – would join Ypres among the battle honours adorning the regiment's colours. The Irish Guards alone would leave 2,350 men in the quiet, isolated cemeteries which a century later still delineate 'the front' along which so much blood would be shed.

In autumn 1914 an old style of warfare was passing, as was the regular army BEF that had taken the field in support of the French army in August. The fighting around Ypres in mid-October was very different to the manoeuvre and counter-manoeuvre of the early months of the war: a prolonged, essentially static grapple in which the two opponents fought themselves to a standstill. By then rudimentary trench lines snaked from the Swiss border to the coast, with no man's land a narrow but extremely dangerous strip that had to be crossed between them. In the First Battle of Ypres and the simultaneous Battles of the Yser and Armentières footsore and battle-weary British, French and Belgian troops opposed fresh German reserve divisions trying to break through to the Channel ports. The fighting of October and November 1914 was intensive, close-quarters combat. Artillery raked the shallow ditches that the frontline soldiers had scraped for shelter before infantry assaults tried to smash through the thin Allied line. 'High explosives, shrapnel, machine-guns and rifles blended into one unending roar,' Captain Harry Dillon wrote home.[2] With shells running short after three months of fighting, it was these hand-to-hand fights with rifles and bayonets and the resilience and bravery of the men who fought them that would decide the engagement. In this confused series of disjointed, local fights for villages, woods and makeshift trench lines – only pieced together subsequently into a 'battle' by official historians – there was desperate glory on both sides, collective effort and individual heroism. 'Twas like a football scrum,' one guardsman recollected. 'Every one was somebody, ye'll understand. If he dropped there was no one to take his place. Great Days!' This was the last hurrah for an old style of man-to-man combat: 'An' we not so frightened as when it came to the fightin' by machinery on the Somme afterwards.'[3]

Over four weeks the Allied line between La Bassée and the coast was thinned and in places pushed back, but it never broke. Appointed to coordinate the three Allied armies at the northern end of the line, General Foch conducted a methodical, if at times knife-edge defence. He could always scrape up reserves to plug gaps in the front or to mount a desperate counterattack. In a battle 'in which Companies had to do the work of Battalions, and Battalions of Brigades, and whose only relief was a change of torn and blood-soaked ground from one threatened sector of the line to the next' the ranks on both sides were quickly thinned by artillery and machine-gun fire as the machines of war asserted their control over the entrenched battlefield.[4] Between 31 October and 8 November the Irish Guards lost 613 officers and men, yet their front line moved only a few hundred yards. Reinforced with fresh drafts, the guards gave much better than they got once they returned to the line: the battalion's war diary estimated that the enemy left 1,200 dead and wounded on the field when they made their final attack on the dug-in guardsmen on 17 November.[5] The guards lost a single sergeant killed. Such was attrition.

The successful defence of Ypres and the River Yser was the first great battle directed by Foch, who was to emerge by 1918 as the Allies' most accomplished military leader. In 1914, like every other commander he was still serving his apprenticeship. Foch was born at Tarbes in the Pyrenees in 1851 and first put on a military uniform in 1870, when he was called up in the *levée en masse* that followed the defeat of Napoleon III's armies and the establishment of the Third Republic. He did not see action, and thereafter completed his academic studies at the prestigious École Polytechnique. After graduating Foch chose a military career, joining the artillery. Despite his deeply held Catholic faith, often a handicap for army officers in the increasingly liberal and secular republic, his career prospered. Ability outweighed dogmatism: the strongly anticlerical premier Georges Clemenceau knew that Foch was the right man to take command of the École de Guerre (staff college) in 1907 and to educate France's future military leaders. As a teacher on operations and tactics at the staff college before the war Foch had imbued the military principles of the great masters – Frederick the Great, Clausewitz and Napoleon – but had the intellect to adapt them to the particular circumstances armies faced in the field, '*la guerre actuelle*' as Foch himself dubbed it. Before the war he had published influential books on military operations based on his staff college lectures, and he reflected constantly on the challenges of future war in the complex – and unresolved – debates between the advocates of firepower and shock action on the battlefield that animated the army before 1914.[6] Foch for his part saw beyond the tactical minutiae to engage with the coming problem of leading large armies in grand battles.

Preparing himself and France's army for the confrontation with Germany that might come had been Foch's life's work. The loss of his only son and one son-in-law in the battles of August 1914 gave him a personal motive to defeat the invader. 'I try to find support in remembering my duty,' he wrote to his friend General Millet. 'The cruel sacrifices which we are enduring ought not to remain sterile. I shall work with all the energy of which I am capable, absolutely confident of the issue of the fight with the mercy of God helping us.'[7]

Nowadays Foch's personality is better remembered than his ability, largely due to his lionisation by biographers immediately after the war. He was certainly a man with personality and spirit, but these were geared to a sharp intellect. Everyone who met him could not fail to be struck by his quirks and gestures. A small man with a thoughtful face adorned with a thick grey moustache set over pursed lips that were usually clamped around a cigar, Foch would talk quickly and animatedly in a truncated gibberish that only became comprehensible to those who learned his style and grew accustomed to his mannerisms. The truth was his brain worked faster than his mouth. But his ideas were generally sound, and he had the acuity to reflect constantly on the circumstance and experiences of war as he lived through them. *Apprenez à penser* – 'learn how to think' – was the aphorism that he inculcated into his students, because he practised it himself.

In 1914 Foch commanded the elite XX *Corps d'armée* (CA), the 'Iron' Corps, a permanently established formation that would cover the deployment of the French army in the event of a war with Germany. Foch's baptism of fire proved abortive and nearly got him sacked for disobeying orders. At Morhange on 20 August 1914 his army corps held its ground until it was thrown back by an enemy using concentrated firepower. Foch, as he was to do throughout the war, learned from that experience. Promoted to command the newly formed Ninth Army in the French centre during the Battle of the Marne, he combined his natural attacking instinct with the massed firepower of his divisions' 75mm batteries to contain and counterattack the enemy's attempts to break through. What Foch showed, like many French generals who were to rise to senior command during the war, was an intellectual approach to the problems presented by the battlefield. As novel operational and tactical challenges manifested themselves from 1915 their complexity initially defeated, and continued to perplex, many commanders. Some practitioners, Foch foremost among them, proved adept and adaptable enough to grasp new principles of warfare and to start to apply them. But this was to be a tentative, stop-start process, since it was necessary, as Foch admitted after the war, to forget what he had learned and taught beforehand.[8] Foch recognised in front of Ypres that breaking the massed ranks of Germany would be neither quick nor easy. It would require hundreds of thousands of men, material in abundance and the willpower to see the fight through to a victorious end, as well as appropriate military method. It was nevertheless possible, if a daunting challenge and likely to take a long time. This was a fundamental lesson of the war. The first stage of the process would be learning how to fight on the new battlefield, something that all armies had to master.

At Langemarck on 22 and 23 October Germany threw a muster of eager but inexperienced wartime volunteers hastily into the offensive. With flags flying and singing patriotic songs, according to the later reports in the German newspapers, three fresh reserve army corps, ninety thousand men, advanced against intermixed French and British positions around Ypres. If one was still needed, it was a final lesson that old-style assaults en masse had no place on a modern battlefield dominated by small arms and artillery fire. Exact casualties are impossible to establish; but they were very heavy, up to 70 percent in some regiments.[9] This *Kindermord* 'massacre of the innocents' in front of the Allied rifles and machine guns scarred Germany in the same way that losses at Verdun and on the Somme would traumatise France and the British Empire.

The first prolonged breast-to-breast struggle in Flanders showed up the essential problems of warfare between mass citizen armies in the industrial age. As well as there being insufficient space in which to manoeuvre such huge forces, the availability of fresh reserves would make battle prolonged and indecisive, as armies only advanced over the corpses of the slain. The characteristics of attritional trench warfare were emerging: strong defensive fortifications; intensive artillery and machine-gun firepower controlling the battlefield; material-intensive warfare; the availability of reserves to sustain prolonged fighting; the struggle for moral dominance over the enemy. Men of flesh and blood would struggle in a shattered landscape dominated by war machines designed to kill indiscriminately and in large numbers. Above all, attritional war was characterised by the cycling of divisions into the battle, fighting them out and replacing them. In total thirty-four German infantry divisions fought in Flanders in October and November: nine British, twelve French and six Belgian divisions opposed them, supported by marines and dismounted cavalry.[10] By the battle's end both armies were exhausted. It meant stalemate not simply on that battlefield where the Allied armies 'demolished all [the German army's] plans by closing in its face the last possible door by which it could break through', but along the whole line that would come down to posterity as the western front.[11] On the eastern front the situation was much the same as winter set in.

The Irish Guardsmen withdrawing exhausted but not dispirited from the first great attritional battle around Ypres 'knew very little of what they had done. Not one of their number could have given any consecutive account of what had happened, nor . . . whither they had gone. All they were sure of was that such as lived were not dead . . . and that the enemy had not broken through. They had no knowledge of what labours still lay before them'.[12] These tough fighters from Ireland under their proud English officers were just a few among the millions of ordinary men now caught up in a vast war machine. It would drive the world for four more years, with the echoes of its powerful actions still resounding a century later. The First Battle of Ypres indicated that a new style of warfare was imposing itself on the battlefield, although it remained to be seen exactly how it would subsume the home front. Bloodier in the West than any that was to come, the first campaign revealed that it was to be a war of sacrifice and slaughter.

Rudolf Binding, a German reserve cavalry officer whose unit held the line at the soon to be notorious village of Passchendaele, noted disdainfully as the battle dragged on:

> I can see no strategy in this manner of conducting operations . . . All I can see in this method is the last degree of clumsiness and lack of imagination . . . Everything on the front is rooted to the same spot. I don't

call it a success when a trench [or] a few hundred prisoners are taken. They have always cost more blood than they are worth. The war has got stuck into a gigantic siege on both sides . . . Neither side has the force to make a decisive push.

This proves that generalship is lacking. Genius looks different and shows itself otherwise than through what we see everywhere.[13]

Binding would not be the last soldier to criticise the military conduct of operations. But as he acknowledged, 'War is a strange business. No one really knows it, and its methods of teaching are cruel, rough, and primitive.'[14]

The essential nature of the war and warfare would teach new lessons. There was much method behind this apparent madness. 'This is a war of attrition; the side that is used up first will lose it,' Binding identified.[15] The societies that participated in this wholesale bloodletting would reorganise temporarily to fight it, engage wholeheartedly in it, change permanently as a result of it and be destined to repeat it. Many more states would join in: the war would not reach its greatest extent until 1917. The real legacy of Europe's Great War would be a new type of war and a world organised to fight it.

JOFFRE, FOCH AND FIELD MARSHAL LORD HORATIO HERBERT KITCHENER, Britain's recently appointed secretary of state for war, met in person for the first time at a hastily organised military summit at Dunkirk on 1 November to consider the battle raging a few miles away. Manpower, the sinews of attritional warfare, was on the agenda. Kitchener, Foch recollected, was anxious: 'Well, so we are beaten!' he greeted Foch. Foch reassured him that all was not yet lost, but asked him to send British reinforcements to shore up the line as soon as possible. Kitchener demurred: 'On 1 July 1915 you will have one million trained English soldiers in France,' he promised the anxious Frenchmen.'Before that date you will get none, or practically none.' These three generals who argued over manpower at Dunkirk above all were to conceptualise, organise and fight the war of attrition which mass mobilisation had inaugurated. Here they debated the crux of the strategic problem facing the Allies as stalemate set in. Would a little more effort at this point bring the war to an end, or was it best to plan for a protracted war in which resources had to be mobilised, deployed and sustained over months or years? Undoubtedly with the benefit of considerable hindsight, Foch concluded his account of their meeting with a posthumous tribute to the Englishman's foresight:

During my conversations with Lord Kitchener I was struck by the accuracy of his conceptions in what concerned the war, which he already saw would last a very long time. Indeed it was his conviction of that fact which had led this eminent organiser as early as September . . . to begin to raise considerable armies throughout the British Empire.[16]

Short-term needs and opportunities seemed, however, more pressing or attractive than long-term provisions over the winter of 1914–15.

Kitchener's farsightedness was in the fullness of time to earn him the deserved epithet 'architect of victory'. In the short term, however, it was to bring him into conflict with both his own ministerial colleagues and his French allies. Foch had flattered Seely in 1912 that Britain's small army might prove more formidable than a big one: 'With your sea power enabling you to send them where you will, [it] may well prove decisive if ever a conflict comes.'[17] This gave a false impression of British power, one that competed through the first eighteen months of the war with Kitchener's own judgement that the British would have to roll up their sleeves and wade into the mass armies brawling on the continent. It was not her maritime power, able to deliver a sudden strike at an enemy's vulnerable point, but her latent industrial, financial and manpower resources which would make the difference in a drawn-out war of attrition. Kitchener often stated when asked how long the war would last that he did not know, but that he knew that it would only begin in earnest after two years, once Britain had mobilised. He had little truck with those who thought that Britain could pursue a strategy of 'business as usual', leaving the continental powers to decide the land war among themselves. This was unworthy of British honour as well as inimical to her interests. But if Britain's strategy of slow military build-up left her strong at the peace table after enemies and allies alike had exhausted themselves in battle, that was all to the good. Although Britain already had the lion's share of the world, she intended to keep it and to take more if it was offered.

For Kitchener was also a British imperial soldier through and through. He had served his military career in the colonies. His peerage and his public reputation had come after his victory over the Mahdists at the Battle of Omdurman in 1898 that avenged the death of General Gordon. Kitchener had gone on to subdue the Boers in South Africa with a considerable degree of ruthlessness. He had lorded over the Egyptians as sirdar of the Egyptian army and later as the British consul general in Egypt. Indeed he was on his way back to his post in Egypt when Asquith appointed him secretary of state for war. It was an experiment, and a hazardous one as Asquith himself admitted for no serving soldier had held office in a modern British cabinet.[18] Like Joffre, Kitchener was by military specialism an engineer, and so might be expected to grasp the technicalities of modern warfare. Kitchener was also used to military command, power and government. But with power and responsibility came imperiousness. When commander in chief in India he had notoriously conducted a long-running dispute with the viceroy in India, Lord Curzon, which had ultimately led to the latter's resignation, and in Egypt he dominated both the British administration and the local ruler, the khedive. Not without good reason had he earned the sobriquet 'K of K', alluding to the biblical King of Kings as much as his title, Earl Kitchener of Khartoum. In a cabinet of strong-willed and opinionated politicians, Kitchener was more than able to hold his own, yet his dictatorial and secretive ways did not endear him to his fellow ministers. By early 1915 the experiment was starting to appear rather rash.

As a Field Marshal with a forceful personality and authoritarian habits, Kitchener could be expected to command Britain's army as it faced up to war, in practice if not de jure in his capacity as a civilian minister. A succession of weak chiefs of the Imperial General Staff at the War Office in the first fifteen months of the war allowed him to take personal control of strategy and mobilisation and by the time stalemate set in the broad parameters of British wartime mobilisation had already been established. A mass army was to be raised, on the voluntary principle that was imbued in the nation and empire, and the War Office would engage with manufacturing industry to equip it. Britain's early mobilisation was perhaps over reliant on one man; a popular hero undoubtedly, with an imposing figure of heavy build and a stern face set with deep blue eyes, and adorned with that famous moustache which surmounted the pointing finger that told Britons that Kitchener 'needs you'. But it seemed to be working. Young men had responded in huge numbers by the end of 1914. Until the New Army was ready to take the field, strategy would have to be evolved for the war they were being raised to fight.

As a strategist, Kitchener had probably a better grasp of the global nature of the war than any other Allied soldier or statesman, and more long-term vision. But as well as dominating British soldiers and overawing many of his cabinet colleagues, he also exasperated Allied representatives with his stubbornness. Given his background and his habit of taking command, Kitchener was not about to be bullied into rash military action by Britain's allies, nor to surrender Britain's freedom of action. It was unfortunate, perhaps, that he was best remembered in France for checking French imperial pretentions in Africa at Fashoda in 1898. But it was also true that as a just-gazetted young engineer officer he had crossed the Channel to volunteer to fight for France against Prussia in 1870. He certainly appreciated that it was above all an alliance war, and that the united front had to be sustained: it would not do if owing to British procrastination one or more of Britain's allies was beaten while the empire was organising itself for battle. But as he mustered his New Army for the eventual showdown with Germany he remained receptive to strategic initiatives that would improve the general military position and British imperial security – as long as these did not draw too heavily on Britain's limited resources during the year of mobilisation, nor leave Britain's allies too exposed.

ALTHOUGH THE WAR HAD STALEMATED, AS THE NEW CAMPAIGNING SEASON commenced in 1915 most still believed that the war would not, could not, last long. A rudimentary knowledge of military history, and practical considerations, suggested that an end was not far off: 'the war will be over in six months' was a common, overly optimistic, refrain, and strategic papers were drawn up to justify this prediction and advocate diplomatic initiatives and military operations that would demonstrate it. At the same time those papers recognised that the war had changed its nature both tactically and operationally owing to the trench deadlock on the land fronts, and strategically after the German diplomatic coup that had brought Turkey into the war on the side of the Central powers in November 1914.

While battlefield tactics and military strategy were adapting to the realities of modern warfare, the diplomatic front was very active. The Entente's leaders had their own diplomatic hands to play in the Mediterranean and the Balkans, in the hope that the enemy coalition could be overstretched by winning new allies. In May that policy paid off, when Italy abandoned its erstwhile allies and declared war on Austria-Hungary. The Mediterranean provided a distraction, a new theatre that offered better short-term prospects than France, Poland or the Carpathian Mountains, and one in which maritime strength could be brought to bear. Turkey, a threat to British imperial interests and a barrier astride the warm water communications between Russia and her allies through the Straits, could be usefully and relatively easily attacked while British force was mobilising: after a century of steady decline, the Ottoman Empire appeared weak and ready for its final dismantling. The Allies' diplomacy among themselves was focused on carving up Turkey. Russia would finally get the Straits that she had always coveted, while Britain and France would be compensated in the Persian Gulf and the Levant. Effort might have been better focused on assessing the enemy and planning military operations appropriately. As it was, the Eastern Mediterranean and Middle East offered false hopes of quick victories. The strategic mind-set of

1914 had yet to reset itself for the war that was actually in progress. The slapdash approach to actually making war which developed with the onset of spring contrasts strikingly with the earnest preparations being made everywhere for mobilising national resources for a long war. Thus in the first half of 1915 Entente strategy and operations lacked coherence and potency. As the war continued to expand the Entente's leaders would stumble through a series of sharp disagreements and false starts towards the shambles at the Dardanelles.

THE WINTER PAUSE WITNESSED AN OUTPOURING OF REFLECTIONS, PROFESsional and political, on the military situation and future war policy. Collectively they offered many options for taking the war to the enemy in the coming year, either on the existing fronts or in new theatres. Where they differed, however, was in the approach to making war that they advocated. Put simply, for politicians forceful diplomacy and clever stratagems would bring the war to a quick, decisive conclusion, while for soldiers it was the proper concentration and application of resources that would determine the outcome of the war in time – and in early 1915 time was of the essence. Politicians expected that the former could be done almost immediately, so even if in pushing forward the early steps of deeper national mobilisation they accepted that this was a war of resources, they failed to engage with its implications. The latter would take a bit more time, although at this point many of the soldiers were still confident that fuller mobilisation and concentration of force on the main fronts would bring the war to an end within the year.

Over the winter staff officers had an opportunity to pause for thought, assess the lessons of 1914 and engage with the military problems thrown up by the stalemate. The papers produced at the War Office, at the British General Headquarters (GHQ) in France and at Joffre's *Grand Quartier Général* (GQG) presented the war as a conflict whose course and outcome would be determined by the respective resources of the two blocs. If powerless to direct strategy now that Kitchener occupied the minister's office, the General Staff at the War Office could rise to the challenge of providing intelligence to guide it. 'Already over the winter of 1914–15, the statisticians were busily at work,' remembered Major- General Sir Charles Callwell, director of military operations at the War Office. 'They had found a bone and were gnawing at it to their heart's content. Individuals of indisputable capacity and of infinite application', who included the former secretary of state for war Lord Haldane and the historian of Wellington's wars, Sir Charles Oman, 'set to work to calculate how soon Boche manpower would be exhausted'. They totted up divisions deployed, counted populations and manpower mobilised to date, assessed the potential to reinforce the ranks in future months and years and

> arrived at results of the most encouraging kind, for one learned that the Hun as a warrior would within quite a short space of time be a phantom of the past, [and that] the adult males within the Kaiser's dominions would speedily comprise only the very aged, the mentally afflicted or the maimed wreckage from the battlefields of France and Poland.

These early attempts to assess manpower and the potential for attrition were inevitably somewhat careless and imprecise.[19] They might also be specious, designed to sway the ongoing strategic debates. Callwell admitted privately that his January 1915 memorandum on the balance of forces was intended 'to prove that the Germans will run out of men within the next few months', although he doubted so himself.[20] It neglected to factor in annual German replacements and men who might be combed out from home-front industries for military service.[21]

Unfortunately, the War Office's calculations gave Asquith and his restive colleagues too sanguine a view of the military position.[22] They too had time over the Christmas and New Year's holidays to formulate views on the war situation and what Britain should do next (and hopefully, although it was not made explicit in their memoranda, what her allies should be persuaded to do). A veritable barrage of papers hit Asquith's desk with contrasting views on how to conduct the 1915 campaign. The first lord of the Admiralty, Winston Churchill; the Chancellor of the Exchequer, David Lloyd George; the Conservative and Unionist Party's representative on the War Council,* Arthur Balfour, and the War Council's secretary, Lieutenant-Colonel Maurice Hankey, submitted a plethora of imaginative ideas for seizing the initiative against the Central powers, from which the ill-fated Dardanelles expedition was ultimately to spring. Since British politicians did not hold a monopoly, or even a prerogative, in the making of strategy, soldiers, sailors and allies would also weigh in to the arguments over strategy and operations that occupied most of January and February and rumbled on through the spring. Balfour, a shrewd statesman with a solid grasp of imperial defence and strategy from his years as prime minister (in 1904 he had established Britain's Committee of Imperial Defence which he chaire towards the end of 1914d), at least ad-

---

*A small Cabinet sub-committee established towards the end of 1914 to consider strategy and war policy.

mitted that his own musings on strategy 'were very casual observations, and you should not take them too seriously'.[23]

Others, Churchill in particular, lacked such self-awareness, as well as the ability to listen to professional military advice. His writings suggested prudence and preparation, his actions inclined otherwise. 'We ought to concert our actions with our allies, and particularly with Russia', he advised Asquith:

> We ought to form a scheme for a continuous and progressive offensive, and be ready with this new alternative when and if the direct frontal attacks in France . . . have failed, as fail I fear they will. Without your direct guidance and initiative none of these things will be done; and a succession of bloody checks in the West and in the East will leave the allies dashed in spirit and bankrupt in policy.[24]

Second only to Kitchener, the first lord of the Admiralty was to drive the making of strategy in spring 1915. Although he maintained a close and apparently friendly relationship with the field marshal, Churchill's schemes and initiatives could not but cause confusion and chaos, and by December he was apologising to the secretary of state for war for the confusion caused by the many irregular formations he had sent to France – 'Winston's Admiralty circus' as it was known – and for communicating directly with Field Marshal French, the commander of the BEF, regarding military operations without informing Kitchener.[25] This was typical of Churchill, who was not one to let practical difficulties or proprieties stand in the way of a bright idea (characteristics that served him well as a forceful war leader in the next war but were vexatious at a time when cabinet responsibility was undermined). As recently as October he had rushed over to Antwerp as a one-man relief force and offered to give up his office and take personal command of the city's defence. By 1914 Churchill had been a soldier and a war correspondent and was also a fledgling writer. Not satisfied with those occupations, he had been a Liberal cabinet minister since 1908, first at the Board of Trade, then the Home Office and lastly the Admiralty. He had crossed the benches in 1903 (not for the last time) and many were suspicious of this young, ambitious, talented yet mercurial chancer. Young Winston showed little of the statesmanlike gravity of his later career. Asquith had admired his vigour and radicalism and promoted him rapidly in peacetime, tasking him in 1911 with getting the Admiralty into shape. With the bit between his teeth in wartime he was an altogether different quantity. Another note to the prime minister opened with the prophetic statement that 'the war will be ended by the exhaustion of nations rather than the victories of armies', but the strategic logic behind this insight evaded him when there was the prospect of adventure on the high seas and in foreign lands to conjure with.[26] Instead of giving guidance and taking initiative Asquith, who was certainly sympathetic to the ideas put forward by his ministers, found himself acting as referee between his cabinet colleagues and military advisers as schemes unrolled and plans unravelled during the winter and early spring.[27]

The strategy in these papers was decidedly amateur. In the most wide-ranging and fanciful, Lloyd George's December 1914 'Suggestions as to the Military Position', the author openly admitted that he 'cannot pretend to have any military knowledge' and that 'the Government should take counsel with the military experts'. Then, with a lawyer's confidence and eloquence, Lloyd George elaborated from 'the little I saw and gathered in France' a grandiose vision for deploying the Entente's growing resources and deciding the war in the Balkans and Asia Minor! What Lloyd George's paper demonstrated and shared to a certain degree with the others was a failure to differentiate between tactics, operations and strategy, while at the same time completely ignoring the logic of resources and the constraints of logistics. All the memoranda recognised rightly that the western and eastern fronts were currently stalemated – this was a matter of tactics and resources – and then proceeded to push strategy along new and speculative lines.

Lloyd George proposed to bring Germany down by 'knocking away the props'. This notorious concept completely overlooked the fact that Germany's allies did not support her – in fact quite the opposite – yet it was to remain a pernicious drag on proper strategic concentration as Lloyd George rose to greater power and influence in Britain, ultimately supplanting Asquith as prime minister in December 1916. Hankey's comparable view that 'Germany can perhaps be struck most effectively and with the most lasting results on the peace of the world through her allies, and particularly through Turkey' was the most illogical sort of wishful thinking.[28] Leaving aside the facts that Turkey did not prop up Germany – throughout the war Turkey was reliant on German loans, armament exports and other supplies as well as military expertise – and that Germany's defeat of a number of belligerents on the Allied side did not destroy the alliance as a whole, at best an early conclusion to the war in the Middle East would have allowed the Entente to concentrate more resources for the war in Europe, where Germany remained undefeated, although this in itself Balfour recognised 'would not finish the war'.[29] By a statistical sleight of hand the chancellor conjured up an army of 1.4–1.6 million men, founded on the British New Army and Territorial Force volunteers and reinforced by the forces of Balkan states, with which to drive against Austria-Hungary and decide the war while 100,000 men contained and defeated Turkish forces in Syria. The fact that 'Germany and Austria between them have 3,000,000 young men quite as well trained as the men of the Kitchener Armies, ready to take the place of the men in the trenches when these fall' seemed to be discounted, except as a reason not to reinforce the stalemated front in France; yet if not engaged in the trenches these reserves were available to be deployed against any attack on Austria. While he mused on the nature of a wider war of 'exhaustion' as he dubbed it, Lloyd George did not, and never could, grasp the operational logic that when there are millions of men in reserve and efficient communications any strategic initiative will result in stalemate.[30] Although these and other strategic wild horses would be spurred on during the spring, as the Entente's war widened across the Mediterranean events demonstrated that stalemate was not a problem in one land campaign, but the common characteristic of them all.

What Lloyd George did identify, however, was the significance of intangible moral factors in a drawn-out war of attrition. If anything, his memorandum was a plea not to waste Britain's 'superb army . . . upon futile enterprises' and to find a way to demoralise the enemy – to undermine as he put it 'an enthusiasm and a spirit, according to every testimony, which cannot be worn down by a two or three years' siege of German armies entrenched in enemy territory'. Resilience and the will to victory were paramount, and this entailed sustaining Allied resolve with 'a clear definite victory which has visibly materialised in guns and prisoners captured, in unmistakeable retreats of the enemy's armies, and in large sections of enemy territory occupied, [that] will alone satisfy the public that tangible results are being achieved by the great sacrifices they are making'. Such a victory, he represented, could only be gained away from the western front.[31] This memorandum and the many others which Lloyd George penned as the war progressed indicated that he fully grasped the problems of fighting the war, yet remained myopic about its true nature.

It was not only British politicians who took a jaundiced view of the stalemate that had set in over the winter. In France future premier Aristide Briand, another lawyer with left-wing social views but strong nationalist credentials – he had passed the three-year army service law when premier in 1913 – argued that even if the Germans were entrenched within striking distance of Paris a broader perspective on strategy had to be maintained. In November he had formulated his own scheme for stirring up the Balkans by landing a four-hundred-thousand-strong French force at the Greek port of Salonika. Perhaps he sought to challenge Russia's influence in the region. Prewar great power rivalries had not vanished with the outbreak of hostilities, and if the war was to be decided quickly then these would inevitably resume. By February Briand and Lloyd George had colluded, and the Salonika plan, much watered down, was being pressed as the best alternative to a Western offensive.[32] Yet other influential politicians in France, notably the socialist war minister Alexandre Millerand who worked hand in glove with Joffre, set themselves against the Salonika scheme.[33] This was typical of the differences between soldiers and statesmen as they debated strategy during the early month of 1915. 'I suppose it will be like a game of nine pins! Everyone will have a plan and one ninepin in falling will knock over its neighbour!' Fisher opined privately to Churchill. 'As the great Napoleon said "Celerity"! – without it – "FAILURE"!'[34]

While commanding on the main front, Joffre had to consider strategy as a whole in the phase of the war that he dubbed 'the war of stabilisation', a period in which the resources on each side were fairly evenly balanced.[35] He had no particular problem with diplomatic or maritime initiatives intended to establish a stranglehold on the Central powers by bringing in Italy and the Balkan states, although he resisted the diversion of troops from the western front, because engaging and wearing down the enemy's military forces had to be a central element of strategy. Still, in 1915 Joffre seemed in a hurry. France was invaded, which set an obvious task for her commander in chief: liberating national soil was a political imperative, as well as an economic necessity. 'I could never lose sight of the responsibility I had assumed of defending the soil of my own country', he later attested, while judging that the advantages offered by secondary operations elsewhere 'were almost wholly theoretical, while the dangers they presented were real and present'.[36] Still believing that the trench lines could be breached with sufficient forces, he strongly deprecated diverting divisions to the Mediterranean and forcefully engaged any politician who suggested it. Personally he advocated maintaining offensive pressure on the German army on the western front, utilising the Allies' growing forces in that theatre to break the stalemate in the spring. As Kitchener had apparently promised when they met in November, he expected British divisions once formed to come to France to take over more of the trench line, freeing French divisions to form a strategic reserve with which he would try to break the German lines if it was not needed to contain a renewed German offensive that was expected in the spring. The need to tie down German divisions on the western front to deny Germany the strategic flexibility to strike at Russia was also an important consideration. Sir John French concurred.[37] Encouraged by the first lord of the Admiralty he was himself planning an offensive along the coast to capture the Belgian ports of Ostend and Zeebrugge, where the Germans had based destroyers and submarines, if Kitchener would send more troops.

France (personified by Joffre) also assumed for herself the mantle of leadership of the coalition, to which her allies only partially acquiesced, and rarely with good grace. Although the Central powers' united front was shaky at times, it did not have the potential to implode or collapse like the Entente's. As 1915's campaign took shape against a background of internal disputes and inter-Allied wrangles, it became obvious that the Entente had one significant disadvantage relative to the Central powers, a problem of coordination, the consequence of geographical separation and divergent political objectives. Under the terms of the Pact of London signed on 5 September 1914 the three Entente great powers had agreed not to make a separate peace with Germany, or to offer peace terms without discussing them first (although the lesser members of the alliance, Belgium and Serbia, were not signatories).[38] This Allied commitment to unity was recognition that Germany and Austria would be hard to defeat, and that there was greater strength in partnership, even if in the pressing military circumstances of September 1914 how to realise that partnership in practice was overlooked. The pact did not commit them to pursuing a common strategy or even consulting on one (or even communicating more effectively than through the existing diplomatic apparatus). This was reflected in the slowness, confusion and tension in the inter-Allied discussions over how to continue the war.

Joffre found it a struggle to reconcile the British to his strategy of mobilising manpower and material for aggressive engagement with Germany. British ministers thought that strategy might still be conducted as a global enterprise – as was customary for a maritime imperial power used to managing coalitions herself, if in the past these were directed against France – and this became especially so after Turkey entered the war in November 1914. Perhaps for Britain's amateur strategists '[bringing] to bear . . . the full power of the British Navy', which the most forceful of them, Churchill, controlled, had too great an appeal.[39] Kitchener at least did not accept the arguments of those who advocated 'business as usual', although he seemed in no hurry actually to engage British forces in the fight with Germany. On the other hand Russia, if willing to engage the enemy, proved much weaker than anticipated. Despite the Entente's obvious superiority in manpower and resources concentration and commitment was to prove much harder than anticipated.[40] It fell to Kitchener to try to reconcile the plans of British soldiers and statesmen and to integrate them with their allies' perspectives and expectations. At the same time Kitchener had his own views on strategy, which he strove to impose. It was an invidious task, the success of which it is difficult to assess.[41] Unlike most, Kitchener maintained a long-term perspective on the conduct of the war, although like everyone else he was uncertain as to how it would develop or how long it would last: 'two or three years at least' was his initial estimation.[42] In response to another tendentious note from Lloyd George he stated to the War Council on 25 February, 'If we are [to be] victorious, the end of the war must come through one of the following causes: (i) By a decisive victory, or a succession of decisive victories, of the Allies . . . (ii) by attrition, for when Germany is no longer able to support her armies in sufficient strength in the field she must sue for peace.' The likelihood of the former seemed remote and he dampened the enthusiasm of the chancellor and others by suggesting that the war would continue into 1917.[43] Kitchener himself was not confident of any success in the West in the short to medium term: Joffre had taken the offensive in mid-December 1914 but had only gained a few hundred yards, and presently the resources to renew the battle there in greater strength were lacking.[44] He adhered to his November statement that the New Army would not deploy before the late spring, although in the interim he felt obliged to mollify the field commanders by trickling out Territorial Force formations to take over more line from the French. Thereafter he anticipated a three-year war of attrition.[45] Kitchener's medium-term strategy for the West entailed an active defence – a 'policy of attrition' as he called it misleadingly – designed to hold German forces there both to stop them from attacking the Russians and to wear them out as the Allies built up their strength for a sufficiently powerful offensive to break the German army. This at least he could persuade his cabinet colleagues to support, if not his allies, and such a policy would not draw too heavily on British reserves.[46] Relying as it did on 'the hope that the Germans will continue to break themselves up by costly attempts to shatter our lines', this strategy too had some element of wishful thinking to it, if also much common sense as British forces were far from ready for sustained offensive action.[47] But Kitchener did expect when the time was right that Germany's armies would have to be engaged with a large general offensive backed by ample reserves.[48] Meanwhile he was sympathetic to initiatives elsewhere that might enhance the Allies' strategic advantages without draining Allied resources unduly. The prospects of other theatres had yet to be explored and so in spring 1915 he endeavoured to fashion a viable short-term strategy that reconciled politicians' and allies' expectations while Britain was still mobilising.

Joffre and Millerand demurred, and there were fraught exchanges in February and March 1915 over how to pursue the war that spring. Joffre wished to undertake an immediate and sustained offensive in the West, partly to support Russian offensive operations he expected in the East and partly to break the battlefield deadlock (which in spring 1915 was still considered by many to be a temporary winter phenomenon) and settle the war quickly. He asked Sir John French to support it with an offensive on the British front and wanted Kitchener to send reserves to France to facilitate this. The principal bone of contention was the 29th Division, Britain's last regular army formation and the only strategic reserve that Kitchener had in hand until his New Army divisions were ready. It was promised to French for the coastal offensive, but when British strategic thinking started to drift towards an initiative in the Eastern Mediterranean, where the 29th Division would ultimately be deployed, Kitchener changed his mind. While Kitchener accepted that a Russian defeat in the East might necessitate defensive reinforcement of the western front, he was reluctant to undertake an offensive there just for the sake of it. He suggested to Joffre that his offensive should be postponed until all Anglo-French forces were ready, and should then take place all along the front. Although Joffre, Millerand, French and Kitchener belatedly met in late March to reconcile their personal differences, this disagreement over operations in the West was not resolved. Joffre postponed his planned March offensive owing to a lack of reserves, leaving the British army to attack alone at Neuve Chapelle. Joffre would not launch his own offensive until May, and then with limited, if enticing, results. By that time Kitchener had made the despatch of the New Army to France conditional on a clear offensive success, and that was not forthcoming.

MEANWHILE, THE WAR IN THE MEDITERRANEAN HAD BEEN EXPANDING. FOR British leaders sea power and diplomacy were the active weapons in the wider war in the first half of 1915 (as far as maintaining good relations with France and Russia would allow). The diplomacy seemed highly traditional in its conduct and outcomes. Diplomats negotiated and secret treaties were signed. Reshaped countries and expanded empires were sketched onto maps as territories that were not yet actually the Entente's to redistribute were partitioned. The underlying assumption seemed to be that this was the way to win the war quickly and reap the spoils. Whether sea power and the small land forces available for the war in the Mediterranean and the Middle East could actually deliver on such ambitions remained to be seen.

What lay behind this diplomatic and military activity was a battle for neutrals. One of Lloyd George's reasons for advocating a victory in the Balkans was 'to decide neutrals that it is at last safe to throw in their lot with us'.[50] (Although, contradictorily, in conjuring a Balkan coalition from thin air his memorandum then suggested that a victory over Austria was partly dependent on the Balkan states mobilising on the Allied side!)

The kaiser's representatives were not neglecting their weapons however, and so the diplomatic battle would be no easier than those on the land fronts with which it was closely intertwined. The Entente scored a diplomatic success equal to Germany's engaging the Ottoman Empire on their side when they brought Italy into the war. The military effort in the Balkans proved stillborn, however, and that directed against Turkey was badly mismanaged.

There was a joke circulating in Paris in the spring that there were two neutrals, Kitchener's army and Italy, the only major European power as yet undeclared.[51] When on 13 May Prime Minister Antonio Salandra presented his plan for intervention in the war to the Italian parliament there were emotive scenes. It represented the climax of nine months of diplomacy and domestic agitation over whether Italy should remain neutral or join in the war: and if so, on which side? On 26 April Salandra had signed a secret treaty with the Entente to join the war against Austria, yet he could not secure a parliamentary majority and tendered his resignation to the king. Cowed by a tide of pro-war street demonstrations orchestrated by Salandra's supporters, the Liberal opposition leader, Giovanni Giolitti, could not muster enough support for a government committed to accepting Austrian counterproposals and remaining neutral. Salandra returned to power, parliament voted by a majority of 407 to 74 to honour the treaty and Italy declared war on 23 May.[52] It was a great coup for the Entente, and representative of the turmoil that the war had caused in Europe's neutral states.

Aligned with the Central powers in a formal treaty of alliance before 1914, but also the signatory of a 1902 treaty of friendship with France, Italy would choose to pursue her own interests when war came. In August 1914 her soldiers felt honour bound to support Italy's allies, her statesmen felt inclined to wait and see how the war developed and her people were generally in favour of remaining neutral after recent divisive and ill-managed colonial wars. Thus Italy was a divided state and also one unready to go to war. This did not deter the self-interested liberal politicians who developed policy in the factional cliques which competed for power in the Italian parliament. It had been foreign minister Antonino San Giuliano, a canny old-school diplomat, who had kept Italy out of the war in August 1914. Thereafter he negotiated with the Entente to see what Italy could gain from coming in and with Italy's former allies to see what she could get for staying out. His preferred outcome of the conflict, he stated privately in September, would have been 'that Austria should have been beaten on the one hand and France on the other'.[53]

His death in October passed responsibility for these complex, drawn-out negotiations to Sidney Sonnino, a Protestant conservative with extensive political experience who possessed, in Lloyd George's judgement, 'a suspicious, bargaining nature'.[54] Presented with competing diplomatic offers from both sides, he weighed Italy's options in the spring of 1915. The Entente offered Austrian territory if Italy joined the war on their side, although the downside of that offer was that it would have to be fought for. Germany was prepared to bribe her (at Austria's expense) with territory to remain neutral and eventually Conrad too came round to accepting that this was a better course than having to defend another front, although with typical bellicosity he expected to be able to retake the lost provinces by force once the war was over. By the time Austria offered something approximating to Sonnino's increasingly greedy claims, negotiations with the Entente were already far advanced. Since Austria refused to cede territory immediately, expecting Italy to receive her rewards for neutrality only at the end of the war, Sonnino opted for the Entente. By the terms of the Treaty of London signed on 26 April Sonnino undertook to intervene in the war within a month, against Austria only, in return for the incorporation into Italy of the regions with Italian populations living under Habsburg rule, the Trentino and Istria, land on the eastern Adriatic shore (also coveted by Serbia) and a share in any future dismemberment of the Ottoman Empire.[55] Only the Austrian lands would be directly fought for: Italy would open a new southern front along the River Isonzo that separated Italy from Austria. This was a great diplomatic coup for the Entente that strengthened the alliance's military forces appreciably and obliged Austria to rush divisions from the eastern and Serbian fronts to her threatened western flank.

What also occupied an excessive amount of time and diplomatic effort through 1915 was the attempt to recruit the uncommitted Balkan states, Greece, Bulgaria and Rumania, to one side or the other. Most Entente statesmen assumed with a blasé naïvety that these states that had been fighting among themselves as recently as 1913 could be united into a Balkan League against Austria with a limited show of force in the region. While this made sense strategically – all three had medium-sized armies recently blooded in the Balkan Wars, and they occupied a crucial strategic position, menacing Serbia on the one hand or threatening the Central powers' open southern flank and Turkey on the other – it ignored the realities of Balkan politics. Asquith, for example, was blithely confident that most of the undeclared Mediterranean states would come in during the spring, which 'would put an end to Austria', after which they could 'round on the Turks'. 'All these little Powers hate one another cordially,' Asquith posited, 'but when the carcase is ready to be cut up each wants as big and juicy a slice as it can get.'[56] Only Balfour sounded a percipient note of caution. 'I'm not sure I see in your proposal for attacking the enemy elsewhere than in the North of Europe any solution of our difficulties', he represented after reading Hankey's memorandum:

> It is not that I deny the advantages of inducing the Balkan states, with the assistance of the Allies, to make a combined attack upon Turkey . . . But the questions involved are, I fear, so difficult that months of preliminary negotiation would be required to allay passions due to events in the past, and to arrange such a division of the spoils as would satisfy these jealous little states . . . Moreover, it must be remembered that Germany is perfectly indifferent to the fate of her Allies except in so far as her own fate is bound up with it.[57]

Ineffective Allied diplomacy throughout 1915 bore out Balfour's scepticism.

The possibly of attacking Austria though her southern flank was mooted, although there were both political and practical problems in the way. In January and February there was much talk of organising an Allied army corps to land at Salonika in Greece to facilitate this. Sixty thousand Allied soldiers showing the flag would potentially bring Greece and Rumania into the war, save Serbia and initiate a victorious march on Vienna.[58] It was not to be. Balkan politics were not propitious. Having laid the groundwork for the Allied deployment, and for a possible Greek military expedition against the Dardanelles, local allegiances shifted. The pro-Entente Greek Prime Minister Eleftherios Venizelos resigned in early March after clashing with the pro-German King Constantine over intervention, negating any possibility of Allied troops receiving a friendly welcome at Salonika. Even without Greek hostility, finding the troops was an issue. For political reasons Joffre eventually spared a colonial division for the Eastern Mediterranean – it would not be good for French interests in the region if Britain was allowed to go it alone or Russia was given a free hand – and shipping Russian troops to the Mediterranean was far from easy. Balfour floated the idea of sending an expedition through the Adriatic via Montenegro (the smallest and most often overlooked Allied state) to support Serbia, but admitted that he had 'no means . . . of forming any conclusion as to the practicability of such an idea'.[59] While apparently vulnerable, Austria was presently unassailable from the South (unless and until Italy was won over), which was one of the factors that led strategists to focus their attention on Turkey and the Dardanelles come the spring.

AS THE ITALIAN EXAMPLE SHOWS, THE MOST OBVIOUS WAY TO INCREASE PRESSURE on the enemy and stretch his resources, while enhancing one's own, was to find new allies; although with new allies inevitably came further commitments and more problems. Germany had had the only such success in 1914 when Turkey, aligned with Germany before 1914, had joined the war in November. Resentful of European interference in her internal affairs and still smarting from the defeat she had suffered at the hands of Greece, Bulgaria, Serbia and Montenegro in the First Balkan War, Turkey's nationalist leaders sought to take advantage of the great powers' falling out among themselves to restore pride and regain territory. Under the control of the Committee of Union and Progress, the modernising Young Turk movement that had come to power in the Ottoman Empire in 1908 was promoting a pan-Turkish, pan-Islamist dogma that underlay the decision to intervene in the war. The militarist leaders who dominated the Committee of Union and Progress – war minister Enver Pasha, interior minister Tal'at Pasha and navy minister Cemal Pasha – saw intervention on the side of the Central powers as a way to throw off foreign domination, and in particular to end the semicolonial financial and commercial 'capitulations' which the European powers had imposed on Turkey since the nineteenth century. War was seen as a way to promote modernisation and reform the weak empire on an ethnic Turkish basis. Although this made ideological sense to the new ruling elite, engaging the empire's multiethnic population with such an agenda would prove impossible.[60] The war would become one for the future of Turkey as much as one for reviving a glorious imperial past. Enver Pasha, the dominant voice and guiding hand of Turkey's bid for revanche, chose to go on the offensive in the Caucasus and in Egypt, to wrest these former Ottoman territories back from controlling foreign powers.[61]

Turkey's enemies had a rather different perspective on the new war they faced in the Middle East. To them it was merely an old war taking on a new lease of life. As their own empires expanded Britain, France, Russia and Italy had been diplomatically and on occasion militarily engaged with the decline of the Ottoman Empire and the political issues were longstanding territorial and imperial ones. The agreement of March 1915 in which France and Britain finally acceded to long-held Russian demands to control the Straits (in return for Russian recognition of her allies' territorial claims elsewhere in the Middle East) was only the climax of this process. None of the Allied empires could therefore afford to allow their partners a free hand in a region where they had been competing for decades. Thus, while nominally waged against Turkey, the war in the Middle East was surreptitiously conducted in a spirit of great power rivalry, another obstacle to effective unity on the Entente side.

Because Turkey controlled or threatened vital sea routes through the Straits, the Suez Canal and the Persian Gulf, defensive measures would have to be taken. Therefore campaigns waged on the fringes of the Ottoman Empire – in Egypt, Palestine, Mesopotamia and the Caucasus – would come to absorb a large amount of Allied attention and resources without being likely to have any great impact on the outcome of the conflict between Germany and Austria-Hungary and their encircling enemies. To that extent the war against Turkey was a distraction from, not an essential element of, the defeat of Germany and Austria-Hungary. It therefore rewarded Germany to keep Turkey in the field more than it served the Allies to try to knock her out: once the needs of imperial security had been met it would have been better strategy to save the Ottoman Empire for later when without German support it would have been much weaker.

To sustain their position in the Middle East all the nations fighting the war in Europe would have to give attention and divert resources eastwards, so to that extent Turkey assisted the German war effort indirectly. Militarily the alliance brought the Central powers forty Turkish infantry divisions, although these were considerably smaller than European divisions and relatively poorly equipped.[62] For her part Germany had reinforced the Ottoman navy with the modern warships *Goeben* and *Breslau* (replacing the two brand-new, British-built battleships compulsorily purchased for the Royal Navy) that would challenge the Russian fleet's control of the Black Sea, and offered a substantial financial subsidy. Turkish forces posed a direct threat to Russia's southern flank in the Caucasus, and also to British imperial protectorates in Egypt and Persia, where the Suez Canal and oil fields had to be defended. The heavy-handed diplomacy of spring 1915 suggested that nobody expected Turkey to put up a fight. Rather than defend against the new adversary, the Entente chose to strike directly at the heart of the Ottoman Empire, through the Straits to Constantinople, to finish off the process of dismemberment that had been going on since the 1820s.

THE MIDDLE EASTERN WAR MIGHT BE COMPARED TO THE PACIFIC WAR against Japan between 1941 and 1945 in the next world war: vital to its belligerents, impossible to neglect, but in effect conducted separately from and waged differently to the campaigns in Europe. In its first phase at least nineteenth-century colonial military operations furnished the model. The most notorious of these was the Dardanelles campaign, although that waged by the British Empire in Mesopotamia (modern Iraq), if less well remembered, was even more inept.

The series of steps that led the Allies to launch a new campaign by landing an Anglo-French expeditionary force on the Gallipoli peninsula at the entrance to the Dardanelles are convoluted and, even a century later, hard to comprehend. Although the outcome was not predetermined, the initiation was certainly flawed. Allied miscommunication was partly to blame. Churchill's enthusiasm for the campaign and Kitchener's tergiversation over how it could be resourced also compromised what had the potential to be a bold, decisive, strategic stroke.

The Straits were an obvious strategic target once Turkey entered the war. They had been a focus of great power intrigue since the 1830s and closed to warships while Turkey was at peace by the Straits Convention of 1841 – the flight of the *Goeben* and *Breslau* to Constantinople, where they were transferred to the Turkish navy, was a direct violation of this convention. The appointment soon after of the German squadron commander, Rear-Admiral Wilhelm Souchon, to command the Turkish navy (its British advisers having been dismissed) was a further provocation. After Turkey closed the Straits to all shipping on 1 October 1914 (which in effect cut Russia's main import-export route and prevented her from exporting grain to raise capital to buy munitions from her allies) reopening them became an obvious objective. Britain and France's first act of war against Turkey, the bombardment by warships of the forts at the entrance to the Dardanelles on 3 November 1914, was a signal of intent, but also a warning to Enver Pasha to reinforce the defences at this key location.[63] How to follow this up was still under discussion when a telegram arrived from the Grand Duke Nicholas, commander in chief of the Russian army, on 2 January 1915, calling for immediate Anglo-French action against Turkey to take pressure off the Caucasus front. Kitchener and Churchill seized on this for different reasons: the one because it raised anxieties about the solidarity of the alliance and the internal security of the British Empire in the Middle East and India should the Ottomans launch a Muslim holy war (he had fought and won one of those already); the other because it would give the Royal Navy an offensive role in the war.

Greece was initially to be enticed to attack the Straits with an army supported by the Royal Navy, but this initiative collapsed in the face of Greek reluctance and Russian opposition: Russian foreign minister Sergei Sazonov felt that the British were using the Greeks to stop Russia from achieving her long-held ambition to control the Straits.[64] In the meantime the navy had determined to go it alone (with Kitchener's support because he had no troops to spare). Churchill pressed for this despite the reservations of Fisher, who had returned to the post of first sea lord in October 1914. While Fisher was all for using ships aggressively, especially outdated battleships that could no longer line up with the Grand Fleet, he appreciated better than the first lord that ships alone could not bring down the Ottoman Empire, and called from the start for a supporting expeditionary force.[65] Nevertheless, an Anglo-French naval attack commenced on 19 February, only to be called off in mid-March as Allied ships started to be lost to shore batteries and mines laid in the narrows at the mouth of the Dardanelles (one French and two British battleships were sunk on 18 March, the last day of the naval attack). The naval forces were in a bind: land forces were needed to clear the shore of the guns that stopped minesweepers from clearing the mines.

If Britain was to take on Turkey directly, Kitchener favoured landing an expeditionary force at Alexandretta in the Levant, indirectly protecting Egypt thereby. The French demurred, Alexandretta being in their sphere of influence in the Middle East.[66] In time he came to accept that troops would be needed to assist the navy in forcing the passage of the narrows by occupying the Gallipoli peninsula, and an ad hoc force of largely second-rate formations was scraped together. Its nucleus would be the regular infantry battalions of the 29th Division, but its mainstay would be the un-blooded Australian and New Zealand Army Corps (ANZAC) that had deployed partially trained to Egypt in December 1914 to reinforce the Canal Zone. With them would go the Royal Naval Division, which Churchill had raised from Royal Marines and naval reservists surplus to the manning requirements of the fleet, and a scratch French army corps predominantly made up of Foreign Legion and colonial battalions. Joffre had not been consulted on this, because Poincaré and his ministers feared he would refuse to release the troops, as he did when he heard of the government's decision; but given their ambitions in the region they were also unwilling to let the British invade Turkey alone and overruled their commander in chief.[67] All the evidence suggests that Kitchener was sending an occupation force, not an assault force, and did not anticipate strong Turkish resistance. The Royal Naval Division had no artillery, while the ships in which the force sailed from England were not packed for an amphibious landing and had to be unloaded and reloaded at Alexandria in Egypt, further delaying the operation. Moreover, General Sir Ian Hamilton, who was appointed to command the Mediterranean Expeditionary Force, was given to understand that the 29th Division was only on loan and that his operation would always be one of 'limited liabilities', not only to avoid splits in the coalition but also because the need to contain and then to engage and defeat Germany and Austria was and would remain the paramount call on the Entente's resources.[68]

But this was an invasion force, and the Turks might be expected to resist yet another European incursion into their territory forcibly, especially one which pointed a dagger at the empire's heart. Under the impetus of the Young Turk movement, Turkey herself was modernising. This national resurgence included significant military reforms under German tutelage. General Otto Liman von Sanders, who had reorganised the army before 1914, now took command of the defence of the Gallipoli peninsula. A stiffening of German troops – the sailors from the *Goeben* and *Breslau* were to be sent to Gallipoli to act as machine-gun companies – and effective higher leadership made the Ottoman army a more formidable opposition than the Entente expected, given its recent defeats in the Balkan Wars and in Libya, which Italian colonial forces had wrested from the Sultan's army in 1912. Moreover, with the exception of the Dardanelles campaign, all the other campaigns waged against Turkey were on the periphery of the empire, at the end of extended supply lines for both sides. In these the Turkish forces generally enjoyed the advantage of being on the defensive.

When they took the offensive, however, the gulf between Enver Pasha's objectives and Turkey's military capability were apparent. In the Caucasus, where Turkey's expansionist ambitions were focused, and into which Enver Pasha personally led an army once war was declared, the offensive went disastrously wrong: Grand Duke Nicholas's fears proved unfounded. The winter 1914–15 campaign there was fought in atrocious conditions; many soldiers on both sides froze to death. After routing the Turkish invasion force in January 1915 a Russian army invaded northern Turkey across extremely difficult mountainous terrain, at the end of long supply lines. Grand Duke Nicholas did not notify his allies of his change of fortune, however, since they were busy trying to take Constantinople for the Russians![69] It would be two years before the border fortress of Erzerum was captured, during which time the Russians lost far more men to poor weather conditions and disease than in battle.

The Turkish threat to Egypt actually proved perfunctory. After some small-scale clashes along the Suez Canal in January 1915 in which they were repulsed by Indian and Egyptian forces the Turks retreated. Thereafter Egypt was secure, at least while the Dardanelles campaign continued.

ANGLO-FRENCH FORCES ATTACKED THE GALLIPOLI PENINSULA AGAIN ON 25 April. The 29th Division landed from improvised landing ships at the tip of Cape Helles, into a hail of Turkish machine-gun fire. By the end of the day they had established themselves ashore, while the ANZAC Corps was clinging to the steep sides of a small cove on the western flank of the peninsula fifteen miles away. Over the next few days reinforcements, guns and supplies would be landed, and the troops would start to push inland. By early May, however, they faced a familiar situation: trenches, barbed wire and machine guns. In a private letter written soon afterwards to Churchill, Hamilton set out the nub of the military problem:

> Here we are . . . fairly lodged within easy striking distance of the enemy's Capital and head-power. This enemy, though much fallen away from his former high state, is still a great empire on a continental scale possessing vast resources. Hence our troops have to contest against three successive armies. As soon as one lot are defeated they are reinforced by fresh army corps. The last lot who have come are Constantinople troops numbering 24,000. Next we shall have to face and overthrow . . . the Syrian Army Corps.70

The Turkish army's reserves would have to be systematically destroyed in trench warfare before the campaign would reach a victorious conclusion, which would entail the engagement of the Entente's own reserves. As at Ypres the intrinsic dynamic of the attritional battlefield determined that bold strategic ambitions were unachievable. More and more Allied divisions were sent to the peninsula over the summer of 1915. At the height of the campaign fourteen Allied divisions were deployed, although the battle lines moved only a few miles during the course of a nine-month campaign of frontal attack and counterattack. While the Allies could find men for such campaigns in 1915, they did not have the necessary guns and munitions to support extended military operations. Churchill's contention that naval gunfire could substitute for field artillery proved false. Indeed when German submarines started hunting the ships moored around the peninsula the warships had to be withdrawn to safe harbours. By the end of the campaign the Allies had suffered 252,000 casualties, many through disease. Moreover they had suffered humiliation: their positions were quietly evacuated over the winter (ironically, the best managed phase of the campaign), with vast amounts of stores abandoned to the enemy. British prestige had been damaged in both the empire and among her allies, and her strategic flexibility suffered in 1916. Turkish casualties were far heavier, certainly 251,000 and maybe as many as 350,000, but their sacrifice had demonstrated that while the empire itself was ancient, it was not yet rotten to the core.[71] Turkish soldiers were stouthearted fighters, patriotic and loyal. Under German leadership they fought doggedly, at least when the nation seemed under direct threat.

'IT WAS A WONDERFUL VIEW. BELOW WERE THE STRAITS, WITH REINFORCE-ments coming over from Asia Minor, and motor cars and wheeled transport on the roads leading to the south of the peninsula. We commanded

Kilid Bahr and the rear of the communications of the Turkish army at Helles,' remembered Major C. J. Allanson, who had led his Ghurkha battalion onto the high point of the Sari Bair Ridge on the Gallipoli peninsula on 9 August.[72] Reinforced by three fresh but un-blooded New Army divisions that Kitchener had sent from Britain, in early August Hamilton's forces were attempting to break out to the north of Anzac Cove, to whose steep, rugged sides the men of the ANZAC Corps had clung since they had landed there on 25 April. Troops of the New Zealand Brigade's Wellington Battalion had seized the top of the Sari Bair Ridge to the north of Anzac Cove. From this vantage point men from 10th and 11th Divisions of the New Army could be seen disembarking in Suvla Bay to the north. There appeared to be few Turkish forces in front of them; now perhaps they would conclude the Dardanelles campaign, force a way through to Constantinople and knock Turkey out of the war. But appearances were deceptive, and the vista proved only a final, fading vision of a quick end to a protracting war.

A vicious battle developed as Turkish reserves organised by Lieutenant-Colonel Mustapha Kemal (Turkey's future leader, Atatürk) counterattacked the parties of New Zealand, British and Indian troops scattered along the ridgeline. They fought bravely for forty-eight hours at close quarters. 'We bit and fisted and used rifles and pistols as clubs; blood was flying about like spray from a hairwash bottle,' Allanson recollected.[73] But under intense artillery and machine-gun fire, facing repeated Turkish charges and shelled intermittently by their own artillery and warships, each battalion deployed on the exposed ridge was decimated. Wounded himself, Allanson pulled the remnants of his command – 240 men from a battalion initially 1,000 strong – back on 10 August after a final Turkish bayonet charge swept away the battalions on either flank. The commanding heights were firmly back in Turkish hands.[74] In Suvla Bay, after getting ashore the inexperienced New Army formations had shown no sense of haste: the men had spent the afternoon of 7 August landing supplies and resting in the fierce Mediterranean summer heat, and the senior commanders had not gripped the unravelling operation. Demonstrating the advantage of land communications over maritime, even at marching pace, by the time a piecemeal advance commenced on 9 August Turkish reserves had deployed and the beachhead was easily contained.[75] This new front had stalemated, like all the others.

The Anzac Cove breakout and Suvla Bay landing, like all the still-born strategic schemes and failed operations of early 1915, was expected to decide the campaign quickly with a bold stroke by a small force, and proved once more that this was never going to happen. Brute force was no alternative. The Allied battalions at Cape Helles assaulted the Turkish lines once again to support the operation farther north. Seaman Joseph Murray of the Royal Naval Division's Hood Battalion recorded a to-and-fro fight typical of trench warfare:

> At 2.30 p.m. a terrific bombardment was commenced by our artillery . . . Just like old times; the left flank was advancing. The returning wounded said they had captured two lines of trenches but had lost a lot of men . . . A repetition of yesterday – this time it was the centre who were advancing. According to a wounded man, they had taken their objective – two lines – without much trouble, but had been ordered to capture another trench about forty yards further on as well . . . they had met extremely severe opposition, so much so that they had been forced to retire to their original objective, the second trench. The Turks had then counter-attacked and forced them to retire still further to the first of the captured trenches. Here they had remained for about half-an-hour while the artillery bombarded the Turks and they then advanced and recaptured the second trench. After a while the Turks counter-attacked repeatedly but were cut to pieces by the artillery . . . I can see the cost of the few yards of useless ground wrested from the Turks on the 6th and 7th . . . I can see the dead lying everywhere. Out in front of the firing line and in between the lines the scene is the same – Turks as well as our own lads lying rotting in the sun. The stench is nauseating and the scene appalling.[76]

THE FIRST PHASE OF THE MESOPOTAMIAN CAMPAIGN – IN WHICH A DEFENSIVE expedition hastily mounted from India to secure the Persian Gulf transmuted into a largely improvised attempt to push inland to capture Baghdad – furnished another example of extreme military mismanagement. Lieutenant-General John Nixon led an expeditionary force from India sent to Mesopotamia in November 1914 to secure the oil wells at Basra. With no explicit instructions on how to proceed thereafter, Nixon mounted an overambitious and under-resourced attempt to advance on Baghdad, 250 miles inland. The advance relied upon the Rivers Tigris and Euphrates for supply and communications, and behind that a lengthy sea passage through the Persian Gulf and the Indian Ocean. By the time Nixon's troops approached Baghdad in late November 1915 they were exhausted, and depleted by disease and the detachment of contingents to defend their supply lines. There they encountered a dug-in Turkish army that they defeated in battle at Ctesiphon on 22 November, although British losses were so heavy that Nixon was forced to withdraw. Following up, the Turks besieged Major-General Charles Townshend's division at Kut-el-Amara, at a strategic bend in the Euphrates. The siege was concluded long before a relief force could be organised. Townshend and twelve thousand men went into captivity. The Mesopotamia campaign was the most inglorious of the early years of the war: like the defeat at the Dardanelles it led in 1916 to an official enquiry to ascertain what had gone wrong. Wherever the blame actually lay, it is fair to conclude that both operations failed because they were attempts to mount nineteenth-century operations in a twentieth-century war.

One new trench stalemate and one impending disaster were all that the Entente had to show from its military initiative in the Middle East in 1915. A quick victory over Turkey proved a desert mirage. The trial and error of these months left a pernicious legacy of personal frustrations and dissipation of effort that was to sway the making of strategy thereafter. There persists an impression that if better executed and successful 1915's peripheral campaigns might have avoided the later bloodletting in France and Flanders. In best-selling war memoirs their advocates certainly argued this after the war, although their case is weak and tinged with a considerable degree of hindsight. Lloyd George's winter 1914 memorandum was a manifesto for victory that denied operational realities – nevertheless, 'After four and a half years of the closest acquaintance with [the problems of war under modern conditions] I stand by the main thesis of this document', he attested more than twenty years later.[77] Churchill grudgingly acknowledged the true nature of the war on resigning from the cabinet in November 1915 to take up a command in France, but later he opined that,

> By the mistakes of this year the opportunity was lost of confining the conflagration within limits which though enormous were not uncontrolled . . . Thereafter events passed very largely outside the scope of conscious choice. Governments and individuals conformed to the rhythm of the tragedy, and swayed and staggered forward in helpless violence, slaughtering and squandering on ever-increasing scales, till injuries were wrought to the structure of human society which a century will not efface . . . But in January, 1915, the terrific affair was still not unmanageable. It could have been grasped in human hands and brought to rest in righteous and fruitful victory before the world was exhausted, before the nations were broken, before the empires were shattered to pieces, before Europe was ruined.[78]

Churchill's postwar evaluation was overwrought, questionable and to a certain extent self-serving, not least because his own decisions lay behind some of the key mistakes. The alternative, that Churchill was to dub 'the blood test', was already engaged, so defeating Turkey was at best a supplemental, not an alternative, strategy. The key error in 1915 was deploying too few men too quickly with insufficient munitions (compounded by initially trying to use ships on their own against a land power): if delayed, carefully planned and better resourced such initiatives might have had better effect. It is highly unlikely they would have ended a still expanding conflict, although they might have defeated Turkey. As it was, what would today be defined as 'mission creep' developed inexorably, dividing the Allies and diverting attention and effort.

The belief nevertheless persists that ingenious 'amateur strategists' conceived plans in early 1915 that might have proved decisive if acted upon promptly and with sufficient force. In fact they were fundamentally wrong about the nature of the war now being fought, and in ignoring professional military advice merely exacerbated the problems of strategy making. For example, it did not strike Churchill that if the Allies could respond to German moves against attacks on their 'vulnerable and vital points' by converting these new fronts into 'a fortified defensive against which he would uselessly expend his strength', Germany and her allies could respond in exactly the same way, forcing the Allies themselves to expend lives on yet another static front. His belief that 'the military mobility resulting from seapower applicable over a large area will counterbalance to a great extent the enemy's advantage of interior lines' no longer held good in the railway age.[79]

Whatever rationale they were given post-war, as conceived in the winter of 1914–15 the naval and military excursions into the Mediterranean were not actually designed as a means of ending the war with Germany but as a way of improving the position of the Allies (and of balancing Allied imperial ambitions) before they had to face that task when fully mobilised. To that extent, the war against Turkey had soon become, and was to remain, an important one, but it was not the real war – that would be fought out on the continent. This was the import of Lloyd George's, Churchill's and Hankey's memoranda, and the basis of Kitchener's strategic policy pending the time when Germany could be taken on with a hope of beating her. That this was essentially a British view put considerable strain on Allied unity in the first six months of the war of siege. Joffre was impatient to engage the enemy directly, not least on account of political pressure to liberate French soil, and Russia was desperate for faster action against the main enemy who had been left free to attack in Poland. At best operations in the Mediterranean and the Middle East would have knocked Turkey out of the war quickly and improved links between Russia and her Western allies. Yet it turned out that land operations in these theatres were to take on exactly the same entrenched characteristics as the military campaigns in the main theatres, and to stalemate in their turn as the essential nature of attrition asserted itself. Italy's declaration of war perhaps offered the best prospect for a speedy resolution of the stalemate, through a rapid thrust into the vitals of the Austro-Hungarian Empire (although since Italy had not yet declared war on Germany and was not to do so until December 1916, even that opportunity still left Germany to be taken on and defeated). As it was, the new southern front rapidly conformed to type, Italy's first offensive being checked by Austro-Hungarian defensive lines along the River Isonzo.

By spring 1915 the war had assumed its exhausting, destructive character, even if it would take some time to recognise and acknowledge that fact. Mired in the muddy trenches of Flanders, Binding was more perceptive than the politicians who had no part of the real war:

> We are entering this period with the knowledge that the end is yet far away. Many believe that the victor will be the one who can hold out the longest. Seeking to build in the spirit, I hope that the War will be decided otherwise than by the effect of the power machine that can hold out longest and work most economically.[80]

In the early months of stalemate, political and military leaders were still learning and had yet to grasp the principles of modern warfare and to work these 'power machines'. Therefore, 1915 was a year of adaptation, in which old forms of warfare, based on historical precedents, vied with new styles of mass warfare. But the tenor of strategy, as Selborne acknowledged, was in one clear direction: 'The war will be a war of attrition, and of attrition pure and simple,' he represented to his cabinet colleagues in August, 'without annihilating military victories on either side.' He expected it to last into 1917 at least.[81] This lesson was reinforced by the campaigns in the main theatres that continued while the Mediterranean and the Middle East distracted attention.

During the year there was much activity on the diplomatic front, with success and frustration on both sides. Overall, events showed that the politicians' idea that attrition could be avoided by diplomacy and diversions was a false assumption – diplomacy was complex and competitive, and under-resourced diversions inevitably ended in stalemate – yet it never quite disappeared from the strategic thinking of those tasked with political rather than military leadership. In the first year of attrition, alternatives still seemed possible and preferable, if old-fashioned, relying as they did on bold military initiatives coupled with dynamic diplomacy rather than the direct engagement of the developing war machines.

Alongside these the actual character of the war, which continued to grow and was still of indeterminable, if increasing, length, was set.[82] By such a process both sides found themselves drawn into a geographically and politically wider war whose demands would have to be reconciled with the main objective: defeating the armies of the rival coalition and ending the European war. As these peripheral campaigns were ongoing societies were adapting to the needs of attritional war. Its mainstays, manpower and material, were being mobilised for a long struggle.

# FOUR

# A PEOPLE'S WAR

I N ITS 6 FEBRUARY 1915 EDITION *THE VIVID WAR WEEKLY*, ONE OF THE
many periodicals that attempted to narrate the course and convey
the nature of the war to an attentive public, a 'British army officer'
endeavoured to explain 'What a War of Attrition Means'. 'How long will
the war last?' was, he noted, the question he was most often asked – 'just
as long as the Prussian militarists can impose their will upon a suffering
nation' was his answer.[1] Implicit in this estimation was the contention
that the people of the Allied nations were fighting willingly against an
aggressive, oppressive state whose own people were reluctant warriors.
But Bethmann Hollweg's praise to the Reichstag in December 1914 for
'the colossal work which has been and is still being accomplished, alike
at the front and at home, by all classes of the population without distinction' that underpinned 'Germany's united will to victory' was probably
a reasonably accurate summation of Germany's domestic situation at the
war's first Christmas.[2]

What the war entailed socially and militarily was becoming self-
evident everywhere. 'This is a war of attrition – attrition in the trenches,
in the home, in the markets, in the workshops, in the counting-houses
and stock exchanges.' The British officer offered no crumbs of comfort
when he outlined the next phase of the war. 'There is no elbow room for
manoeuvre, it is just a matter of slaughter and maiming and sickness for
months and months, until at last the combatant men are thinned down
to a lesser density' and a military decision might come about. It was a
wake-up call for the 'trial of endurance' that was just beginning: 'It is the
nation and not merely the Army which has to face the music. There are
millions of people in these islands who even now do not realise what this
war means; but they will do before we are through with it.'[3]

\* \* \*

EUROPE'S ARMIES AND THE SOCIETIES THAT BACKED THEM WERE MADE UP OF millions of individuals, each of whom wrestled with his or her conscience as the war developed. This was particularity the case for those who took up arms. Conscripts of course had no choice but to go to war and a fair few would react against it when its bloody reality became evident. The vast majority of those called up accepted their destiny, at least with dutiful resignation and frequently with genuine commitment to the cause (some did choose to evade the call up, but the penalties for doing so were harsh). The many volunteers, from all nations including neutrals, made a more conscious, reasoned choice to fight, or to work for the war effort as far as their capacity allowed. It proved a remarkably popular war, despite its horrors, once the people had been persuaded that the cause was just and the effort worthwhile.

To popularise it, the mass media would come into its own. The printed media – daily and weekly newspapers, printed books, magazines, illustrated part-works such as *The Vivid War Weekly* and striking poster art – predominated between 1914 and 1918, supplemented as the war went on with dramatic documentary and feature films. In the early twentieth century the media was privately owned and just starting to exert the influence on popular opinion and state policy that it was to develop during the century. Newspapers and periodicals, in the hands of so-called 'press barons', represented all shades of political opinion and worked to win popular support and to influence or challenge the policy of governments. In less liberal societies the state's scrutiny of the media remained close, with censorship and, on occasion, the forcible closure of publications. Concomitantly, the media in less liberal societies still retained a high degree of deference to the state and its leaders.[4]

The extent to which newspapers (or their proprietors) remained loyal supporters of the war effort, or took sides in disputes on strategy and policy, was to be tested as the relationship between the state and the media evolved to meet the needs of the war effort. In France and Britain the media had close links with the political establishment and newspaper owners were influential men. In the Third Republic politicians' relationship with the press was intimate: many – such as the Radical leader, scourge of early war ministries and eventual wartime premier Georges Clemenceau – were or had been editors. What was striking about the press in wartime France was the strident loyalty of periodicals of all political perspectives: to demonstrate its patriotism, in 1916 the leading left-wing journal *La Guerre Sociale* renamed itself *La Victoire*. Even those journals on the pacifist left acknowledged the right of an invaded state to defend itself, while still condemning war as a means of policy and calling for its speedy end. More patriotic proprietors and editors could agree on the iniquity of German invasion and rally their readers to the cause of national defence while criticising aspects of the war effort and politicising French war aims.

The British press was less variegated than that in France, and its owners exerted more indirect political power and influence. British press barons exercised their influence as much through the personal relationships they maintained with senior political figures as through the words that they published. Large-circulation national newspapers had emerged toward the end of the nineteenth century, setting a national agenda (although local newspapers remained the main conduit of information for many of the population). Lord Northcliffe, proprietor of the establishment daily *The Times* and the more populist *Daily Mail*, stood preeminent among the media owners in England. Max Aitken (later Lord Beaverbrook) who owned the mass circulation *Daily Express* was another influential figure, with close personal ties to Winston Churchill and Lloyd George. George Riddell, proprietor of the populist *News of the World* who sat on Britain's wartime Press Committee, had such a close relationship with Lloyd George that when raised to the peerage for wartime service he took at his title Baron Walton Heath, the village in which he had built the prime minister a country house![5]

The German and Austro-Hungarian presses were also nominally free, but more deferential to the state than in liberal France and Britain: at least the more conservative journals were, and these usually acted as the compliant mouthpieces of the military. For all their professions of support for the *Burgfrieden* social peace, left-wing journals would have to be more closely monitored. The State of Siege Law enacted in Germany during wartime imposed limitations on popular expression.[6] The establishment of a Central Office of Censorship in Berlin early in the war set the tone for state-media relations that would be repeated elsewhere. Patriotic 'self-censorship' was the desired arrangement and the war ministry had sanctions at its disposal if it was not.[7] The government's reaction to the socialist daily *Vorwärts*'s criticism of the invasion of Belgium was typical: thereafter the newspaper was put under strict censorship and unable to take an independent editorial line.[8]

Censorship, the regulation of the media by the state, the suppression of information and the restriction of public liberties, remains a dirty word. It was anathema to liberals in particular, but in the early twentieth century wartime censorship was generally acknowledged to be necessary, for reasons of military security if nothing else. The relationship between the state and the media in peacetime varied according to political structures. In republican France the media was free to speak its mind, or at least to propagate the opinions of those who controlled it. It had shown its power to make or break governments on numerous occasions, most notably during the notorious Dreyfus Affair at the turn of the century. At the other extreme in Russia, by contrast, the media was closely regulated in order to quiet those reformist or revolutionary elements that challenged the tsar's authority. Between these two extremes the peacetime press enjoyed varying degrees of liberty in expressing views and influencing public opinion. All states included immediately enforceable measures of press censorship and restrictions on public activities in their 'state of war' legislation. France's for example, put control of the media and public associations in the hands of the war ministry. Public meetings and periodicals 'judged to be of a nature to excite or encourage disorder' were banned, and military information that did not originate from official sources was not to be published. Ostensibly intended to sustain military and public morale, the restrictions extended to publishing material on France's allies, interviews with French generals, details of military technology and so called 'peace propaganda'.[9] With nuances, similar legislation was enacted across Europe. Ironically, it did not extend to newspapers in neutral countries which were soon judged to be a better source of accurate war news than those produced at home: in the Swiss *Journal de Genève*, the French philosopher Alain remarked, 'the military reports are admirable and everyone agrees that our journals are ridiculous by comparison'.[10]

From the beginning the powers existed to control political dissent and muzzle criticism of the conduct of the war, but these proved largely unnecessary in its first months. Beyond limiting the supply of information and vetting what was published, control of the press was unsophisticated. In practice the state could rely on all but the most antiwar periodicals to exercise a degree of self-censorship. The desire to support the war effort, coupled with the fear of loss of revenues if censured by the government, or in the most extreme cases of being closed down, acted as a deterrent to unrestricted criticism. In practice most journals adopted the stance of 'loyal opposition' in their commentaries on the war effort: criticism of the conduct of the war was intended to sustain support and promote more effective war management while also championing the cause of a particular political faction. In France the Radical journal *L'Homme libre* (*The Free Man*), edited by former premier Georges Clemenceau, himself a trenchant critic from its outset of the running of the war by France's parliamentary cliques, set the tone for populist pro-war journalism. Following temporary suppression in September 1914 after breaching the censorship regulations it adopted a new name, *L'Homme enchaîné* (*The Chained Man*).

Censorship's dubious counterpart propaganda, a means with which to seed the media and mould public opinion, was also an option. In 1914 propaganda techniques were in their infancy, but like so many other things this untried tool would develop in response to the evolution of the war once the state took over from the privately owned media responsibility for fashioning and sustaining public opinion and the popular will to victory. An age of mass media and literate consumer culture had dawned in the second half of the nineteenth century. Yet if educated to read and write – essential skills in the modern technological economies of the early twentieth century – the mass of the population were not educated to think for themselves. The wartime consumer of information sought knowledge and reassurance rather than criticism and disinformation: *The Handy A.B.C. of the War* and *Little Stories of the Great War*, published in three-penny popular editions, were typical of the genre.[11] Although receptive to war stories, relatively few quested after accurate war news like Alain. Those who did were the governing classes and the intelligentsia. They themselves controlled and wrote for the printed media which the masses consumed, and some, such as Michel Corday (an author who did his war service as a civil servant in France's ministry of war), expressed a degree of contempt for the ordinary man's acquiescence in the war and duping by the media: consumed with 'petty complaints, petty hopes, petty anxieties . . . so narrow-minded, so short-sighted. And that is why this vast herd can be kept on the threshold of slaughter'.[12] Corday's private critique of France's war was exceptional, not typical: hence its publication among the outpouring of antiwar literature as a new world war loomed in the 1930s. But Corday was not alone in decrying the *bourrage de crâne* (head stuffing) nonsense that the French gutter press turned out to incite the people.[13] In September 1915 a humorous satirical weekly, *Le Canard enchaîné*, appeared to offer an antidote to 'the deplorable mania of the day'. '[It] will take the great liberty to insert only, after meticulous verification, news that is rigorously inaccurate,' its opening editorial proclaimed.[14] In a free society such ribaldry was permissible, perhaps necessary, during wartime. A scourge on the censorship and government, it was also a necessary outlet for the frustrations of the governed.

Germany was industrious in trying to manage public opinion. By October 1914 there were twenty-seven separate official and semiofficial agencies reporting to a central propaganda office: bureaucratisation was the way in information management as it would be in so many dimensions of German wartime life.[15] Such offices produced propaganda to promote the justice of the cause while defaming and disparaging the opposition in a tit-for-tat war of words that was customarily vituperative, frequently

mendacious and occasionally absurd. If the Allies did not need such a centralised system of information control in the early years of the war, it was
in part because the enemy did the propagandists' work for them. Germany's actions, even if they might be seen as legitimate acts or inevitable
consequences of war, sustained Allied indignation and added neutral con-
demnation for good measure. They were to engender a four-year litany
of illegality and 'barbarity': the use of poison gas on the battlefield in April
1915; the sinking of the *Lusitania* in May 1915; the execution of nurse
Edith Cavell in October 1915 and Captain Charles Fryatt in July 1916;
the devastation of Serbia, Rumania and the Oise; ultimately the punitive
Peace of Brest-Litovsk with Russia in March 1918; the ongoing trials of
refugees and those living daily under German occupation; naval bombardments and zeppelin raids of British towns (a murderous stratagem but
'merely a fighting tonic to the British race' in *The Vivid*'s gung-ho opinion).[16] Clearly one unforeseen but positive consequence of being invaded
was the advantage it gave in the propaganda war. The Hun remained
beastly, and if this alone was not enough to sustain the will to victory on
the Allied side, it certainly hardened anti-German feeling. After the first
use of gas against French troops Mildred Aldrich noted a change in France.

> Up to now, the hatred of the Germans has been, in a certain sense,
> impersonal. It has been a racial hatred of a natural foe, an accepted evil,
> just as the uncalled-for war was . . . But this new and devilish arm which
> Germany has added to the horrors of war seemed the last straw, and
> within a few weeks, I have seen grow up among these simple people the
> conviction that the race which planned and launched this great war has
> lost the very right to live . . . even if the war lasts twenty years, and even
> if, before it is over, the whole world has to take a hand in it.[17]

Thereafter, the redress of German barbarism and the extirpation of German militarism remained valid rationales for fighting on (and were to be
reprised twenty years later). Indeed so legitimised was this image of Germanic brutality, criminality and rapine that when a new ally entered the
fray in 1917 it could be reworked for an American audience already famil-
iarised by Allied propaganda and their own press with the atrocities,
annexations and aggressions committed in the name of German Kultur.
After all, it was yet another manifestation of these, unrestricted submarine warfare, which catalysed America's declaration of war.

In practice there was no national media strategy in any of the belligerents in the early months of the war beyond limiting the release of
potentially sensitive military information. Partly the army would keep
war news 'official' by issuing a daily communiqué summarising military

developments, and partly the military censor's office would vet newspaper articles to ensure that these did not reveal military secrets. It soon became apparent, however, that the official military information provided was insufficient to satisfy public curiosity or to allay the rumours and atrocity stories that ratcheted up popular hatred of the enemy. Moreover, home and international news was not subject to the same scrutiny as war news. Political debates, domestic developments, diplomatic coups and economic events – both at home and abroad – were all endlessly reported and reflected upon, and formed the staple of wartime press reporting in the absence of 'military' headlines, through which the shifting fortunes of peoples' war could be weighed.

There existed therefore a surprising and unexpected juxtaposition between governments anxious to restrict and play down military war news and the private media desperate for information to engage their readership (and of course to increase their circulation and profits). In the early phase of the war, therefore, presses were doing the governments' work of stirring up wartime patriotism for them with only the gentlest of steers from those who ran the war. Lord Kitchener had only to give one newspaper interview, published in *The Times* on 15 August 1914, to present to the nation his view of the nature of the war and to set in motion Britain's war mobilisation.

In the first half of the war government media strategy was focused abroad rather than at home, as a supplementary weapon of war on the diplomatic front. In neutral and enemy states a form of wartime propaganda developed, managed at one remove from government by the foreign ministry's *Maison de la presse* in France and the War Propaganda Bureau (colloquially known from its offices as Wellington House) in Britain, funded by but not part of the Foreign Office and headed by the ex-Liberal member of parliament and writer Charles Masterman. The task of such agencies was to encourage support for and intervention in the war in neutral countries (in which of course foreign governments could not be seen to be taking a direct part, hence the creation of arm's-length 'public' bureaux), especially the United States. Come 1917 their task was complete (but in that year propaganda had to be turned to domestic and enemy audiences as the issues of the war and the reliability of its warriors came into question).

War enthusiasm was not as widespread a phenomenon as was mooted at the time and subsequently. War acceptance, however, if not universal, was extensive and all-pervading in the war's early months. Engaging people with the war had been relatively unproblematic since, with the exception of a few marginal extreme left-wing publications that would soon fall victim to the wartime censorship regime, newspapers and periodicals rallied to the cause. The publishing industry followed suit, commissioning and rushing out war-related material of better or worse quality to satisfy a voracious demand for information. The war could not be ignored given the deluge of books and illustrated part-works that appeared in all countries. The reality, however, was that few people wished to ignore the war, and this literature was lapped up as the means to engage vicariously with the experience of sons and brothers at the front. With their many black-and-white photographs and line-drawings and simple, positive text, war-surveying part-works such as *The Vivid War Weekly* appear quaint and condescending in today's multimedia environment. In them tales of individual heroism and great victories, the staples of populist military history, proliferated. Such inspiring martial tales were juxtaposed with a genuine effort to explain the nature and needs of a people's war, one that had to be fought in a way in which heroism and victories were actually at a discount. 'Every man, woman and child playing their part,' *The Vivid*'s anonymous army officer enjoined, 'making his sacrifice of life, of luxury, of money as may be demanded . . . It will come gradually, this realisation of what is demanded of us – slowly the government will direct our efforts and organise our energies.'[18] 'The Inspiring Story of the Canadians'; 'The Conversion of Britain and the Establishment of Complete National Service'; 'Triumph of British Science and Invention in the War'; 'Isolating the Enemy: How the Central Empires Were Blockaded' – such chapters in the part-work *The Great War* explained what the nation and empire were doing and how they were doing it.[19] Nor did periodicals shy away from depictions of the battlefield, death and combat, bringing the nature of modern war into sharp focus (something that documentary films only tentatively animated as the war went on, and rarely for public consumption).[20] The aim was simple – 'every man, woman and child . . . playing his part in the national process of attrition' – and while it would be hard, it would be worthwhile, since 'purged by self-sacrifice, ennobled by hardships', the nation would win not just a military victory but gain 'a greater understanding and a noble conception of national and personal duty'.[21] This was an uplifting message, and in 1915 generally an appealing one, although how it might be sustained and what it would lead to in practice remained to be seen.

What was becoming evident was that the media had a role in channelling the public mood, volatile as it might be, and also in sustaining wartime spirit.* On a day-to-day or week-on-week basis the public mood (like a soldier's disposition) might change from elation to indignation or

---

*Clausewitz had identified that mood and spirit were the components of military morale, and the same model might apply to civilians in a mass society at war.

despondency according to events trivial or grand: the rising price of bread, a wounded loved one, another enemy defeat on the battlefield reported in the newspapers. Spirit modulated on a longer wavelength and really determined whether society would stick it out: a winter with little but turnips to eat; heavy losses over a campaigning season; a change of government; the defeat of an ally. In essence the public and their uniformed brethren were responsive to a mixed and changing litany of home news and war news, mediated by the press and government and increasingly monitored for its impact as the war progressed.[22]

The people's will to victory was founded on a just cause, valiantly fought for. On both sides, resistance to aggression laid the moral base for engaging with a righteous cause, distinct from the diplomatic ambitions of statesmen and the military objectives of generals and admirals.[23] Reaction to atrocity (grossly exaggerated by the media early in the war, but with an incontrovertible core of truth) provided the grist for the mill of mutual hatred that was soon turning.

Germany's leaders could justify the war in terms of self-defence; Austria for her part was punishing Serbian 'aggression'. Bethmann Hollweg had announced portentously as Germany mobilised that the war was being waged to defend Germany's right to stand supreme among the great powers, against jealous rivals who wished to bring her down.[24] He saw no irony in the fact that in waging this war Germany was sending her armies into enemy and neutral countries, since the Russians' incursion into East Prussia in August 1914, reportedly burning and pillaging as they came on, and the invasion and occupation of Galicia thereafter could be seized on by the press as sufficient justification for Germany's fears and actions.[25] Germany's socialists certainly seem to have been taken in by this explanation (a situation that Germany's leaders had deliberately orchestrated so that she would not appear as the aggressor). But beyond the immediate needs of defence in August 1914, come autumn there was a need to build a political consensus behind the long two-front war, Germany's strategic nightmare, which now seemed inevitable.

That need was not beyond the comprehension of Germany's more enlightened statesmen, but the political structures and deep-rooted social divisions in the empire would make its realisation problematic. Bethmann Hollweg saw opportunity as well as danger in the domestic situation Germany now faced. The most progressive of William II's chancellors, Bethmann had acknowledged that Germany was changing socially and that the empire's political structure would in time have to adapt to the reality of mass society. He had of necessity, if not from conviction, found himself working with socialist Reichstag deputies to pass the military service bill in 1913, and this gave him the impression that despite their anticapitalist dogmas, the moderate democratic socialists at least appeared also to be good Germans and might be brought into the fold. The war would be a test of their patriotism, but there might be fair rewards for their cooperation in time. Persuading Germany's nationalist and conservative groups to accept this would, however, be hard. The kaiser certainly saw war as a test of the people's loyalty, although he had no intention of rewarding it.

Such rewards as would come to Germany would be her due now the malevolent designs of her enemies had been challenged. World power might yet be won by the sword, since it had never been forthcoming by peaceful diplomacy. Those who would win her just rewards were her soldiers and the financiers and businessmen who equipped the army for its all-or-nothing struggle – Germany's nationalists, who did have to be compensated. In early September 1914 Bethmann drew up a draft war aims programme should Germany emerge victorious, just when the expectation of a quick, decisive war was disappearing as Moltke's manoeuvre through Belgium and France came unstuck. The September Programme, with its schedule of territorial annexations and scheme for postwar economic dominance in Europe, Asia and Africa – security guarantees as Bethmann euphemistically and disingenuously identified them – was not for public (or neutral) consumption.[26] It was certainly not a document that acknowledged that in Germany 'social peace' had broken out and that socialists were partners in the kaiser's war. It was an ideal to be aspired to by Germany's conservative, militaristic elites; its economic aspirations were heavily influenced by Walter Rathenau, the businessman who assumed control of Germany's newly established War Raw Materials Board through which Germany's industrialists would take their share in managing the war effort.[27] Its achievability in practice was moot, not least because it would be the efforts of the people in uniform and the workplace that would make it happen. Thus Germany began the war with the capitalist and imperialist objectives of businessmen, the army and government juxtaposed with the patriotic yet pacific spirit of her people. They would dutifully defend Germany, territorially and as a cultural ideal, with their lives should it come to it, yet they had been hoodwinked into accepting legitimate defence as a cloak for national aggrandisement.[28] As the war dragged on, with German troops encamped abroad everywhere and occupied territories subject to Prussian-style martial law, sustaining the will to victory on the home front on this false premise would prove increasingly difficult. The socialists and their antimilitarist allies in the democratic Catholic Centre and liberal parties would in time find a voice with which to challenge that reactionary imperial agenda.

To the Allies, conversely, 'Prussian' power in both its abstract conception and practical application was something against which public opinion could rally. Germany's perceived hegemonic aspirations could be denounced – more easily since German deeds on the battlefield and in occupied regions endorsed long-standing suspicions. Just as Bethmann Hollweg was sketching out Germany's war aims programme, the Entente powers were signing the Pact of London. A shared opposition to German expansionism could bind three powerful empires together, setting aside, temporarily at least, their own diplomatic and cultural differences. Unity among the Allies had to be matched with unity within them. The German invasion of Belgium famously provided the pretext for British unity and resolve: a tense Liberal cabinet crisis over intervention gave way to almost complete ministerial support for foreign secretary Sir Edward Grey's ultimatum to Germany demanding immediate withdrawal from Belgium. The Unionists, who as the war went on would become the bedrock of the political will to victory, backed firm action from the start. 'Remember Belgium' was the first rallying cry for the British people. It convinced even strong pacifists such as the Oxford University scholar and later advocate of the League of Nations Gilbert Murray of the justice of war against Germany's 'dishonest government . . . unscrupulous and arrogant diplomacy [and] spirit of "blood and iron" ambition which seems to have spread from Prussia through a great part of the nation'. This did not fatally undermine his belief in the inherent decency of Germany's ill-led people.[29] As German armies crossed that country gory and sensationalist (and often untrue) tales of the execution of civilians, the rape of women and the murder of children sustained the first wave of voluntary military recruitment. The destruction of the library of Louvain University was true and represented the first affront of German *Kultur* to that of her enemies. France too witnessed the brutality of advancing German armies, anxious to avoid a repetition of the *franc-tireur* incidents of 1870–71 in which armed civilians had ambushed and killed Prussian soldiers.

Some might see this as legitimate, or at least necessary, acts of war. Binding certainly noted matter-of-factly as he deployed on the battlefield at Ypres:

> The fact that the enemy is near makes the villagers dangerous as well. I was fired on quite unpleasantly from some house. The prescribed procedure in this event – to burn the houses in question – is nonsense, increasing the confusion and the resistance, and almost always strikes the innocent. I had two men shot whom I found in two houses from which we were fired on. This had the required effect.[30]

Summary executions, burning down villages and looting private properties were certainly effective ways of imposing the invaders' will on the civilian population, although grist to the mill of sensationalist Allied journalists. (Similar incidents of French troops taking reprisals against uncooperative civilians in August 1914 during their short-lived invasion of Alsace and Lorraine could be quietly forgotten once the battle lines settled down on friendly soil.)[31] Acts of violence and destruction perpetrated by Russian troops in the East were seized on by German newspapers in the same way that the Allied press denounced German atrocities. Later, however, a German official report admitted that 'Russian atrocities have . . . turned out to be grossly exaggerated'. With a few notorious exceptions, Russian troops generally behaved correctly towards civilians – they treated the Polish Jewish population much worse than the enemy during the early campaigns – and much damage to property was a direct consequence of military action.[32] Collectively, such early war outrages and their regular repetition in other guises as the war went on became a new weapon operated by the media which always seized on a lurid, paper-selling story, fuelling the mutual hatred that competed with rational judgment in wartime. Since war is bestial, it would bring out the beast in soldier and civilian alike.

Hatred of the enemy and moral outrage at his actions was one important reason to engage with the war, but belief in the cause was perhaps a more potent and more affirmative reason for deciding to fight, and to fight on: hatred was after all common to both sides, as were frightful acts of war, but purpose had to be different. Both sides strove to create and sustain a sense of moral righteousness, coupling it with a worthy rationale. In Germany cultural superiority was assumed and its protection emphasised. The enemies were at the gates and if not resisted the vibrant, superior Germanic tradition was in danger of being submerged by the decadent French, aided by the brutal, bestial Slavs and the rapacious Anglo-Saxons. Germanic *Kultur* had to be preserved against such an unholy alliance. For the Entente, whose enemy had breached the walls, this very *Kultur*, manifest in barbarity and militarism, had to be humbled for the future peace of Europe. By the middle of the war Allied resolve to fight on would crystallise around a single, clear purpose, which justified the method adopted: fighting 'until the military domination of Prussia is wholly and finally destroyed' necessitated even more intensive mobilisation, Chief of the Imperial General Staff (CIGS) Sir William Robertson forcefully reminded the British cabinet in November 1916.[33]

WHAT MOTIVATED INDIVIDUALS TO ENGAGE WITH THE WAR INEVITABLY varied from person to person and place to place. But engage they did. J. B. Priestley, the English author who was to turn like so many educated

Englishmen against their war when they realised its consequences, volunteered in September 1914. He intimated that the moral cause counted for less than the call of war: 'I was sorry for "gallant little Belgium" but did not feel she was waiting for me to rescue her.'[34] The cause of 'king and country' moved him much less than a strong, manly impulse to go to war, he later intimated.[35] The author and poet Siegfried Sassoon, who post-war would become the most notorious British objector to the conflict as it wore on, had an equally strong desire to fight: 'Like most of the human race I had always wanted to be a hero.' He enlisted as a trooper in the territorial Sussex Yeomanry the day before Britain declared war: 'I'd got to go and be a soldier and knew nothing about how to do it when I got there.'[36] Others wrestled longer with their conscience before making the decision to enlist. The writer Edward Thomas waited for nearly a year before enlisting in the Artist's Rifles (28th Battalion, the London Regiment) in July 1915.[37] A mature, married man, Thomas lacked the gung-ho enthusiasm of youth, and his decision to fight was made on moral grounds. The diarist Bruce Cummings desperately wanted to fight like his brother, but chronic ill-health prevented it.[38] It is the voice of this type of man, the literary intellectual, middle-class and educated, that captured the spirit of the war for posterity. Such men, however, were untypical of the volunteers of 1914–15.

For many putting on a uniform in wartime was an unexceptional progression from peacetime. Oliver Lyttelton (later Lord Chandos) and a number of his contemporaries were promptly promised commissions by Lord Salisbury, patron of the Bedfordshire Regiment, on the outbreak of war. It was expected that the sons of aristocrats would take up arms in times of national danger and Lyttelton would seem to have accepted his new life without demur. He already had some rudimentary military knowledge from his time in the Eton College Officer Training Corps, and he happily set to training Kitchener volunteers in drill and musketry.[39]

Volunteerism, although quintessentially a British phenomenon, was not confined to nations without conscription. The Germany army enlisted many volunteers who had escaped the draft before 1914, in that year and subsequently. The most notorious of these was Adolf Hitler, who in 1908 had emigrated from Vienna to Germany rather than be conscripted, but returned to join up in 1914: when the Austrian recruiting officers classified him as 'too weak; incapable of bearing arms', he recrossed the border to enlist in the Bavarian army.[40] Many others were motivated by a similar sense of duty encouraged by a belief in the justice of the cause and values worth defending. Erich Maria Remarque, author of the famous war novel *All Quiet on the Western Front*, represented the 'iron youth' of 1914 as gripped by an unhealthy blend of mass hysteria and indoctrination; yet such a generation was exactly what the German state had worked hard to create in peacetime and was geared up to exploit in time of war.

The potency of the moral message, as well as the appeal of the adventure of war, spread beyond the belligerents. Volunteers from neutral countries flocked to the ranks on both sides (but predominantly to the Allies). The famous French Foreign Legion readily accepted volunteers from neutral states. Between thirty thousand and forty thousand non-French volunteers served with France's armies, the majority in the legion's *battalions de marche*.[40] If this was a drop in the ocean of wartime man-power, it represented a significant propaganda advantage, especially since Foreign Legion battalions were raised from Eastern European separatists, Czechs and Poles. The majority of foreign volunteers, some 29 percent, were Italians (who were recalled to the Italian army when that nation entered the war, producing the peculiarity that the last surviving French Great War veteran, Lazare Ponticelli, was in fact an Italian).

Although the United States adopted a diplomatic position of strict neutrality in 1914, the issues being contested in Europe could not be ignored. Many Americans considered that it was not their quarrel, but most still had sympathies with one side or the other. A number felt sufficiently stirred to fight. The young American poet Alan Seeger, living in Paris in summer 1914, immediately enlisted in the French Foreign Legion because the chivalric idea of going to war appealed to him so much.[42] As he left for the front he sought his mother's blessing:

> I hope you see the thing as I do and think that I have done well . . . in taking upon my shoulders, too, the burden that so much of humanity is suffering under, and rather than stand ingloriously aside when the opportunity was given me, doing my share for the side that I think right.[43]

She gave it.[44] Others probably made more measured and less emotional judgements. 'I have a rendezvous with death' Seeger's most famous poem began: he was to be killed on the Somme in 1916. Seeger was not the only American who chose to fight for the Allied cause. He is listed among the twenty-three legionnaires who gave their lives for France on the memorial to American volunteers in the Place des États-Unis in Paris. Other Americans joined the volunteer Lafayette Squadron of the French army, raised largely as a propaganda exercise in 1916 and named after the general who had led French troops during the American War of Independence: perhaps some felt a residual moral obligation to France. The vast majority of American volunteers crossed her border with Canada and enlisted in the Canadian army that was being raised for service in Europe. The most common American response at the beginning of the war, however, was humanitarian. The American Red Cross raised field ambulances and hospitals staffed by American volunteers for the Allies and funds for Belgian refugees, as well as organising relief for civilians in German occupied France and Belgium. It was clear early on which side American liberals favoured, and the Allied propaganda machines quickly geared up to exploit this.

With the many complex motives behind volunteering to fight, it must be remembered that the vast majority of the war's participants did not make a conscious choice to take up arms (or indeed to 'serve' on the home front, where employment in 'war industries' as often as not represented the continuation of peacetime work, or a chance for better wages and conditions in a manufacturing sector crying out for labour). Writing about the war to come, the French military theorist Commandant Jean Colin had identified patriotism as the root of an army's cohesion and discipline. The same might apply to a nation at war. Although the nations of Europe were different, patriotism motivated both sides. An idealised image of 'hearth and home', of a noble culture and values, and of people, both combatants and civilians who embodied those values pervaded all societies: both British and German recruitment posters depicted an inviting, sunny, verdant and pastoral homeland worth defending (only the enemy was depicted attacking on posters). Thus whatever the individual motives of citizens and soldiers, a shared sense of patriotic duty and willingness to make sacrifice – of time, of effort and potentially the supreme sacrifice of life in the greater cause – held together the vast majority of the people in their war. In August 1914 serving conscripts and reservists reported for duty with much less demur than authorities expected. When it came to calling up annual contingents thereafter, absenteeism was still limited, although it increased as the war dragged on. That these conscripts went willingly to fight, possibly to die, may seem surprising in today's individualistic age. At the turn of the twentieth century, however, societies were very different. When *la patrie* or *der Vaterland* needed them most young men were prepared and willing to answer the call. But Colin issued a prophetic warning to those nations, like Russia, where patriotism was weak or public opinion divided: 'Where patriotism is beginning to die in a nation, that nation has but the semblance of a military force; it keeps up a more or less brilliant façade which will crumble at the first shock.'[45] In this war it was not just the bodies of the soldiers that would have to be managed but their hearts and minds as well.

The immediate fear in 1914 was for the loyalty of the left. But even the socialists whose philosophy denounced war between nations as inimical to the interests of the international working class demonstrated that they were patriots first and comrades second. Most workers accepted the justice of a nation's right of self-defence when attacked, and also their obligation to serve.[46] It perhaps surprised national governments that social democratic parties everywhere and the trade unions that supported them called upon their members to do their patriotic duty, either in uniform or the workplace. A certain degree of pragmatic political calculation by workers' leaders has been suggested – loyalty in the short war that was expected would hopefully secure them longer-term political influence and social rewards once peace returned (although the German example suggests that this was a rather optimistic assessment of the situation in the conservative empires at least). But this is to deny that in pre-1914 society the workers and their leaders were inculcated with the values of state and nation like everyone else, sufficiently so at least when an enemy threatened and invaded. Yet there remained a few socialists of principle in 1914 who opposed war in all its forms. Ramsay MacDonald, a future Labour prime minister, opposed the war from the start, even while privately admitting the morality of the cause Britain was fighting for. Nevertheless, he cautioned his parliamentary colleagues on 3 August 1914 as they voted for war credits, 'no war is at first unpopular'.[47] Other opponents of the war were more pragmatic. Recently disgraced former premier Joseph Caillaux – the trial of his wife for shooting dead a newspaper editor had both captivated and scandalised the republic while the July Crisis was unfolding elsewhere in Europe – soon emerged as the leader of a pro-peace faction in the French parliament. Around such men would form in time a more coherent, if never widespread, opposition to the continuing musters of young men to feed the guns. Broadly, however, this was to be a participatory war, whatever the consequences.

WHILE THE PROSPECT OF THE OUTBREAK OF WAR HAD FILLED THE PEOPLE OF Europe with horror in July 1914, the actual war, with all its concomitant dislocation and atrocity, quickly engaged them, '[galvanising] the sense of national community and involvement in politics that had been growing in the previous half-century'.[48] It had not taken long for both sides to establish that the war was justified, worth fighting, and would be continued until one alliance was broken. Essentially innate nationalism, a sense of patriotic duty, revulsion at the actions of an invading enemy catalysed by a loyal media and widespread curiosity as to what a major war actually entailed came together. It did not require statesmen to give more than the most general incitement to war, by means of justificatory speeches and appeals to a sense of honour and duty in the cause of national defence, to rouse their people into action, and once the passions of the people were stirred the war became collective. Although war broke out over the interests and rights of great powers, the cloak of a mass participatory war soon covered the belligerents, although its shade varied from country to country, some people and interest groups wrapped themselves in it more fully than others, and a few refused on grounds of conscience to don it. Moreover, it was a shroud of 'genuine hatred . . . as Europeans developed new, often dehumanizing views of their enemies'. While a growing sense of disenchantment with a war that had promised quick, glorious victory was already setting in by its first autumn, thereafter that garment could be richly embroidered or restyled according to the year's fashion.[49] This ensured that enough of the people would remain clothed in war colours whatever the trend of events.

Early, indignant, unconditional support for the war was relatively short-lived; it ceased around the time the trench lines that came to signify a long, brutal and uncertain conflict appeared. But disenchantment with the nature of the war did not mean disillusionment as to its purpose. The peoples of Europe had turned on Germany by 1915, although for now at least her own people seemed firmly behind the war effort. The interaction between patriotic sentiments that had been inculcated pre-war and Germany's actions in its early months ensured that Britons and French would set themselves determinedly to resist and defeat the 'barbaric Hun'. Russian liberals thought the same, although the empire's masses were harder to motivate with anti-German and anti-Austrian sentiment. Although Russian Poland was invaded, the vast bulk of her landmass was not menaced, unlike Belgium, which was almost completely occupied, and France, whose northern *départements* hosted the foe.

In both liberal societies and the monarchies there were strong patriotic drives motivating men to fight on or women to 'do their bit' in the greater national endeavour. Such criticisms as there were were starting to be directed at those who were managing the war, an indication that public opinion wished the war to be fought more intensely rather than to be concluded prematurely and that societies still had some way to go in adapting to the circumstances of wartime.

This is what the people's leaders had primed them for. 'It should be assumed,' Kitchener had posited drawing an analogy with the four-year long American Civil War, 'that before Germany relinquishes the struggle, she will have exhausted every possible supply of men and materiel.'[50] The Allies would have to respond in kind. Since the feared 'people's war' had come about, it was to the people that statesmen and military commanders turned. Young men of military age, workers in factories and fields and the great untapped resource, women, would all be mobilised as the war took on its definitive shape during 1915. Thereafter it would be events on the battlefield or the other fronts that rallied public opinion behind the war effort. This presented governments with new challenges in the use of information and the management of public opinion as the true nature of the war and the sacrifices expected by all revealed themselves. The commanders embarking on a war of attrition could, however, be fairly confident of the reliability of their troops, individually and collectively, at least if the war was properly managed and its values remained clear and worthy. What they could be less sure of was that their manpower resources would be sufficient to achieve a victory.

# FIVE

# MOBILISING MANPOWER

FIVE WEEKS AFTER ENLISTING IN THE FOREIGN LEGION, ALAN SEEGER wrote to his mother from barrack at Toulouse, on the eve of his departure for the front: 'we are entirely equipped down to our three days' rations and 120 rounds of cartridges. The wagons are all laden and the horses requisitioned. The suspense is exciting, for no one has any idea where we shall be sent.' After six weeks of hard drilling – twelve hours a day, seven days a week – he claimed to 'have learned in six weeks what the ordinary recruit in times of peace takes all his two years at', and all for the modest sum of one sou a day.[1] Seeger could drill, march and shoot, but he was not yet ready to fight: he would go through a few weeks of tactical training on the old Marne battlefield, within the sound of the guns, before going into the trenches in Champagne in late October. Seeger was impatient to see action: 'Imagine how thrilling it will be . . . marching towards the front with the noise of battle growing continually before us . . . I go into action with the lightest of hearts.'[2] Like many thousands of others in 1914 and afterwards, his transition from civilian to soldier would be rapid and intense, as the battles raging across France demanded fighting men at an unprecedented rate. The battles that Seeger would fight in, culminating on the Somme in 1916, chewed up soldiers and spat them out, often maimed and broken, once the grinding military machine started to process its 'cannon fodder'. Hundreds of thousands, Seeger included, would never come back, and lie today in neat rows of graves in the well-tended war cemeteries of northern France and Belgium, or are listed on the many memorials to the missing who have no known grave, eternal monuments to the manpower-intensive, humanity devouring military system that defines the Great War. But Seeger like so many was 'happy and full of excitement over the wonderful days that are ahead'.[3] Although his confident prediction that he would be back home safe by next summer proved false, he remained a happy warrior, despite the grim ordeals of battle. In his last letter, on the eve of the Somme offensive, he assured his friend: 'I am glad to be going in the first wave. If you are in this thing at all it is best to be in to the limit. And this is the supreme experience.'[4] Seeger expressed one of the eternal paradoxes of this or any war. A man facing adversity, terror and potentially death remains anxious to fight and determined to conquer: his enemy to the front, the new recruit who would replace him, and the nation that spawned him.

In simplest military terms, this war would be all about manpower, which became what Clausewitz characterized as the 'centre of gravity' of the war. Eradicating the enemy's manpower reserves would determine its outcome. Attritional strategy on land would be predicated on destroying the forces that the enemy could deploy faster than he could replace them. Military tactics, operations and strategy were all geared to wearing down the enemy's reserves to a point that his army's power of resistance would break. Frontline companies that held trenches and reserve battalions that counterattacked attacks designed to capture them would be eliminated in battle. During campaigns divisions and army corps held in strategic reserve to reinforce threatened sectors of the defensive front would be drawn into battle and defeated. Behind them the untrained manpower available for replacing losses year-on-year would have to be whittled down over the course of several campaigns. This became evident in 1915, although then the military methods to achieve it effectively were rudimentary. One of Seeger's legionnaire comrades, a Bulgarian who had fought in the recent Balkan wars, missed the open warfare and bayonet charges of that conflict: 'It is ignoble, this style of warfare, he exclaims . . . We are not . . . leading the life of men at all, but that of animals, living in holes in the ground and only showing our heads outside to fight and to feed.' But the trenches were there to protect him and his comrades from the 'precise and scientific struggle of the artillery' raging constantly overhead and the small-arms fire that made the open battlefield uncrossable, and their existence would complicate and prolong the process of battlefield attrition.[5] Such conceptions of warfare in which manoeuvre, decisive battles and the conquest of territory determined success persisted beyond their usefulness. Statesmen and soldiers still advocated them and people expected them. When he visited the Somme front in 1916 Asquith bemoaned to Lieutenant-General Alexander Godley,

> The fact that what the British public wanted to hear of was geographical gains of towns and territory, on a large scale, and large bags of

prisoners; and that a successful fight that only involved an advance of a couple of thousand yards and the slaughter of a large number of Germans did not appeal to them. They wanted something tangible.[6]

Attrition was controversial as a strategy then, certainly misunderstood, and morally questionable ever after; but the slaughter of a large number of Germans and the reciprocal sacrifice of Allied troops determined the nature, course and outcome of the war more than anything else.

As the war of attrition got underway in earnest, fresh soldiers such as Seeger were at a premium. In autumn 1914 his raw regiment deployed into a relatively quiet sector where the novelty and incongruity of war could be savoured. 'How beautiful the view is here, over the sunny vineyards!' he reported of his arrival at the front. 'And what a curious anomaly. On this slope the grape pickers are singing merrily at their work, on the other the batteries are roaring Boom! Boom! This will spoil one for any other kind of life.'[7] Elsewhere, however, the war raged on: Seeger was well aware of the heavy losses in the battles around Ypres.[8] Joffre ended the year with a final concerted push to break the German defences in Artois and Champagne, but without success. The battle settled down into small-scale fights for villages and trenches over the winter, while soldiers adapted to the conditions of the trenches: 'The real courage of the soldier is not in facing the [shrapnel] balls, but the fatigue and discomfort and misery,' Seeger opined, although it was not long before he and his comrades had made themselves cosy for their winter hibernation.[9] He had ceased to be a civilian and was now a soldier whose destiny was no longer in his own hands. This did not trouble him, he reflected in a rare moment of solitude away from the bustle of the regiment: 'This life agrees with me; there will be war for many years to come in Europe, and I shall continue to be a soldier as long as there is war.'[10] While Seeger was adapting to living outdoors during a cold winter, Joffre was arranging his fate, and that of many others, come spring.

THE EFFORT ON THE LAND FRONT WAS STILL FOREMOST IN STRATEGISTS' minds as they planned the first campaigns of 1915. Joffre was anxious to renew the fight as soon as possible, and for this he needed soldiers, his own and those of allies. The balanced utilisation of manpower would become the central issue of strategy as the war developed, and for France it would always be problematic due to a large extent to Joffre's costly and aggressive offensive strategy in 1915 that, coming on top of the heavy casualties of 1914, strained France's own manpower resources. In January 1915 Joffre was still calculating that he could end the war quickly with a 'push' – his army's ranks were full and the enemy had not yet entrenched as solidly as he would by the end of the year – if he could maximise military potential quickly. As France and all the other belligerents would find during 1915, however, war was now a much more complex undertaking than simply massing men into huge armies to slug it out in decisive battles.

Reviewing the strength of his army at the beginning of the new campaigning season, Joffre was perturbed. France had few undeployed reserves from earlier annual contingents in her depots, which had been emptied of all but the half-trained remnants of the 1914 class and older territorial-age reservists. Joffre resorted to incorporating naval conscripts, surplus manpower from the artillery and supply services and younger territorials from line-of-communications battalions into the frontline infantry. The whole of the 1915 class were designated to replace infantry losses in the coming campaign, while those regions whose depots retained a manpower surplus were directed to send men to others. Younger recruits and reservists were to be allocated to active units and older reservists and territorials to reserve divisions.[11] By these expedients Joffre would start the new campaign with ranks full and reserves for another year of war. Further heavy losses during 1915 – 465,000 killed or captured by the end of November – demonstrated that the parameters of prewar military manpower policy were unsustainable. Joffre had gambled that it would not need to be if Germany could be beaten quickly and lost.

In the short to medium term France could expand her army (to a lesser extent than Germany, which had recruited a smaller percentage of men before the war into each annual contingent and therefore had more untrained manpower to call up). The GQG formed independent battalions of *chasseurs* and foreign legionnaires into new divisions, raised new battalions from trained men from earlier annual contingents and recruits of the 1914 and 1915 classes and expanded the territorial reserve (older men who could hold quiet sectors of the front or labour behind the lines). At the end of the year Joffre commanded 134 divisions, compared with 84 infantry and 10 cavalry divisions in August 1914. But this was a risky manpower strategy predicated on a relatively quick end to hostilities. Annual classes were being called up early – the 1915 class in December 1914 and the 1916 class in April 1915 – and by 1916 the forty-nine-year-olds of the 1886 class were in uniform.[12] So far the conscription system was working smoothly, with contingents cycling through military training one after the other. But a pattern of demand that did not tally with supply was already evident. Training was being curtailed when faced with the voracious human demands of the front, and so most new recruits went to the front only partly prepared and in need of acclimatisation and further instruction. The need for infantry seemed paramount in 1915, although that would soon change. As warfare became increasingly mechanized more men would be required for the technical branches – artillery, engineers, signals and later aircraft, tanks and mechanised transport that required skilled drivers, pilots and mechanics – which entailed longer periods of technical training for a greater percentage of the recruits. At the same time, more manpower would be needed to manufacture and service these modern technologies of war.

In France, war minister Millerand was on the whole a staunch supporter of the commander in chief when it came to strategy and politics, but the question of manpower divided them. The strategy adopted to meet the mass of the German army in battle in the short term was proving inimical to mobilisation for a long war: in order to match German numbers in the field in 1914 France had put large numbers of industrial workers into uniform (and, inevitably, many had become casualties). As the second year of war commenced Joffre wanted as many men as possible for the fight, representing that this was the way to end the war quickly; Millerand recognised that if the fight was to be conducted with explosives and steel rather than flesh and blood, then munitions production lines had to be kept going and expanded, and the rest of the economy serviced. Since there seemed to be more than enough reservists and recruits still in the army's depots to fill existing gaps in the ranks and to replace anticipated losses in the coming campaign, Millerand, whose ministry ran the war economy as well as the army, put pressure on the GQG to release mobilised workers to factories, otherwise the weapons and munitions the army needed for trench warfare would not be forthcoming. Joffre conceded the principle, but in practice throughout 1915 the manpower needs of armaments factories would compete with those of the front.[13] Millerand endeavoured to regularise manpower policy in spring 1915, advocating extending conscription to seventeen-year-olds and men above conscription age (for home-front not military service) and the categorisation of conscripts into skilled workers and others. A system of individual examinations ensured skilled workers remained in the factories, which was formalized by the August 1915 Dalbiez Law establishing the numbers of men needed in the various categories of the war economy. A rigorous examination of rear-area workers would produce 650,000 men eligible for frontline service.[14] Yet around 500,000 men eligible for uniformed service were deployed on the home front thereafter. No more could be spared, although Millerand and his successors would find themselves 'caught between Joffre's incessant and growing demands for war material and the complaints of industrialists short of manpower, raw materials, and machines'.[15] Thus France's manpower policy took shape during 1915. There were echoes here of the disagreements between advocates of state intervention and 'business as usual' in Britain. Similar dialogues on principle and practice were engaged in all states during 1915 as the realities of manpower mobilisation and the competing demands for military manpower and industrial labour became apparent.

FRANCE PLACED GREAT HOPE IN THE MASSES THAT HER OLDEST ALLY COULD potentially put into uniform. Unfortunately, Russia's manpower situation was deceptive. Paper population figures suggested a vast pool of recruits and the ability to expand her forces rapidly. Soon, however, those who observed the Russian recruitment system in action started to report concerns about the gulf between assumed potential and practice. There was, British military Attaché Colonel Alfred Knox noted scathingly, a popular wartime joke in Russia: 'An Army is an assembly of people who have failed to evade military service.'[16] In truth Russia's conscription system had never fulfilled its avowed objective to make, in the words of the 1874 military service decree, 'the business of defending the fatherland . . . the general affair of the people, when all, despite distinction of title or status, unite for that holy cause'.[17] While Russia had a huge population, and many patriots among ethnic Russians at least, the vast multinational empire did not really have a people united and willing to serve the national cause, and the conscription system itself had done much to guarantee this. The prewar system was more remarkable for the numbers it let avoid national service than for the size of the force it raised or the efficiency of the military instrument it created. For one reason or another, up to three-quarters of draft-eligible men were exempt, or liable only for territorial army service: only sons, sole breadwinners and men who had younger siblings to support, those who had brothers already serving or had lost close relations in military service and economically exempt workers all escaped the call-up. Educated men, and paradoxically those who passed the officers' exam, had their period of service reduced. Certain non-Russian ethnic groups were exempted from service altogether. Others, such as the Poles, whose territory would be the likely theatre of a future war, were subject to stringent restrictions. Although in theory exempted men could be conscripted in wartime, prewar practices persisted, making it hard for the army to expand after 1914. Much of the paper-strength of the Russian army was actually the territorial reserve, semi-trained and equipped with obsolescent rifles and artillery and incapable of frontline service. Only 30 percent of the Russian army was fit to take the field, Knox calculated, and only 30 percent of those eligible to be conscripted actually served in any capacity.[18]

Russia's manpower situation was exacerbated by huge casualty bills in 1914 and 1915, essentially caused by matching an ill-equipped army against one with more guns and shells. The army suffered between three hundred thousand and four hundred thousand casualties per month, which there were insufficient trained reserves to replace. Consequently many Russian units fought seriously under-strength, and many men were sent to the front only partially trained. When Austria-Hungary launched a winter offensive the seven hundred thousand recruits of the 1914 class, called up in October, were deployed after only three months of training. The 1915 class took their place in the depots in February 1915, eight months early, and the age of frontline service was raised from thirty-two to thirty-eight, adding another seven hundred thousand reserves. Various largely ineffectual expedients were tried to limit the heavy rates of surrenders, desertions, self-inflicted wounds and illness among the rank and file. By 1915 the Russian army was suffering from a crisis of morale and leadership. Harsher discipline could only achieve marginal improvements, while there were few incentives to encourage soldiers to fight for their country: a land grant to veterans was suggested, but never legislated for. Officers and NCOs were also in short supply, further compromising military efficiency. Secondary school teachers, previously exempt from conscription, were rushed through intensive four-month officer training courses and sent to the front, but the regime baulked at further changes to the conscription system until military events – the Germans' May 1915 advance into Poland – obliged a rethink of military manpower policy.[19]

In the short-tem, however, crisis-management measures only exacerbated the problem. By the end of June 1915 the number of Russian casualties had doubled, as unit after ill-equipped unit was deployed to slow the German advance. The 1915 class was deployed after three months of basic training, and after them the 1916, 1917 and 1918 classes after only one month in training. Not surprisingly casualty lists continued to lengthen, while surrenders and desertions mushroomed. At the start of September Tsar Nicholas took personal command of the field army and immediately declared most existing exemptions cancelled. It was expected that this would produce a reserve of 9–10 million men who could be trained over the winter. This was exactly what the liberal opposition in the Duma had been advocating, and it represented a concession to the modernisers that the tsar's own ministers were reluctant to implement. Moreover, the people themselves were resistant: there were anti-conscription riots and large-scale evasions over the winter of 1915–16.[20] Wartime had proved Russia's peacetime military system outdated and unadaptable. Political conflict, bureaucratic inefficiency and popular resistance meant that its deficiencies were impossible to reform – at least not without seriously weakening the whole structure of the tsarist state.

ALTHOUGH RUSSIA WAS PROVING AN UNEXPECTED MILITARY DISAPPOINTment, her other ally offered unexpected, more immediate and more useful reinforcements for France's battles. On 22 January 1915, in typically British winter weather, sleet slow and a biting wind, Millerand had toured the home counties inspecting the volunteers who had responded to Kitchener's call to arms. His tour started at the Epsom racecourse, now a vast tented camp, and ended at Aldershot, the historic home of the British army. He inspected 140,000 men from five newly raised divisions in all, an impressive display of Britain's growing military might: although what he thought of the men playing leapfrog to keep warm is not recorded.[21]

Prewar France had only anticipated (and never counted upon) a small reinforcement from Britain in the form of her regular army expeditionary force.[22] The announcement in August 1914 that Britain would raise a mass army was therefore greeted with considerable surprise and satisfaction, although many thought the war would be over long before Kitchener's New Army would be ready. As Kitchener had found out when he met Joffre and Foch in November, the French were impatient to get British forces into the line in France. To Joffre, Kitchener's military manpower policy proffered salvation – a regular flow of reinforcements and in time a continental-sized army to take on the invader (if France had not driven the Germans out herself beforehand). To Kitchener himself a mass army meant power and influence – a force with which to engage the enemy certainly, but also to sway Allied military policy. Britain's New Army (and her other military resources, domestic and imperial) was a panacea perhaps, but also a slow-working and untested asset. How many divisions she could raise and equip, when they would be ready and where they would go were still unknowns. It could not be expected that Britain's resources would be placed without exception at France's disposal since Britain had to concern herself with home and imperial defence and strategic interests beyond the continent.

Kitchener's first call on 7 August had been for one hundred thousand men, before hostilities commenced in earnest, the first contingent of an initial five hundred thousand recruits authorised by parliament. J. B. Priestley was one of these, volunteering on 7 September: he would be commissioned from the ranks and wounded three times before being classed unfit for active service in September 1918.[23] Once the first contingent had been raised by the end of September, hundreds of thousands more followed when any limit on recruitment was lifted, as volunteers responded to the unfavourable development of the war in autumn 1914.[24]

Kitchener ultimately settled on the ambitious if somewhat arbitrary figure of a seventy-division metropolitan army.[25] Alongside the raising of Kitchener's New Army (made up of five armies and thirty divisions in total), Britain's reserve army, the Territorial Force, was expanded (fourteen pre-war divisions became thirty-one, although not all left the British Isles. Men of the Territorial Force were accustomed to the military life, and a large number of them quickly took the oath of foreign service requested by Kitchener after war broke out – some seventy battalions in August 1914 alone.[26] Although Britain had no conscription, it had a tradition of part-time soldiering that would more than meet its requirements for military manpower in the short term, as well as a pride in its 'volunteer army, instead of an army of slaves driven to the slaughter'.[27] Excepting a number of second-line Territorial Force divisions retained in England for home defence and as depots for the fighting divisions, it was intended that all these newly raised formations would follow the regular army overseas. The New Army, it was presumed, would deploy to France once equipped and trained: individual Territorial Force battalions had been sent out to reinforce the BEF since November 1914, and four newly organised divisions of regular battalions recalled from imperial garrison duty and replaced by territorials went out by the end of January, before Kitchener started to reconsider his strategic policy. Thereafter some units were trickled out to appease Joffre, but others went to India, Egypt and the Dardanelles as imperial security needs resurfaced.

British military mobilisation was the first manifestation of the profound changes that war would bring to British society. The country had not raised a mass army from scratch before, and structures and resources were lacking. Under the auspices of a newly established all-party Parliamentary Recruiting Committee local dignitaries, municipal authorities, businesses and sporting clubs raised whole companies and battalions of 'pals', men who were pledged to serve together, for the New Army, organised into divisions by the War Office.[28] In order to instil some identity and esprit de corps into what were essentially wartime scratch formations many of the new units were given regional or military identities: 9th (Scottish) Division; 14th (Light) Division; 18th (Eastern) Division; 35th (Bantam) Division; 36th (Ulster) Division. Over one million men had enlisted by November, by which time the strains of uncontrolled enlistment were starting to show. Even after racecourses, public parks and country estates were requisitioned by the military for camps and training grounds there were too many volunteers to be accommodated and trained over the first winter of the war: a mass army needed a lot of space. Many men had to be sent home until they could be inducted into the army. Inevitably the supply of equipment lagged behind recruitment.

Many early recruits temporarily wore 'Kitchener blue' uniforms while Khaki uniforms were being manufactured. It was all a great improvisation, typical of the British way of waging war but inimical to national efficiency. By the time more thoughtful reflection suggested that there should be some sort of central management of Britain's wider manpower effort, the damage had been done.

The battles of 1914 had severely depleted Britain's prewar regular army. Casualties had been heavy, and the vast majority of the trained special reserve had been deployed before the end of the year. Old soldiers had been summoned back to the colours to train the new battalions, and retired officers and Indian Army officers on leave in England were drafted into command positions. University students and schoolboys from the Officer Training Corps took command of platoons and companies in the newly raised battalions. In this way a new citizen army took shape, although it would need the experience of the regular army to make it battle ready. Wounded men from the front would find themselves assigned to training roles in the depots once recovered, teaching about the actual conditions of war. There was a lot more to military training than the notorious bayonet-fighting drill mocked by many later writers. Musketry, route marching and tactical schemes were designed to teach soldiers how to use their weapons and how to operate on the battlefield. But there was no real substitute for battle experience and Kitchener's army would not really get a feel for war until it had undergone a baptism of fire.

It was becoming clear that the war was going to take a steady and heavy toll of British manpower. By mid-April, before any New Army divisions went to the front, there had reportedly already been 140,000 British casualties.[29] Although the recruiting officers were still doing a brisk business – voluntary enlistments revived in spring 1915, inspired by further German 'barbarity', the use of poison gas at Ypres and the declaration of unrestricted submarine warfare resulting in the sinking of the liner *Lusitania* – many were realising that to sustain losses on that scale the voluntary principle was inadequate. This presented a challenge to Britain's communitarian values: 'One volunteer is worth three conscripts,' the Liberal Lord Chamberlain Lord Sandhurst asserted.[30] Nonetheless, administrative measures to better organise the flow of British manpower were becoming essential. At the very least a more efficient registration system was needed, 'a stocktaking of the whole nation – men and women, and then parcelling them out – soldiers – industrials – ticket collectors etc. etc.',[31] so that manpower resources could be properly assessed and utilised. A political movement for so-called 'National Organisation', with Lloyd George to the fore, started to agitate in the summer for a policy that better balanced military and industrial manpower needs. The first cabinet subcommittee on War Policy, chaired by the Lord President of the Council Lord Crewe, was set up by Asquith to engage with departmental conflicts over labour resources. It only served to highlight the deep divisions over both principle and practice. Belatedly other government departments were waking up to the fact that the War Office had stolen a lead on them in securing the lion's share of a limited pool of young men – but at the same time a vociferous minority of the subcommittee represented that the introduction of compulsory service was essential to raise and sustain Kitchener's seventy-division army.

First of all, however, available manpower had to be counted and categorised or no centralised manpower policy was possible. In late summer 1915 a national register of men aged nineteen to forty-one still in civilian life was prepared by the Local Government Board. Some 1,563,000 men were registered, although Ireland was excluded. By September 1915 there was starting to be some knowledge of how many men were actually available, although getting them to serve, either in the military or in appropriate home-front occupations, was still some months and several administrative and legislative changes away. Compulsion was looming, but before that in a last forlorn attempt to preserve voluntarism, Director of Recruiting Lord Derby inaugurated an attestation scheme through which men would register their willingness to serve if summoned (by age contingent), single men before married. Yet this was a stopgap measure to appease liberals like Sandhurst who resisted compulsory service on principle. When 650,000 married men failed to register, it became clear that to initiate a practicable manpower policy Britain would have to join the continental states in adopting conscription.[32]

Before the war the National Service League had mounted a sustained campaign advocating conscription, but with a Liberal government firmly in power had got nowhere. From May 1915, however, Britain had a national coalition government with pro-conscription Unionist ministers (and Liberal converts such as Churchill) on the front bench. The political arguments about conscription rumbled on against the background of the increasingly troubled Dardanelles campaign during the summer and autumn of 1915. Kitchener himself did not favour the introduction of conscription while there remained a steady stream of volunteers. Over the summer, as casualties mounted from offensives and day-to-day attrition, so-called 'trench wastage', the number of men joining up steadily fell: in September 1915 recruitment reached a new low of 71,617 men, well short of the 35,000 volunteers needed per week to keep existing units up to strength.[33] Perhaps the two developments were not unrelated. Early enthusiasm for the cause was starting to be tempered by greater awareness of the nature of the war. Yet in Kitchener's estimation the war was not even underway in earnest. The battles that his armies were recruited to fight in 1916 would be on a grand scale, with a potential rate of losses that the supply of volunteers could not be expected to sustain. It was partly because recruiting was not meeting actual requirements by late 1915, but also because needs were anticipated to become much greater in 1916, that conscription of single men was put on the statute books in England, Wales and Scotland in January 1916. The first conscripts joined the army in May. Belatedly, and necessarily, Britain had committed to an intensive war of attrition with the human costs and centralised management of manpower that it entailed. But even then Kitchener's military ambitions were not entirely realisable. Another cabinet subcommittee on the coordination of military and financial effort which met in January 1916 concluded that even with conscription a sixty-two division army was all the country could keep up to strength, let alone afford: the Treasury had argued for only fifty-four divisions. Military manpower requirements were finally being assessed systematically, but proper engagement with the manpower needs of the home front was only just starting.

BEHIND THE MOTHERLAND, COLONIAL EMPIRES WERE MOBILISING. UNIQUE among the belligerents' empires the British Empire included a number of self-governing settler colonies, the Dominions of Canada, Australia, New Zealand and South Africa, governed at one remove through the Colonial Office and a London-appointed governor general. Their domestic affairs were run by locally elected parliaments but they had no independent foreign policy and London declared war on their behalf in August 1914. Increasingly integrated into a system of imperial defence before 1914, they were expected to provide forces for their own local defence and the imperial war effort. It had been Kitchener who had established the parameters for military cooperation between Britain and the Dominions, giving some substance to then Secretary of State for War Richard Haldane's embryonic scheme for an imperial army of thirty-four divisions.[35] He had toured the empire in 1910, reviewing local defence arrangements and advising on military organisation, training and command appointments.[36] This scheme was incomplete in 1914, but it at least allowed Britain to deploy Dominion forces organised, equipped and trained along the lines of those of the motherland, which could in time be integrated into the wider war effort. By December 1914 the ANZAC army corps of one New Zealand and five Australian brigades had been despatched to the northern hemisphere to reinforce Egypt. After fighting at Gallipoli it expanded threefold for service on the western front, each brigade serving as the nucleus for a division. Canada sent its first formed infantry division to Britain in autumn 1914, which deployed to France in February 1915. By 1916 the Canadian Corps comprised four divisions, plus an independent cavalry brigade. As the most recently established and least integrated Dominion, South Africa only raised one brigade for the war in Europe, although two divisions served in campaigns on South Africa's northern borders.

Overall, the Dominions' contribution to Britain's fighting strength would be significant, increasingly so as the war went on: 458,000 Canadians (of whom a fair number early on were actually American volunteers), 332,000 Australians, 136,000 white South Africans and 112,000 New Zealanders served, many of them overseas.[37] But the Dominions' self-governing status was in one way inimical to the full mobilisation of manpower. After conscription was imposed in Britain, the Dominion governments had to face up to the reality of attritional warfare. Having raised forces for Europe, their numbers had to be maintained, and by 1916 the voluntary system was proving inadequate. Australia held two conscription referenda, in autumn 1916 and autumn 1917. The former divided the nation, and split Prime Minister William 'Billy' Hughes's governing Labor Party. Thereafter he led a new National Party committed to all-out war 'to the last man and the last shilling'. Conscription was defeated on both occasions.[38] Canadian Prime Minister Robert Borden belatedly passed conscription legislation through parliament in August 1917, but not before forcing a divisive general election that brought a realignment of politics around wartime issues. The measure would keep the battalions of the Canadian Corps up to strength, but was strongly opposed by the population of French Canada and the trade unions. Only New Zealand accepted conscription without a political crisis, in July 1916.

Similarly Ireland – still a part of the motherland but anticipating a measure of independence after the long and hotly contested home rule legislation was placed on the statute books in September 1914 for implementation once war was over – was both a source of military manpower and potentially a political powder keg. Irishmen had always been a mainstay of the British army (and mainland workforce), largely owing to the rural poverty endemic in their homeland. By a quirk of fate it turned out that Ireland had a ready pool of semi-trained manpower that could be drawn on: paramilitary Irish Volunteers from the Catholic south and Ulster Volunteers from the Protestant north had been raised in anticipation of a civil war over home rule. With home rule granted and a real war in progress, men from both sides of the sectarian divide took the king's shilling. Germany could be identified as a common, worthy foe, even if Ireland's divisions were reflected in the units that were raised. In Kitchener's New Army the 10th (Irish) Division was largely composed of southern Catholic volunteers, while the 36th (Ulster) Division drew on the manpower of the loyalist Ulster Volunteers.

Irish sensitivities prevented the full mobilisation of the island's manpower, while war radicalised nationalist political opinion. The April 1916 Easter Rising, during which Irish republicans had seized government buildings in Dublin and fought British troops for control of the city, indicated to Asquith that compelling nationalists to serve the cause of the hated British was only likely to exacerbate an already fractious political situation. Conscription in Ireland was belatedly passed into law in spring 1918, although it could never be applied. Military manpower had to be quadrupled to maintain civil order in Ireland in the face of protests, more than cancelling out any gains that the measure would have brought.[39] Between twenty-seven thousand and forty-nine thousand Irishmen died in the war (the actual figure remains disputed), yet proportionate to the population of the British Isles as a whole this represented a lesser sacrifice. Politics remained a drag on full manpower mobilisation, both nearby and far from home.

In South Africa, a recently formed and fragile union of British colonies and the previously independent Boer republics, racial issues shaped the response to the conflict. The colony's defence forces' first campaign turned out to be a counterinsurgency operation against Boer rebels who hoped to take advantage of the motherland's European difficulties to challenge the shotgun union of 1909's South Africa Act. After the uprising was suppressed, volunteering made little impact in the former Transvaal and Orange Free State territories and conscription was impossible. While the former Cape Colony and Natal could raise white volunteers for the crown, South African recruitment was secondly handicapped by the fact that the majority of the population were of native black or immigrant Indian and mixed race. Non-Europeans were not to be armed: a combination of racism and fear of the nonwhite majority that was to underpin the rise of apartheid ensured that South Africa's military contribution would be circumscribed. Yet non-Europeans would not escape the white-man's war. If they could or should not fight, black Africans could work, and as the war progressed they were increasingly conscripted or indentured into auxiliary roles to sustain imperial field armies.

MANPOWER POLICY IN THE ENTENTE IN THE FIRST TWO YEARS OF THE WAR was chaotic, as administrative structures were set in place to mediate the competing demands between army, war industries and the wider economy. This was the way liberal states made war: as departmentally based government expanded its reach it often resulted in counterproductive turf wars. In Russia's case inefficient bureaucratic autocracy struggled to

adapt to the demands of a people's war. Comparatively, in Germany –
where the army held sway – manpower policy would be better managed
early in the war and the mobilisation of personnel would match that of
the Entente. Yet the competition for men between army and industry
would trouble Germany as it would the other belligerents. In Austria-
Hungary, manpower problems were emerging by the beginning of 1915
and would become acute by year's end.

The State of Siege Law enacted in Germany when war broke out
vested local authority in the deputy commanding generals of Germany's
army corps districts. This included responsibility for military recruitment
and labour supply. This decentralisation, which left each general free to
conduct his own policy within his district, contrasted with the centralising
tendencies of the wartime state, which entrusted responsibility for military policy, and in practice manpower distribution and industrial mobilisation, to the Prussian war ministry. Germany would have its own turf
wars, particularly between the various arms of the military bureaucracy,
especially the Prussian war minister and the chief of the General Staff
who each reported directly to the kaiser.[40] Perhaps this structure gave
Germany a head start in organising for mass war – crucially in 1914 General Erich von Falkenhayn held both key military positions – but it had
inherent long-term weaknesses.

The bravery of Germany's soldiers had carried them forwards
against a numerically superior enemy, Bethmann Hollweg pronounced to
the Reichstag with confident bombast, but having 'conquered strong and
secure positions' sacrifices would have to continue until the resistance of
the enemy was broken: 'The world must be taught that no one may with
impunity do injury to a German.'[41] (Such speeches of course were unlikely
to convince Germany's enemies that there was little justice in their cause.)
Despite occupying enemy territory on both fronts, Germany's leaders were
quite aware of the vulnerability of their strategic position. They accepted
that they were now engaged in a protracted defensive war: the State of
Siege Law was appropriately named. Falkenhayn certainly conceived the
war in such terms, one of *Ermattungsstrategie* (strategy of attrition) and
*Stellungskrieg* (position warfare).[42] Germany would need to man the ram-
parts of her continent-bestriding fortress, sallying forth on occasion
against her enemies in the hope that localised military successes might
weaken their resolve to continue the war. For Germany that meant two
things. 'The German talent for, and love of, organisation are ever revealing
themselves under new forms', Bethmann explained:

No man or woman seeks to escape his or her self-imposed duties, no
big recruiting propaganda needs to be made – and all such duties are

cheerfully performed in view of one great object. The aim of everyone
is to sacrifice everything he or she possesses – whether life or wealth –
for the country of our ancestors and for the future of our descendants.[43]

On the first point he was certainly correct. In January 1915 the pressing
need was to organise Germany's resources to fight for her life.

The most populous nation in Europe after Russia, Germany had
considerable potential to increase the size of her army. In peacetime only
50 percent of her manpower received military training, compared with
85 percent in France and 35 percent in Russia.[44] Already in 1914 she had
mobilised *Freiwilliger* into new divisions in an attempt to overwhelm
France's dwindling forces before the year was out, and over the winter
of 1915 she expanded her army further in anticipation of a long struggle.
As well as trained reserves for her field and territorial armies, Germany
could call upon the ersatz reserve. She could also conscript men who had
received no peacetime training. Her well-developed war industry had the
potential to supply the expanding army as long as the voracious need for
military manpower did not fall too heavily upon industrial workers, who
had largely escaped the draft before 1914 because of their presumed socialist allegiance. But manpower policy was ill-organised and chaotic,
and on Germany's home front a 'battle for manpower' would soon develop between military authorities and civilian producers. By autumn
1914, when Germany faced a munitions crisis as prewar shell stockpiles
ran out, the issues that would dominate labour mobilisation in all the
belligerents surfaced. Producers demanded the return of skilled machin-
ists from the front while protesting the supply of unskilled female and
youth labour with which the deputy commanding generals hoped to meet
the labour shortfall. In some regions the producers were successful, in
others not: in some districts the generals even sent further contingents of
factory workers to reinforce the army.[45]

At the start of the year the manpower position was comfortable.
Although the General Staff calculated that 180,000 men were needed
each month to keep the field army up to strength, men of the 1915 class
and older contingents were available.[46] However, the anticipated rate of
wastage proved optimistic. In fact 300,000 replacements were needed
per month in 1915, while the supply of military manpower was starting
to be disrupted by the growing number of exemptions being granted to
industrial workers essential to the war effort. The appointment in January 1915 of the businessman Richard Sichler to head a war ministry
agency to oversee exemptions policy turned out to be a bureaucratic compromise that merely added to the chaos in the short term. By May manpower policy was being handled by the reserves section of the war

ministry, centralising the assessment of manpower needs and its allocation between army and industry. The deputy commanding generals retained the power to draft or exempt individuals, however. It was not until
January 1916 that Sichler's office was tasked with working alongside the
reserves section, and even then the military dominated. No common manpower plan was drawn up. Sichler's struggle to maintain industrial labour
exemptions ensured that by early 1916 1,200,000 men were allocated to
factory labour, although during 1915 the army had geared exemptions
policy in such a way that older exempt civilians or released soldiers were
favoured over younger men for the war economy.[47] Meanwhile the army
took as many as it could of the young and fit. The 1915 class had been
deployed before the year's end, the 1916 class was called up in the autumn, and the 1917 class at the end of the year. By such measures the
army remained at full strength and expanded during 1915, but a manpower crisis was already looming before the war of attrition commenced
in earnest.[48]

The Habsburg armies had been very badly handled by the Russians
and checked by the small, battle-hardened Serbian army, and had lost
nearly 1,000,000 men, killed, wounded and prisoners by the end of 1914.
Over the winter the ongoing fighting in the inhospitable Carpathian
Mountains claimed another 750,000 men: in addition to battlefield casualties, many succumbed to illnesses or frostbite, froze to death or committed suicide as morale plummeted. The fall of Przemyśl in March added
another 120,000 prisoners to the total.[49] From an early point, keeping
Austria-Hungary in the field would become a concern for Germany's
leaders. Austria faced a different sort of manpower crisis. As in Germany,
her war industries would require skilled labour, but these were relatively
undeveloped compared with Germany's, which would have to supply allied as well as domestic needs. The 1912 War Productions Law allowed
the state to conscript men for war production if they were unfit for military service and to deploy conscripts to factories at the same rate of pay
as combatants. There were 953,000 exempted industrial workers by
spring 1916. In contrast there were 13,000,000 exempted agricultural
workers who were seen as critical for supplying food to the empire and
Austria's allies. But military manpower needs were pressing: in the first
four months of the war 800,000 men who had not been called up when
their classes had originally been trained had been incorporated into the
ranks, and thereafter recruiting officers resorted to various expedients to
keep them full. Gypsies, who previously had not been allowed to serve,
were now drafted, and men exempt from conscription in peacetime on
health grounds were reexamined. Ultimately conscription was extended
to all men from ages eighteen to fifty.[50]

It was not just numbers, but quality, that declined. Austria's official historians judged that as early as spring 1915 Austria was fielding a '*Landsturm* [territorial] and militia army' composed predominantly of older reservists, partly trained recruits and inexperienced junior leaders.[31] The first campaigns had decimated the trained reserve of officers and NCOs. Thereafter various improvisations were resorted to: commissioning educated and decorated NCOs; combing-out the police force and rear-area commands; and drafting previously exempt teachers into NCO training, to be replaced in schools by invalids.[52] Moreover, early in the war draft dodging became endemic in the Habsburg Empire as willingness to serve in the face of appalling losses and growing tensions between the empire's ethnic groups threatened the war effort as a whole and the army's ability to keep its ranks filled.[53]

Although not subject to call up like men, women also stepped into new roles as part of the war effort. By summer 1915 Paris was reportedly 'a desert and this usually the fullest time . . . no men – female cab drivers, females at all the *caisses* in the big shops where open. Female conductors on trams and omnibuses; hardly any employees in the Hotel Crillon except old men and boys'.[54] Such substitution of female labour in traditional male occupations was an early consequence of able-bodied men being called to the front. It had been women, old men and children who had gathered the harvests in autumn 1914, and thereafter they remained the mainstay of the agricultural sector. In Britain (where the predominant continental system of peasant families tilling the soil had largely died out) boys from Rugby School were paid two pence per hour to gather hay in 1915, and by 1918 a Women's Land Army sixteen thousand strong had been raised from urban volunteers by the Board of Agriculture.[55] Opportunities for women to work in the expanding industrial war economy would develop as the conflict continued, particularly in the munitions industry. As often as not it was economic necessity – or opportunity, since industrial jobs paid far better than traditional female occupations in shops or domestic service – rather than a sense of patriotic duty that brought more women into the war economy. Working-class women would take over male industrial roles – by the end of the war nearly 40 percent of Krupp's workforce would be female – while middle-class women would move into administrative and clerical posts, particularly in the state bureaucracies that burgeoned as the war effort became better organised.[56]

When war broke out, however, women's active roles were limited. Nursing was the principal female profession that would be immediately drawn on in wartime: it more than used up available trained nurses and many volunteers were needed. Although she was a socialist with strong antiwar convictions, Toni Sender became a hospital assistant, recording the details of wounds and treatment. She volunteered out of compassion for the wounded, but on realising that she could not 'go on . . . helping to cure men only to have them sent out anew as cannon fodder' she left to return to her job in a metal company (which actually provided raw material for the machines with which to kill other men – there was no escaping the war).[57] Britain's First Aid Nursing Yeomanry sent not only nurses but also female ambulance drivers and hospital managers to France. Many trained nurses and unskilled women who would serve as orderlies – the most famous of whom was Vera Brittain, author of the wartime nursing memoir *Testament of Youth* – would apply to work in the field ambulances and hospitals sponsored by the Red Cross and other institutions that proliferated, raised by both belligerents and neutrals. Women could offer their services in numerous ways: Germany's National Women's Service was an umbrella organisation for the many female charities and associations that offered to help in wartime administration. Through such initiatives (which were not only a female preserve, for churches and other civilian organisations such as the Salvation Army and Young Men's Christian Association were also active in fund raising and charity work) soldiers' welfare organisations burgeoned behind the lines and on the home front. Civilians staffed canteens, reading rooms and bathhouses which formed part of the troops' unofficial support services. Less worthy and respectable opportunities for women existed in the *estaminets* and brothels that sprung up to cater for soldiers' baser needs. This the armies sanctioned, but came increasingly to regulate as escalating rates of venereal disease became a huge drain on ever more scarce manpower.[58] On occasion, over-enthusiasm or naïvety threatened to blur the distinction between the two in prudish society. The mayor and ladies of Deal in Kent set up a club and canteen for sailors; although the Baptist minister's daughter caught sitting on a sailor's knee was obliged to resign her position![59]


IN 1915 THE FRONT REQUIRED MEN IN GREAT NUMBERS, AND SO MILITARY manpower was prioritized. Gaps in the ranks from 1914's and later 1915's heavy fighting had to be filled, and all armies were expanding in response to the spread of the war. By the end of the year, when the nature of fighting was more evident, it had been recognised that for the men in uniform to fight effectively home-front labour in sufficient numbers was essential to produce growing quantities of weapons and munitions. If the balance was never quite right – there would never be unlimited manpower available, and competing needs would always have to be measured and prioritized – the manpower policies in place from 1916 onwards were more appropriate to the drawn-out war being fought. By then France had realised that her own reserves were finite, and also that those of Russia, Britain (and later Italy) were hard to tap effectively.

A tendency to resent and resist the impositions of the state and the sacrifice, often to death, that it demanded (if not yet to question the justice of the cause) appeared relatively early on in the less populist societies of Eastern Europe, Russia and the Habsburg Empire. Here the personification of the state in the figurehead of the emperor inspired a basic degree of loyalty, although respect for the crown did not necessarily translate into willingness to follow the orders of imperial functionaries who placed the amorphous and escalating needs of the war effort above the concerns and interests of ordinary men and, in time, women. The reality of mass war – that it eroded individual rights and liberties and offered few rewards in return – was becoming evident at the same time as the demands of war mobilisation intensified. The nations that could both 'mobilise their material and human resources on an unparalleled scale and secure the active participation of all social groups in the war effort' while maintaining social cohesion would have a better chance of seeing the conflict through.[60]

COLIN CONCLUDED HIS 1911 REFLECTION ON MODERN WAR WITH THE OBSERvation: 'When armies of the same value, commanded by good generals, are facing each other, it is numbers – the material element – which is the deciding factor.'[61] Attrition, in its essence, is a numbers game, and strategy entailed maximising the men who could be brought to bear against the enemy. Whether manpower could be better employed in directly fighting him or producing the weapons with which others would fight him, however, became the crux of manpower strategy. In 1915's land campaigns, the former perception prevailed, in the hope that powerful offensives might decide the war swiftly.

The raw totals of men mobilised and casualties suffered that were gathered by bureaucrats during the war and later collated by historians highlight the bleakest aspect of attrition as a strategy: it was predicated on killing or disabling men on account, while attempting not to lose men at an unsustainable rate. This seems to suggest a lack of strategic imagination or human compassion, charges which have consistently been laid against its practitioners. Recognising attrition as its determining strategic principle, it is easier to understand why the First World War assumed the nature and took the course that it did.

In practice, the forces deployed were in all cases a mixed bunch, whose constitution changed as the war went on and casualty rates mounted. In this war of diminishing reserves, it was not only the absolute number of soldiers but also their skill and their morale, their willingness to fight on, that came into play. Colin recognised three types of troops: national recruits, animated by patriotism, were the best, when well-led and trained; professional troops, soldiers by trade, were second best; some way behind them were 'militia, who serve against their will, and are destitute of all training'.[62] Such militiamen increasingly made up the rank and file as the war went on, although the hope persisted that they might be turned with experience into the better categories, at least if losses were not so devastating as to de-skill or demoralise a unit. Since these problems were shared by all armies, this made the assessment of advantage more difficult, because new conscripts were inevitably less well-trained than prewar soldiers. As Joffre himself acknowledged early on, care would have to be taken in utilising military manpower: 'The French soldier has lost none of the military qualities of his race; he retains all of his offensive ardour, but these same qualities need to be wisely directed on the modern battlefield or they will lead to a rapid wearing out of forces.'[63] As the war dragged on ordinary soldiers, thinking and feeling individuals but collectively 'cannon fodder' as they quickly came to identify themselves, would start to pass judgment on the nature of their war and its conduct by their generals. That would be in the future. At the end of 1914,

> In the chill trenches, harried, shelled, entombed,
> Winter came down on us, but no man swerved.[64]

# SIX

# WAGING WAR

AT CALAIS RAILWAY STATION EARLY IN THE MORNING ON 6 JULY 1915, Joffre and Kitchener, the two generals who after eleven months of war controlled the strategy of nations and empires and determined the fate of individuals, talked privately in the saloon car of the train which had brought the French delegation to the war's first formal Anglo-French summit. They had differences to resolve, and face-to-face they were able to thrash out an agreement that balanced French needs with British interests. Joffre left the discussion happy: Kitchener had agreed to provide him with a timetable for despatching British divisions to France, for which Joffre had been pressing for months. He could now prepare further offensive operations against the German trenches.[1] Later in the morning the prime ministers of Britain and France finally met for the first time, with ministers and military chiefs in attendance. Viviani allowed Asquith to open the meeting with a short prepared statement, delivered in halting French, setting out Britain's position, which the cabinet had determined a few days beforehand. France was to be considered the main theatre for British forces, and 'we shall support the Allied armies there with all the available strength we can command as our New Armies become complete in men and equipment', although the government was to retain a degree of freedom to react to events elsewhere. Nevertheless, the French were to be encouraged to delay resuming offensive operations in France.[2]

The Calais summit was a belated recognition that strategy needed to be made in concert, not conjured up in London and Paris and poorly coordinated through slow, peacetime diplomatic channels and hasty, confrontational ministerial meetings. The Calais meeting did not resolve Anglo-French tensions immediately or conclusively, nor did it show that the united front was established and effective: no formal minutes were taken at the conference and both delegations left thinking that their view had been accepted by the other. But it did represent a new commitment to conversation, compromise and common sense in strategic planning. The short-term consequences would be played out in the autumn, when Joffre mounted offensive operations on a grand scale in Champagne and Artois, with the British army supporting them at Loos. These battles proved no more decisive than Joffre's spring offensive and suggested that his policy of large-scale operations to try to break the German lines in France was misguided. Indeed breaking the line, essentially a problem of tactics, was one thing – beating the German army, a matter of operations and strategy, quite another. While nations were still mobilising fully, it certainly appeared premature to expect a decision, although there were military and political imperatives that obliged an aggressive policy nonetheless, with two other fronts in the land war – in the East and, after Italy entered the war, in the South – to be factored into the strategic equation.

The short-term consequences of this Calais compromise have been generally regretted; its impact on the direction of Allied strategic policy has largely gone unrecognised, since the formal record was patchy. Asquith's sense of occasion and his penchant for confiding in pretty young ladies, however, left a glimpse of the real import of this meeting for posterity. He posted his scribbled notes to Sylvia Henley, who had replaced Venetia Stanley in his affections after the latter contracted to marry one of his ministers. It is clear that both sides laid their cards – in Britain's case the actual number of division they had in training – on the table, and the French explained the nature of their strategy: intensifying attrition. The Germans, Joffre stated, had enough men to last another seven months. Rather than merely 'breaking through' the German defensive lines in France, which would change the lie of the trenches but would not necessary destroy the German army, the idea that they might be 'overthrown' with 'simultaneous attacks on as large a number of fronts as possible' was mooted for the first time; Millerand specifically identified the objective as 'killing men'.[3]

The conference committed Britain and France to a common policy of military attrition, even if how and when the land war should continue remained unresolved. Thereafter, its slow, steady working remained prone to turbulence from unpredictable events in a still-expanding war. The Entente belatedly adopted a concerted, resource-based strategy in the middle of 1915, after the misadventures of the first half of the year. Then Britain's civilian war leaders had enjoyed the luxury of detachment from the battlefronts in France, Poland and Hungary (and the misfortune of military advisers too weak to guide and control them). Meanwhile, France, Germany, Russia and Austria-Hungary had been getting on with the war.

THE STRATEGIC DIRECTORS OF THE TWO SIDES IN 1915, JOFFRE AND FALKEN-hayn, had to address the military situation promptly and directly. When there were no longer plans to follow, or opportunities to manoeuvre, there were statistics to fall back on. As he planned the first campaign of trench warfare, Joffre hoped that it would be the last. He was optimistic because the GQG's calculations indicated that the Entente's numerical advantage was substantial and potentially decisive if properly mobilised – perhaps unduly so since there were still many millions of enemy soldiers to engage and defeat. But in January 1915 his army's depots were full of trained reserves and fresh conscripts to fill gaps in the ranks. On Germany's other flank stood the masses of Russia and behind them Britain was raising the New Army that had been promised for the western front. This numerical advantage in troops would only increase, while the Allies' populations (which included the people in the French and British Empires) vastly outnumbered those of their enemies. These figures indicated that sooner or later the Allies would prevail. But for France, a certain degree of caution was required, not least because she had already suffered over one million casualties. Since military strategy was based on destroying the enemy's reserves at a faster rate than they could be renewed it was clear that France could not sustain the war with her own resources indefinitely. That would not matter too much if by deploying men en masse the enemy could be beaten and the war ended quickly: this chimera persisted well into 1915. The fighting in 1914 was exceptional in scale, intensity and destructiveness, but it suggested that one year's fighting (in fact little more than one-third of a year in 1914), could potentially exhaust all and more than one year's new recruits. The central question of strategy that Joffre faced in January 1915, therefore, was how much more fighting would be needed to exhaust Germany's manpower reserves, and where could he muster the forces to achieve this? France's prewar diplomacy had been geared to winning reliable allies and ensuring that they brought effective aid to her in wartime, both to avert defeat in a short war and enable victory in a long one.[4] Reviewing the situation at the start of 1915 it was evident that this policy had to be sustained in wartime.

Linked to this were the questions of what sort of military campaign Joffre should undertake, and how he could best coordinate with France's allies. For both political and military reasons, France adopted an offensive strategy against Germany's entrenchments. An extensive tract of northern France was occupied, and liberation of *la patrie* was a priority that all Frenchmen could agree on: when Lloyd George asked Second Army's commander General Noël de Castelnau whether this was possible now that the war had become one huge siege, his laconic answer was simply 'we must do it!'[6] Three of his six sons were to be killed before it was done. An offensive was the only way to break the German lines and push them out of France: it would, if nothing else, contribute to attrition. The alternative of waiting for the Russian masses to sweep eastwards was too contingent and, moreover, uncertain. Unionist politician Lord Selborne speculated:

> Suppose that the Russians are not able to beat the Germans to their knees, quite a likely supposition. Our obligation of honour, and indeed for our own existence, still compels France and England to thrust Germany clean out of Belgium. Well that will be a tremendous task. It will be us who will be compelled to take the offensive against a series of immensely strong prepared positions. When France has equipped her men she can have no more to bring forwards. We may want *every man* just the same and you cannot get every man without compulsion.[6]

Selborne did not know it, but at the end of 1914 he was predicting the course of the land war to come. Although Russia and Austria were still heavily engaged in the East, the prospect of Russia attacking Germany in the near future was slim. In fact as the spring went on the imperative to remain active in the West to stop Germany moving troops eastwards for a large-scale offensive against the Russians increased.

As for the British, Kitchener shared Joffre's view that Germany's manpower reserves would have to be engaged and destroyed. When presented with the War Office's calculations of relative manpower resources, 'Lord Kitchener displayed some interest in these mathematical exercises and was not wholly unimpressed when figures established the gratifying fact that the German legions were a vanishing proposition', Callwell recollected.[7] But in spring 1915 he was in no hurry to take on Germany in the West. He accepted that German forces there had to be tied down to protect the Russians, and for that reason Britain's military commitment in France and Flanders had to be maintained. Beyond that, he counselled patience until all Allied resources were mobilised and they could take on the enemy with a realistic hope of victory. Given this fundamental disagreement, Joffre and Kitchener's relationship in 1915 would be marked by a simmering battle of wills over where and when to engage the enemy.

Kitchener's dilemma cut to the heart of the problem of fighting a coalition war of attrition. How much would he have to pander to Allied wishes, and to what extent could he retain a degree of strategic independence? By the time the BEF was reorganised into two armies in January 1915 France had already received twice as many troops as she had been led to expect in 1914: ten regular army and two Indian Army infantry divisions held a relatively short sector of the joint front in Flanders and France, supported by five cavalry divisions. Eventually Britain would deploy five armies in France. But that was still eighteen months away: individual divisions were the bones of contention in early 1915. France's greatest reserve for her fight with Germany lay in Great Britain and her empire, but in the short term Joffre's ability to increase the number of divisions in the field gave Kitchener a reason for not rushing British divisions out to France in spring 1915.[8] Millerand's visit to England in January 1915 had the purpose of persuading his British opposite number of the need to send British troops to France – in the short term to take over more of the defensive line while Joffre's armies renewed the offensive; in the long term to shift the balance of forces decisively in the Allies' favour on the western front and decide the war on land.[9] Kitchener did not object in principle, believing as he did that to end the war the German army would have to be beaten and knowing that British troops were essential to do so. However, it was premature to think that the Allies were ready to beat Germany. His long-term perspective, that it would take two years to train, equip and deploy Britain's armies, clashed with Joffre and Sir John French's impatience to reengage the enemy after the winter lull.

ALTHOUGH IN THE LONG TERM HIS POLICY PROVED THE RIGHT ONE, JOFFRE did not really have enough resources for taking the offensive with a realistic prospect of success in 1915, so to a degree Kitchener was right to counsel caution and steady attrition. But Joffre was quite right that at the start of the year his enemy was overstretched because the Central powers were engaged on many fronts, and that this situation would only worsen in the longer term because their manpower was vastly outnumbered by that of the Allies. The Central powers' strategic director in 1915 appreciated this. Like Joffre, Falkenhayn would hope for a quick end to the war, because he knew that the Central powers could never win a long one against a coalition with an overwhelming resource base. Moreover, he was held in a strategic bind, having to fight a two-front land war with insufficient forces. He felt that at best the army could inflict costly defeats on Germany's enemies such that they would judge the price of victory not worth paying and seek a negotiated peace.[10] At least in the New Year he still retained the initiative, but whether he could strike a decisive blow that would bring the Entente to terms was questionable.

Falkenhayn had been the Prussian minister of war before 1914 and was an obvious successor to Moltke, if an unwelcome one: Moltke's supporters and others who disagreed with Falkenhayn's strategic policy were to make his tenure as chief of the General Staff difficult. They felt that he was a political general, and Falkenhayn certainly had the confidence and support of the kaiser, who had sponsored his accelerated promotion to the higher ranks of the army after he had distinguished himself as chief of staff to the force sent to relieve the European legations in Peking during the Boxer Uprising. This meant that he also had military experience, unlike most of his contemporaries in the German army. Fifty-three years old, he was younger than all of Germany's army commanders in 1914. Falkenhayn was a military man by heritage and upbringing, with a soldier's bearing and strong will. He had undoubted talents as a strategist and commander (which he was later to demonstrate in a lightning campaign that defeated Rumania in 1916). In 1915, however, he had a problem. 'I cannot imagine anything less unlike the situation forecast for the end of October by the German General Staff than that which actually confronts them in the west and east,' Selborne crowed.[11] Falkenhayn, more realistic than many of those who served under him, fully appreciated the difficult position that Germany found herself in now that her strategic nightmare of a two-front war had come to pass.

Germany's strategic problem was much simpler than her enemies'. When Prussia had last faced such a situation during the Seven Years War in the eighteenth century, she had prevailed by breaking the coalition ranged against her and this principle had not been forgotten. In a rare moment of perception after the Anglo-Russian Entente had tightened the strategic noose around Germany, the kaiser had identified that if it came to war 'we must be guided by the example of Frederick the Great who, when hemmed in on all sides by foes, had beaten them one after the other'.[12] This was Germany's plan (and the basis of the Central powers' strategy for the rest of the war). In early 1915, Russia and France looked too strong, and Britain unassailable – only Serbia was small, isolated and vulnerable. As it turned out, Falkenhayn's long-nurtured plan to eliminate Serbia would have to be delayed time and again, as the greater powers had to be contained in the East and the West, and later the South.[13] It meant that Falkenhayn and Conrad would spend 1915 bickering over strategy and diplomacy and ultimately engage front-by-front in a succession of momentarily effective yet indecisive offensives in a vain attempt to break the enemy's stranglehold.[14] Serbia would not be attacked decisively until the autumn.

Falkenhayn's strategy was also attritional, although it was conceived differently to Joffre's and aimed to break the cohesion and will of

Germany's adversaries, individually and collectively by destabilising their united front. Like a besieged garrison, on occasion the Central powers' armies would sally forth in an attempt to break the circumvallation. Engaging their enemies' forces in battle and inflicting heavy losses might encourage negotiation – at the same time their home fronts could be attacked with sea power and primitive air warfare. Falkenhayn appreciated (unlike some of his subordinates) that Germany's relative military effectiveness during 1915's battles while the Allies were still mobilising their resources was unlikely to break her enemies' huge armies. But she had no alternative while she retained the initiative in the European war than to try to reduce the growing threat that the Central powers faced.

While confident in their overwhelming resources in the long term, the Allies could not expect any immediate manpower advantage, since while they were expanding their armies, Germany would be doing the same. Lieutenant-General Sir Henry Rawlinson, in command of IV Corps in Flanders and recently director of recruiting at the War Office, identified that initially the growth potential of the two sides would cancel each other out: he warned Kitchener that even with 30 British and additional French divisions in the field by the summer, the western front would likely remain stalemated.[15] He was right. The OHL was reorganising Germany's forces to make new divisions. By reducing each German infantry division in the West from 4 to 3 infantry regiments and each artillery battery from 6 to 4 guns, 14 new division were formed during the spring (fewer than the 24 Falkenhayn had hoped to raise). More divisions were raised from men of the Ersatz reserve, allowing Germany by the end of the year to deploy 161 infantry divisions in 53 army corps. A shortage of supplies rather than men delayed the deployment of new units over the summer, but new divisions still took the field into the autumn.

Falkenhayn raised new divisions to give himself a degree of strategic flexibility: as an operational reserve behind the lines in the West, security against a French attack in the spring, and to sustain offensive operations. The Balkan imbroglio distracted his attention too. During the winter and spring twin fears about the dependability of his allies and the menace of uncommitted neutrals obliged him to look southwards. He would have preferred to resume the offensive in France before the expected arrival of Kitchener's armies gave the Entente a significant numerical advantage there. But Germany currently lacked the reserves to decide that campaign with a powerful general offensive, such as Kitchener contemplated for later in the war.[16] General Staff studies indicated that such an operation would take time to plan and resource. In the West in the spring the army could at best mount limited attacks 'that would raise the morale of the troops, who for months had been exhausting themselves in a war of attrition',[17] such as that by three divisions north of Ypres on 22 April, notorious for the first deployment of chlorine gas. The bulk of the reserves Falkenhayn could muster were drawn inexorably towards the East and the South to support the Austrians in Galicia and drive back the Russians in Poland.

Mirroring Germany's strategic position, Austria faced a two-front war against Russia and Serbia and was not doing well against either. For Falkenhayn, keeping his hard-pressed ally in the field was a priority in spring 1915. To that end he wanted to relieve Austria's southern flank with a powerful offensive against Serbia backed by German troops. This too would ward off his real fear, that Rumania and Italy together would take up arms against Austria, in which case, he warned Conrad stoically, 'We shall be deprived of the certain expectation of terminating the war victoriously along the entire line. The consequences of a defeat, however, are self-evident: the position as a great power of Germany as well as that of the Dual Monarchy would be ended.'[18] But menacing Russian armies in Galicia denied him the chance to strike at Serbia in the spring. Nor could he persuade Austria to make the necessary territorial concessions in time to prevent Italy joining the war. His strategy at least dissuaded Rumania. What reserves he could spare over the winter were formed into a new *Südarmee* to support the Austrian forces in Galicia directly, although it could not intervene in time to relieve Przemyśl, which fell on 22 January 1915. A costly, indecisive campaign continued in horrendous winter conditions into the spring, when a new Austro-German offensive launched with fresh forces at Gorlice-Tarnów on 2 May broke the Russian Third Army, forcing a general retreat into Poland. Przemyśl was recaptured by Austrian forces on 3 June. Although Rumania was cowed into staying neutral by this success, Serbia remained undefeated and Italy had engaged the Austrian army on a new southern front in the meantime. Falkenhayn's spring campaign had staved off the prospect of crushing defeat – both sides still viewed the eastern front as the one on which a decisive Entente success might occur – but it did not improve the long-term strategic prospects for the Central powers. Germany's two-front war continued, to her temporary advantage with her defeat of the Russians, but Austria now had to find reserves to contain the enemy on three fronts.

WHILE FALKENHAYN WAS CONTAINING RUSSIANS AND WORRYING ABOUT Italians and Rumanians (and Austrians) Joffre was planning Germany's demise. The political objective of liberating France dovetailed with the military objective of destroying the German army and demanded the resumption of the offensive. But operations would have to be conducted with due caution. In an ex post facto rationalisation of military policy in his memoirs, Joffre suggested:

> The object we had in view was victory, and since the Germans had undertaken a war of attrition, it was for us on our side to conduct it with due economy, and turn the situation to our advantage by making attacks only when we could profitably assume the role of attackers. In this way we would cause a melting of the enemy's reserves and reduce his front to nothing more than a thin barrier which, if we economised our own reserves, could be broken down by the combined blows of the Allies, and permit the passage of our victorious battalions. In this game it was certain that we would also suffer wastage, but the enemy would be worn down; the whole question lay in conducting our affairs with such wisdom as to enable us to last longer than he did. In war it is the final battalions that bring victory.[19]

Expressed more pithily in *The Vivid*, this thinning-out process became the guiding principle of military operations for the Allies, the essential means by which a better resourced and more numerous coalition would overcome powerful but weaker adversaries after military operations became stalemated. It would take a lot longer than expected, partly because the proper technique for doing so was in its infancy as Joffre renewed the offensive.

Wisdom is something that comes with experience, and the French army's leadership was wise enough to learn from experience. The task of managing France's first large-scale offensive in spring 1915 was entrusted to Foch, who now commanded a provisional army group on the northern end of the French line, adjacent to the British. The armies that he directed faced for the first time an age-old military challenge in a new form: trench warfare. Ever since David slew Goliath with a slingshot, battle had been a contest between firepower and shock action. The former could prevent manoeuvre and inflict heavy casualties; the latter was essential to capture ground and overthrow the enemy. The battles of 1914 had demonstrated that armies equipped with modern weapons could dominate the battlefield with firepower: these gave an inestimable advantage to the defence. If infantry were to leave their protective trenches they would be massacred unless the enemy's machine guns and artillery could be silenced. The means to do this was to fight fire with fire. That was obvious as a tactical principle but difficult to realise in practice in early 1915 because the attackers generally lacked firepower.

In planning his offensive to capture the Vimy Ridge, the Second Battle of Artois, Foch drew on his experience at Ypres. 'The conduct of battle will be determined by the problems and methods of siege warfare,' Foch posited. 'Every activity, capture, occupation, organisation and defence . . . must be founded upon the use of our artillery superiority, properly supplied. One should address the matter of artillery first of all.'[20] In 1915 during the Artois offensive General Philippe Pétain, the future commander of the French army, coined the adage, 'the artillery conquers, the infantry occupies'. With constant refinement in technique thereafter, this remained the core principle of warfare as armies fought in trench systems. This had been learned from the gruelling battles over the winter that had taken place in Artois for the dominating hill Notre-Dame-de-Lorette, and in Champagne. In both locations the French had found themselves engaged in costly close-range fights for fortified villages or sections of trench. Such small-scale attritional fighting – *grignotage\** – would be a feature of trench warfare: merely the bubbles on the surface of the war, as Binding observed in a striking metaphor.[21] It was a frustrating and unsatisfactory way of proceeding, but lack of munitions made it difficult to launch large-scale operations before the spring. But by the time the Battle of Artois started, the French had adopted appropriate techniques for integrating the supporting fire of artillery with the offensive power of the infantry that could be tested in combat.[22] As the war went on the techniques of bombardment, to protect the attacking infantry and to break the power of the enemy's defence, adapted, becoming more complex, scientific and potent. Concomitantly, the number and types of guns would multiply, while munitions production swelled and diversified. Here above all the mobilisation of science and industry was integral to warfare, producing, transporting and applying the means for artillery to control the battle-field.[23] Siege warfare, like everything else, proved adaptable to the technologies and productivity of modern capitalism.

The British army was also learning its first lessons of trench warfare. When Rawlinson's IV Corps and the Indian Corps attacked Neuve Chapelle village on 10 March there were only enough shells for a hurricane thirty-five-minute barrage.[†] This did the trick, and the village was seized: despite the enemy watching day and night tactical surprise was still possible if the defence could be paralysed by bombardment just long enough for assault troops to enter their trenches and evict them. However, over the next couple of days many men were lost trying to exploit this success against a reinforced German defence with insufficient artillery support.[24] These early battles indicated that at the start of an offensive it

---

*A French concept, this involved repeated small-scale offensives to (translated literally) 'gnaw' the enemy's strength.
†Joffre had declined to attack at the same time owing to shortage of reserves since Kitchener had withheld the 29th Division.

was relatively easy to capture an objective with acceptable casualties if the bombardment was effective. Following up against an alert defence, however, was likely to be costly.

Fighting successfully from trench to trench was one thing; engaging army against army required a different set of skills. Foch's experience at Ypres also suggested that a long, drawn-out battle would be likely, and that winning it was not merely a matter of effective assault tactics but also of operations – that is, the careful preplanning of battle and the control of large formations during a prolonged fight for superiority. Foch's large, cumbersome armies would have to be engaged appropriately, so that the offensive would achieve strategic objectives. The first blow would be the heaviest, and all that could be done to make it effective was done before zero hour. Thereafter, the battle would unfold in a way that neither side could predict and would have to be managed in the same way as 1914's operations. Reserves would have to be fed in as needed, just into a smaller space, and potentially for a longer time.

The Second Battle of Artois showed that although the enemy's trenches could be captured in places, his defensive positions as a whole were impregnable, and techniques for controlling the drawn-out offensive battle were as yet rudimentary. Between 9 May and 18 June General Victor d'Urbal's Tenth Army attempted to take the Vimy Ridge and the rest of Notre-Dame-de-Lorette. The Germans had sited their defences on strategic high ground wherever possible in 1914, and so most Allied offensives had as immediate tactical objective ridges from which their lines were overlooked. Because indirect artillery fire was a central element of the new tactics, observation was vital. The Allies would have to counter the Germans' advantage of holding the heights by developing aerial observation platforms, aircraft and tethered balloons, without which the task of mastering the German defences with carefully targeted artillery fire would have been all but impossible.

On 9 May XXXIII CA, commanded by Pétain, spearheaded the assault. Its divisions were among France's best – the Moroccan Division was composed of North African and Foreign Legion regiments, and the *70ème* and *77ème Divisions d'infanterie* (DI – infantry division) were commanded by Fayolle and General Ernest Barbot respectively. The offensive started very well. The prolonged and carefully monitored preliminary bombardment had cut the wire and all but cleared the trenches immediately opposite the centre of the attack, where the Moroccan Division's assault troops burst through, advancing four-and-a-half kilometres in the first rush and establishing themselves atop the Vimy Ridge. 77 DI's leading brigade occupied Givenchy village, at the northern end of the ridge. But it was not a story of universal success. Fayolle's infantry to the north and battalions from XX CA attacking farther south were checked after a relatively short advance, or found themselves caught up in an energy-sapping fight within the enemy's complex trench system: not for nothing were the positions assaulted by XX CA's 11 DI known as 'the Labyrinth'.[25] The well-planned and thorough barrage, which destroyed large sections of fixed defences and cut much of the enemy's barbed wire, represented the first experimental use of more 'scientific' artillery techniques that would become standard. Fire was carefully controlled and monitored, and governed by meticulous trigonometric calculations of range and trajectory: ballistics was to be one area in which military science made substantial progress from 1915. But where the bombardment failed to cut the wire or left machine guns un-silenced the defence generally held. More munitions and guns, especially heavy guns, were seen as the answer to this, plus a longer bombardment to ensure that all targets were properly engaged. The attack also demonstrated that infantry élan still counted for much in the assault. It also confirmed that the momentum of an attack was best sustained by pushing deeply into the enemy's defences, rather than getting bogged down fighting for the front lines. These principles would form the foundation of First World War offensive tactical doctrines.

Shock action still worked at the start of a battle, but firepower still determined its course and outcome. The Moroccan Division's rush onto the Vimy Ridge had appeared spectacular and gave false hope that the trench lines were breakable. Yet the speedy advance had come at the expense of proper control. Once established on their objective, the troops could not be properly organised for its defence or resupplied and reinforced. Mainly this was a consequence of the primitive nature of battlefield communications, particularly beyond the French front line where the elaborate telephone networks with which armies were managed did not exist. By the time news of the Moroccan Division's success filtered back to commanders in the French lines and orders to push reserves forward in support had been issued, too much time had been lost: the defence had reacted and isolated the French penetration. Similarly, once troops became bogged down in trench fighting control was rapidly lost and confusion set in. The Germans' control mechanisms remained relatively intact, so they could bring reserves forward to contain and counterattack faster than the French could reinforce. The French breakthrough on a narrow front was contained from its flanks and isolated with an artillery counter-barrage that hampered reinforcements and supplies getting through. Machine-gun and artillery fire whittled down the numbers of the *poilus*, legionnaires and *zouaves* who clung desperately to their gains on the exposed ridge: fire was coming from all sides and General Barbot himself was killed by a stray shell on 10 May. Over three days a succession of local counterattacks pushed in the apex and flanks of the French penetration, thinning the ranks of the defenders still further and regaining control of the Vimy Ridge.[26] Operational technique was clearly deficient at this early point. Command and control was weak, and it was obvious that it was impossible as yet to overmaster the defence to the extent that it could not mount an effective counterattack.

For the rest of May and June an offensive that had promised so much revealed the reality of fighting against an alert, reinforced and reorganised defence. As Fayolle identified, 'It must always revert to siege-warfare and wearing down the enemy, and that's why the war will be terribly long, and Europe will come out of this gigantic struggle exhausted and ruined.'[27] Throughout May *grignotage* attacks persisted, before the Tenth Army renewed the general attack on the ridge in mid-June. But in practice the fighting had become localised around strong points such as the Labyrinth and Neuville St Vaast and Ablain St Nazaire villages, which sucked in and decimated French infantry battalions one after the other. Attritional warfare had reverted to type, except unlike the earlier battle at Ypres it was now the French who were sacrificing lives in a forlorn attempt to follow up early success and break through fixed defences.

To the north General Sir Douglas Haig's First Army, spearheaded by Rawlinson's IV Corps, had launched an offensive against the Aubers Ridge in support of the French attack. A sustained methodical preliminary bombardment had been attempted for the first time, but it failed to master the enemy defences and machine guns and artillery decimated the attacking troops. The first attack on 9 May suffered eleven thousand casualties with no permanent gains, and later operations showed little improvement. The defeat triggered political repercussions, the 'shells scandal' which obliged Asquith to broaden the base of his ministry and appoint a minister of munitions. Militarily, however, British attacks in early 1915 furnished uncertain lessons.

WHILE BRITISH AND FRENCH TROOPS WERE LIVING UP TO CHURCHILL'S PRE-diction that they would inevitably '[chew] barbed wire in Flanders' as long as the 'fine and terrible army' in front of them held reserves in hand, Falkenhayn's armies were developing their own offensive techniques on the eastern front.[28] They appeared to be much more successful, although appearances could be deceptive. At the start of their May offensive, in the Battle of Gorlice-Tarnów, a short but intensive preliminary bombardment broke the enemy's defences. Against a relatively weak and undeveloped defensive system such a bombardment could prove effective, and the immediate effect was devastating (there would be similar instances in 1916, 1917 and 1918). But, as Churchill had also identified, 'withdrawn into their own country [the Russians] can hold their own', once the Germans got beyond the railway communications on which their forces depended for supply and mobility.[29]

Although on a grander scale – and hence very worrying for Allied leaders – the fighting in the East was governed by the same dynamics as that in France. While artillery predominance enabled them to defeat the Russians they attacked, the Germans could no more overwhelm them than the French could overwhelm all the defences in Artois. German offensives would also lose momentum since the Russians could and did trade space and lives for time, a pattern that repeated itself through the summer and autumn campaign in Poland. Warsaw might fall by August, but there were still many Russians, and a great expanse of Russia, in front of the Central powers' forces. Churchill's further prediction, that 'the war will be ended by the exhaustion of nations rather than the victories of armies', seemed astute. Even stunning offensives, such as Gorlice-Tarnów that destroyed a whole Russian army and forced a general Russian retreat, did not redress the wider strategic stalemate. In 1915 commanders everywhere had ambitions that were beyond the capabilities of their forces and their field commanders. As long as battlefield and strategic objectives remained overambitious, translating tactical success into strategic victory would prove impossible. At the same time, as Mildred Aldrich acknowledged, 'In the spirit I have caught from the army, "All these things are but incidents, and will have no effect on the final result. A nation is not defeated while its army is still standing up in its boots, so it is folly to bother over details."'[30]

IF ANY FURTHER REINFORCEMENT OF THESE LESSONS WAS NEEDED, THE Italian army's first campaign provided it. Italy possessed a large army sustained by a relatively weak industrial base. Its commander, General Luigi Cadorna, had been carefully studying the land war since August 1914, but since appropriate lessons had yet to crystallise from the ongoing fighting, it should come as no surprise that his army's early operations were costly and relatively ineffective. Cadorna was a professional general, but turned out to be a poor leader of men. He came from a Piedmontese military family – his father had led the Italian armies that had seized Rome from the pope in 1870 – and he had enjoyed a steady, if unremarkable rise through the ranks to become chief of staff in July 1914 after his predecessor died suddenly, just before Europe erupted into war. An artilleryman and trained staff officer, he studied the military art seriously and published tactical studies before the war (which were inevitably out-dated by the time he tried to apply them in 1915). A staunch conserva-tive, Cadorna disliked liberal politics and politicians. He believed in untrammelled military authority over strategy and army management during wartime and was not shy in confronting ministers who interfered. Such authoritarianism extended to his management of the army and his treatment of troops. He had never seen active service, but following a protracted war against Turkey in Libya he understood the weaknesses of the army that he took over and advised the government not to intervene immediately. Thereafter he began to reform and reequip the army, and to plan intervention against the Austrians, which he thought was both desirable and inevitable.[31]

When that intervention came, however, the army was still unready: it was short of machine guns and heavy artillery in particular. Cadorna felt that the Austrians were fully committed on their other fronts and could muster few troops for the Italian frontier, so the advance into Aus-tria would be more or less unopposed. He chose to attack on the southern end of the Italo-Austrian border: the mountains in the higher Alpine re-gion were impassable for large bodies of troops. Two armies would seize Gorizia and Trieste, open the road to Vienna and hopefully eliminate Austria from the war.[32] Mountainous frontier territory between Italy and Austria lent itself to defence, however, and the first Italian offensive in June 1915 proved disappointing.

The objective was to cross the border, seize the crossings over the River Isonzo and push onto the Carso Plateau beyond. Events conspired against Cadorna's plan. Rather than the Italian advance coinciding with supporting Russian and Serbian offensives, by the time his armies were underway the Russians had been checked at Gorlice-Tarnów and Conrad was able to send reserves southwards. Instead of a scratch defence of militia and training and convalescent battalions, the Italian advance guards came up against the battalions of the new Austrian Fifth Army, commanded by General Svetozar Boroević, an experienced and practical defensive commander who had cut his teeth in Galicia. His divisions had been redeployed from Serbia and their men were practiced in the tactics and used to the rigours of mountain warfare. The Italians were allowed to cross the Isonzo Valley, but got little farther: in early June their advance guards were cut to pieces in the foothills of the Julian Alps beyond the river. The full-scale offensive that followed in late June and early July, the First Battle of the Isonzo, proved no more productive. The Austrians held the high ground in increasing force and the Italians lacked the artillery to blast them out of it – Cadorna expended many lives, perhaps thirty thousand, to demonstrate this.[33]

Although active, 1915's fighting on the Italian front was essentially localised, and was not intense by eastern and western front standards, since the Italians lacked the resources for sustained warfare. In four offensives Italy lost 66,000 dead, and the Austrians only 28,000, a fraction of their casualties on the Russian front: the line merely rippled along the eastern bluffs of the Isonzo Valley.[34] The Austrians certainly got the better of the early fights along the Isonzo, while Italy's commanders and forces were waking up to the reality of material-intensive battle. The frontline troops would then have to endure a grim winter in exposed mountain positions. Cadorna at least used this hiatus to good effect, equipping and training his men for the renewed offensive that was to come in the spring. Cadorna was aware that he lacked the heavy guns and other resources that would give the army a fighting chance in the mountains.[35] He had also become aware of the true nature of the war he had been given responsibility to conduct: as he wrote to his daughter despondently, 'This war can only be ended through the exhaustion of men and resources . . . It's frightful, but that's how it is.'[36] He had still to persuade the government and the nation that a long, grinding campaign was inevitable. Like Joffre in France, by the end of 1915 he was being criticised by Sonnino and the war minister, General Vittorio Zupelli, who had done much to get the army ready for war, was having to manage Italy's own munitions crisis and who now wished to get more control over Italian strategy.[37] In the ensuing political crisis Cadorna triumphed and Zupelli was forced to resign.[38] Italy was committed politically to a war of attrition, and Cadorna was committed to justifying it to political and military critics as the campaign developed. The truth was that from summer 1915 the new southern front was stalemated just like the others.

THERE WAS, ASQUITH CONFIDED TO SYLVIA HENLEY AFTER THESE EARLY offensives, 'unrest and forebodings [in] London' as to the current military situation and likelihood of a quick end to the war.[39] Selborne, who had always had a very realistic view of the nature and likely course of the war, confided to his sister in June:

> If the great French attack on Arras* does not succeed in breaking the German line we shall have to play the waiting game for many months more. We all have immense confidence in Joffre. Thank God I think that the French and British peoples thoroughly understand that if we do not go through with this job now no matter how long it may take, it will all come again and worse and worse and worse within a generation.[40]

---

*Selborne's geography was a bit shaky – Arras was behind the Allied front line.

Asquith was certainly becoming sceptical. 'The Frogs' Joffre and Foch visited the GHQ on 2 June to brief him on the military situation shortly before the Calais summit, but he did not share their 'resolute, confident, imperturbable optimism . . . that we have the Germans in the hollow of our hands'.[41] Kitchener was looking east after the failure to take the Aubers Ridge. On 16 May he cancelled the first New Army's deployment to France.[42] In the West he would maintain his policy of attrition – if the Germans obliged by attacking the Allied lines – while seeking a decision at the Dardanelles.[43]

Nevertheless, at the midyear static review in Calais the British government essentially caved in to the French. Joffre won the broader argument about concentrating forces on the western front. Kitchener thought that he had persuaded Joffre to delay further offensive operations there until British troops had been committed in strength, and in the meantime he could send troops and munitions to Gallipoli to finish that campaign. Yet enemy actions and inter-Allied politics would undermine that resolution over the coming months, while distractions – particularly the entry of Bulgaria into the war on the Central powers' side in early October – would oblige further hasty strategic initiatives before the end of the year. What the Calais conference and its aftermath acknowledged was that there were no quick, easy routes to victory – although they would continue to be pursued, at least against Turkey. As Balfour, one of the more realistic cabinet ministers who had replaced Churchill at the Admiralty in May, accepted, 'There is no prospect, I believe, of the allies obtaining an old-fashioned victory over the Germans at this stage of the war.'[44] But in the West at least an interim policy of *grignotage*, rather than large-scale and costly offensives during the summer, appeared to be settled, allowing the Dardanelles campaign to be prosecuted to a conclusion.

ALTHOUGH THE POLITICAL AND MILITARY SITUATION WAS TURNING AGAINST Germany by the summer it was by no means desperate. Italy's attack had been easily contained, as had the Anglo-French spring offensive in the West, while Hindenburg's armies were making steady progress against the Russians in the East. However, Germany's fundamental strategic problem was already apparent. Since she could not mass sufficient forces in the East or the West without dangerously weakening the other front she could never eliminate one of her major adversaries. Falkenhayn could always move forces around in dribs and drabs and win local victories such as those at Ypres and Gorlice-Tarnów, but a 'campaign deciding' offensive would always be impossible owing to a lack of reserves.[45] Germany's two-front strategic nightmare therefore lay at the root of her ultimate defeat. Yet such a method would serve her well in defence, making Allied strategy problematic: while Germany and her allies maintained large reserves offensives on the principal fronts could be contained, as could initiatives on new fronts.

Owing to this Serbia could not be eliminated quickly as Falkenhayn had wished, and so the resources of the Balkans remained in play throughout 1915.[46] Ultimately Germany was the beneficiary. Bulgaria had lost territory to her neighbours in 1913's Second Balkan War after they had fallen out over the spoils of the first. By the terms of her alliance with Germany Bulgaria would get a large war loan and was promised her lost territories at the end of a victorious war. Germany could finally open a direct railway route to Turkey, enabling her to send munitions to the Dardanelles. Bulgaria's entry into the war in October brought eleven infantry divisions into the eastern military balance and placed Serbia in an untenable strategic position. Deterred, Rumania and Greece remained neutral. Like Turkey, Bulgaria brought manpower to the Central powers, if little industrial capacity: the new alliance represented another draw on Germany's munitions industries. It was another diplomatic shift that expanded the war and complicated the strategic choices which faced leaders on both sides: for the Allies, yet another distraction from the central problem of engaging and defeating Germany.

Although the Russians were not represented at Calais, they were certainly not forgotten: anxieties about the Russian situation had preoccupied Kitchener and Joffre all summer.[47] One strategic principle Joffre and Kitchener did agree on was that Russia was vital to the stranglehold that needed to be maintained and tightened to defeat the Central powers. Expectations that Russian armies were going to push inexorably on to Vienna or Berlin had long since been abandoned, but they were certainly fighting a large part of the German army and most of the Austrian, and inflicting heavy, if not proportionate, casualties. Therefore the subsidiary purpose of an offensive strategy in the West, 'to lighten the pressure on our allies in the East by undertaking actions which would be as powerful as the state of our matériel permitted', increased in importance as the Central powers followed up after Gorlice-Tarnów.[48] The fall of Warsaw and the occupation of Poland appeared bad for the Allies in the crowing German newspaper reports, even if it was only a tiny fraction of the vast Russian Empire. But Russia's heavy losses and flagging Russian resolve were more serious factors in a coalition war of attrition. Therefore aid to Russia, the nineteenth-century 'strong man' whose weakness in modern war was starting to show, became the determining feature of strategy in the autumn.

At the same time, the intrinsic dynamic equilibrium between the two sides as each continued to mobilise was becoming evident: 'The struggle on the Western front during 1915 presented the aspect of a race between our offensive matériel and the German defensive organisations, both of which increased in strength with every week that passed,' Joffre later noted.[49] A contest of reserves and resources was emerging as the crux of a developing war of attrition, which would entail greater effort to break the stalemate. Joffre's plans for renewing the offensive therefore envisaged doubling its intensity, with attacks on two separate sectors of the western front, hopefully with British support on one. Of those resources that could be drawn into that contest in the middle of 1915, Kitchener's armies were the only potentially decisive element, so Joffre won a significant victory by drawing his ally's army into the attritional struggle that he was waging.

'The same question is being asked everywhere: What are the French doing?' France's ambassador to Russia reported on 14 August.[50] Joffre was doing what he always did, forcing his strategy through in the face of political and Allied reluctance. Joffre's fears that Russia's commitment to the united front might be weakened without Anglo-French action to relieve military pressure in the East were real. While not sharing Joffre's conviction that an offensive would significantly change the overall military situation, Kitchener concurred. When the two leaders met next on 17 August Kitchener assented to renewing the offensive in September 'to relieve pressure on Russia and keep the French army and people steady', even though he reported himself 'far from sanguine that any substantial military advantage will be achieved' – not doing so risked 'serious and perhaps fatal injury to the alliance'.[51] As well as anxieties about Russian staying power, for Kitchener and the cabinet concerns were also emerging about French defeatism as political crisis (of a sort familiar in France but worrying to the British) broke out in Paris.[52] Thus France's biggest offensive to date, the combined Battles of Artois and Champagne, supported by a British offensive against the mining village of Loos, was born out of political necessity rather than military conviction. Kitchener's principle of building up resources for the attritional war remained sound, but Joffre's conception of a dual-fronted strategy and political imperatives to push the Germans from France prevailed once more in autumn 1915.

In the interim the Dardanelles campaign had stalled, and Britain was gripped by its own drawn-out political crisis as Kitchener came under attack for his management of the campaign and the war effort more generally. Essentially the question of conscription, interconnected with the huge cost of mobilising for mass war, had stirred up criticism of his policy of attrition from domestic factions. One group, which included Lloyd George and Attorney General and Ulster Unionist leader Edward Carson, who resigned from the coalition cabinet in October, thought that Britain was not doing enough, while another led by Chancellor of the Exchequer Reginald McKenna thought that she could not afford to do as much. Kitchener and Asquith tried to steer a steady course between the two. 'We had to make war as we must, and not as we should like to' was Kitchener's stoical view of his summer troubles.[53] Events in France were to justify his pragmatism.

ON THE EVE OF THE CHAMPAGNE-ARTOIS OFFENSIVE, JOFFRE ISSUED A general order to his armies:

> During the past months we have been able to increase our numbers, and resources, while our adversary has been using up his. The time has, therefore, arrived for us to make a victorious attack . . . Thanks to your fellow-men, who have worked night and day in our factories, you will be able to advance to the assault behind a storm of shellfire, along the whole of the front, and side by side with the Armies of our Allies. You will carry all before you. In one bound, you will break through the enemy's defences and reach his artillery. Give him neither pause nor rest until victory is gained. Forward with good heart to free the soil of our Fatherland, and in the name of justice and liberty.[54]

This was a hyperbolic and unfortunate bulletin intended to inspire his troops to a victory that might possibly decide the war. It reflected the shifting strategic balance in an attritional war accurately, although the offensive itself proved that despite the expansion of armies and munitions production military capability did not yet tally with strategic ambitions.

After the early success in Artois in May, the belief persisted that the German line could be broken. In practice, however, 'breakthrough' would not work because defensive lessons were also being learned. Put simply, the defences could be continually strengthened and deepened in response to better offensive techniques. As the war went on attacks would become more rapid and penetrations into defensive systems more extensive, but they would always be containable. Moreover, deeper, stronger fixed defences also economised on manpower, which could be held back to counter-attack rather than be exposed in forward positions, thereby making attrition more slow and difficult. The first lesson that the Germans learned in Artois was that a second defensive position needed to be constructed behind the first to contain any successful enemy assault,* ideally

---

*A 'position' consisted of a series of interlocking trenches. Typically one had three lines of front, reserve and support trenches connected by communication trenches and reinforced with barbed-wire entanglements, fortified strongpoints, underground shelters and intermediate defences.

on a reverse slope where it could not be observed and targeted by enemy artillery. This defensive adaptation would check fresh French and British attempts to break through deepening defensive positions. Only when that goal was abandoned would offensive attritional warfare start to become truly effective.

The autumn 1915 offensives demonstrated that the basic tactical principles of infantry-artillery cooperation were effective, at least when it came to taking the enemy's trenches – holding them against enemy countcrattacks was still problematic. Operational ambitions could not be realised given tactical realities. It had been Joffre's intention to fix the German army in Artois while breaking through in Champagne to menace the enemy's lateral railway communications behind the front and precipitate a general retirement. Unfortunately, the first phase of that bold scheme, breaching the enemy's fortified lines, proved beyond his army's capacity. In Champagne Joffre massed 26 French infantry divisions supported by 2,164 guns in de Castelnau's *Groupe des armées du centre*. Castelnau planned to break through on a 28-kilometre front, create an open flank and manoeuvre against the enemy in open country.[55] Farther north the Tenth Army was to renew its attack on the Vimy Ridge. Joffre had ordered Foch to 'rupture' the front as well, to draw in German operational reserves so that they could not be sent eastwards to contain the Champagne breakthrough. In practice, however, this attack with 19 divisions supported by 1,090 guns was to proceed methodically.[56] The renewed Artois attack was to be supported by a British offensive against a cluster of mining villages north of Loos.

The extended and strengthened bombardment in Champagne offered initial hopes. 'The noisy racket reached an extraordinary crescendo. It bore heavily on our limbs and robbed us of all willpower . . . We were sitting in absolute Hell,' German Unteroffizier Haferkorn remembered. 'All the roads, crossroads, level crossings, the entire rail network and the villages were being bombarded in accordance with a sophisticated plan, which covered the whole area and was directed from the air . . . Out in front everyone was pinned inside their dugouts.'[57] The bombardment largely cleared the barbed wire in front of the first position, but not its defenders, and the French troops had to fight hand to hand to capture its forward trenches. But there was a clear success in the centre of the front of attack on 25 September, where XIV CA and II *Corps d'armée coloniale* penetrated the German first position to a depth of four kilometres, from which they could assault the second position. Thereafter, attempts to exploit this 'break in' repeated most of the errors made in Artois in May. One of XIV CA's brigades secured a temporary foothold in the German second position the next day, but overall the day belonged to the Germans, whose artillery and machine guns did heavy execution among the French infantry attacking where the wire had been insufficiently cut. On 28 September another breach in the second position was reported, into which regiment after regiment was thrown the next day. Since unsilenced artillery and machine-gun positions in support trenches still covered the breach, many battalions were destroyed in the attempt. The murderous folly of 'forcing a breach' was confirmed: the offensive had collapsed into chaos and disorder.[58] After a fortnight the offensive, which had inevitably degenerated into a number of localised struggles against a reinforced defence, was wisely halted.[59]

Those 'who heard and cheered the order of Joffre to the army before the battle', the call to liberate the country, could only be disappointed. The offensive itself did not go badly compared with earlier battles. 'We broke their first line along a wide front, advanced an average of three or four kilometres, took numerous prisoners and cannon,' Seeger reported proudly to his mother. 'We knew many splendid moments, worth having endured many trials for.' But the larger aim of 'piercing their line, of breaking the long deadlock' failed. Seeger took comfort in the fact that at times during the American Civil War the North had fared equally badly on the battlefield, 'though in the end of a similar *guerre d'usure* they pulled out victorious'.[60]

The British learned a similar, painful lesson at Loos. The results of the initial attack had been mixed. For the first time Haig's First Army was using gas to support its offensive: gas itself was a new, barbarous and as yet uncertain addition to the technologies deployed on the industrial battlefield. A cloud of chlorine gas released from fixed cylinders was blown across the German lines, substituting in part for a heavy bombardment as the British army still lacked the guns and munitions to support their attacks on the scale enjoyed by the French army. On the day the wind was barely enough to disperse the gas: indeed in places it lingered in the British trenches and gassed the waiting infantry crowded into the British forward lines. But in several places, at least where the bombardment had cut the enemy's wire, the assault troops captured their objectives with relative ease. The next day's events, however, turned a competent if unspectacular attack into a disaster. Poor command and control was partly responsible, but once again this was essentially a consequence of over-ambition. Three reserve divisions – the 21st and 24th Divisions, two fresh New Army units that had yet to see any real action, and the Guards Division – had been held back some miles behind the front under the personal control of Sir John French, who released them to Haig too late to exploit penetrations into the German defences on the first day. Congestion behind the British front lines further delayed their move forwards.

Nonetheless the decision was taken to push them forward on 26 September in an attempt to exploit disorganisation in the German defence. Overnight, however, the enemy had had time to reinforce and reorganise. In the morning the massed infantry of 21st and 24th Divisions advanced towards the German second position with very little artillery support. The German wire remained largely uncut and their machine gunners were waiting. They scythed down 8,200 men in a little over an hour, and the raw New Army divisions broke and fled. Only the deployment of the Guards Division prevented a rout as German counterattacks recaptured much of the ground lost the previous day.[61] Events such as those of 26 September were rare, but tragic, and ever after have epitomised the futility of trench warfare. Yet they were neither typical, nor unique to the British. Moreover, they were mere blips in the steady progression of attrition.

The Tenth Army had greater success through using less aggressive methods. Accepting how strong the German defences had becomes since the last attack on the Vimy Ridge, Foch's divisions were committed more systematically against specific sectors of the German defences saturated by artillery fire. Although some attacks failed for the usual reasons, they had the cumulative effect of driving the French forces into the German positions stage by stage. There was no stunning initial penetration as there had been in May, and the advance was stopped short of the crest of the Vimy Ridge, but by the time the battle ended the French had secured a clear advantage over the defence, with key positions that had been disputed since May now firmly in French hands. In his post-battle summary, Foch acknowledged that the results of the attack had not been remarkable. They had nevertheless been steady and positive: 'Against certain particularly strong positions . . . persistent actions, sustained until the enemy's will is broken, ought to succeed,' he concluded. 'Not requiring large numbers of infantry, they are above all costly in artillery munitions; all the same such a form of attack should not be rejected. They should find a place in our methods.'[62] This was perhaps the first clear example of how armies could operate effectively on the constricted, firepower-dominated battlefield, wearing out the enemy physically, materially and morally, with acceptable cost to themselves.

QUITE BY SURPRISE, IN LATE SUMMER THE FRENCH PRESENTED A POSSIBLE resolution to the stalemate at the Dardanelles. To settle their latest civil-military crisis a new Army of the Orient was to be formed, to be commanded by General Maurice Sarrail, one of Joffre's army commanders with political connections whose sacking in July had caused a furore. Six French divisions were to land north of the peninsula and decide the campaign – although not, Joffre had insisted, before his autumn offensive had endeavoured to do the same in France. That plan was never tested, since Bulgaria's declaration of war obliged the Allies to divert Sarrail's army to Salonika and to reinforce it with British divisions from France and the Dardanelles. The objective was to support Serbia. Falkenhayn, whose strategy throughout the year had been to contain the Western Allies while making gains at Russia's expense in the East, retained the initiative at the end of the year. German, Austrian and Bulgarian armies struck decisively before any meaningful assistance could arrive and forced the Serbian and Montenegrin armies to retire through Albania. Falkenhayn had finally broken one of the adversaries ranged against him, if the weakest – although the Serbian army took ship for Corfu, and thence to Salonika, where it remained in the field until the end of the war – yet the eastern, western and southern fronts still contained the Central powers. Conversely, the Entente had very little to show for its ambition and manoeuvre. The Salonika front quickly stalemated like all the others, leaving the Allies with two running sores: one diplomatic because the landing infringed Greek neutrality, and one political because thereafter the British and French (and Italians) argued constantly about the utility of and resources needed for the campaign. The Dardanelles campaign was wound down over the winter. Anzac Cove was evacuated in December and Cape Helles overnight on 8–9 January 1916. The Entente had had few victories in 1915, and Germany and her allies, if battered, remained far from beaten.

INTERIM CIGS, LIEUTENANT-GENERAL SIR ARCHIBALD MURRAY, POINTED out to the cabinet in his end-of-year strategic review that,

> Large allied forces cannot be removed from existing fronts in France and Russia, to conduct a campaign elsewhere, without the enemy's knowledge. Consequently, with his superior communications, their removal to a new theatre would enable him either to launch an attack against the front so weakened or to transfer an equivalent force from that front in ample time to meet the new attack . . . while any offensive on a minor scale against the Central Powers, on an independent line of operations, would almost certainly lead to the detachment employed being held up, sooner or later, by an entrenched position, if not enveloped and destroyed.[63]

The Allies had endured this strategic bind throughout 1915 and it would not go away: it dictated the increasingly fixed channels into which strategy was slipping.

Allied strategists who hoped to avoid taking on Germany directly had had no more success in the second half of 1915. But the war had been turning inexorably in the Allies' favour as France and Russia (with some British and Italian help) started to engage and erode the Central powers' fighting strength. Killing Germans was inherent, and became explicit, in the Western offensive strategy during 1915. The main weakness of Joffre's strategy, that Kitchener realised and that became obvious as the year went on, was that attrition was not yet cost-effective since material was lacking. Moreover, attrition was not a strategy that suggested empathy. Binding for one observed the process with concern:

> It seems that every headquarters, down to the Company Commander, gives returns on their losses and asks for reinforcements. These drafts, in the immediate communications between the unit in the field and the draft-finding units, are given over to fresh losses without reservations . . . No one perhaps considers the capital of lives, unless it be the Higher Command. Everybody takes it into consideration in secret; but when the order comes from above "We will attack," or "The position will be held," it puts a stop to all considerations. Then it costs what it may.[64]

The fact that soldiers had simply become yet another war material was starting to be felt, and resented.[65]

Although not yet ready to undertake a full-blown war of attrition, both sides had to devise a strategy in 1915 that would facilitate this objective – and what became clear by year's end was that old-style war was redundant and attrition was inevitable. Although it seemed to Binding 'that there is not a single General alive to-day who knows how to use armies that are numbered in millions',[66] objectives and methods were slowly adapting to their use – but using them up had become the watchword of the war. Strategy for both the Allies and the Central powers involved balancing military efforts in the East and the West, engaging diplomatically with still-neutral states and developing strategic possibilities on other fronts, in particular in the war against Turkey. Coordination was as yet rudimentary, which meant that 1915 would be a year of false starts and dashed hopes. But it would be a year of valuable experience. Come winter the strategic position was very different, the nature of the war was better understood and forces and societies were better mobilised to pursue attrition.

Expectations of a quick decision were fanciful while the war and the armies that were fighting it were still expanding, although the events of 1915 established the pattern of the rest of the war. France, the effective leader of the Allied coalition, strove to mobilise manpower and material fully, and to organise her allies for a long war. Britain, with some false starts, followed suit in her ongoing mobilisation, although she proved recalcitrant when it came to following French leadership. Much weaker than supposed, Russia proved a disappointment, needing support rather than giving it. Nonetheless, by the end of the year with the recruitment of Italy (another disappointment) and engagement in the Balkans the Central powers were menaced from many directions. Anticipated as easy prey, Turkey proved robust, and would thereafter tie down significant Allied forces, principally British. Since decisive battles were not going to happen – Germany's Eastern offensive and events on the Italian and Dardanelles fronts had demonstrated this – holding and wearing down the enemy's armies was prioritized, not least to support hard-pressed allies as the united front started to wobble. Yet if not properly managed, this stratagem offered no better prospects than a 'peace of exhaustion' when both sides had sacrificed men and treasure.[67]

It became apparent through 1915 that this was a war of resources, and in particular of reserves. The course and effectiveness of a strategy of attrition would be determined by how many men could be put in the field, how well they could be supplied and the extent to which casualties could be replaced, either by new recruits or recovered wounded. Raising more divisions would secure the front, since there would be reinforcements available to contain any enemy attack. This also gave some strategic flexibility, as sustained offensives could be mounted against the fortified front, and new campaigns could be engaged elsewhere. Too many divisions, however, would overstretch manpower resources in time if the war dragged on. It was already obvious that the Central powers were in a position of inferiority and were making war accordingly. Falkenhayn also strove to maximise manpower and material, partly by exploiting the resources of occupied territories. Beyond that he had to hold Germany's beleaguered allies to the common cause while endeavouring to split the hostile coalition by striking limited blows at their encircling adversaries one after another. There were early signs of strategic overstretch. The Eleventh Army that Falkenhayn created in spring 1915 for a strategic counterstrike, which he planned to use in the west or against Serbia, ultimately went eastwards to relieve the pressure on the Austrian army by striking back at the Russians. Although Germany could pick off smaller powers like Belgium and Serbia, her great power rivals proved more resilient. At best she could hope to wear down her enemies' military strength and will to fight on to final victory: the 'peace of exhaustion' had already been acknowledged by Falkenhayn as Germany's best hope. The fact that the occupation of Belgium and Serbia failed to force either of these states to make peace suggested that territorial conquest alone was not going to bring the war to an end.

Meanwhile, Joffre mustered France's reserves and demanded British reinforcements to sustain a prolonged operation to break the German defence in France.[68] Neither he nor Falkenhayn could deploy reserves in sufficient numbers to force a military decision in 1915, although during the year they locked themselves into a tit-for-tat expansion of armies and mobilisation of resources. The concomitant decimation of forces on both sides established the essential nature of military strategy. On the battlefield the enemy's forces had to be beaten, in an offensive his strategic reserves had to be used up – longer term, his military depots had to be emptied. Husbanding reserves was the other side of the equation, which of course would not be easy in the prolonged, intensive battles that characterised attritional warfare. The whole process would take time, not least because armies were still growing and more nations were joining the fight. Thus as 1916's campaign was planned it still remained to be seen which side would be exhausted first.

In the first year of stalemate, military techniques were adapting, quite quickly, but painfully. The French army adopted appropriate tactics during its early battles (although in 1915 it remained deficient in the vast amounts of war material they required). Directing large formations in prolonged military operations proved more difficult. The German army proved adaptive when on the defensive and equally quick learners when on the attack. An unforeseen feature of the process of adapting to trench warfare was that all armies would be able to achieve more on the battlefield more quickly as the war progressed. Paradoxically, this ensured that a dynamic military deadlock would continue, so that the land war would still be decided by the balance of loss between the two sides. The military cycle was to fight for a year, to evaluate that fighting and then to codify new methods, to train and equip to use them, and then to repeat the process in the next campaigning season. The first cycle, in which large-scale offensives failed to break the stalemate in the West and along the River Isonzo, was experimental but also informative: the challenges presented by the industrialised battlefield became apparent, while experience identified an appropriate tactical response and better operational methods. In the second cycle these methods would be tested, and in the third armies would be educated, trained and equipped to practice them. In 1918's fourth cycle, the war came to an end.

The fundamental principles of how to balance firepower and manoeuvre became evident during 1915's battles and would be refined and applied thereafter. To onlookers then and later, however, there seemed to be something fundamentally misguided in a strategy based on engaging the enemy's main army in increasingly big and prolonged battles. 'Had they been men of genius – which they were not – they could have adapted

themselves more quickly and effectively to the new conditions of war,'
Lloyd George later asserted of his generals.[69] Around the same time the
novelist C. S. Forester, who had been rejected for military service himself
on health grounds, published a successful novel, *The General*, that presented one of the most memorable and enduring images of British commanders and their approach to the challenges of the industrial battlefield:

> In some ways it was like the debate of a group of savages as to how to
> extract a screw from a piece of wood. Accustomed only to nails, they
> had made an effort to pull out the screw by main force, and now that
> it had failed they were devising methods of applying more force still,
> of obtaining more efficient pincers, of using levers and fulcrums so that
> more men could bring their strength to bear. They could hardly be
> blamed for not guessing that by rotating the screw it would come out
> after the exertion of far less effort; it would be a notion so different
> from anything they had ever encountered that they would laugh at the
> man who suggested it.[70]

The generals of the early half of the war were not poor generals per se,
even if their political contemporaries and later critics were to blame them
for the long casualty lists inherent in industrialised attritional warfare.
Whether grand strategists like Kitchener or field commanders like Joffre
and Falkenhayn, they understood the nature of the conflict they faced.
But none was able to make a decisive, dynamic intervention at a time
when the war was still being shaped. Partly this was because, on the Allied side at least, they did not agree on how best to pursue the war; mainly
it was because military doctrines had only just started to adapt to the actual circumstances of the battlefield. The problem of turning the screw
would be solved, bit by bit, although given the size of the armies engaged
the fundamental costliness of mass warfare would never go away.

It was not the commanders' objective to wear out their own troops,
but an awareness that this was the enemy's objective had to govern military thinking, as did recognition that friendly troops would be worn out
too. Ultimately the land war would be decided when one side developed
the ability to inflict casualties on the enemy at a rate that could not be
replaced with reserves. After some false starts, and consequently and regrettably some disastrous if localised massacres, by the end of 1915 this was
becoming the guiding axiom of military operations. In attritional warfare
armies ideally needed to inflict loss on the enemy at a rate that matched
or exceeded that which they suffered (although larger force might still win
even if the casualty rate was disproportionate). For most of the time the
defence possessed an advantage, although as time passed it was eroded as

material replaced manpower on the battlefield, and appropriate methods were developed and inculcated into armies, a process in its infancy in 1915. Their early set-piece offensives were to cost the Anglo-French forces relatively heavily, while Russia, outgunned, was to suffer even more. In spring 1915 the French and British armies lost 1.88 and 2.22 casualties respectively for each one they inflicted on the enemy, a proportion that did not improve in the autumn. Nevertheless, the experience gained in these battles, harsh though it was, was fundamental to victory on land. Come 1918, when the German army was finally beaten, those figures had dropped to 1.15 and 1 per German casualty.[71] That the land war was to cost so many lives in between was a consequence of the nature of the war itself. In the war's first cycle, casualties were high because the operational ambitions of commanders were still attuning to the tactical realities of the battlefield, and because the defence still possessed an obvious material advantage. Over the winter of 1915–16 the Allies developed techniques that resolved this battlefield conundrum, suggesting that the fortunes of war might go better in the second cycle of attrition. But the German army remained a powerful adversary, suggesting that the land war would still be difficult, and a great deal more effort would be needed to decide it.

Returning from Paris to Germany on the outbreak of war, Toni Sender had encountered a confident French officer who had predicted, 'It would be a war of technique and material, and we will crush them.'[72] Technique developed in 1915's fighting. Material, its mainstay, was, however, lacking while the war machines with which the war was fought were mobilising. These factors meant that Joffre was too ambitious in 1915, entailing further heavy casualty bills with relatively little to show for them. But this harsh baptism of fire was necessary to establish the ways and means to fight the land war efficiently and to win it. While certain politicians seemed able to guess at what was going to happen on the land front, their suggestions as to how to avoid it were impracticable. They had pretensions to make war, but soldiers understood war, and this war, better than statesmen. When Lloyd George first met Foch, at the height of the Battle of Ypres, Foch had reassured him that 'there will be no more retreats'. When pressed whether there would be any more advances, Foch had replied, after reflection, 'That depends on the men and material you will be able to throw into the battle line.'[73] Foch articulated the guiding principle of attritional warfare: the mobilisation of manpower and material with which to defeat the enemy along his battle line. How the latter could be done eluded the generals early on. While he conducted the attritional battles in Artois Foch himself was learning all the time. The former was engaging the politicians with similar tentativeness. Their effective combination would not be seen until the second year of the war.

# SEVEN

# WAR MACHINES

'NEED FOR SHELLS: BRITISH ATTACKS CHECKED: LIMITED SUPPLY the Cause', ran the headline in *The Times* on 14 May 1915, above an article penned by the paper's military correspondent, Charles à Court Repington, just returned from a private visit to GHQ in France. Prompted by Field Marshal French himself, Repington reported that 'the want of an unlimited supply of high explosive was a fatal bar to our success' in the ongoing offensive to capture the Aubers Ridge.[1] Rumours about Britain's lack of military preparedness had been widespread during the spring, as had ministerial denials. 'All we need is shells, shells, shells,' one recent visitor to the GHQ had assured a public meeting on 13 April.[2] Reports that guns had been restricted to firing two or three rounds per day (in fact an essential economy to build up ammunition reserves for the coming offensive) heightened the anxieties of backbenchers, and some ministers were also starting to question the management of the war.[3] On 21 April Asquith himself had felt obliged to assure the House that 'there is not a word of truth in the statement that we or the Allies have been hampered by our not being able to provide sufficient ammunition', a blandishment that would be exploded by Repington's exposé.[4] The 'shells scandal', coming on top of other criticisms of the fledgling war effort, helped put an end to Britain's last Liberal government, which was toppled precipitously by the simultaneous resignation of the first sea lord, Fisher, who had grown tired of Churchill's interference in matters of naval strategy. Conservative and Unionist Party leaders joined a re-modelled coalition government committed to prosecuting the war more vigorously, which included Britain's first Labour Party minister, Arthur Henderson who took the Board of Education.

Asquith's reshaping of his ministry represented only the continuance of old-style party-political manoeuvring.[5] Nonetheless, the shells scandal inaugurated a modernisation of the practices of government. A new Ministry of Munitions was created to manage the production of war material, taking over from Kitchener's War Office: this Lord Beaverbrook later suggested was the real objective of anti-Kitchener press agitation following Repington's revelation.[6] The field marshal had given essential momentum to Britain's war mobilisation at its start, but now the energy of 'K of Chaos' as some were beginning to disparage him was no longer enough, since it also brought friction, notably in the allocation or manpower between the army and industry. The war effort would need management, and that required specialists.

Lloyd George took on the new munitions portfolio, a significant step on his ascent to wartime leadership. War engaged the former radical liberal social reformer after he threw off his pacifist mantle in August 1914. Industrial mobilisation was one facet of modern warfare that he understood. 'This is an engineers' war, and it will be won or lost owing to the efforts or shortcomings of engineers,' he had pronounced. 'Unless we are able to equip our armies our predominance in men will avail us nothing. We need men, but we need arms more than men, and delay in producing them is full of peril for this country.'[7] The 'Welsh wizard', as the press dubbed him, represented a new sort of war leader, populist, practical and hands on: a 'man of push and go' in the phrase Lloyd George coined himself. Lloyd George had a reputation for getting things done, and for fighting tooth-and-nail for his beliefs. He had forced through his modernising 1909 'people's budget', provoking a constitutional crisis in the process. This marked his out as the people's champion, someone who was needed as the patrician political class that controlled liberal Britain engaged a popular war effort. This did not make him a better war leader than Asquith, but he was certainly a very different sort. He was a strong orator and a striking figure, able to rouse a crowd with his expansive hand and head gestures and shock of white hair waving with the effort. Unfortunately, 'The Man Who Won the War', as a section of the press later dubbed him sycophantically and inaccurately, was prone to strong opinions, expressed with a lawyers' conviction but based on a shaky grasp of what was possible.[8] Soldiers would find him hard to handle, since his strategic impressions mixed a sound grasp of the nature of the war with fanciful notions of how it should be conducted. To the home front Lloyd George was an asset, to the land war less so. He was also a consummate political intriguer. His surprise appointment to the War Office after Kitchener's untimely death in June 1916 was perhaps misguided, but by then Asquith was keen to placate the minister who was the most consistent critic of his management of the war and was clearly after his job. Even after the war, Lloyd George continued his vituperative skirmishes. The impression conveyed in his tendentious *War Memoirs* that he was right and most other politicians and soldiers were wrong persists against the accumulation of contrary evidence.[9]

The Ministry of Munitions was the first new department established to manage the practices of modern war in Britain. Ministries of Labour, Shipping, Blockade (all December 1916), Reconstruction (July 1917) and Information (February 1918) all followed, and a minster for food, or food controller, was appointed in December 1916. In each new ministry a new bureaucracy was set up, drawing on professional civilian expertise. After Lloyd George became prime minister in December 1916 technical experts were brought into government. For example, after serving as deputy director of munitions supply and sorting out the army's transport problems in France, the railway manager Eric Geddes became first lord of the Admiralty in July 1917. His brother Auckland, in peacetime an academic and part-time soldier, who served as director of recruiting in Lloyd George's War Office, became the new minister of national service in August 1917. Newspaper magnates Lord Beaverbrook and Lord Northcliffe became respectively minister of information and director of propaganda in enemy countries in 1918. If they were to remain on the front benches, old-style party politicians, who directed the war in its first year, would have to adapt their notions of war, government and civil-society as Lloyd George had done.

Asquith's government reshuffle merely reinforced, rather than changed, the course of mobilisation. *The Vivid* had told its readership in February that 'we have almost reached the first stage of Armageddon, that of the nation *in arms*; were are now preparing also for the second stage, that of the nation *in work* . . . Slowly the Government will direct our efforts and organise our energies'.[10] Britain and the empire were moving towards a continental model of home-front war organisation that entailed great disruption to individual lives and collective enterprises as state power extended inexorably into all dimensions of the war effort. Such was national mobilisation – a novel, initially suspect and inevitably inefficient expedient in liberal Britain that was to take two years.[11] Manpower, and in particular raising armies, had been the preoccupation during the earliest phase of mobilisation. After stalemate set in economic management and industrial productivity would become its other mainstay; central to this was weapons and munitions production and distribution. Waging war became an increasingly technocratic process. The skills of science and industry, business and communications management became vital components of the war effort, while making war became the essential function of big government that increasingly controlled the private-enterprise domestic economy and its workforce. As a consequence, workers and women would be drawn firmly into the war effort: Henderson's promotion to the cabinet acknowledged unionised labour's place in the national partnership. Engaging and sustaining popular participation in the home-front war effort while ensuring consent and consensus would thereafter increasingly occupy governments.[12] Motivation was all-important, although a certain amount of coercion was inevitable.

The interrelationship between workers' productivity at home and the effectiveness of the army in the field was becoming apparent. In the House of Lords debate on the Munitions of War Bill introduced shortly after the shells scandal to legislate the relationship between private producers and labour, Lord Stanhope, just back from the front, reported that French trenches were held by the fire of very superior artillery and few rifles, while our artillery was inferior and the trenches held by rifle fire – the former being very expensive in ammunition, the latter in life – and secondly, that what the soldiers said was they wished we would wake up in England and send more big guns.[13] England was belatedly awake, although the intent to press on with mobilisation took time to translate into actual physical output. The munitions that were being delivered in bulk by early 1916 had actually been ordered by the War Office before the Ministry of Munitions was created.[14]

Sir John French had raised the question of munitions with Kitchener in 1914, and in March a special committee to look into War Office procurement practices had been established, chaired by Lloyd George. The War Office was doing all it could to expedite the production and delivery of munitions when the shells scandal broke. But as well as the forces in France and at the Dardanelles, an army expanding tenfold and allies also had to be supplied. Facing unprecedented national mobilisation, all the War Office was doing would never be enough until the inherent problems of redirecting a peacetime economy into wartime channels had been engaged with and overcome. First, future needs had to be calculated and orders placed. Where productive capacity did not yet exist it had to be developed, either by converting related industries or building new factories. Machine tools then had to be manufactured before gun and shell production could begin. Labour too had to be found and organised, which required the cooperation of trade unions that found their power and influence greatly enhanced in wartime. All the while new ways of making war obliged constant adaptation and invention, placing science, engineering and technology at the heart of industrial mobilisation.[15]

The time lag between demand and supply that resulted from mobilisation was common to all the belligerents, although its impact was heightened in Britain, which did not possess the prewar infrastructure for equipping a mass army. But all war ministries had hugely underestimated the munitions required for modern warfare and were finding that manufacturing more and heavier guns, and vast numbers of shells to shoot from them, demanded labour, raw materials, money and above all time. Home-front mobilisation became the second front of the war effort from 1915. While it was ongoing, field armies were effectively fighting each other with one hand tied behind their backs. This was another reason why battlefield losses in 1915 were out of proportion to battlefield success, something that was redressed after mobilising fully.[16]

THE GERMANS COINED A WORD FOR THE MECHANISM WITH WHICH THE ALLIES ground down the fighting power of their armies in a vast, unceasing war machine: *Materialschlacht*. Germany would have to match her enemies as best she could in this new way of making war that, alongside the management of manpower, required the mobilisation of science and industry, capital and labour. She could never outpace them. Germany's mobilisation problems were not managerial, since the military-industrial complex could adapt swiftly to wartime needs. Rather, Germany's problems would relate to supply and labour.

Germany started the war better prepared than the Entente. Peacetime planning had anticipated the needs of a long war (if not of one that was to last more than four years), and some key raw materials had been stockpiled in anticipation of an economic blockade: Krupp had two years' worth of nickel and one of chrome, plus copper and its own iron-ore producing capacity should foreign imports dry up.[17] Germany's armaments industry was the largest and most advanced in Europe. Provision had been made to increase munitions production in wartime, giving German artillery and machine gunners a temporary advantage on the battlefields of Poland and France in the first year of the war. But Germany too quickly found that provisions for shell production were inadequate. By the end of the Battle of the Marne prewar shell reserves had been exhausted, and at the height of the First Battle of Ypres, one operations officer at the OHL noted that the army only had enough shells for six more days' fighting at the current rate of consumption.[18]

The German military establishment was tasked with ensuring the army's needs were met – it now became the greatest and most demanding consumer in the state. Yet unlike in Britain, German civilians would begin and remain subordinated to the military bureaucracy, which became the policy maker and managing agency for Germany's war effort. Germany's patriotic industrialists slipped willingly into the military orbit. The All-German War Committee on German Industry, formed by Germany's two largest employers' associations when war broke out, exercised an advisory role, and individual industrialists took on managerial and administrative tasks as the state mobilised. German heavy industry was highly cartelized before the war, and this central management model proved adaptable to wartime. By September the army had established a War Materials Section (*Kreigsrohstoffabteilung*, KRA) headed by the industrialist Walter Rathenau, the head of Germany's leading electrical firm, AEG. Under the KRA's general supervision a growing number of corporations representing various private producers regulated the supply and distribution of raw materials – coal, iron and steel, metals and chemicals for example – in a close economic relationship with the state, which invested in what were essentially wartime joint-stock companies. This system allowed production for the army to be prioritized and expanded, while the private producers, who managed the corporations and channelled contracts to their own firms, were guaranteed a 5 percent profit. Twenty-five corporations had been formed by the beginning of 1915, nearly two hundred during the war.[19] This functional relationship between the state, the army and big business benefited them all, although it relied on workers, the third element of a wartime 'corporate partnership', to deliver the goods.

The question of workers' loyalty was one that would preoccupy Germany's war managers, especially given the fear of socialism's inexorable rise that poisoned prewar politics. Toni Sender faced like so many a difficult individual choice as she took her place in the war effort. Not that she could have avoided some form of war work in wartime Germany where, she recollected, 'almost all economic life was concentrated on war purposes . . . nobody working for a living during the World War could escape some work connected with production of war materials'. After giving up her nursing appointment she was recruited by the German metal firm that she had been working for in Paris before the war to set up a new department. It was interesting work, '[dealing] with the most confidential records of manufacturing and financial transactions. Its scope included relations with the war ministry . . . the building of new plants for war purposes . . . [and] the operation of plants already owned by the company'. But as well as being a war worker, Sender was a socialist who would become an increasingly active antiwar agitator. She found herself in a position of responsibility in which she learned 'many secrets that would have interested the anti-war movement'. Yet despite her political convictions she would not betray the confidence placed in her by her employer.[20] Moral conscience plus a fair degree of job satisfaction that an intelligent, liberated young woman might not have found in peacetime persuaded Sender to work diligently for the war effort even while condemning the war. Nor was she unpatriotic, despite her opposition to the kaiser's regime. It remained to be seen how long such wartime compromises would continue. Like many other socialists, for many months Sender found herself torn between loyalty to the SPD that supported the war and the belief that they were betraying the interests of the working class by doing so – splitting the socialist movement seemed another disastrous consequence of war that ought to be avoided.[21]

Germany certainly had a head start in shifting from a peacetime to a wartime economy, although her early efforts were not without problems. Cast iron was substituted for steel in shell casings early on to expedite the supply of field-gun ammunitions, which led to poor-quality munitions being produced. The experiment was abandoned in July 1915 as steel became more plentiful.[22] Germany's domestic reserves of the basic raw materials required by modern heavy industry, such as coal and iron ore, were substantial, although there was an inevitable lag before they could be developed to substitute for imports cut off by the Allied blockade. Germany's early military successes had won her extra assets – most of Belgium and a productive area of France. Her spoils included the Longwy-Briey basin that before the war produced much of France's iron and steel; the coalfields, steel and chemical works of Southern Belgium; and the textile mills of the Lille-Roubaix-Tourcoing agglomeration. These 'occupied' resources – industrial workers and manufacturing capacity, as well as agricultural land – could be integrated into her war effort in the same way that they would be in the Second World War. They came under direct military administration and were to be exploited thoroughly. Over the course of 1915 Germany was to add much of Russian Poland to her spoils, and further gains in Eastern Europe thereafter, notably Rumania in 1916. For this reason Germany had little to fear in a short war, because she could sustain industrial productivity at a rate that matched her enemies' and generally address shortages thorough developing domestic production or foreign conquest. Austria's occupation of Serbia at the end of 1915 eased shortages in the supply of manganese for high-quality steel production for example.[23]

In the war's early years, therefore, Germany developed a strong war economy and had a clear head start over the still-mobilising Allies. In the war between the home fronts, however, she would be overmastered by the Allies in a long conflict as her war economy reached saturation point more quickly. The intertwined processes of restrictive economic blockade, with its concomitant popular unrest, and her enemies' mobilisation of their greater resources would eventually tip the balance decisively in the Allies' favour – when could not be foreseen in 1915, but unless Germany could win on the battlefield beforehand, inevitably it would happen.

\* \* \*

FRANCE HAD DONE LITTLE TO PREPARE FOR A LONG CONFLICT. HER POPULATION imbalance relative to Germany necessitated mobilising large numbers of industrial workers on the outbreak of war: many valuable skilled workers were killed and maimed in 1914's costly battles. France did have a strong, modern industrial sector. Her domestic heavy industries such as iron and steel were not comparable in size to those of Britain and Germany, although in recent years yet she had made real progress in developing the newer light engineering industries that would come to the fore in wartime. Before the war France produced the most advanced artillery pieces, such as the world-leading 75mm field gun and the 155mm Rimailho howitzer. France also possessed the world's largest and most advanced aircraft manufacturing sector. Her aircraft engines would be vital to the Allied war efforts. Thus, when it came to designing and producing new weapons France would prove the most effective of the belligerents.[24] In its early stages, however, France's industrial mobilisation was improvised and unsystematic: such was not unusual in the early months of war.[25]

Joffre recognised immediately that his forces were ill-equipped to take on the better-armed Germans. After the first encounter battle in Alsace in mid-August 1914 he requested that War Minister Adolphe Messimy increase shell production at once, from 8,000 to 100,000 per day! By October he was demanding large numbers of the modern, quick-firing 105mm and 155mm heavy artillery pieces that inventors had designed at the turn of the century, but which had only been purchased in small numbers before the war owing to budget restrictions and bureaucratic infighting. These were excellent guns, which in time would prove themselves on the battlefield, but in early 1915 there were only a couple of hundred of them in service. Three hundred and forty more heavy guns had been ordered, some only in June 1914, but the order was not due for completion until 1917. As late as 30 May 1916, on the eve of the Somme offensive, Joffre still had occasion to chide the war ministry over the inefficiency of heavy artillery production while at the same time demanding another large increase in the output of guns and shells. Modern guns in significant numbers would not start to arrive until 1916 and their systematic serial production would not be organised until 1917. The need for munitions and more and more 75mm field guns – the mainstay of the French artillery, but which were failing in large numbers by 1915 owing to overuse and a significant increase in barrel explosions caused by hastily manufactured, poor-quality shells – had to be prioritized as the armaments industry was expanded. As a stopgap the army pressed obsolescent fortress guns into service. This produced 7,500 medium and heavy guns to support 1915's offensives – but one of the

factors that obliged slow, steady, prolonged bombardments in those battles was that the supporting guns were hard to position and manoeuvre
and were slow-firing and difficult to aim accurately.[26]

As in Germany, industry hurried to respond to the unprecedented
requirements of battle, although the war ministry's chaotic placing of orders and the rapid acceleration of demands in the early months of the
conflict gave an overall impression that French industry could not meet
the needs of the military.[27] Rather than the industrialists themselves taking control of economic management, in bureaucratic republican France
local authorities and civil servants stepped in. Departmental committees
were established to coordinate supply and demand, labour and resources.
Mayors in particular set about bringing together local businessmen and
trade unions in their personal fiefdoms – they of course had often risen
to local power on account of their own economic success.[28] The broader
problem of early economic mobilisation lay in coordinating the army's
needs with industrial capacity. Around the time that Britain was putting
its munitions programmes on a more systematic footing France tackled
the problem by promoting socialist deputy Albert Thomas, who was assist-
ing Millerand with munitions procurement, to the post of undersecretary
at the war ministry. He would take over responsibility for armaments
from the director of artillery, General Louis Baquet. Under Thomas's
pragmatic direction the 'socialisation' of production would take a back
seat to the coordination of industry and labour. Working with employers'
organisations – such as the influential *Comité des forges*, which represented iron and steel producers – Thomas would strive to reconcile supply
and demand, labour rights and industrialists' reasonable profits in the
wider interest of keeping the army fighting and the home front producing,
thereby winning the war. By a different route France had settled on a similar corporatist system to Germany. Raw-material monopolies were regulated by the industrialists themselves, while the war ministry directed
labour – so called 'military workers' released from the front but still subject to direction within the war economy – under the provisions of August
1915's Dalbiez Law.[29]

LIKE HER ALLIES, RUSSIA TOOK NEARLY A YEAR TO ADDRESS THE CHAOTIC
early phase of mobilisation. In the tsar's empire the challenges of war
would prove too much for conservative political structures and inefficient
administration. By the middle of 1915 it was clear that the Russian war
effort was in crisis and that if the regime did not bend, it would break.
While power lay with the tsar and his appointed ministers, such public
opinion and reformism as existed was expressed through the 'progressive'

liberal factions in the Duma. The peacetime placemen who still ran the war effort were an easy and deserved target for criticism. The defeat at Gorlice-Tarnów obliged change. Mikhail Rodzianko, leader of the liberal Octobrist Party and president of the Duma, received more than three hundred letters from the provinces,

> pointing out how alarmed and indignant the country is. In every corner there is the same complaint: the bureaucracy is incapable of organising the industrial activities of the nation and creating the war machinery without which the army will go from disaster to disaster.

Dismayed by the defeat, on 31 May he sought an audience with the tsar:

> I had little difficulty in proving that our administration is powerless to solve the technical problems of the war unaided and that recourse must be had to the assistance of private sources to rope in all the live forces in the nation, augment the output of raw material, and coordinate the work of the factories.

Tsar Nicholas agreed to set up a Munitions Council, comprised of four generals, four members of the Duma and four metallurgists, including the preeminent armaments manufacturer Putilov. Dining with the latter two days later, the French ambassador, Maurice Paléologue, was dismayed to record that Putilov 'almost revelled in describing the fatal consequences of the imminent catastrophes and the silent work of decadence and dislocation which is undermining the Russian edifice'. Tsarism's days were numbered, he predicted: 'It is not merely a technical problem, a question of labour and output which has to be solved. The whole administrative system of Russia must be reformed from top to bottom.'[31]

Russian industry was slow to adapt to the needs of wartime, owing to the inherent inefficiencies of the Russian way of doing things. Allied commentators universally noted that the Russian war effort was hamstrung by bureaucratic infighting, political rivalries, vested interests and corruption. Negley Farson, an American contracting agent for the Manchester subsidiary of an American engineering firm, recollected his Petrograd contact's explanation of business practices:

> He gave me a brief but, as I afterwards learned, very realistic description of how one went about getting orders from the great Russian War Department. The first rule was never to go to the War Department at all. One found an intermediary. The intermediary knew the right people, he knew how much each official would take, and which official –

if he did not get that much – would see that the order went to somebody else. Or that there would be no order at all. Neither the needs of
the Russian soldiers being slaughtered at the front, nor the quality of
the goods supplied, mattered in the very least.

When Farson found his intermediary, he was informed that the minister
of war himself took 2 percent of every contract. And he was far from
alone in his pursuit of a profit. Expecting lengthy negotiations, Farson
took lodging in the Hotel Astoria where his intermediary held court.
Here, one French munitions expert explained that among 'the galaxy of
officers, diplomats and courtesans . . . are all the general staffs of the
world and all the beautiful cocottes that the Germans have kindly driven
out of Poland'.[32] This was good for Farson, who would linger for three
years in Russia enjoying the pleasures that Polish hospitality had to offer
while manoeuvring to secure supply contracts, but disastrous for Russia.

Tales that Russian soldiers advancing into battle had to pick up the
rifles of fallen comrades had a certain degree of authenticity.[33] As well as
small arms shortages, however, where the Russians were really outclassed
by Germany in 1915 was in artillery, both in quantity and technique. While
in absolute terms Russian industry could produce large amounts of
weapons and munitions, in practice due to graft in the Technical Department of the War Office – and also a lack of railway capacity that meant
that even when supplies were available these could not always be shipped
to where they were needed – it did not during the first two years of war.

Powering up the 'steamroller' required reform in Russia and assistance from allies and neutrals. Although this was obvious early on, the
tsar only took action once Russia's armies started to retreat in spring
1915. Venal war minister General Sukhomlinov was replaced on 26 June
by his former deputy General A. A. Polivanov, who started to issue the
necessary contracts that his predecessor's corruption and obstructionism
had delayed.[34] Polivanov was also accustomed to working with the Duma
and was well regarded by the progressives. War organisation seemed to
presage political modernisation as the adjunct of efficiency: a reconvened
Duma started to press the tsar for 'a government of public confidence'.[35]
The new Munitions Council was able to engage with and partially solve
the technical and productivity bottlenecks that were hampering the Russian war effort, ensuring that the situation improved significantly during
1916. If Russia's armies could buy time meanwhile, come 1916 they might
be able to counterattack the enemy on more equal terms.

Expansion of responsibility for wartime management beyond the
traditional bureaucracy by measures such as establishing the Munitions
Council endeavoured to bring professional expertise into the war effort.

In practice, however, such devolved responsibility merely heightened existing political tensions. In June 1915 Russia's Association of Trade and Industry's annual congress set up its own War Industries Committee to coordinate supply and production nationwide, in direct rivalry to the state bureaucracy. It was not greatly effective, but its very creation was provocative. In response the state set up further fuel, food and transport councils, thereby undermining the possibility of cooperation between the 'progressives' of the Duma and the capitalists of the Association of Trade and Industry. Wartime Russia remained a society of competing interest groups, albeit now patriotic private enterprise was redressing some of the state's deficiencies, or at least encouraging reform. Although patriotic businessmen were not above making a good profit from the war contracts they were now sharing among themselves.[36] Moreover, as the war went on Tsar Nicholas became personally identified with the success and failure of the war effort: in September 1915 he assumed supreme command of the army in a bold if misguided attempt to inspire Russia's masses. In doing so he ensured that the fortunes of the Romanov dynasty would become dependent on success or failure in the war. Moreover, his opposition to further political concessions remained strong. Polivanov was soon replaced by the more compliant General Shuvayev, a supply expert, which was certainly needed, but no politician.[37]

Although less subject to the vagaries of Russian internal politics, assistance from outside was liable to be slow and limited. In time 'Britain became Russia's financier and armourer to an extent both unimagined and unimaginable before 1914', but it was a difficult transition due to Russian intransigence as well as Britain's own inability to provide war materials in adequate quantities for the huge Russian army in the vastness of Russia.[38] Allied resources were initially needed for their own mobilisations. Buying from neutrals was an alternative, and there were many contactors like Farson hunting a lucrative opportunity in Petrograd. Any purchases had to be paid for, and war with the Central powers had seriously restricted Russia's access to world markets for her foreign currency earning exports, principally grain, which before 1914 had been shipped through the Straits. Russia quickly exhausted her assets abroad and thereafter relied on loans from allies, principally Great Britain.[39] These loans would be used to purchase goods from allies and neutrals, tying the long-term stability of the international economy closely to a Russian victory.

Getting foreign weapons and munitions to Russia was a logistical nightmare. Japanese goods – mainly rifles and small arms ammunitions – would have to be shipped to Vladivostok in the Far East, at the end of the 5,700-mile-long trans-Siberian railway. American and Allied goods would have to come through the northern ports of Archangel and Murmansk, ice-bound for five months a year, from whence there would be a lengthy and slow railway journey to the factory or the front. Farson visited Archangel in spring 1915 to try to expedite the unloading of an inbound cargo. He found the port 'smothered under layers of lead ingots, steel bars, rusting motor-cars, bales of soggy cotton and broken crates of machinery of every description'. Shortage of wharf space meant ships might sit in the harbour for weeks, waiting for permission to unload. Things were no better after unloading: the overused single-track narrow-gauge railway 'was literally sinking into its own road bed' under the weight of traffic. A picaresque gang of international representatives competed for scarce dock space. 'One silent little Scotchman', a Mr Dodd who was responsible for trans-shipment of flax for the British aeroplane industry, seemed to have mastered the Russian way of business. 'A man with an amazing grasp of detail and unashamed effrontery . . . he knew every official of the port of Archangel and his weakness.' Decked out in a self-styled 'uniform' of Russian breeches, British tunic, Italian military cloak, French beret and over-large cavalry sabre, he lied, bullied and cajoled his ships in and out of the port. Dodd was 'a perfect example of what a man can do with just a little will power alone', Farson remembered. 'We called him the Emperor of North Russia.'[40] Farson's own excursion to Archangel proved wasted: the American ship he was awaiting had been intercepted as a blockade runner and diverted to the prize court at Portsmouth.[41]

Physical distances, political and economic backwardness and administrative chaos together contrived to make Russian mobilisation the biggest and least solvable problem of Allied war management. However, by the time Kitchener took ship for Russia in June 1916 to engage with the problem directly at an inter-Allied munitions conference, progress was obvious. Russian armaments production had increased ninefold, reaching 397,000 tons in 1916, compared with 43,000 in 1914.[42] The lean and chaotic year 1915 had given rise to bounty, as domestic contracts placed then started to deliver. A new port, fatefully named Romanov, had been opened on the Kola Inlet to ease the supply bottlenecks in North Russia. Yet it still took three days and nights to get to Petrograd, and the new railway could only handle 13 percent of the goods that could be landed in the new docks: some problems, particularly of transportation, were indissoluble.[43] In June 1916, as Russia's armies belatedly went on the offensive, railway limitations meant that the Putliov works and other Petrograd private engineering firms were only receiving half the coal they needed to maintain full production.[44] Foreign assistance too had still to make any real impact on Russia's war effort. Only some 2.3 percent of Russian war expenditure in 1916 was on imported war materials.[45] Kitchener's own plan to take a grip on the Russian war economy in summer 1916 sank, literally. He was drowned when HMS *Hampshire* carrying the Allied munitions delegation which he was leading hit a mine north of the Orkneys.

ALTHOUGH HE DID NOT LIVE TO SEE IT, BY THE SUMMER OF 1916 KITCHENER'S prediction that it would take two years for the Allies to mobilise sufficiently to engage the Central powers in an attritional struggle with some hope of success was being tested, in the general Allied offensive from June to November. Although they were still far from lavishly equipped, by then all Allied armies had sufficient guns and munitions, as well as the extensive paraphernalia of modern war, to engage in sustained attritional operations. The armaments programmes that Joffre had set in train in autumn 1914 were finally producing modern heavy guns and shells in sufficient quantities to allow his armies to engage the enemy in two prolonged battles at Verdun and on the Somme. Yet his renewed demand for heavy guns after May 1916, some 6,720 of all calibres, indicated that early war calculations of need were significantly deficient. The fact that only 1,312 of these would be delivered within a year confirmed that although shell production could be expanded reasonably quickly and easily, manufacturing the complex machines that fired them in large numbers was a greater challenge.[46]

British munitions started to arrive in increasing quantities during 1916. At the opening of the Somme offensive British artillery fired its heaviest bombardment yet: more than 1,500,000 shells from around 1,500 guns over a seven-day period before 1 July. This represented an impressive rate of progress since the shells scandal in May 1915, although such a rapid expansion of production was not without its problems. Notoriously, owing to hasty production and poor quality control in the expanded munitions industry, a large proportion (some estimates suggest as many as one-third) of British munitions failed to explode. But quantity was never lacking thereafter thanks to the efforts of Lloyd George's Ministry of Munitions and Britain's (and America's) industrial workforce. In later years British armies could engage in battle confident that there was sufficient material for operations, and as munitions became plentiful the rate and scale of material-intensive offensive operations could increase.

POTENTIALLY, THE WORLD'S RESOURCES WERE AT THE DISPOSAL OF EUROPE'S mobilising nations: control and exploitation of global resources, whether derived from imperial power or international commerce, was central to economic strategy, as was denying or restricting the enemy's access to resources and markets. British, French, Belgian and Italian imperial resources were immediately available to the Allies, who controlled the world's sea-lanes. Such control also enabled them to seize or interdict Germany's global assets quickly. Fighting would spread into Africa, Asia and the Pacific in 1914 as expeditions were mounted to seize German colonies. Fascinating as military campaigns, and waged against nature as much as the enemy, these were colonial small wars on the edges of the real thing. With the exception of German East Africa, which held out until 1917, the wider imperial war was over quickly. Such campaigns had some value to Germany since they could be sustained with local manpower and materials and were a drain on Allied resources disproportionate to their size and strategic importance. Even after German East Africa was occupied General Paul von Lettow-Vorbeck's forces managed to tie down a large number of South African troops by continuing a guerrilla war from Portuguese East Africa until the armistice was signed in Europe (indeed for two days longer, until the news that hostilities had ceased reached him).

Colonial campaigns were not going to have any significant impact upon the outcome of the war in Europe. At best for the Allies occupied German colonies would provide tropical raw materials for the war effort. In this dimension of the war, however, the Allies already had an immense advantage, since much of the world was in practice 'European' and therefore belligerent. Britain and France were the greatest colonial powers, with the largest and most developed extra-European empires linked to the motherland by extensive shipping and telegraph networks. Russia's empire was also huge – although contiguous, it was more difficult to exploit commercially owing to the problems of land transportation over vast distances and Russia's relatively restricted access to the world's sea-lanes after Turkey entered the war. To this could be added the tropical resources of the vast, although as yet poorly developed, Belgian Congo, and in time those of Italy's North and East African colonies.

The global contest was not over imperial assets: the Allies had won the colonial war before the European war had really begun, and thereafter imperial manpower, raw materials and overseas production would increasingly supplement that at home. Since the world's trading systems were highly integrated before 1914, a contest for neutral assets would develop. Although not in the war, sovereign neutral states would find themselves embroiled in the conflict raging around them because the war was in them from its start. Neutral governments had to decide on and take steps to defend their status, while political parties and the press set about manipulating public opinion in favour of neutrality or intervention, or cultivating sympathy for one side or the other. But this was diplomacy – meanwhile, economics had free reign.

There was much potential profit in a war that pitted industries against each other and relied on the world's trading systems. That applied to both belligerents and neutrals. As an enterprising and ambitious young businessman Farson wanted his share of 'the mushrooming war order business'. After learning the ins and outs of doing business in Russia for a year, he went into partnership with an enterprising Scandinavian merchant who had been sent to America to purchase foodstuffs on behalf of the Swedish government. While their main endeavour was to sell American motor vehicles to the Russians, 'Landby and Farson Inc.: New York-Stockholm-Petrograd' was not averse to trading with Germany too, since the profits were better.[47] A world war would reach everywhere in its voracious need for manpower and material. Farson and his employers were not alone: American businessmen, Swedish merchants, Argentinean cattle ranchers, Chilean miners, Chinese labourers, Danish merchant sailors, Dutch farmers, Japanese steelworkers, Portuguese fishermen, Spanish textile workers and Swiss bankers would all be going to war.

Before she became a belligerent, America was a war profiteer: 'The major role the United States was destined to play in the First World War was that of economic powerhouse and supplier of munitions, food and money to Britain and her allies.'[48] By 1916, 40 percent of British war expenditure was spent in the United States, with harmful effects on Britain's balance of payments and the stability of the currency. It meant that during the course of the war America was to supersede Britain as the world's leading financial power. Such was the price of fighting and winning a world war: $83 million per week by the time America entered the war. A large part of the profit went to American bankers and businessmen. In January 1915 the banking house J. P. Morgan and Co secured a concession as the War Office and Admiralty's sole purchasing agent in the States. By the end of 1916 $20 billion worth of trade had been commissioned at 2 percent commission on the first $10 million of purchases and 1 percent thereafter.[49] J. P. Morgan also acted until February 1917 as the financial agency for dollar war loans raised on the American markets, much of which would then be spent on American goods. Expertise flowed the other way after the Ministry of Munitions established resident missions across the Atlantic to manage production facilities for the Allied war effort. Although the volatility of American public opinion – divided between pro-Ally, pro-German and pro-neutrality factions – obliged this economic activity to be carried on at arm's length from British diplomacy as a private commercial rather than a public enterprise, in effect before America entered the war the two economies had become intricately linked. This situation gave president Wilson a certain amount of diplomatic leverage, and Britain a limited degree of deference and a great deal of concern should America pull the plug on its supply and financial life-lines. Indeed by the end of 1916 Britain had liquidated most of its assets in the States to pay for war purchases and was teetering on the brink of bankruptcy unless a new loan could be raised in New York. To that extent American entry in spring 1917 came at just the right time to ensure that their new allies did not lose the war economically before they won it mil-itarily. Thereafter financial and commercial relations could be put on an official footing and conducted through the Treasury and the Foreign Office, while Britain could, with some relief, pass on financial responsi-bility for the coalition to the American Treasury.[50]

The commercial and economic imperatives of war drew in all neutral states. Sweden, for example, was at an economic and diplomatic cross-roads between the rival alliances that contested for Scandinavia resources. She would engage therefore on all fronts except the military. King Gustav V, who was married to a cousin of the kaiser, and his government were sympathetic to Germany, with which the nation had strong commercial and cultural links and political affinities, and hostile to Russia. Because of her geographical position, Sweden could never take sides against Ger-many, which had diplomatic leverage backed by the threat of military force. She 'traded with the enemy', both of the Allies and the Central powers: Swedish iron ore was a vital commodity to both alliances' war industries.[51] Diplomatically she negotiated with the Allies over blockade, although they never made as much progress with the Swedes in restricting exports to Germany as they did with the Dutch, Danes and Swiss.[52] By 1917, the value of Sweden's export trade with Germany had risen from £10 million to £18.3 million.[53] In fact, she acted as the intermediary through which trade with the enemy flowed both ways: chemical dyes from Germany to the Allies, and rubber and foodstuffs from the British Empire to the Central powers.[54] Her merchant ships carried goods for both sides and their owners did handsomely out of the trade. Travelling from New York to Stockholm in summer 1916 on the Danish passenger liner *Danske Fly*, Farson found himself part of 'a travelling circus of the war tycoons of that time'. Prominent among them were three Scandina-vian shipping barons. One, Louis Hannivig, had made $40 million selling out his shipbuilding contracts to the British in New York, while Johann-son's ships were earning as much as they had cost to build from one month's charter. They were living in 'a typhoon of wealth' and the champagne flowed before breakfast.[55] Sweden was a conduit for goods to Russia, which gave her some bargaining power with the Allies. Also for intelli-gence: Captain Montagu Consett, British naval attaché in Scandinavia and head of the Secret Intelligence Service there, provided a wealth of useful statistical information to the Admiralty's fact-starved blockade department (and infuriated his diplomatic colleagues in the process).[56] The Swedish diplomatic service provided a message service for German diplomats in other neutral nations. But as the Allied blockade tightened, Sweden's golden period came to an end and fuel shortages and Entente-imposed import restrictions plunged the economy into recession by the end of 1916. Food rationing had to be introduced. Sweden's war experience mirrored that of the belligerents. Some businessmen made healthy profits, but ordinary Swedes experienced similar privations to civilians living under German rule in Europe: public disorder would spread across Sweden as everywhere else during 1917. The political realignment this forced brought a liberal government to power, and thereafter Sweden inclined towards the Allied side. Physically, Sweden lost 290,000 tons of shipping and 9,800 lives.[57]

Sweden's experience is illustrative of that of the smaller neutral states. Other countries would fare better or worse according to their situation and utility to the belligerents. To be neutral was to be a pawn in the diplomatic game between the wartime alliances. At the same time, after the world's commercial systems reformed around the needs of the Allied war effort following their initial dislocation, neutrals and their citizens became agents at a time when both the risks and rewards of commercial capitalism were exaggerated. Although Allied maritime power and blockade policy increasingly constrained the possibilities for truly free trade and submarine warfare threatened maritime commerce physically, individuals, businesses and some nations would do very well out of servicing the war machines.

By 1917 Sweden was also a haven for those who sought peace. It was in Stockholm in summer 1917 that socialists tried to gather for an international conference to debate peace terms (although many were refused passports by their government). National governments' anxieties about a pacifist left wing that would undermine the war effort, while valid, were slow to bear fruit. By the time peace started to feature on the domestic political and diplomatic agendas in 1917, socialists could find a certain amount of common ground with others who were tired of war, although the nature of the peace was disputed. Before then, belligerent social democrats imposed other terms for their cooperation in the war. Workers' rights, and capitalists' profits, became the battlegrounds on which labour's representatives would make a stand.

As the shells scandal unfolded, the Lord Chancellor, Viscount Haldane, acknowledged that workshops, and the labour that manned them, were becoming the centre of gravity of industrial war. 'It is no use saying these things in the House of Lords, where they do not echo far enough,' Haldane protested as the political debate unfolded. 'They should be said in the great industrial centres, in the factories and the workshops, and the shipyards.'[58] This was already becoming a war of labour, and politically that entailed compromises with socialism and constraints on capitalism. A war machine relied on the cooperation of private manufacturers and workmen and needed human producers in their millions, and it was becoming the government's role to mediate between employers and employees in the interests of national solidarity and efficiency.

Although international socialism's pretence to being antiwar had been immediately exposed in July 1914, the labour movement's attitude to war, as it was to most things, remained conflicted. Socialism's structure, philosophies and objectives certainly differed from nation to nation, while within each country there was little consensus. Essentially, two broad strands of socialism competed for workers' loyalty. Social democratic trade unions and political parties advocated working within the existing political and economic system to improve labour's working conditions and political influence. In Europe's more progressive liberal states labour parties participated in the electoral system. Indeed in France where socialism had made the most political progress the so-called Radical Party, the left-wing opposition from the early years of the republic that now sat firmly in the centre ground of French politics, had become the mainstay of most Third Republican coalitions, while members of the *Parti socialiste français* had taken ministerial portfolios in prewar governments. Certain core goals of social democracy such as the eight-hour working day had still to be won. For Germany's social democrats in particular the war presented an opportunity. Loyal support for the war effort might at last remove the stigma of disloyalty to the nation, and mobilisation might present an opportunity to press for organised labour's cherished workplace demands.[59]

Protecting and enhancing workers' rights would be central to social democracy's wartime political agenda, as in time would be the restriction of capitalists' profits. Antiwar agitation would be confined to the left-wing fringe, those parliamentary socialists who had voted against war credits in 1914 on grounds of conscience or conviction, and those revolutionaries who advocated armed class struggle to bring down the capitalist system in its entirety. The fact that capitalism and imperialism were ranging abroad as two global horsemen of the apocalypse inevitably and predictably galvanized radical opposition. As more and more money was spent on war making, and the voracious need for manpower forced more and more men to take up arms or tools in the capitalists' war, the ideologues of the revolutionary left issued their own calls to arms. At the antiwar socialists' Zimmerwald Congress in September 1915 Leon Trotsky issued a declaration for peace. Rather than collaborate in the capitalists' war, the world's workers should unite against the conflict.[60] Such sentiments were marginalised in the early patriotic frenzy, although they would in time find their champion. The anti-Tsarist Russian revolutionary Vladimir Ilyich Ulyanov (better known by the pseudonym he adopted in 1901, Lenin) would eventually emerge as the most vituperative critic of capitalism's war. In 1915, however, revolutionary socialism had yet to agree on its stance on the war.

In spring 1915, Lenin revealed his divisive agenda at a congress of antiwar socialist women in Berne in Switzerland. He persuaded the Russian delegation to propose an immediate split with the social democrats. On that occasion Lenin failed: 'We did not want to separate ourselves from the masses by order of Lenin,' Toni Sender recollected, 'for it was among these masses that our agitation for peace must be conducted.'[61] Lenin persisted, declaring war on capitalism and the perfidious social democrats who sustained its warmongering. Lenin saw the war as the ultimate crime of capitalism, but he also saw in it the seeds of his class enemies' downfall.[62] In *Imperialism, the Highest Stage of Capitalism*, published in Zurich in 1916, he argued (in measured terms, in order not to fall foul of the censor) that monopoly capitalism and the competitive imperial system that it encouraged had caused the devastating global war. Free of the restrictions imposed by the press he was more forthright. Lenin turned on the social democrats and 'organised labour' who were conniving in the mass slaughter. He looked instead to the proletariat, workers who had been duped by the bourgeoisie and their social democratic class-traitor allies into toiling for the capitalists' war or sacrificing their lives in the trenches. He would build his postwar utopian society on the one group apparently untainted by war guilt.

None of this would have mattered much if Lenin had remained a brooding exiled revolutionary in Switzerland. He had been exiled from Russia (again) after the 1905 revolution. Revolutionary sentiment there was far from quelled, although socialism was far from united. Lenin's own Social Democratic Party, that sought to seize power on behalf of the urban workers as advocated by Karl Marx in *The Communist Manifesto*, was itself divided between a democratic 'minority' Menshevik wing who advocated working within the existing Russian political system and Lenin's 'majority' Bolsheviks, who were organised into a revolutionary cadre dedicated to seizing power in Russia by armed insurrection. They remained for now a marginal force in imperial Russian politics, although on occasion, as when they blocked workers' participation in the activities of the new War Industries Committee, the Bolsheviks showed that they had some power to obstruct a truly national war effort.[63] When Lenin did return to Russia in spring 1917 he found a very different country – one in which his extreme rhetoric and philosophy would find an attentive audience.

Labour began the war a divided movement, which had to debate and formulate its stance on the unfolding war. Revolution, however, was not on the cards. While revolutionaries brooded, powerless in the onrush of capitalism's crowning folly, social democrats seized their opportunity. In Britain and France the opportunities were real, as labour joined wartime governments. In Germany and Austria-Hungary they remained hypothetical. Bethmann Hollweg could profess to the assembled Reichstag deputies, following the kaiser's lead, that there were 'no more parties, only Germans', but rhetoric was no substitute for real power and influence – particularly since the chancellor went on to assert that such a 'marvellous spirit' should be sustained once Germany had won 'a glorious and happy peace'.[64]

SINCE WAR WAS GOOD FOR BUSINESS, CAPITALISTS COULD BE EXPECTED TO BE more committed to the war effort. The businessmen who owned factories, mines, railways and shipping companies engaged actively with war making from the start, as did bankers and investors. Reconciling producers' and financiers' interests with those of their workers and customers as much as anything determined the mushrooming of war-related ministries and government-sponsored management organisations, which were designed to reconcile competing interests in the cause of efficient, cost-effective and above all harmonious concentration on defeating the enemy. A reasonable level of profit was accepted, although restriction of excess profits was one thing that socialists and liberals might agree on – the former out of class conviction, the latter since profligacy was inimical to an efficient war effort. In wartime Germany offshoots of the Ministry of War or the army would take responsibility for managing wartime business relations, whereas in Britain, France and Italy it would generally be civilian ministers and civil servants, liaising with but not controlled by the military. In Austria-Hungary too the military and state bureaucracy generally held sway, whereas in Russia as has been indicated, the state and private interests competed in a chaotic, inefficient power struggle.

Prewar preparations for managing the war economy had not been entirely neglected, but these were inconsistent and piecemeal, and generally directed towards immediate wartime needs rather than long-term war planning. After the nation's poor showing in the South African War Britain had created a standing Committee of Imperial Defence, which sat under the prime minister's chairmanship from 1902. Its secretariat managed a 'War Book' that laid out the steps to be taken by government departments when war broke out. The Defence of the Realm Act that established the principle of extended government powers in wartime would come into force on the outbreak of war, though how it would be applied in practice remained to be seen. Gradually ministerial power and civil service management would be extended into economic activities previously determined by the market, and professional businessmen and technical experts would be brought in to advise and assist. For example, within a week of the outbreak of war the government set up a Cabinet Committee on Food Supplies chaired by Home Secretary Reginald McKenna to purchase foodstuffs in bulk and passed the Unreasonable Withholding of Foodstuffs Act to prevent food hoarding and profiteering.[65] In this perhaps Britain was more advanced and perceptive than Germany, where 1851's outdated State of Siege Law handed power to local military satraps with little understanding of economic practices or business and labour organisations.

In invaded France civil-military divisions were enshrined in both the organisation of the country and its management practices. In the *zone des armées* behind the front martial law and military authority held sway, while civilian administration persisted in the rest of France. Military needs had to be channelled through the war ministry's bureaucracy. Following Millerand's dismissal in November 1915 generals were to hold the portfolio of minster of war until March 1917, although the ministry (and parliament) continually restrained the wartime powers of the army rather than acting as its instrument.[66] Perhaps this was inevitable in a state in which a precedent for wartime military dictators existed: certainly there was widespread fear among politicians that Joffre aspired to such as role.

In Germany, in contrast, by the terms of the State of Siege Law elements of military law and authority – administered by the regional military commands – were imposed upon civilian life. Occupied territories also came under military administration, tying the whole domestic and over-border war effort to the OHL. Nominally the kaiser, who deployed himself to army administrative headquarters at Koblenz for the duration of the war, was supreme war lord.[67] As the war went on, however, real power passed to the chief of the General Staff at the OHL, where strategy was planned and from which the war economy was increasingly directed. After the duumvirate of Hindenburg and Ludendorff took over responsibility for strategy and war management in August 1916, an effective military dictatorship had come about in Germany. In Austria things went the other way. For the first half of the war Conrad had near-dictatorial powers, in the Austrian half of the empire at least. A new emperor and continued failure led to his demotion to an army command in 1917.

\* \* \*

ENGAGING WITH THE OUTBREAK OF WAR HAD HELD GOVERNMENTS' ATTENTION in August and September 1914. Since they were essential for military mobilisation and deployment railway companies were brought under state control from the outset, although managed in different ways. A Railway Executive Committee of railway-company managers came into being in Britain in August 1914. This short-term mobilisation expedient persisted for the rest of the war. In Germany, where national rail policy always had a strategic dimension, much of the network was already state-owned and run. The General Staff had a railway logistics department, charged pre-war with constructing the infrastructure needed for invading Germany's Western neighbours quickly and working out the details of mobilisation and deployment with Germany's railway managers.[68]

From October to December 1914 the expectation that with a little more effort there might be a military decision had gainsaid much long-term economic planning. The immediate needs of the armies at the front, for reinforcements and munitions, took precedence. From early 1915 the model of wartime economic management started to take shape. Once governments woke up to the reality of the war and hurried to mobilise effectively there was a spring of opportunity for both capitalists and workers. Contracts mushroomed, not just for raw materials, weapons and munitions from armaments manufacturers and other engineering concerns, but for food, clothing, shipping and more prosaic items such as telephones and typewriters to sustain the expanding military and civilian bureaucracies behind the war effort. The initial rush to order war materials from domestic producers, allies and neutrals was an unregulated free-for-all. Problems of access to external markets became apparent, partly financial and partly practical, as shipping was taken up at unprecedented rates. High prices could potentially be charged by manufacturers as demand outstripped supply. High wages could also be expected as the rapid economic expansion (coupled with the mobilising of young men) put an end to unemployment. The response, common to all the belligerents, was twofold: legislation to regulate the marketplace, wages and prices, and direct state intervention in the workplace. On the whole, governments were able to exploit workers' support for the national cause, expressed in a voluntary renunciation of industrial militancy and restrictive practices, to negotiate significant workplace concessions with trade unions, for the duration of the war at least.[69]

Britain's economic mobilisation followed the model already evident in France and Germany. 'Business as usual' as the British government disingenuously dubbed its economic strategy actually 'implied an unusual level of government intervention'.[70] The March 1915 Shells and Fuses

Agreement, for example, legislated for dilution of labour – the employment of unskilled workers in munitions factories – for the duration of the war. For their part, employers undertook to revert to prewar conditions once the war was over and not to dismiss skilled workers or reduce wages as a consequence of dilution. The Treasury Agreement that followed effectively introduced a truce in the struggle between capital and labour for the duration of the war. The unions accepted dilution and agreed not to strike, while the government undertook to administer compulsory arbitration in labour disputes.[71] Yet in part this agreement was a response to an outbreak of strikes and labour unrest on the Clyde in February. As with socialist parties, trade unions had their militant elements willing to push the socialist agenda forcefully despite hostilities. Concessions such as a guarantee to maintain wages for skilled trades and even for unskilled workers employed in them, as well as restrictions on the level of profits in war industries, had to be made to the unions.[72] But with such economic concessions came a new degree of social compulsion. The July 1915 Munitions of War Act, introduced soon after the new ministry was set up, imposed restrictions on munitions workers' freedom of movement in the labour market, thereby acknowledging the principle of labour conscription. In future a munitions worker wishing to change jobs would have to obtain a 'leaving certificate', and therefore he could not sell his labour to the highest bidder in a free market.[73] Significantly too, the government became a large-scale employer of war workers in its own right. The rapid expansion of the munitions industry depended on the spread of national factories: thirty-four were set up by 1916. Similarly, the Munitions of War Act allowed the Ministry of Munitions to take control of private firms producing munitions, as well as to manage fuel supplies, raw material contracts and imports for shell production centrally.[74] It was a model of state management that could be adapted for other sectors of the war economy as the conflict intensified.

OVER THE COURSE OF THE WAR PUBLIC EXPENDITURE ROSE THREEFOLD IN Russia (until 1916, and it would have risen further thereafter had revolution not intervened), four-and-a-half times in France, fivefold in Germany and more than five-and-a-half times in Britain by 1918, growth figures indicative of the relative economic strength of the principal belligerents.[75] Bloch's prediction that war would bankrupt modern states proved wide of the mark. It did, however, oblige radical financial measures to pay for it.

Inter-Allied cooperation first took shape in the financial sector, where after stalemate set in the matter of credit for war purchases had to be addressed. Selling foreign assets was one way of financing purchases abroad, but by the end of 1914 Russia had all but exhausted her foreign holdings and gold reserves. Allied finance ministers first met in February 1915, establishing a close liaison between their central banks and agreeing on a policy for joint foreign loans and credit to lesser allies. Thereafter Britain started to extend credit to France and Russia, and Italy after she joined the war. France in turn lent to Russia, Belgium and Serbia (generally charging higher rates of interest than she was paying to her British creditor – some elements of capitalism remained sacrosanct). This indicated that international war finance was to function through bilateral credit exchanges rather than gold-backed transactions. It was the same among the Central powers. Germany assumed Britain's role of credit banker to her allies, while Austria-Hungary made subsidiary loans to Bulgaria and Turkey; the settlement of inter-alliance debts was to be held over until the end of the war when, hopefully, indemnities extracted from the beaten enemy would ease the repayment burden.[76]

Laying the financial foundations for a long war took time. Funds could be raised on the domestic and international markets, but in both cases there had to be a balance between credit and revenue, since to pay for the war from revenue alone would have bankrupted all the belligerents in short order. Revenue could be raised by increasing domestic taxes, which all belligerents did, but the main source of domestic funds was further credit raised through war bond issues. Patriotic citizens initially rushed to invest in government bonds issued everywhere in the early weeks of the war: interest rates were good, and they were confident in the national cause and the likelihood of a quick victory. In practice this meant that the wealthy at least would add a financial investment in the war effort to their emotional one, although how much this contributed to intensifying belligerency after stalemate set in is impossible to judge.

The sums involved in financing the war were astronomical on both sides. Despite some anxious moments, credit never dried up, even if it was much less easy to secure by the second half of the war. With some 35 percent of Allied early-war purchases in America being financed on the New York exchanges, some $2.4 billion in total, by 1917 the Allies had mortgaged themselves heavily to the United States, whose investment in Allied victory had to be sustained. After America entered the war Britain's almost exhausted credit line was extended further, with almost 69 percent of Allied purchases being financed on credit thereafter.[77] This suggests how everywhere war credit, belligerent or neutral, represented an investment in a future victory. Therefore only one side would get its money back (with interest), unless the war ended with a negotiated peace, in which case all belligerents would remain in hock. Following the precedent of nineteenth-century wars it was expected that ultimately the loser would pay – war reparations to the victors would be added to the debt accumulated by the vanquished, leaving the defeated enemy economically prostrate and unable to challenge the verdict of the battlefield for the foreseeable future.

ALL THIS ECONOMIC ACTIVITY WAS DIRECTED TOWARDS EQUIPPING ARMIES and navies properly and prosecuting the war more vigorously and effectively. As well as counting men, general staffs counted guns and shells and all the other paraphernalia of modern warfare. Material was the factor which when integrated with manpower would determine the outcome of battles and the nature and course of the war. The big battalions might win, but they would win more quickly and at less cost to themselves if they were better equipped than the enemy. Indeed, as the Germans demonstrated early on even the smaller battalions could win if better equipped.

By 1916 Lord Northcliffe could appositely observe after a visit to the British front in France that 'everyone in an army knows that he is part of an intricate machine, and that although his part may only be a small one, it is essential to the whole'. Northcliffe could report with awe on the vast assemblage of war material behind the front: shells stacked in their millions, huge dumps of food, clothing and small-arms ammunition, thousands of motor vehicles to transport everything, vast tented camps and 'literally miles of hut hospitals' put up along the Channel coast to deal with the large numbers of wounded and sick. The 'impression that one gets is that now war has settled down to a regular business, it proceeds at the bases with the clockwork regularity of a great business'.[78] And an 'army behind the army' existed, of mechanics, telegraphists, doctors and nurses, store men and clerks, keeping the whole war machine running. Weapons had to be maintained and repaired, troops and goods transported to and from the front, casualties recorded and personal effects returned to families; and in a commendable effort to reduce the escalating costs of modern war men of the Salvage Corps searched recently captured enemy lines for unused bullets, scrap metal, damaged but repairable military equipment and even old rags, which could be sold at fifty pounds per ton.[79] Clearly by the middle of 1916 when Northcliffe was writing it had become a war of industry, both at home and at the front.

It had been Northcliffe's newspapers, including The Times which broke the shells scandal, that had been Asquith and his ministers' most persistent critics: indeed even as he toured the army's lines of communication Northcliffe could speculate that 'owing to their burning desire or by the pressure of the authorities men who, in the end would have killed more Germans by the use of their own particular skill in the workshop have left the anvil, the tools, the lathe, or the foundry for the firing line', a final dig at Asquith's chopping and changing mobilisation policy which before the introduction of conscription failed to direct manpower appropriately. Not long afterwards, Northcliffe's papers would back Lloyd George in his bid for the premiership and his intention to mobilise the nation's and empire's resources still further, to prosecute what had become 'the horrible, grim, mechanical business' of war to which those war machines were devoted.[80]

It had taken two years for the British war machine to take shape and to start to produce war material in sufficient quantities to sustain an expanded army and deficient allies in the field. Although British mobilisation had not been a thoroughly efficient or well-managed process, no other prime minister might have done better during those early months of improvisation and false starts. Lloyd George liked to take credit for the mature war machine while downplaying the foundations laid by Asquith's other ministers and the importance of earlier, faltering steps towards national mobilisation. Asquith's style of government, departmental and consensual, was looking increasingly unsuitable for managing modern war by the time he left office. Lloyd George offered the country only 'a system for enrolling the whole nation for war works of sorts, more or less on the German idea as a reply to Germany's action in the direction.' The 'great ovation' that Asquith received from his parliamentary colleagues at the same time was an acknowledgement of the contribution he had made to setting Britain on the right path to a functional war effort.[81]

By the end of 1916, the 'year of attrition', both sides had recognised that it was a war in which the efforts of the men in uniform had to be sustained by the sweat of workers and the regulation of private enterprise on the home front. During that year the public-private Allied war effort caught up with and overtook Germany's increasingly militarized 'state of siege' economy. Germany's response, the December 1916 Patriotic Auxiliary Service Law to which Lloyd George was referring, introduced directed labour-service for all male workers aged seventeen to sixty, a belated recognition of the fact that the Allies would always overmaster the Central powers economically unless they could be defeated on the battlefield quickly. This measure probably came too late and could make little difference. By this time there were very few men who had not already been inducted into the army or the war economy, and despite calls for female conscription German women would not be mobilised by law in the same way as men. Yet it represented more than a further extension of state power over labour. The law allowed the army to concentrate industrial production by closing nonessential private businesses and turning others over to manufacturing for the war effort.[82] Germany, true to Prussian historical tradition, was once again becoming 'an army with a state'. The fact that socialists and trade union representatives were called on to implement the new law in the workplace, moreover, indicated that the state was finally willing to acknowledge social democrats as partners in the war effort.

THE TRANSITION TO A WAR ECONOMY WAS NOT A SMOOTH PROCESS, SOCIAL democratic labour's patriotic support notwithstanding. Every nation faced mobilisation problems, if not as acute as those in Britain which had to create a mass army and the war industries to sustain it from scratch, and each needed an 'organiser of victory' to engage the home front in the war effort, be it Thomas in France, Polivanov in Russia or Rathenau (and later First Quartermaster-General Erich Ludendorff) in Germany. Great Britain found Lloyd George, who approached war mobilisation with vigour and was not shy of overturning old-fashioned an inefficient practices in the pursuit of fuller mobilisation. It is hard to judge exactly when mobilisation ended and the mature war machines were functioning: perhaps it never did, since production everywhere went on increasing into the final year of the war. By the time Lloyd George handed over the Ministry of Munitions in June 1916 there was still some way to go to reach full mobilisation, although the proper systems were in place and functioning. Productivity would increase exponentially thereafter as the military machine's voracious need for weapons, bullets and shells grew apace. While 1915's improvisations led to a twelvefold increase in shell production that year, there was to be another twelvefold increase by 1917, when 76,200,000 shells of all calibres were manufactured.[83]

Schlieffen's prediction that an attritional strategy was unworkable because of its costs proved mistaken. While there were political mistakes and social frictions during mobilisation, European economies and societies proved adaptable enough, with labour willing, private enterprise able and financiers skilful enough to remodel practices to fit wartime needs relatively quickly and with the state taking overall responsibility for the transition. By the end of the first year of stalemate the trench lines along which the fight for supremacy would take place separated command economies gearing up for all-out war. Although the pacifist philosopher Bertrand Russell was appalled by his observation that wartime economic policy had the objective of 'maximum slaughter at minimum expense' he was essentially correct, and the time was coming to test that hypothesis.[84]

Inevitability, the principal land fronts would become the proving ground of war machines. A strategy of attrition involved engaging them directly: this became Allied policy in 1916, ratcheting up the costs and consequences of war. The war machines that were operating by then were not perfected, but they functioned well enough to enable the armies to fight attritional war in France and Flanders and along the Italian front. Here railway-based communications allowed armies of millions of men armed with the increasing amounts of war material they required to be engaged. Alternative strategies focused on secondary fronts had proved ineffective by then. At Salonika where the Allies began a new campaign in October 1915, for example, half a million men would be deployed, but the railway infrastructure and military wherewithal required to mount anything more than localised offensives could not be provided before 1918. No wonder that the German high command considered the Salonika front their largest prison camp.

# EIGHT

# CONTROLLING
# THE SEAS

J
UST AFTER MIDNIGHT ON 1 APRIL 1916 THE ARMED TRAWLER *OLIVINE*
and two drifters of the Royal Navy's Auxiliary Patrol weighed anchor
and steamed out into the Thames estuary to engage an unidentified
vessel. After issuing a challenge which went unanswered, the patrol ships
opened fire. 'We surrender; have no arms. Come alongside,' came a pan-
icked voice. The *Olivine* launched its dinghy, and on closing with the
adversary its commander Lieutenant Mackintosh was surprised to see a
vast balloon emerge out of the darkness, with a Prussian officer in full
uniform adorned with the Iron Cross standing amid the wreckage. Worthy of an April Fool's joke, this was probably the only time a naval vessel
captured a German zeppelin! Seventeen surviving crewmen were taken
prisoner and the airship taken it tow, although it collapsed and sank before landfall.[1]

The capture of Zeppelin L15, which had ditched in the sea off Essex
after being hit by antiaircraft fire while returning from a bombing raid,
was one extraordinary, memorable incident in an otherwise routine naval
war along the coasts and in the narrow seas around the British Isles and
in the Mediterranean. Stopping and inspecting merchant vessels; minelaying and minesweeping; the 'cat and mouse' hunt for enemy submarines; scouting and patrolling: these were the daily duties of hundreds
of small ships (fishing vessels, pleasure boats, yachts and paddle-steam-
ers) now commissioned, armed and manned by Royal Navy reservists.
Between 1914 and 1918 they were they the eyes and ears, and to a great
extent the claws and teeth, of the world's most powerful navy.

The Royal Navy flotilla labouring night and day, year round and
in all weathers in the North Sea and the English Channel made a vital,

yet generally unrecognised, contribution to defeating the Central powers. The action of naval power – the 'blockade' as it was dubbed, applying a not entirely accurate term from the preindustrial age to modern economic and maritime warfare – was slow, steady, always working, rarely dynamic and only after some time really effective. Commercial warfare was not glamorous and its practitioners with humdrum roles, destroyer and submarine captains, naval ratings and merchant seamen, intelligence officers and statisticians, generally went unrecognised. But blockade and counterblockade characterised the naval war between 1914 and 1918 and had a growing impact on both home and fighting fronts.

'THE ATTITUDE OF WAITING' THAT A NAVY IMBUED WITH THE AUDACIOUS offensive spirit inculcated in naval officer since Nelson's time had been forced to assume galled everyone from the first lord of the Admiralty downwards, yet a fleet action remained elusive.[2] In December 1914 the German Imperial High Seas Fleet steamed out to challenge to the Royal Navy at a time when British numerical superiority had been temporarily weakened by mechanical problems and the detachment of three battle cruisers to deal with von Spee's squadron. Battle cruisers bombarded the coastal towns of Scarborough, Whitby and Hartlepool – another atrocity to add to Germany's growing list – in an attempt to lure the Royal Navy's Grand Fleet out and draw the pursuing British warships onto a line of waiting submarines. The commander of the Grand Fleet, Admiral Sir John Jellicoe, took the bait only partially. He sent one of his three battle squadrons out to trap the German battle cruisers, which in turn was nearly surprised by the whole German battle fleet. The German battle cruisers got away and the few cruiser encounters that did occur were badly handled. If anything, the incident highlighted the problem of finding enemy ships and bringing them to action, which would not go away. The 'Dogger Bank action' in January 1915, an attempt to trap the next German battle cruiser raiding squadron, was equally muddled. SMS *Blücher*, an armoured cruiser bringing up the rear of the German squadron, was caught and sunk, but in the ensuing confusion the other German ships escaped.[3] Thereafter, the Germans curtailed capital ship incursions into the North Sea for nearly a year.

Churchill famously quipped that Jellicoe was 'the only man on either side who could lose the war in an afternoon', but he was wise enough not to put his ships at too great a risk. The waiting game could continue once German surface raiders had been swept from the high seas and the Royal Navy had demonstrated which fleet dominated the North Sea. The Allies' navies would steadily undermine the Central powers' home front prosperity and civilian morale with economic blockade while their armies were worn down on land. Germany could only fight back with the other weapons in their naval arsenal, the submarine and the mine. These would now determine the course of the maritime war, which by 1915 was starting to focus on disrupting the supply of war materials rather than naval battles.

THERE WERE CERTAIN RULES – THEY LACKED THE STATUS OF INTERNATIONAL laws since not all states had ratified them, and they remained subject to interpretation – that governed the conduct of commerce warfare. By the terms of the 1856 Declaration of Paris belligerents were expected formally to announce the blockade of a port and to maintain warships at sea off that port. 'Blockade runners' would have to take their chances with the cordon of patrolling ships. Captured ships carrying contraband cargo could legitimately be committed to a maritime prize court and sold. What worked in the age of sail, however, was problematic now that torpedo boats and long-range shore batteries could drive off the ships that maintained such a 'close blockade'. Instead the Royal Navy instigated 'distant blockade' in August 1914. Standing patrols were established in the northern approaches between Scotland and Norway and across the Strait of Dover, through which merchant ships coming across the Atlantic would have to pass on their way to Germany or the neutrals through which she traded. While far safer for the blockading ships, distant blockade made control of trade in the North Sea less tight. Scandinavia, for example, was beyond the reach of the physical blockade. Its legality was also dubious.

The more bullish warriors at the Admiralty chafed at the navy's inability to attack Germany more directly. Fisher fully appreciated that Germany had adopted Frederick the Great's Seven Years War defensive strategy of '[using] his interior position to deliver violent attacks beyond each of his frontiers successively', thereby holding the hostile coalition at bay until it had exhausted itself and split. Sea power, he argued, might redress Germany's advantage on land. The only real threat to Frederick had been from a Russian landing on Germany's Baltic coast, and Fisher pressed to recreate such an operation, risky though it was in the age of mines and submarines.[4] Churchill agreed: 'The Baltic is the only theatre in which naval action can appreciably shorten the war. Denmark must come in, and the Russians be let loose on Berlin.'[5] Once stalemate set in and speculative strategic memoranda began to flourish, various elaborate schemes were floated for seizing an island off the German coast to enforce the blockade more closely, to mine German coastal waters and to push

British naval power into the Baltic.[6] Submarines and mines could bottle up the High Seas Fleet, and had not the Royal Navy 'Copenhagened' enemy fleets in the past?* Yet this was no longer the age of Nelson and, perhaps fortuitously, the distraction of the naval expedition to the Dardanelles, Fisher's resignation and Churchill's demotion from the Admiralty in May 1915 ensured that such operations were never tried. Fisher was undoubted right in recognising that 'passive pressure of our fleet' would only exhaust Germany very slowly, but it was improbable that active naval measures would have brought Germany to her knees, and the cost to the Royal Navy would undoubtedly have been heavy.[7]

THE MARITIME WAR THEREFORE BECAME BY DEFAULT ONE OF STEADY COMmercial and economic strangulation, as far as neutrals would allow. As the war intensified Britain unilaterally extended the range of merchandises that could be considered contraband. 'Conditional contraband' goods such as foodstuffs and coal, and 'civilian' commodities such as cotton, rubber, fertilizers and metallic ores were placed one by one on a growing list of goods that the Royal Navy would confiscate if they were bound for Germany. By applying the long-established principle of 'continuous voyage', whereby ships bound for neutral ports could be detained if the final destination of their cargo was a belligerent state, intermediaries' trade with the enemy could be constrained further. The fact that the Board of Trade purchased goods seized at a fair market price might mollify businessmen (they were after all useful for the Allied war effort too), but the arbitrary rewriting of international treaties and interference with neutrals' property at sea would anger statesmen – America's president Woodrow Wilson in particular.

By 1915 a more pragmatic, conciliatory approach was adopted. Wherever possible the Foreign Office sought to negotiate bilateral agreements by which neutrals would voluntarily restrict their trade with the Central powers. The Netherlands Overseas Trust, an association of Dutch importers who agreed not to send goods on to Germany set up in January 1915 by agreement between the Foreign Office and the Dutch government, furnished a model for voluntarily limitation of the reexport trade that was copied in Switzerland and Denmark. Some neutrals – such as Sweden that had a more lucrative trade with Germany – refused such restrictions. This measure might limit onward transmission of imported commodities, but it did not stop neutrals from exporting home produced

---

*In 1801 and 1807 the Royal Navy had carried out pre-emptive attacks against the Danish fleet at Copenhagen.

goods, foodstuffs in particular, at a premium and replacing them with cheaper substitutes purchased on the world market. To limit this Britain tried to impose import quotas calculated on neutrals' prewar domestic production and consumption, as well as to prepurchase neutrals' produce for themselves. Ultimately, by the terms of December 1915's Trading with the Enemy Act, the Foreign Office drew up 'black lists' of neutral firms trading with the Central powers, with which British shipping firms were forbidden to do business; of neutral shipping lines conveying cargoes to Germany, whose ships were subject to confiscation if intercepted; and of banks and other firms financing enemy trade.

Owing to the commercial acumen of neutrals and the self-interest of many Allied businessmen, although blockade reduced imports and exports compared to prewar levels, Germany and her allies seemed perfectly able to function in a restricted wartime global trading economy. By 1915 it was becoming evident that the Board of Trade lacked clear statistics on exactly how much trade had been conducted with and by the enemy and neutrals before the war and how much was still getting through, directly or via neutrals. Without such information, there was no way of assessing how the blockade was functioning. The data the Board of Trade had cobbled together by June 1915 actually suggested that the blockade was having very little impact on Germany's ability to make and pay for war. Moreover, uncontrolled recruitment of workmen into the army was having a negative effect on Britain's own balance of payments. The logical conclusion drawn by advocates of 'business as usual' was that the blockade should be abandoned.[8] As with other aspects of the British and Allied war effort, it was not until mid-1915 that systems were even in place that were able to assess the effectiveness of economic warfare against Germany, and then they only served to prove Fisher's contention that maritime blockade alone would not 'bring Germany to a state of hopeless exhaustion . . . within a reasonable time'.[9]

As the war entered its second year, the over-ambition of the Admiralty's plan to bring Germany to her knees with economic warfare was obvious. If anything, the maritime war, in which naval efforts had focused on engaging the enemy's fleets or mounting amphibious operations, lagged behind the military one. Private enterprises and commercial bodies and ministries had certainly not been properly prepared for such a struggle in peacetime. The domestic limitations on blockade in it early years were as significant as uncooperative neutrals, which might of course have been anticipated. Too many competing agencies, divided responsibilities, poor inter-Allied coordination and unclear legal expedients combined to make blockade another slow, grinding weapon, just as it had been in previous wars, rather than the stab into the enemy's heart that the Admiralty had represented it to be pre-war. That the blockade was not going well was apparent to many come 1915, but what could be done about it was not obvious.

It was not until February 1916 that Asquith appointed Lord Robert Cecil minister of blockade. His job was to pull together and streamline the activities of the various maritime and commercial agencies distributed across government departments.[10] This reorganisation was part of the belated acknowledgment that 'business as usual' was an inappropriate economic strategy for prolonged war and heralded greater government interference with private businesses and overseas trade. 'The vital thing is to succeed in stopping German commerce,' Cecil pronounced, adding:

> I believe we have a perfect right to do that by every principle of international law. I believe it is perfectly legitimate for a belligerent to cut off all commerce from his enemy and to destroy and injure it by economic pressure exerted to the fullest extent . . . With that I think we ought to combine absolute respect for the rights of another nation.[11]

Thereafter, however, diplomatic niceties would impinge far less on economic and commercial warfare, potentially setting the Allies on a collision course with the United States. In July 1916 the 1909 Declaration of London that supposedly governed the conduct of war at sea was formally repudiated,* the precursor to deepening the blockade and pushing home the advantage secured in the first two years of the economic war.[12] By now various orders in council issued on matters of contraband and other high-handed interference in the international trading economy had effectively nullified the Declaration of London as anything more than a document on which neutrals could found their protests. This and other measures, such as the addition of many American firms to the Foreign Office's black lists, provoked Wilson's anger, and he appealed to Congress for powers to deny Allied shipping access to American ports.[13] Yet by September 1916 when such powers were granted, such retaliatory action in principle promised in practice to do considerable harm to United States' businesses since by then American economic activity was much more bound up with the Allied than the German war effort. This ensured that in the second half of the war the mature blockade would start to strangle Germany, working alongside Allied military forces to intensify attrition. America's entry into the war would merely enhance it.

By 1916 the Allied blockade had become familiar to neutrals (and their own businessmen) even if they did not like it and did all they could

---

*Although all the major belligerents had signed it, it was never ratified and therefore had only moral rather than legal force.

to evade or limit its operation. Measures such as the introduction of 'navicerts' (certificates issued by British embassies to merchants endorsing the legitimacy of their cargo and allowing them to pass freely through the blockade patrols) removed some of the more onerous obstructions to the flow of legitimate trade.[14] An international trading economy adapted to an ongoing war of attrition between two powerful coalitions had stabilised by 1916. Trade in scarce commodities with Germany and her allies might prove lucrative, but it was also more risky given Allied inspections and prize courts. The blockade was tight enough that few ships could evade inspection.[15] On the other hand, trade with and among the Allies was regular, more certain and equally likely to turn a profit, if subject to other risks as Germany's commerce raiders and submarines took their toll on merchant shipping. A lot of what the Allies did in the name of economic warfare was of questionable legality, but to a certain extent it was a matter of might is right, at least when that might was not applied indiscriminately. For at least in comparison to Germany's maritime strategy, the Allied blockade maintained some veneer of civility, and some pretence of respecting neutral rights. Moreover, when their own relations with the United States started to become strained, the Allies could always rely on Germany to do something worse to redress the balance.

GERMANY HAD ONE WEAPON, THE U-BOAT, AND ONE STRATEGY, UNRESTRICTED submarine warfare, that enabled her to challenge the Allies' command of the sea and control of global shipping and commerce. Like so many of Germany's strategic expedients, this was a controversial policy, and one that her diplomats shied away from until it became clear that the army was not going to win the war quickly. For the first six months of the war Germany largely restricted submarine attacks to warships, hoping to erode the superiority of the Royal Navy. Thereafter, in the tit-for-tat war on trade Germany raised the stakes. Her first declaration of unrestricted submarine warfare on 4 February 1915, by which she threatened to sink without warning any merchant ship entering the 'war area' around the British Isles, while provocative, was militarily ineffective. Germany had too few submarines to make an appreciable impact on British trade. Only twenty-one vessels were sunk before the declaration was rescinded. Diplomatically, unrestricted submarine warfare proved a disaster. Protests inevitably followed when American lives were lost in the notorious sinking of the liner *Lusitania* on 7 May, and again after the steamer *Arabic* was sunk on 19 August. The campaign was suspended on 18 September.[16]

During 1915, U-boats were railed overland in sections to the Austrian navy's Adriatic bases and reassembled, allowing the submarine war to be extended to the Mediterranean. At the end of May *U21* scored a notable success at the entrance to the Dardanelles when she sunk the elderly British battleships *Triumph* and *Majestic*. British warships supporting the land operations had to be withdrawn to safe harbours. Thereafter, troop ships, merchant vessels and even hospital ships fell prey to German and Austrian U-boats: the enclosed and relatively calm Mediterranean Sea turned out to be a particularly rich submarine hunting ground. Thirty-two Allied ships (100,000 tons) were sunk by U-boats or submarine-laid mines in the Mediterranean between January and March 1916, two-thirds of the ships sunk during that period. The situation worsened thereafter: 100 ships (149,000 tons) were sunk between April and June; 155 (312,000 tons) in the third quarter; and 129 (428,000 tons) in the final quarter of 1916. Moreover, over 400 Allied vessels were tied up in antisubmarine warfare.[17]

Falkenhayn pressed strongly for a resumption of unrestricted submarine warfare to coincide with his Verdun offensive in spring 1916, believing that this was the best way to attack the British while his land forces invested the French. The second time around, Bethmann Hollweg prevaricated – with few U-boats at Germany's disposal he was not confident that Britain could be starved into submission and feared permanently alienating the United States. After more American lives were lost when the unarmed liner *Sussex* was sunk on 24 April, another strong American protest obliged Germany to declare that she would abide by prize rules thereafter, Falkenhayn's threat to resign notwithstanding.[18] In practice, U-boat captains continued to sink merchant ships without much compunction through 1916, but with reelection looming Wilson could not exercise his threat to break off diplomatic relations with Germany while 'limited' submarine warfare was ongoing.

Certainly the Allies were getting the better of the sea war in its first phase. German surface raiders and U-boats could predate merchant shipping steadily, but Allied tonnage was not lost at an irreplaceable rate, or one that threatened to interrupt the supply of food or raw materials for the Allied war machine. A little over 6 percent of British merchant shipping was sunk in the first year of the war.[19] Germany's merchant shipping had been all but eliminated: indeed, such was the sense of commercial isolation that the German navy started to build large oceangoing submarines with a view to using them to run the blockade.

The presence of supporting battle fleets on both sides made the commerce war in the North Sea and the Atlantic possible, but they had little influence over its course and outcome. When the fleets did confront each other again in the North Sea in the Battle of Jutland from 31 May to 1 June 1916, the result was indecisive. Jutland was not a real battle, as the main fleets barely came to blows. Vice-Admiral Reinhard Scheer was hoping to engage and defeat a part of the British fleet, thereby improving the balance of naval force: with thirty-seven Royal Navy battleships and battle cruisers ranged against his twenty-one it was a brave strategy. Beatty's battle cruiser squadron came off worst in the first encounter, losing two modern ships to powerful internal explosions caused by a design fault. When the Grand Fleet appeared the outgunned High Seas Fleet steamed for port, after a short engagement in which another British battle cruiser was sunk and one German battle cruiser was crippled. The Grand Fleet gave chase, but as night fell the German fleet was able to evade its pursuers who feared torpedo attacks in the darkness. Jellicoe turned his battleships back to Scapa Flow, secure in the knowledge that the German fleet had returned to its self-imposed prison after assaulting its jailer. Both sides claimed victory. The fact that the German navy sunk more capital ships caused initial alarm, although this had little impact on the balance of naval power in the North Sea.[20] British naval mastery was acknowledged: thereafter the German fleet never ventured out of coastal waters or the safety of the enclosed Baltic Sea. Even if the fleets had come to blows, the mutual destruction of capital ships would not have ended the war in an afternoon. An overwhelming British victory would have strengthened the blockade, but that was hardly necessary, and this would not have brought the German army leadership to terms. A German victory would not have given them control of the seas: even if a substantial part of the High Seas Fleet had escaped destruction in a melee with a superior fleet, there was still a Franco-Italian battle fleet to defeat (the Royal Navy might not have wished to acknowledge the fact).

The naval war in the Mediterranean was a microcosm of the bigger picture. The escape of the German battle cruiser *Goeben* and heavy cruiser *Breslau* to the Straits at the start of the war was a naval nuisance (but of more political than military significance as it encouraged Turkey to join the war). But the ships themselves could be bottled up by superior Allied force. In 1915 an Anglo-French fleet was able to operate against the Dardanelles unimpeded by enemy capital ships: once again it was mines and submarines that took a toll on the Allied vessels there. In the Adriatic, at the Straits and in the Black Sea, where a Russian fleet contested control with the 'Turkish' *Goeben* and *Breslau*, a naval stalemate that mirrored that on land persisted throughout 1915.

THE ALLIES' CONTROL OF THE SEAS GAVE THEM GREATER STRATEGIC FLEXIbility, although sea power did not prove to be an antidote to land power. It did, however, encourage and enable so-called 'sideshows'. Without sea power the war against Turkey would have been difficult and the Salonika campaign impossible. More importantly, however, sea power allowed manpower and supplies to be brought from the British and French Empires for the battles in France. The apparent flexibility offered by sea power belied the fact that in the railway age peripheral sea movement had lost its edge over land communications. Amateur strategists such as Churchill and Lloyd George failed to grasp the implications of this change, no matter how often sailors and soldiers tried to explain it to them: 'The idea of an easier way round seems to be based more on impatience than on careful examination of evidence,' CIGS Murray had to remind them again at the end of 1915.[21] Although British statesmen brought up on the exploits of the Pitts and Nelson were the main culprits, enough French politicians condoned such manoeuvres to ensure that they were a distraction at the start of, and in the case of the Salonika campaign a nuisance throughout, the war. To Murray and his successor Robertson, however, peripheral campaigns supplied from the sea were anathema. The 'fundamental principle of war which can never be neglected without serious detriment namely the principle of concentration [of force] at the decisive point' was being flouted, Robertson warned the War Committee in June 1916 as the Somme offensive was in preparation, adding: 'The maximum number of men must be placed on the main fronts and commitments in all other theatres reduced to a minimum, even to the extent of taking considerable risk in those theatres.'[22] Ships were also essential for supplying offensives in the main theatres, so tying up increasingly scarce shipping on subsidiary operations, not to mention the threat from predatory U-boats in the Mediterranean, galled military strategists. Domestic politics and imperial strategy nevertheless meant that Joffre, Robertson and later Foch would all have to accept campaigns beyond Europe despite the fact that they would stretch Entente shipping resources, alarmingly at times.

Using naval force to project military power on land was rarely tried. Although often mooted, capturing an island off the German coast or landing troops on the Belgian coast were never attempted. The small-scale amphibious landing at Tanga on the African east coast in November 1914 proved a debacle.[23] The only successful amphibious operations, the two landings on the Gallipoli peninsula, turned out to be the precursor to stalemated land campaigns supplied by sea. This campaign as a whole, the only one that tried to integrate land and naval forces, demonstrated that modern warfare was more complex and liable to mishaps than that in the preindustrial age, although it might be speculated whether the Dardanelles campaign could have enjoyed greater success had it been launched after full mobilisation could sustain it.

As well as for supplying home fronts and the armies in France, Italy and Russia, by 1916 shipping had to be found to move men and supplies into and out of Egypt, Salonika, the Middle East and Africa. Longer journeys to the Mediterranean and the Middle East placed a proportionately greater strain on finite shipping resources than the relatively short crossing between Britain and France. Come April 1917 Robertson persuaded Lloyd George to argue for a reduction in the number of British divisions at Salonika because there was insufficient shipping to supply them. The campaign required 150 merchant ships even when there was no offensive underway, and 22 had been sunk in the Mediterranean in that month alone.[24] By 1917 a plan had been hatched to develop a railway supply route between Calais and Brindisi on the heel of the Italian Peninsula, so great was the need to relieve the pressure on shipping resources.[25]

By then shipping had become another resource managed centrally, initially through Allied shipping ministries, and later through joint boards of control such as the Allied Wheat Executive, which from December 1916 apportioned shipping for this vital foodstuff. This was the precursor to a more general shipping agreement that created an inter-Allied chartering bureau in London.[26] Such diplomatic agreements regulated the fair distribution and efficient take-up of this essential resource: acting rather like a lubricant, the coming and going of merchant vessels – troopships, tankers, bulk-carriers, refrigerated ships carrying meat and other fresh produce, tramp steamers, fishing trawlers – kept the Allied war machine operating. By the time an Allied Supreme War Council was established to direct coalition strategy in late 1917 such central control of vital war commodities and pooling of resources had become commonplace. In fact the Allies' united front had been solidifying for some time around such commercial and economic cooperation, notwithstanding the intergovernmental and civil-military disagreements over military strategy that rumbled on. Soon after an Allied Maritime Transport Council came into being to regulate imports and exports and to ensure shipping was not being wasted on goods that were not vital for the war effort. This belated but necessary government intervention in the working of the private commercial economy was 'a decisive stage in the economic history of the war' in the recollection of French Minister of Commerce Étienne Clémentel, one of its architects. It would ensure that in 1918 American men and supplies would flow freely across the Atlantic during the war's decisive year.[27]

It took the Allies until 1918 to master the methods of controlling supply in wartime. They took nearly as long to get to grips properly with how to interdict the enemy's supplies. Blockade therefore was not going to provide a rapid solution to the stalemate. It might at least strengthen the Entente's grip on Germany and her allies, and begin to impact on their ability to conduct the war on the home and fighting fronts. Controlling the seas and interrupting German trade was relatively unproblematic for the Allies and became increasingly effective. The military application of sea power proved much more difficult.

THE BLOCKADE'S EFFECTIVENESS SHOULD BE MEASURED BY THE IMPACT THAT it had on Germany's ability to make war. Into 1916 Germany's war industries seemed to be functioning without undue hindrance. She was self-sufficient in coal, while many prewar imports on the Allies' contraband list could be replaced with domestic substitutes or found in occupied countries. There were few commodities that Germany could not get access to, but tropical raw materials were one category of goods whose supply was becoming increasingly restricted. Rubber for tyres and gas masks was in very short supply by 1917. The innovative German chemical industry turned out ersatz synthetic rubber but could not meet all of Germany's needs. German army trucks had to run on iron-rimmed tyres, reducing their speed and mechanical reliability. Jute for sacking and sandbags that came from India became virtually unobtainable, the army resorting to using paper for the latter. Yet these were peripheral commodities, significant but not vital for the war effort. Essential for the manufacture of explosives and as fertiliser, nitrates were one commodity that Germany was going to have difficulty replacing. The chemical industry could produce synthetic nitrates, but these were prioritized for the munitions industry. Short of fertiliser, German agricultural productivity declined steeply, exacerbating a growing wartime food crisis.

British blockade measures had gone some way to restricting the unlimited flow of goods through neutral entrepôts by 1916, although Germany was still a long way from crisis. There was still enough food and other commodities coming in via Scandinavia and Holland to meet basic requirements, although prices had risen and supply to urban areas was becoming erratic. Cereal grains were the first commodity to become scarce, not least because imported fodder had been declared contraband and so they were being fed to animals instead. In a development that mirrored those in the industrial war economy, in November 1914 the state established a wheat corporation to oversee grain supply. Oat and potato supplies were also managed centrally from 1915, and other commodities thereafter. By 1916, a Food Control Office and a War Food Office oversaw the supply and distribution of foodstuffs and managed a comprehensive system of rationing.[28] Notwithstanding the proliferation of food agencies and the civil servants who staffed them, a dual food economy was effectively developing in Germany. Country folk who produced food still enjoyed a reasonable standard of living, while townsfolk who relied on external supplies were starting to go hungry. Similarly, with Germany still largely governed and administered locally, conditions and supplies varied significantly from region to region. Bread rationing was first introduced in Berlin in February 1915, with meat rationing, meat-free and fat-free days to follow. Quality was also declining. Unpalatable wartime 'black bread' became commonplace. Richer urbanites could redress the imbalance with weekend excursions to the countryside to buy overpriced food from the producers. The urban poor had to resort to bread queues when foodstuffs were available: food riots broke out if they were not. In mid-1915 the government stepped in to prevent profiteering, introducing price controls for vital commodities. Around one thousand items were to be regulated in this way: but yet another solution that increased bureaucracy rather than addressing actual shortages was no real solution.[29] As an example, an order in spring to slaughter pigs in large numbers because feeding them was putting too great a demand on the nation's potato supplies served only to glut the market. The price of pork plummeted, then rose excessively in the ensuing pork shortage. To cap it all, the Imperial Potato Office calculated soon afterwards that Germany had far larger potato stocks than was thought![30]

The state had responded to being blockaded by tightening the national belt and taking control of supply and demand in order, in principle, to ensure equality of experience and sacrifice for all. This theme the press rehearsed week after week, although in practice all knew that there was one rule for the wage-earning worker and his family, quite another for the farmer and rich businessman with produce to sell and money to spend on the flourishing black market. One of the principles of the *Burgfrieden* that Bethmann Hollweg constantly stressed was that all Germans were in the war together, but the steady play of the blockade gradually undermined any sense of common duty and shared hardship. But hunger itself was no deterrent. 'If hunger is all that we have to face, even the hunger of millions, the momentary impossibility of effecting a decision, cannot justify our throwing up the sponge,' Binding avowed. Only starvation, which was a long way off, should force Germany to capitulate.[31]

'THE MORE CLOSELY THE HISTORY OF THE WAR IS STUDIED,' HANKEY suggested after the war, 'the larger does the factor of sea supremacy loom.'[32] A former Royal Marine and determined navalist, and a forthright supporter of Lloyd George in his disputes with Robertson and Haig over strategy, Hankey was prominent among those who after the war discounted the efforts of armies and industries, suggesting that the strangulation of Germany and her allies by maritime power was the decisive weapon. The cumulative impact of the Allied blockade on their adversaries' home fronts and military operations was certainly significant, particularly from 1917. But while Britannia ruled the waves and the trade and finance that flowed across them, Germany bestrode the continent with a powerful economic bloc of her own. In occupied Europe there were sufficient resources to offset interdiction of her maritime commerce.

The other dimension of the picture is the Allies' reliance on sea power: '*La guerre, c'est le Shipping*,' was how Clémentel expressed it, in language that suggested that by 1918 the Anglo-French sense of coalition had imbued maritime affairs like so many others. Without sea power the land campaigns in France, Italy and Eastern Europe could not have been sustained for four years. Churchill was very proud of the fact that the Admiralty had conveyed 809,000 men and their equipment across the Channel in 1914 without any loss to the enemy.[34] After the commencement of submarine warfare in earnest such good fortune would not continue, but the passage of troopships, supply ships, merchant steamers and colliers always sustained the Entente's war effort even on the many land fronts. The war could not be won on the maritime front alone: navies could never defeat armies or overthrow nations, as the Dardanelles campaign had shown. But it seemed to both sides that it could certainly be lost there, if the popular will to victory should be fatally undermined and if the supply of vital resources for feeding and equipping armies and paying for the war could be sufficiently degraded.

Over the winter of 1916–17, when the potato crop failed and the nation was reduced to a diet based on turnips, there was a prolonged period of hunger and misery in Germany: in that at least everyone shared equally. Temporarily, this ordinary root vegetable had a huge impact on a world war. Toni Sender remembered,

> The worst winter, that of 1917, when almost all food consisted in whole or in part of turnips . . . Bread made of flour mixed with turnips, turnips at luncheon and dinner, marmalade made of turnips – the air was filled with the smell of turnips and it almost made you vomit! We hated turnips and had to eat them. They were the only foodstuff obtainable in abundance.
>
> I soon realised that a great change in the mentality of the people was taking place. They had lost their confidence in Hindenburg and Ludendorff, in the whole General Staff.[35]

# Are **<u>YOU</u>** in this?

*Propaganda played a significant role in mobilising people for the war effort. This British poster from 1915, designed by the founder of the Boy Scout Movement Robert Baden-Powell, portrays military and civilian service as equally important to the war effort, and suggests everyone—man, woman and child— could make a contribution.*

General Franz Conrad von Hotzendorf, Austrian Chief of Staff, 1914–1917, was spoiling for war before 1914, even though he knew that it was likely to bring down the Habsburg empire.

Field Marshal Lord Horatio Kitchener, British Secretary of State for War, 1914–1916, is best remembered for the citizen army that he raised to fight a war of attrition, and that bore his name.

General Joseph Joffre (at center), commander in chief of the French army, 1914–1916, was the architect of the Allies' strategy of attrition.

*Men and women worked side-by-side in munitions factories and navy yards such as these two throughout the war.*

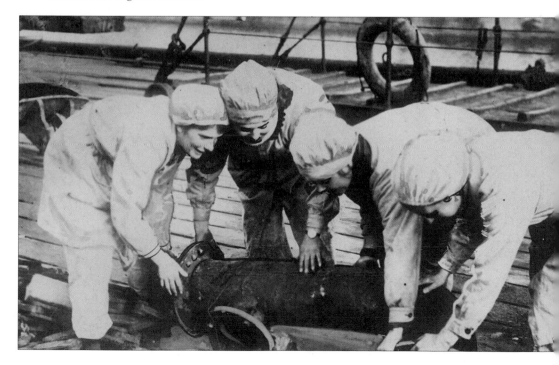

*Russian infantrymen line the trenches in the forests of Sarikamish in the Caucasus during the winter of 1914.*

*One of Russia's greatest strengths lay in its nearly endless supply of manpower.*

ABOVE: *French soldiers lying in hastily dug personal trenches along the Western front in 1915*

BELOW: *The Second Battle of Artois in May 1915 took its toll on the village of Carency in Northern France.*

LEFT: *A German 'giant' bomber aircraft from 1916, the Zeppelin-Staaken R-IV. Zeppelin airships and long-range bombers were used from 1915 to terrorise Allied civilians on the home front.*

ABOVE: *The Red Cross brought Americans to the front long before their nation joined the fight. The ambulance seen here is on its way to the battlefield at Verdun in 1916.*

RIGHT: *Austrian positions in the Julian Alps offered a natural fortification against invading Italian forces.*

ABOVE: *After a demoralizing defeat, Italian troops retreat through Caporetto on 24 October 1917.*

RIGHT: *German soldiers round up Italian prisoners of war during the Battle of Caporetto.*

ABOVE: *Canadian machine gunners dig in on the Vimy Ridge that was finally captured during the Battle of Arras, the most successful phase of the April 1917 Nivelle Offensive. The attack plan was ambitious but, as in earlier western front offensives, early success degenerated into a prolonged attritional struggle with heavy casualties and little change in position.*

BELOW: *French Schneider tanks being unloaded in railway sidings. The French army made very effective use of these new weapons of war during its last year.*

A section of the Hindenburg Line at Bullecourt, viewed from the air. This formidable 1916 defensive position could be stormed by the Allied armies in a week come 1918.

Nicholas II of Russia, the last tsar, was an autocrat who failed to inspire a popular war effort in Russia and paid with his throne and his life.

Vladimir Lenin, leader of the Bolshevik Revolution, condemned the imperialist war in Europe and also offered a new agenda for peace, one that appealed to Russia's disillusioned masses, but less so to social democrats elsewhere in Europe.

ABOVE LEFT: *Enver Pasha, Turkish war minster and the strongest advocate of Turkey's entry into the war on the side of the Central powers, visiting the Dome of the Rock in 1916 with navy minister Cemal Pasha.* ABOVE RIGHT: *David Lloyd George, British Prime Minster, 1916–1918, was a strong populist war leader, but was handicapped by a weak grasp of military strategy.*

ABOVE LEFT: *Field Marshal Sir Douglas Haig, commander in chief of the British armies in France and Flanders, 1915–1918, engaged his forces in a costly and controversial offensive campaign to defeat the German army on the western front.*

ABOVE RIGHT: *General Paul von Hindenburg, German Chief of the General Staff standing with General Erich Ludendorff, First Quartermaster General, 1916–1918. The two men inherited a losing war after the Allied general offensive began in 1916, and thereafter resorted to increasingly desperate strategic expedients to try to save imperial Germany.*

ABOVE: *The German cruiser SMS Seydlitz was severely damaged during the Battle of Jutland, but did not sink.*

RIGHT: *Woodrow Wilson, President of the United States, 1912–1920, offered a new, liberal agenda for peace after America entered the war. This was not to the liking of European leaders, but appealed to many of their people.*

ABOVE: *This drawing, made for the* New York Herald *and the London Sphere, shows the* Lusitania *as a torpedo from a German U-Boat tears a gaping hole in the hull.*

BELOW: *British battle cruiser HMS* Invincible *explodes at the Battle of Jutland, 31 May 1916.*

# ONLY THE NAVY CAN STOP THIS

The United States was appalled by the sinking of civilian vessels like the Lusitania,
and papers throughout the country ran cartoons like this one, portraying the Germans
as savage pirates slaughtering civilians.

Financing a truly global war was a daunting challenge. Posters, such as these from the United States and Canada, encouraged citizens to invest in war bonds, often restyled as "Liberty Bonds" for maximum patriotic effect.

LEFT: *General Phillipe Pétain, commander in chief of the French army, 1917–1918 with General John Pershing, commander in chief of the American Expeditionary Force, 1917–1918. Pétain reorganised the French army to fight modern material-intensive warfare effectively. Regrettably, Pershing's attention was focused more on alliance politics than military efficiency and his forces would repeat many of the mistakes made earlier in the war when they took the field.*

BELOW: *A twenty-one centimetre German gun captured by Canadian forces in the Battle of Amiens, 1918.*

ABOVE: *Georges Clemenceau, French premier, 1917–1918, offered the war-weary French people 'war, nothing but war', but they were quite prepared to fight on to liberate their country from the German invader.*

LEFT: *Marshal Ferdinand Foch, Allied generalissimo, 1918, grasped the problems of fighting on the entrenched battlefield better than any other First World War general, and put his experience to good use in a sustained campaign of attrition that broke the German army.*

Although in straightened circumstances and on short if still sufficient rations, Germany and her allies were still a long way from being brought to their knees by economic and maritime pressure. By this point, however, the economic war, like the military war, was getting into its stride. It was not the overabundance of turnips alone that dismayed the German people, but also the facts that the fleet was confined to port and the army was now on the defensive. The nation's solidarity was starting to waver, just as the high command's grip on the war was starting to slip.

# NINE

# ATTACK

THE 1916 CAMPAIGNING SEASON OPENED AT DAWN ON 21 FEBRUARY 1916, when the German bombardment of Verdun began. A huge 380mm railway gun landed a shell in the courtyard of the Bishop's Palace – it missed its target, a bridge over the river Meuse – heralding artillery fired on a scale not yet seen. One thousand two hundred guns pulverised the French forward defences from three sides, up to forty shells per minute raining down in places, while new gas shells blanketed French gun positions. The next afternoon, German infantry pressed forward, penetrating between the isolated pockets of dazed French soldiers who had survived the bombardment. The Frenchmen fought back aggressively, contesting their shattered trenches a few metres at a time, but were gradually overwhelmed by infiltrating assault troops armed with grenades, light mortars and another new and terrible weapon of trench warfare, portable flamethrowers for clearing undamaged bunkers. The first days of the offensive went well, as they usually did when guns were concentrated, troops were fresh and enemy reserves were dispersed. Combining artillery and infantry effectively in the first assault was something that armies were starting to get right now lessons from the previous year's tactical experimentation had been absorbed. German observers were confident. 'I have a feeling that the attack at Verdun must succeed,' Binding noted:

> Not because of the number of guns and attacking troops, but because of the more general reason that war must be directed in the last resource, not against positions and armies, not against a State, but against human weaknesses. When they appear there is no more hope . . . The French are abandoning absolutely impregnable positions . . . no

Council of War, no talk of glory, and no Army Order can prevail against that . . . When Verdun falls – and I believe, subject to reserves, that it will fall – the Frenchman will lose the butter off his war-bread . . . and I doubt whether he will still care to eat it then.[1]

By 25 February the heights east of the Meuse were in German hands, and Fort Douaumont, the supposed key to the Verdun perimeter defences, had fallen without a shot being fired. But, Binding was well aware, 'It may take a long time yet . . . this feeling does not portend the end of the War by a long way, particularly against a coalition.'[2]

It was Falkenhayn's objective to bleed the French army white in front of the fortress; it soon became Joffre's intent to wear down the enemy among the ruins of Verdun's outer defences, until the Allies could organise themselves to counterattack and destroy the German army once and for all. Like all the other battles, the Verdun offensive was to slow once the rhythms of campaigning asserted themselves. Within a fortnight the defence of Verdun had organised. Councils of war, army orders and motivations to death or glory prevailed, and French resolve toughened. *Tenir* became the watchword of army and nation: Verdun would hold on, and so would France, until her allies came to her aid. Guns and fresh troops were hurried to the battle, and Second Army commander Philippe Pétain was rooted out of a hotel room where he was entertaining his mistress and sent to organise the defence.

Today Pétain is better remembered for his notorious second career as head of France's collaborationist Vichy regime during the Second World War. The reputation that allowed him to take the helm in France during an acute national crisis was made on the battlefields of the Great War, and particularly at Verdun. He had earlier been professor of infantry tactics at the École de Guerre (at the same time Foch and Fayolle had also been instructors) and so understood the problems of tactics and operations that he met on the battlefield. In 1914, Pétain was a colonel of *chasseurs*, France's elite light infantry, in command of an infantry brigade. He was one of those promoted when Joffre purged the French high command following the army's disastrous first engagements, taking command of 6 DI. He ascended rapidly thereafter, taking command of XXXIII CA in October 1914 and, having made his reputation as one of the best corps commanders in the army in the Second Battle of Artois, the Second Army in June 1915. By that point he had recognised that the French army was engaged in a war of attrition and would have to husband its reserves. This principle he applied to the Verdun battle, where he organised a sector-based system of defence sustained by a continuous cycle of reinforcement and supply along the road and light-railway corridor – the famous *voie sacrée* (sacred way) – that connected the fortress with the front, stabilising the situation.[3]

Another future French leader passed that way. On 1 March, Captain Charles de Gaulle led his company of the *33ème Régiment d'infanterie* into the maelstrom, taking up scratch positions in shell holes and among the ruins of a village, from where his men beat off repeated German attacks. Last seen leading the remnants of his company in a charge against another wave of advancing German infantry, de Gaulle was awarded the *Légion d'honneur* 'posthumously': in fact he had collapsed after being wounded and was to spend the rest of the war a German prisoner.[4] Now backed by their own concentration of heavy artillery, by early March fresh French divisions had checked the German advance. 'The offensive has got stuck at its beginnings,' Binding quickly recognised.[5] Thereafter the battle would grind down both armies in the longest continuous engagement of the war. Phases of relative calm separated brutal close-range fights when one or other side went on the attack. All the time, the guns kept firing, while the infantry cowered below the earth. In that respect, Verdun represented the new way of fighting now that the war machines were mobilised.

THE STRATEGIC REVIEWS OVER WINTER 1915–16 WERE BETTER INFORMED and much more realistic than those a year before. Overall Germany's military situation still looked comfortable, with Serbia defeated and the other Allied fronts contained, although the General Gtaff at the OHL appreciated that the Allies' stranglehold on Germany was noticeably tighter than it had been at the end of 1914. The blockade was starting to have an impact on the home front, and it was incumbent on the army to relieve that pressure somehow. But the land victories of 1915 had not brought the Allies to terms: if anything, they seemed to bring them closer together, while their resources were developing all the time. The effort to break the enemy coalition would have to be hastened and increased, for time was not on Germany's side.[6] The majority of the German army had to remain deployed in the West to contain Britain and France, and so Germany could never build up the necessary preponderance of force to smash the Russian army once and for all, although Falkenhayn had been obliged to contain Russia in 1915. Despite the advance into Poland, Russia was far from broken as the new campaign commenced. If anything, she was strengthening. In 1915 Germany had possessed a decisive material advantage over the Russians on the battlefield, which Allied mobilisation was likely to negate in the coming campaign. For all these reasons – and for personal ones too, since Falkenhayn resented the home front's glorification of the eastern front's successful commander, Hindenburg –

Germany's strategic focus turned westwards in 1916. Her strategic method changed too, from annihilation to attrition.

'The bottom line,' the kaiser was informed on 3 December, 'is that a decision can only be reached with a blow in the West for which all available forces must be staged!'[7] If he could not break Russia, Falkenhayn calculated that he might break France.[8] Falkenhayn's calculations were wrong, and his assumptions false. The OHL's intelligence staff estimated in November 1915 that the French could at the current rate of wastage sustain the war until September 1916, before having to call up younger classes ahead of schedule. France had four hundred thousand fewer replacements in her depots than in August 1914 – by that estimation a long, gruelling campaign was in prospect. Moreover, the expanding British army, if not yet efficient, would in time balance any French losses, while the German army enjoyed no local superiority in the West, with only twenty-five fresh reserves divisions against twenty-seven Allied. Central to Falkenhayn's strategy was the belief that the French army's morale was weak after its 1915 checks and losses, that civilian commitment to the war was wavering and that France's will to victory would break if put under sustained pressure.[9] Given this inferiority, the enemy's morale was the obvious target – it might be broken before Germany's military strength, and this was a chance that Falkenhayn had to take because Germany would never win the manpower and material contest as it stood.[10] Knocking France out of the war might split the alliance ranged against Germany. But France showed no signs of capitulating without a fight: tentative peace feelers extended in September had been rejected out of hand.[11]

To break France's army, Falkenhayn chose to attack the strategic fortress complex at Verdun, which the French would have to defend to the last drop of blood. Falkenhayn reasoned that in this salient, which could be fired into from two sides, attrition could be conducted cost-effectively, since he could draw the French army's reserves onto his concentrated guns. This plan acknowledged what the German army could achieve on the battlefield, although it was not a realistic stratagem for ending the war quickly, which was a fundamental flaw, since 'the longer the war lasted, the longer the Entente would be able to bank on the fact that the Central Powers would exhaust themselves militarily and economically'.[12] German losses in 1915 had been heavy, if sustainable: 612,000 in total. Austria-Hungary had suffered far more heavily, around 2,100,000 men killed, wounded or captured fighting Russians, Serbs and later Italians.[13] Falkenhayn was naturally starting to worry about the staying power of his main ally. The 'horrible sacrifices in blood' were starting to tell on the home front, where a 'tenacious determination' was now substituted for early-war enthusiasm. 'Time favoured the enemy in an alarming, ominous way', although as yet 'the will to prevail was unbroken'.[14]


THE ALLIES ALSO CHOSE A STRATEGY OF ATTRITION IN 1916, REPLACING THE disjointed, speculative operations of the first phase of the war, which would manifest itself in a long anticipated 'big push' against the German lines in France, supported by offensives in Galicia and Italy. It would take considerable effort and much negotiation to get there, but the process indicated that the Allies' united front was consolidating around a shared objective and agreed method for taking on and defeating the Central powers. It offered better prospects than the 1915 campaign, although the test would only come once battle was joined.

The Allied plan was hatched at a strategic conference at Joffre's GQG at Chantilly in early December 1915. Joffre presided masterfully and with authority over three days of deliberations in the ballroom at the Hotel du Grande Condé that served as French military headquarters. He recognised the need for the Allies to work more closely together, and his political masters agreed. By then Joffre had triumphed in the civil-military battle of wills that had hobbled French strategy throughout 1915. The most recent round of civil-military discord in Paris brought a new premier, the wily lawyer Aristide Briand, to power and also toppled Millerand, Joffre's closest political ally, from the war ministry. Briand replaced Viviani after the latter lost a parliamentary vote of confidence following the confused opening of the Salonika campaign. Like Viviani, Briand was no war leader – he is most famous today for the interstate peace plan, the Kellogg-Briand Pact, that he went on to sponsor between the wars – but he could operate the Republican political system deftly. Briand would be France's longest serving wartime prime minister, holding office until March 1917, while ministers came and went and the fortunes of war shifted. The new leader could not immediately sack his commander in chief, so instead Briand terminated the crisis by enhancing Joffre's authority. In the heated arguments over exactly how the war should be carried on after the loss of Serbia, Joffre at least offered a clear view of the nature of the war and a plan for winning it. The GQG would now control the campaigns outside France, and implicit in this reorganisation of the high command was an expectation that Joffre would also offer strategic leadership to the coalition. The Salonika crisis had made it clear that the Allies were being outmanoeuvred for want of a coordinating strategic authority, so this and formalizing the ad hoc system of inter-Allied political-military conferences that had developed during 1915 seemed to meet this need. The new system for coordination, if not perfect, would at least make Allied collaboration more speedy and consensual than it had been during 1915, strengthening the united front.[15] It showed immediate results in the strategy agreed for 1916.

Joffre's appointment suggested that after the strategic flailing of amateurs, in 1916 the military professionals would be given their chance now that the war machines were properly ready. Military plans would, however, be subject to scrutiny and approval by the Allies' political leaders. Reflecting on 1915's campaign, Joffre was aware that a quick, decisive victory was not possible in an attritional war. Germany had so far held her own in the West against two strong Anglo-French offensives, had weakened if not broken the Russian army and had better organised her resources for a long, slow war. Germany had gained a new ally in Bulgaria, while Allied diplomacy had faltered in the Balkans. The war against Turkey had proved a shambles, and the Italians had disappointed, while Serbia had been defeated, relieving some of the pressure on Austria. But despite these achievements, there was much that suggested that the Central powers were no nearer victory than they had been in 1914. Allied unity and concentration of effort was the key to beating Germany, and she had not made much progress towards breaking it. If anything, her enemies had recognised this and were starting to draw closer together.

Allied preparations for the 1916 campaign, more systematic and realistic than they had been a year before, aimed to escalate Germany's blood sacrifice and undermine national will. By concerting the Allies' superior resources, Joffre reasoned, the strategic flexibility which the Central powers had enjoyed in 1915 would be curbed.[16] This was the basis of the general Allied offensive, essentially Joffre's plan, agreed to at Chantilly in December 1915. The military leaders of the four main Allies pledged to 'undertake a simultaneous combined offensive with the maximum of troops possible on their respective fronts, whenever they are in a position to undertake it, and where circumstances appear favourable . . . Up to that moment the war of attrition will continue'.[17] The agreed objective, 'the destruction of the German and Austrian armies', was simple.[18] It was calculated that the Allies' manpower and material superiority would now allow them to seize the initiative and engage and defeat their enemies' reserves, at least if 'these offensives were to be launched simultaneously, or at least on dates sufficiently near each other to prevent the enemy moving his reserves from one front to another'.[19] This agreement suggested that a dose of reality had been taken: the Central powers' military strength could not be broken quickly in this way, but systematically and decisively, over a prolonged campaign. Joffre admitted that 'the decisive moment of the war may still be far off'.[20]

The Chantilly meeting produced an expression of strategic intent, from which a workable plan was expected to follow. Attrition of the enemy's armed forces was set as the goal of 1916's military campaign: how and when this should be done remained to be decided in further military and political meetings. Joffre's role thereafter became to muster his allies as the vagaries of war diverted their attention and buffeted their resolution. He kept the plan together, but it lost momentum during the spring after Germany attacked, such that when the general Allied offensive was launched it was to fall considerably short of Joffre's ambition. Civil-military disagreement and unpreparedness undermined British engagement; the Russian were willing enough, but reluctant to take on Germany directly; the Italians remained weak.

AT CHANTILLY JOFFRE HAD MADE IT CLEAR THAT AFTER TAKING ON THE greater burden of fighting the war throughout 1915 the French army was weakening, and that it was time for his allies to take a greater share in beating the German army. In particular, their armies should undertake a preliminary phase of attritional operations, while France husbanded her fighting strength for the decisive offensive later in the year. This would be the main sticking point for the British.

Kitchener had always intended what Joffre now planned, to engage the enemy directly once his armies were ready. Moreover, there were indications that amateur strategists were coming to appreciate the nature of a modern war. In his speech of resignation from the cabinet in November 1915 Churchill acknowledged his own change of heart:

> There is no need to be discouraged about the progress of the war . . . while all the appearances of military success attend her arms, Germany may be defeated more fatally in the second or third year of the war than if the Allied Armies had entered Berlin in the first.[21]

Churchill had gone to do his own small part in that military effort, taking command of a New Army battalion at the front. Others would still need persuading, although in 1916 the General Staff's case was much better made, being founded on experience and having the weight of statistics to support it. After returning from Chantilly Murray presented a memorandum to the War Committee (as the Dardanelles Committee was renamed in November) that explained in clear, stark prose the actual situation of the war. It would be a slow war of attrition fought and decided in the main European theatres. 'In this . . . war the resources of the Allies are sufficient to enable them to wear out the enemy and finally to beat him, if only the will to conquer and a sound direction of their united efforts and resources are not wanting': the choice, Murray represented, was now between 'assault and investment' of the Central powers' defensive lines, and he advocated the former. With manpower more or less fully mobilised and munitions production now sufficient, if not yet ample, the time had come for 'strong, vigorous, simultaneous and sustained pressure by all the Allies on existing main fronts' that would deny Germany the freedom of manoeuvre she had enjoyed in 1915 and bring her armies to battle. With between four-and-a-half and five million Germans and Austrians under arms with reserves to sustain them in the field for some months yet, that would certainly be a slow, risky strategy, Murray admitted, adding: 'The prospects of success are considered at least sufficient to justify the attempt . . . such an effort . . . stands at least a fair chance of pushing back the enemy's armies. They may break badly'.[22]

William Robertson, Murray's successor as CIGS, hailed this memorandum as 'the bible of the war'.[23] It would fall to him to implement the 1916 plan, and to hold politicians to these principles thereafter. It would be a tough job, but the army now had at its head a common soldier who would fight its position robustly. Robertson did not shy from an argument, as Lloyd George was to find. The new CIGS was a bluff, no-nonsense farmer's son from Lincolnshire. He holds the distinction of being the only man in the British army to rise from the rank of private to become a field marshal. He did so by dint of intellect, hard work and professionalism. Before the war he had been a staff officer, mastering supply, intelligence and operational matters. That made him a natural choice as commandant of the Staff College, Camberley from 1910 to 1913. He went to war as quartermaster-general of the BEF, and replaced Murray as Sir John French's chief of staff in January 1915 after Murray fell ill. Once it was recognized that the General Staff in London needed strengthening to ensure a better military grip on strategy than in 1915, the choice lay between Robertson and Haig. Robertson came home, insisting on powers in his new role that would ensure that he, not Kitchener, would direct the war. Kitchener acquiesced since he and Robertson were broadly agreed on how the war should develop. Haig would stay in France to execute their plans, at least if the government concurred.

In December 1915 some doubters in the British cabinet remained to be persuaded: both the method and likely outcome of the Chantilly plan were questionable. Lloyd George and Balfour remained determined to hold Kitchener and the General Staff to account over the details of military planning. On the other hand, Kitchener was now less tolerant of the schemes of his more maritime-minded colleagues, not least perhaps because they had all come to nothing. He agreed with Robertson that anything not now essential for imperial defence should go to France: he had raised an army for that purpose and in 1916 it was ready to take the field. This also brought to a head the clash over the affordability of Kitchener's strategy, since 'business as usual' was incompatible with maintaining a mass army through conscription.

Supported by Robertson, Kitchener presented the case for concentrating effort in France to the War Committee on 28 December 1915. The Chancellor of the Exchequer McKenna demurred, and was backed up by Lloyd George and Balfour, who after the costly autumn 1915 offensive were concerned as to the methods the army would employ and the potential for heavy losses. The War Committee endorsed Kitchener's proposal to take the offensive in France – but with reluctance. Military unanimity, it appeared, had mastered amateur strategy, the bane of 1915, although there were aftershocks.[24] At its next meeting on 13 January 1916, at which Balfour represented that British and Russian forces would not be ready to attack until the summer, the War Committee added the proviso to their earlier endorsement that a final decision remained to be taken.[25] Only on 7 April, after Asquith presented his colleagues with a stark update of the state of Allied opinion after visiting Italy and Paris, was the decision to take the offensive in France confirmed.[26] Despite political misgivings, the British army had an inevitable appointment with the German army at some place and at some time, because strategy had become simple. As Repington noted, matter-of-factly, 'I don't think we have anything to do but go on steadily killing Germans in the west.'[27]

It would fall to General Sir Douglas Haig, who had replaced French in command of the British army in December, to implement this decision. Haig remains notorious, the British general associated with attrition more than any other. 'The greatest soldier that the empire possessed', as his obituarist in *The Times* lauded him, has been ill-served by history.[28] In 1916, he was both the best-qualified man for the job and a commander still moulding his army and adapting to fighting industrialised war. His reputation as a skilled, professional soldier started to slide after his death, at a time when a scapegoat was sought for Britain's wartime sacrifice. The novelist C. S. Forrester amplified the developing perception of British command in alluding to the arrival of Sir Douglas Haig at the GHQ:

> The personality of the new Commander-in-Chief was already noticeable in his selection of his subordinates, and so through them to the holders of the lesser commands. The men who were wanted were men without fear of responsibility, men of ceaseless energy and of iron will, who could be

relied upon to carry out their part in a plan of battle as far as flesh and blood – their own and their men's – would permit. Men without imagination were necessary to execute military policy devoid of imagination, devised by a man without imagination. Anything resembling freakishness or originality was suspect in the view of the plan of campaign.

By 1936, when Forester was writing, the reputations of British commanders had been increasingly tarnished by memoirs and histories written by politicians: by Lloyd George because he never accepted Haig and Robertson's attritional strategy, and by Churchill, who was disappointed because his own former cavalry-lieutenant's military intuition had proved less perceptive than the generals'. There is illogicality in such critiques of Haig's performance, in that he was castigated for seeking to replicate 'mobile' operations in the inappropriate conditions of positional trench warfare while being condemned for not finding a supposed 'magic' solution, Forester's elusive screwdriver, which might restore dynamism to the battlefield.

Haig was an educated and trained professional seeking to remodel military science and the military art in novel circumstances while actually having to prosecute operations at the front and manage the largest army Britain had ever deployed. Strategy was one thing (and never Haig's to decide, although he fully accepted the attritional nature of the war), tactics quite another, and operations that linked the two, Haig's real responsibility, problematic. In his solutions Haig was certainly not as freakish or original as Foch, for example, but he was up to the task of leading and managing his army as it grew, learned and adapted. Costly and tragic mistakes were made: the second day of the Battle of Loos, for example, and the notorious first day of the Battle of the Somme. Such mistakes have been dwelt on by subsequent generations thereby obscuring the steady evolution of warfare and the growing effectiveness of Haig's army in fighting it. It should be remembered that in the dynamic of combat the effectiveness of the enemy's defence was significant for the outcome of an attack, and the real killer on the battlefield. Attributing disaster to poor planning and lack of imagination alone is misguided and narrow-minded.

Haig was a meticulous planner and a thoughtful and adaptable soldier who wrestled with and mastered the administrative and operational problems he faced. His admirers liked to eulogise him as 'master of the field', acknowledging that the armies he commanded were instrumental in the final defeat of Germany. Haig had a particularly difficult and unique task: he had to build an effective mass army on the cadre of a small professional force. The latter he understood, since he had helped to create it in a successful staff career before the war. Haig had advised war minister Richard Haldane as a modern British army was organised after 1906. Endeavouring within the limitations of the voluntary system to maximise the number and efficiency of the forces that Britain could deploy in a future war, Haldane and Haig created the BEF, the second-line Territorial Force and imperial contingents. Haig also managed the drafting of *Field Service Regulations 1909*, the army's new war-fighting manual. In August 1914 he had advocated keeping the British army at home and building up its strength to intervene later in the campaign: to that extent he agreed with Kitchener that it would be a *'war of several years'* for which Britain would need a proper army.[29] Haig led I Army Corps to war in 1914 and commanded it in the Battle of Ypres. Promoted to command the First Army in January 1915, he directed it in 1915's clumsy, under-resourced battles for the Aubers Ridge and at Loos. He had the widest experience of command in battle and a growing professional understanding of what was and was not possible on the battlefield when he assumed the chief command. Haig agreed in principle with the Chantilly strategy. To beat the German army would require engaging it on a larger scale than had been possible in 1915. His prewar staff training had inculcated the principle that battlefield operations consisted of a series of phases – manoeuvre, attrition, decision, exploitation – and he recognised that the immediate task facing the Allies was to 'employ sufficient force to wear down the enemy and cause him to use up his reserves'.[30] It did not suit that the British should undertake the attritional phase on the coming campaign alone, however.

Robertson apprised Haig of the political mood in London, and in particular of ministers' fears of a return to the costly, indecisive offensives of 1915. Joffre's proposal that the British carry out the attritional phase of the offensive before the French army delivered the coup de grace appeared to be both bad politics and bad strategy: it meant that the British army would do the hard work while the French took the glory if the general Allied offensive proved decisive, and it dissipated rather than concentrated the Allies' growing strength in the West. Between December 1915 and February 1916, in a series of complicated and often tense negotiations, Haig forced Joffre to abandon the attritional phase of any western front offensive. Any preliminary British operation would now directly precede the main Anglo-French attack. This at least would mollify the politicians, although Haig's chopping and changing angered Joffre who determined that the British must attack alongside the French army rather than alone in Flanders towards the Belgian coast, which would have been more palatable to maritime-minded British strategists.[31] Thus the Battle of the Somme, the main element of the intensified strategy of attrition, was conceived and the fate of Britain's new armies was decided. After a plan was agreed upon its implementation remained subject to developing events. Haig argued thereafter that the attack should be delayed until his armies would be properly trained and ready. Joffre refused to countenance such a delay given general Allied and France's own military difficulties. The eventual compromise was that the Somme offensive would be launched in the last week of June.

The Russians also proved hard allies to direct. After Russia's mauling in 1915, Russian commanders were aware that they could not engage the German army on equal terms. They could certainly beat Austrians, however, and the strategic principle adopted at Chantilly left them a loophole to do so. Russia's representative at the conference, General Yakov Gilinsky (the head of the Russian military mission in France), had tabled the Russian chief of staff, General Mikhail Alekseev's, plan for a concerted campaign to knock out Austria. This was thrown out because, in Joffre's estimation, it was logistically impossible to deploy the eight hundred thousand English, French and Italian troops Alekseev expected to support the Russians in the mountainous Balkan Peninsula.[32] Yet the development of events on the eastern front meant that come the summer the Russians would default back to Alekseev's plan.

IT TURNED OUT THAT THERE WOULD BE AN ATTRITIONAL PHASE TO THE 1916 campaign and that it would be carried out by the French army. At Chantilly the Allies agreed in principle to be ready to attack in the spring in order to forestall a renewed enemy offensive. It soon became clear that Russia would not be ready by then. Once Falkenhayn struck at Verdun, the strength of the Chantilly agreement was to be tested. In the event of one ally being attacked the others were expected to mount relieving offensives. It turned out that Britain was unready and unwilling, that Italy was willing but barely ready and that Russia was willing but unable.

Rather than mount a relief offensive, Haig agreed to take over more of the front in Artois (which he had so far declined to do in order to train his army for the summer offensive). On 11 March Cadorna launched Italy's first offensive of 1916, after Joffre appealed for a relief operation after Verdun was attacked. The Italian army was better prepared for the new campaign. Cadorna's army was growing (it expanded from thirty-five to forty-eight divisions during 1916, as the call-up was extended to older classes) and new tactics appropriate to close-range warfare were being adopted. Machine guns, hand grenades, trench mortars, wire cutters and other trench stores, including the first steel helmets, were now arriving in proper quantities. Heavy artillery was still lacking. Italian industry was not producing guns quickly enough to equip newly raised field-, mountain- and siege-gun batteries, an indication of the intention, if not the ability, to adapt the Italian forces for fighting attritional warfare in the mountains. In February Cadorna asked France to provide heavy guns, but French industry was tied up producing weapons and munitions for France's own forces.[34] The Fifth Battle of the Isonzo did not amount to the large-scale preparatory attritional operation that Joffre had expected his allies to mount. The Italians suffered thirteen thousand casualties in seven days' fighting that advanced the line only a few hundred metres in isolated sectors, the Austrians only a few thousand casualties.[35] The offensive indicated that the Italian army was prepared to fight, although Cadorna himself regarded it as little more than a demonstration, and winter weather forced a rapid halt to the battle. Thereafter he would turn his attention to arming and training his army for the general Allied offensive that was now postponed until the summer.

More was expected of the Russians; but perhaps the Western Allies still expected too much from Russia. British military attaché Knox's reports had been pessimistic about the prospects of Russian offensive action – too pessimistic in Robertson's view – but it was evident that 'the rearmament of Russia is the main problem of the winter months'. Knox accompanied a Russian delegation which visited the Ministry of Munitions in London and attended an inter-Allied munitions conference in Paris. This betokened greater cooperation, but French and Japanese small arms ammunition and British howitzers would take time to manufacture and deliver to Russia.[36] Knox noted that there was still a great misunderstanding of Russia's actual capabilities: 'Competent authorities in the west seemed to expect from Russia a continued effort based on the size of her population, without taking into consideration the limitations imposed by actual conditions of armament, communications and power of organisation.'[37]

Joffre now appreciated that Russia was not the makeweight that had been thought. The GQG calculated that Russian rifle strength was only 1,300,000, even though Gilinsky had represented at Chantilly that Russia had 2,700,000 men under arms. This was evidence, Joffre recollected, 'that a clear lack of confidence reigned between the Russian General Staffs and ours' and that ordinary Russians did not share the emperor's commitment to the Allied cause.[38] Joffre was realising that Russia would be slow to engage and hard to direct. Russian military headquarters effectively ignored a French military mission under General Paul Pau, Joffre's predecessor as French chief of staff, that went to Russia over the winter to investigate the military situation. Senator Paul Doumer's simultaneous mission to arrange for surplus Russian manpower to be sent to France where it would be equipped to fight with the French army did little better. By the end of 1916 one Russian brigade had come to France and two others had reached Salonika.[39]

Russian unpreparedness obliged Joffre and Robertson to postpone the date for resuming the offensive until April, and only then to relieve Russia if Germany attacked in the East. The date of the general Allied offensive would, ultimately, depend on when Russia was ready.[40] In fact, it was the Russians who were obliged to mount a relief offensive themselves, at Lake Naroch in March. Joffre was right. General Alexis Kuropatkin's hastily organised and poorly led attack on the German Tenth Army in appalling winter conditions failed disastrously, despite his forces outnumbering the German defenders six to one. Another failure of artillery-infantry cooperation condemned the Russian infantry to an attack on largely undamaged enemy defences. The Russian suffered 112,000 casualties, including 12,000 from frostbite, while the battle inflicted only 20,000 on the enemy. Now that they were on the offensive, Russia's field commanders began to appreciate that the German army should be broken with firepower rather than by sacrificing manpower, but it had taken a costly operation in 1915 style – which aimed to force a breakthrough that could be exploited by cavalry – to realise this.[41] But since guns and shells were still lacking, 'Lake Narotch was, despite appearances, one of the decisive battles of the First World War. It condemned most of the Russian army to passivity.'[42] Thereafter, the prospect of Russia not attacking at all started to concern Joffre. In fact the Russians remained broadly faithful to their commitments. Yet they declined to take on the better equipped and effective German army in the summer offensive, defaulting once more to an operation against the Habsburg armies, akin to Alekseev's rejected plan. Such an offensive equated better with Russian territorial and imperial ambitions, and on past evidence was more appropriate to their military capability.

The united front was still consolidating in spring 1916. The British still seemed reluctant to engage the enemy. Despite her weaknesses and previous losses, Russia had little choice but to soldier on, although the rapid check of her March offensive reinforced her wariness of fighting Germans. Italy had no real alternative to supporting a coalition strategy on the success of which her own fortunes now depended, although how determinedly she would fight remained to be seen. Nor could she engage Germany directly. France was battered but still determined. Joffre strove to rally these diverse, discordant forces for her liberation while the enemy disrupted his planning by grinding down the Allies' principal fighting instrument, the French army.

COME MID-MARCH, THE VERDUN OFFENSIVE WAS DEVELOPING INTO THE usual prolonged slogging forwards against reinforced defences stiffened with artillery. Blocked on the east bank and enfiladed by new French bat-

teries deployed across the river, on 6 March Crown Prince William's Fifth
Army struck again, with far less success, on the west bank of the Meuse.
Here a back-and-forth fight for the heights at Côte 304 and Mort
Homme ensued for three months. With its cycle of attack and counterattack, its rhythmic artillery fire that rose intermittently to a crescendo as
small infantry units sought to wrestle a trench or a bunker from the
enemy, Verdun epitomised attritional battle. It is impossible to know how
many men passed through Verdun, 'the Meuse mill' that ground up men
and spat out their bodies smashed, maimed or traumatised. They were
sucked into the salient's churned, featureless lunar landscape, occasionally relieved by a shattered tree stump or remnant of human habitation.
There mud caked everything. The noise of near-constant shelling; thirst
and hunger; a troglodytic existence among dismembered bodies and
decaying, flyblow cadavers; the stench of mortal decay mingled with nox-
ious chemical fumes was their lot, even if they avoided the fears and dangers of mounting an assault. Such was the theatre of attrition, with its
sights, sounds and smells, which men would experience as their unit took
its turn through the mechanical battle. The lucky ones would come out
some days later, mentally exhausted if physically unharmed after a tour
of duty. Many would depart prematurely, wounded and evacuated; others
repose in Verdun's ossuaries and all-enveloping soil. But even the lucky
ones were aware that if spared this time, inevitably their turn to endure
would come again, and that next time they might not be so lucky. To
have 'done Verdun' became a badge of honour among French soldiers; a
widely distributed one, but also one that they relished. As it seemed that
his division would take its turn in June, Seeger reflected:

> That would be magnificent, wouldn't it? – the long journey drawing nearer
> and nearer to that furnace, the distant cannonade, the approach through
> the congested rear of the battle-line full of dramatic scenes, the salutations
> of the troops that have already fought, "bon courage, les gars!" and then
> our own début in some dashing affair. *Verdun nous manque.* I should
> really like to go there, for after the war I imagine Frenchmen will be
> divided into those who were at Verdun and those who were not.[43]

Falkenhayn's plan to break their morale was coming unstuck. Rather
than collapse, after the initial shock Pétain's defence rallied public opinion
and steeled the army for a grim, tenacious resistance: 'They know that
they are saving France, but also that they are going to die on the spot,'
one military censor reported approvingly.[44]

For German soldiers, in contrast, initial elation was to turn increasingly sour. In the defence of the western heights from March to May the

French extracted a substantial toll for the ground. The German army lost as heavily as the French: Mort Homme, the key position, was aptly named.[45] After the battle flared up again on the eastern heights in May, Fort Vaux fell on 7 June after a long siege. This local victory marked the height of German success. Thereafter the French contained and counterattacked the Fifth Army once the general Allied offensive got underway, drawing off German reserves from Verdun. It was not until 18 December, 303 days after the battle had begun, that the gunfire finally slackened off for the winter. By then the guns were predominantly French, and Douaumont and Vaux were both back in French hands after a successful late-autumn counteroffensive directed by Pétain's successor, General Robert Nivelle. Meanwhile attrition had done its work in the spaces between Verdun's scattered forts, the epicentres of the battle. The Germans had inflicted by French reckoning 377,000 casualties on their army, of which 162,000 were killed. The Germans themselves suffered 337,000 casualties. Other imprecise estimates put the total casualties both sides suffered around Verdun over four years as high as 1,250,000.[46] These are the stark facts of attrition in practice.

While Verdun ground down his army, Joffre strove to organise his counterattack, the Somme offensive, which would be the principal Anglo-French action of the general Allied offensive. As France's reserves diminished Joffre encouraged, cajoled and sometimes tried to bully his allies into accelerating their preparations. Verdun's positive, knock-on effect for Germany was that by wearing down the French army it would lessen the blow that the Allies were preparing against the German army. Falkenhayn's offensive had seized the initiative back from Joffre, whose intention to mount the general offensive in the spring had been thwarted by his allies' unpreparedness. Falkenhayn reasoned that his sustained attack on Verdun would force the Allies to mount hasty relief offensives, thereby using up Allied reserves more generally, although it would also reduce the reserves Falkenhayn had in hand to meet Joffre's counterattack when it came.[47] Falkenhayn was right, in that Russia and Italy did mount hasty and easily checked attacks in March. Thereafter Joffre had to play a waiting game, offsetting his army's losses at Verdun (and the enemy's) against the increasing potency of the pending general offensive. In a war in which material predominance was starting to become the determining factor in battlefield success, it made sense to delay the offensive until all armies were armed and ready, a deduction that the early phase of the Verdun operation affirmed. Haig certainly let Joffre know whenever he had the opportunity that the longer the Somme offensive was delayed, the better armed and trained his army would be. But when Haig started to suggest that his forces might not be ready to attack before mid-August, Joffre became anxious, for while his allies built up their strength, France's army was wasting away.[48] Joffre recognised even before the Chantilly conference that France's military manpower policy – 134 infantry division were in the field by November 1915 – was unsustainable in the long term. As reserve divisions were cycled into and out of the 'Meuse mill' through Pétain's *noria* (bucket waterwheel) system, at a pace calculated not to break their fighting power irreparably, Verdun only served to emphasise that manpower would be the crucial issue for France thereafter.[49] Defending Verdun forced Joffre to deploy the reserve divisions he had husbanded for his own offensive and to call on the British to take over more of the line from the French, shrinking the reserves available for the general Allied offensive. A 67-division battle conceived in February – to involve 42 French and 25 British divisions – shrunk in scope and size.[50] By the end of May, when Joffre and Haig agreed to launch the Somme offensive in late June, it would engage initially only 21 British and 18 French infantry divisions, some 60 percent of those available in February. Although the Somme offensive was to be the biggest Anglo-French battle yet, its shrinking as a consequence of Verdun would make attrition, which depended on its scale for defeating multimillion-man armies, much less effective. Fayolle, who was to command the French Sixth Army on the Somme, speculated that an attritional offensive that resulted in 200,000 casualties might still not bring the war to an end.[51] Indeed Joffre himself seemed to recognise this, defaulting like Falkenhayn to the expectation that a prolonged battle would break the enemy's morale more rapidly than it used up his strength.[52]

The prospect of victory depended partly on how much the German army had been worn out at Verdun, and partly on the respite Verdun had given the other Allies while preparing their part in the offensive. To that extent France herself had carried out the attritional phase of the Chantilly plan at Verdun. Allied intelligence, monitoring the state of the German army, started to tick off its reserve divisions as they were consumed on the Meuse. As the general Allied offensive got underway in June, the GQG concluded that the attritional process still had some way to go: German reserve divisions were reported moving eastwards to contain the Russians who started the offensive in early June. The GHQ calculated that there were now very few fresh German reinforcements to halt its advance if the defensive crust was breached, and scaled up the British attack on the Somme accordingly. During June Haig's plan evolved from one for a steady attritional battle to one that anticipated the decisive phase of operations.[53] In the Verdun counterattack, as the Somme offensive was starting to be perceived, his forces might now break the thinned

German front once and for all. If Italians and Russians took their share of the fighting, the general offensive could beat an overstretched German army, although not without weeks and months of heavy fighting. An offensive of *durée prolongée* (drawn-out – Foch's expression) was in prospect however well the first attack went.[54]

ITALY'S SHARE WAS BY NOW UNCERTAIN, SINCE THE AUSTRIAN ARMIES, WHICH had been quiescent since the defeat of Serbia, had taken the offensive. Like Falkenhayn, Conrad was fearful of 'a war of exhaustion' that the 'well-provided Entente' could impose on the Central powers in 1916. Over 2,000,000 casualties in 1915, including 775,000 prisoners of war, furnished brutal evidence of the war Austria-Hungary was engaged in. The punitive expedition in the Balkans that her July 1914 ultimatum to Serbia had set in motion seemed to be concluded; on the other hand, a levy of 3,000,000 recruits over the winter had been needed to refill the army's ranks for the next campaign against Russia and Italy. Nevertheless, Conrad remained misguidedly optimistic about the way the war would go in 1916.[56] With renewed confidence after driving back the Russians and beating the Serbs, Conrad was inclined to disregard the support that Germany had given to these successful operations. Indeed Austria found a new independent spirit in 1916, and relations with Germany became strained.[57] While Falkenhayn had been drawn eastwards by the threat Russia posed to his principal ally in 1915, Conrad in his turn was disinclined to look westwards. Instead his attention was focused south. The time for Conrad's long-desired reckoning with treacherous Italy, Conrad's personal bête noire, had come.

While Falkenhayn planned to grind down the French at Verdun Conrad was separately planning to smash the Italian army with a strike southwards from the Alpine front, the so-called *Strafexpedition*,* that would trap Italy's armies against the River Isonzo defences and destroy them. Conrad retained unrealistic expectations as to what was possible on the battlefield – a sketch of his 'plan' envisaged six daily twelve-mile advances, culminating in the occupation of Venice – but nonetheless this would be his first independent offensive since that which had gone so disastrously wrong in August 1914. Falkenhayn had firmly refused to send German divisions to support the Austrian surprise attack, which he considered a selfish diversion. Moreover, Germany was not yet officially at war with Italy. Piqued, Conrad deployed reserves of his own from the Galician front.[58]

---

*Literally 'punishment expedition', a term coined by a journalist: the idea of punishing the upstart lesser powers that challenged Austria died hard.

The Trentino offensive was a 'map offensive', planned at Austrian headquarters six hundred miles away at Teschen in Silesia. The operation's objective was to advance forty-five miles and occupy Padua, the main railhead supplying the Isonzo front. It could not take place until the spring thaw in the Alps, and even then conditions on the lines of communication did not allow forces and supplies to be built up properly. The Italians were forewarned – hiding such a build up of forces from the enemy's intelligence network was always difficult – and Cadorna deployed reserves northwards. Nevertheless, with no experience of being attacked in this way, Italian forward defences were poorly sited and overmanned: the First Army commander General Roberto Brusati made the rudimentary error of using the reserves Cadorna sent to reinforce the front lines (for which Cadorna sacked him on the eve of the offensive) rather than manning his strong defences in depth and keeping reserves in hand to counterattack. This meant that if the defensive crust could be cracked, which was always possible with a powerful artillery preparation, the softer interior could be penetrated.[59]

The attack therefore opened with some success on 15 May, although it still took the Austrian Eleventh and Third Armies two weeks to defeat the Italian First Army and occupy the Asiago Plateau. In all an advance of some 12 miles was made, on a 20-mile front, which looked impressive but was far from decisive. Cadorna proved as imperturbable in a crisis as Joffre. The dogged defence gained him time to reinforce his threatened northern flank and to organise a new Fifth Army to contain and counterattack the Austrian penetration. Between 6 and 16 June the Italians recaptured much of the lost ground. The battle cost the Austrians 81,000 casualties, the Italians 147,000 (including 56,000 prisoners, a worrying sign of uncertain morale).[60] It cost the Italian prime minister his job too: on 10 June Salandra lost a vote of no confidence in parliament after he tried to blame the initial Austrian breakthrough on Cadorna.[61] In a belated recognition that Italy was really at war his successor, Paolo Boselli, a respected if undynamic 78-year-old parliamentary veteran who could reconcile Italy's political factions, organised a national unity government. The failure of the *Strafexpedition* finally disabused Conrad of any lingering expectation of quick victory. If he did not relish the potential consequences, it was evident now that there was no alternative to all-out war and to backing the alliance with Germany come what may. The only alternative, a compromise peace, would mean the end of the Dual Monarchy.[62]

BY DIFFERENT REASONING BUT THROUGH THE INEXORABLE LOGIC OF THE war, at roughly the same time both sides established that prolonged attrition was necessary to bring the land war to a decision and accepted that they would suffer losses in consequence. Heavy casualties would certainly occur; domestic support would probably waver; military authority and political legitimacy might be questioned. Commanders on both sides now understood that they could use material to inflict casualties and swing the balance of losses in their favour, although since both sides had reached the same conclusion this would merely result in the intensification and mechanisation of carnage on the battlefield, where rather than other men machines would now kill men. Since battles became lengthy and attritional in 1916, casualties remained high absolutely, but they were decreasing in proportion to time and space as infantrymen dispersed. During 1916 commanders' overambitious operational expectations were scaled back now that they appreciated better what their troops could achieve in positional warfare. The material balance also started to shift towards the attacking army, at least in the first phase of an offensive. The development of *Materialschlacht* was also shifting the balance of morale in the attackers' favour.

By 1916 warfare had become a matter of calculation – of manpower resources, of weight of shell per metre of front, of how many trains could supply an army on the offensive with munitions, of how many casualties and prisoners it would take to break the enemy once and for all – and the dual western front killing machines of 1916, the Battles of Verdun and the Somme, would come to epitomise the worst of attritional warfare. At the same time in Russia and Italy more men were being put into the mincer more rapidly in an attempt to decide the war.

That was how the war had become by mid-1916. 'The War does not move, and peace is farther away than ever,' Binding opined. It had become

> a stupid senseless brawl without any trace of justification from necessity, from superfluous energy, from outstanding policy, from the creative power of any one person: that will be written of this war! It is not mania but stupidity that rules that which was left of the spirit of mankind two years ago, and what is still left of it after two years.[63]

Binding's 'self-deception' about the glory and justice of the war was starting to evaporate, as was so many others'.[64] It was against this very different, volatile background that Joffre was to launch the general Allied offensive, his own endeavour to win the war now that Falkenhayn's had clearly failed.

TEN

# COUNTERATTACK

O N 4 JUNE 1916 THE GALICIAN FRONT ERUPTED SUDDENLY, SPECTAC-
ularly as General Alexsei Brusilov's South-western Army Group
began the general Allied offensive. For Austrian troops grown
accustomed to watchful calm, the impact was devastating. For three days
heavy artillery bombardments and aggressive infantry attacks rippled
along the 150-mile front south of the Pripet Marshes, probing for weak
spots and confusing Conrad and his subordinate army commanders as
to where their reserves should be deployed. Inevitably, sectors of the front
were penetrated, destabilising the defence. By 7 June the Fourth and Seventh Austrian Armies on the northern and southern ends of the Galician
front had been broken, and the First and Second Armies and the German-led *Südarmee* between them were starting to lose ground as their
lines were infiltrated. With the front collapsing, a general retreat ensued.[1]
In the offensive's first week the Russians captured 216 guns and 190,000
prisoners and inflicted at least 100,000 casualties.[2]

Brusilov's success indicated that Russia was belatedly mobilised to
fight modern war and that she had found commanders who knew how
to operate a modern war machine.[3] Brusilov, 'a general whose common-
sense amounted to brilliance', had surrounded himself with a coterie of
young, efficient staff officers who demonstrated a growing appreciation
of how infantry and artillery should work together on the battlefield, and
of the need for thorough preparation.[4] The Brusilov Offensive's tactics
were innovative and anticipated to a certain extent those of 1918, but
they also drew heavily on those developed in the West in 1915. Careful
monitoring of the bombardment's progress from the air ensured that it
cleared a way for the infantry effectively – the infantry in their turn
sapped their lines forwards to within close assaulting distance of the
enemy's front. They practiced the assault on mock-ups of the enemy's po-

sitions beforehand.[5] While highly effective, these tactics were not in themselves decisive, or an alternative to 'the stage of sacrificial *Materialschlachten*' that was taking place on the western front.[6] While they precipitated a smashing collapse of a lengthy section of the front (a genuine 'rupture' of the sort that was talked about in the West but proved impossible given the limited space for manoeuvre in that theatre), this was nothing new in the East with its lower concentration of forces and longer lines of communication along which reserves had to be moved.

However devastating it was to a part of the Habsburg army, Brusilov's attack was not in itself going to decide the war: that would be a matter of operations and strategy. Brusilov had a momentary advantage in June 1916, partly and paradoxically because he had not amassed sufficient reserves of his own to give the enemy the impression that a large-scale attack was being prepared, but also because the overstretched Austrians also lacked reserves in the theatre. Since the winter, when an offensive by Brusilov's predecessor, General Ivanov, had largely failed, the Galician front had been quiet. Then the Austrian defences had proved strong, and their defenders well-equipped with artillery and machine guns.[7] Thereafter manpower at the front had been thinned and however solid, field defences were only defendable with men and guns. Falkenhayn had turned his attention westwards, stripping reserve divisions from the temporarily quiescent eastern front for his sustained assault on Verdun, thereby largely removing the stiffening of German divisions that had sustained the Austrian forces in 1915. Conrad had redeployed six veteran divisions and heavy artillery batteries to reinforce the *Strafexpedition*, replacing these with newly raised, semi-trained formations.[8] Also, in December 1915 Ivanov's attack had been concentrated on a short section of the enemy's front, while Busilov opted to engage on four army fronts at once, testing weakened Austrian defences over a long distance. Reserves simply did not exist to contain or counterattack the many and widening breaches that Brusilov's troops forced in the Austrian front.

Brusilov's offensive obliged Falkenhayn to go to the aid of his hard-pressed ally once again, stretching his reserves even more thinly. It took ten days to redeploy German and Austrian divisions from other fronts, but by mid-June a new Austro-German army group was being formed under German General Alexander von Linsingen to contain and counterattack Brusilov's northern advance. Falkenhayn had gripped the crisis situation (and re-gripped his allies, much to Conrad's consternation); for the remainder of June, while the rest of the Russian army remained static, Brusilov's troops would have to push against stiffening resistance. While the scale of Brusilov's battle was greater than any seen since 1914, its development conformed to the established pattern of attritional operations.

\* \* \*

THE ALLIES' SUMMER 1916 OFFENSIVE, LIKE SO MANY FIRST WORLD WAR military operations, began well. Brusilov's initial success was certainly striking and raised hopes on the Allied side to fever pitch. Now the Russian 'steamroller' was finally moving and the 'big push' that had been the subject of speculation and rumour for many months was underway. Yet this was merely the first phase of operations that might last until the winter. Such a sustained engagement with the enemy's armies over several months might eventually break the Central powers' forces through concerted, cumulative attrition.

Joffre's broad ambition, 'the destruction of the German and Austrian armies', if reduced in scale and less focused, might yet be achieved. The German army had already been worn down appreciably at Verdun; and while Russia was not attacking Germany directly yet, Brusilov's success had obliged Falkenhayn to send German reserves to support her wavering ally, including five divisions from the western front.[9] The Austrian army was certainly gripped and suffering casualties at Italian and Russian hands at a rate that it could not sustain. Operations in Italy and the East would not be directed at the German army itself. This was expected in Italy where the war was with Austria, but Russia's reversion to Alekseev's plan for an attack on Austria that had been rejected at Chantilly, in an attempt to break the Habsburg armies once and for all, dissipated the concerted effort that Joffre had planned to exercise against Germany. In fact, Alekseev had given orders to renew the attack on the northern section of the Russian front, and Brusilov's blow, hasty and speculative in its conception, was only envisaged as a short-term 'auxiliary attack' intended to assist the French and Italian armies that were then under attack and to draw German reserves southwards.[10] Its success took everyone by surprise, Alekseev included. Brusilov had only a small numerical superiority in men and guns on the southwestern front, while General Aleksei Evert's armies to the north had more than three-to-two superiority in divisions.[11] But while Alekseev naturally chose to reinforce Brusilov's success, stripping divisions from Russia's northern army groups, Evert stalled when ordered to attack to support the operation to the south.[12] He would after all be taking on the German army, not the Austrians, and after Lake Narotch was chary of the likely outcome.

THE NEXT EFFORT, THE ANGLO-FRENCH ATTACK ASTRIDE THE RIVER SOMME, would complete the encirclement and intensify the process of attrition. In his last briefing to the field commanders Joffre identified that the offensive might develop in one of two ways: either the enemy's weakened front would be 'ruptured' or a prolonged battle of attrition would ensue. Either way, 1 July 1916 marked the start – not the end – of the destruction of the German army: *'Knocking out the German army on the Western Front, or at least an important part of their forces'* was going to take time.[14]

For the denouement, Joffre had chosen his most trusted subordinate. Foch now had the chance to apply the lessons he had learned from 1915's fighting. What mattered to Foch at this point was not objective but method – in particular, how to take proper control of the battle, which he saw had become prolonged and would be unduly costly if infantry were squandered indiscriminately attempting to follow up early success.[15] The battles Foch had fought in Artois had shown that the enemy's trenches could be taken as long as a sufficient weight of supporting fire was brought to bear effectively and the infantry was properly armed and organised: holding on to them proved more difficult. Cutting the wire was vital, as was silencing the enemy's machine guns. Eliminating the defending garrison with artillery fire alone, however, was difficult as most would be sheltered underground during the bombardment. Therefore the infantry would have to fight for control of a position: it was not so much that the artillery could conquer and the infantry occupy but rather, as Joffre formulated it, 'the artillery suppresses, the infantry overwhelms'.[16] During spring 1916 French infantry were trained to do just that: to advance quickly behind the barrage and to sweep through the enemy's forward lines to more distant objectives while the supporting waves mopped up the remains of the defence behind them. The depth of an attack, meanwhile, would be limited to the range of effective artillery cover.[17] Increasingly effective tactics were the first element in solving the military problem that was trench warfare: systematic, 'scientific' operations were the second. By ensuring that cohesion was not lost and that any blow struck by his armies was not wasted Foch would make offensive warfare effective again. His methodical approach, determined by the capabilities of technology and the skill and stamina of the infantry, proved better than one which staked all on surprising and smashing a defensive system with one huge blow (many other commanders, unfortunately, had yet to reject that sanguinary method). In the Somme offensive, the French forces would proceed systematically through the enemy's defences using weight of artillery fire to advance the infantry steadily, step-by-step, through successive German defensive positions. In the modern war machine soldiers were the less durable component, and reducing losses was becoming the watchword of the French army's methods after the bloodletting of 1915 and Verdun.[18]

In Fayolle, who was to lead the Sixth Army in the offensive, Foch had an experienced subordinate who was able to execute such methods on the battlefield. 'We have understood that we cannot run around like madmen in the successive enemy positions,' Fayolle noted as he started to prepare. 'Doctrine is taking shape. For every position there must be a battle, following each other as rapidly as possible. Each one needs a new plan, a new artillery preparation. If one goes too quickly, one risks being checked; too slowly and the enemy has time to make more positions. That is the problem, and it is serious.'[19] Fayolle, however, doubted that attrition on the scale that was now possible would prove decisive.

Moreover, the Allies' main instrument for the first assault was not the increasingly skilled French army but Haig's largely untried and partially trained divisions, whose role in the offensive had been increasing as Verdun shrank that of the French army. Haig took planning for the battle seriously, and Fourth Army commander General Sir Henry Rawlinson, who was to direct the offensive on the ground, also prepared assiduously to 'kill Germans'.[20] But planning went awry in its later stages, and the British troops, although keen, lacked the professional skill and military means to execute Haig's overambitious plan. Copying the French, Rawlinson prepared a steady, systematic assault against successive German positions. But a combination of factors led Haig to reject Rawlinson's plan in favour of an attempt to take the enemy's defensive positions in a single rush and exploit the breakthrough with mobile forces in the direction of Bapaume. This was more in keeping with Joffre's overall conception, to take on and beat the German army in a major offensive, and erroneous intelligence reports in June suggested that German reserves had been thinned to the point that the 'decision' phase of operations could be mounted with some hope of success.[21] Privileging operational objectives – the desire to break the German lines and capture ground – over tactical capabilities proved a recipe for disaster.

The Somme offensive notoriously started very badly for the British army, which was obliged to attack some weeks before Haig had wished because of the pressure on Verdun. The opening of the Battle of the Somme cost the German army 25,000 casualties, so intense was the seven-day Allied preliminary bombardment. This was a small number absolutely, but greater than in any earlier Anglo-French attack. Although the British army had more guns and shells than ever before, the munitions produced by a rapidly expanded war industry proved of poor quality, which, coupled with Haig's plan, condemned Britain's raw troops to a bloodbath. The British bombardment was too diffuse and so failed to cut all the German wire or to silence the enemy's machine guns and counter-barrage, which fell on the infantry as they left their trenches. On the right of the British line adjacent to the French attack the enemy's first position was taken, but not without a prolonged fight which exhausted the attacking formations. Farther north there was little to show for the first day's fighting but casualties, once the initial assault collapsed into chaos under the concentrated fire of German guns. The blow to the British army's strength and prestige, if not irreversible, was profound. Its 56,886 casualties killed, wounded or missing on the first day of battle have ever after stood as shorthand for the folly of attrition. This was a consequence of tactical and operational mistakes that might have been avoided with more careful preparation, rather than the fault of the strategy per se. Fayolle's Sixth Army, attacking alongside the British, demonstrated that it was perfectly possible with adequate guns and shells and appropriate tactics to inflict a smashing blow on the enemy in the first attack and to follow it up rapidly with a successful assault on the enemy's second position. His troops were fully confident of success. 'Think of me when you read the first big communiqué, which we shall have a brilliant share in the making,' Seeger bragged to his *marraine*.[22]* Within four days Fayolle's divisions had advanced five kilometres south of the river. It was touch and go whether the enemy could contain the Anglo-French assault after 1 July: the German commander certainly judged that the offensive had torn a huge hole in his defences, and only the tenacious localised resistance of small parties of infantry survivors had prevented a disaster.[23] Seeger was to lose his life on 4 July, as the legionnaires stormed the village of Belloy-en-Santerre, south of the river. This was to be the high point of the Sixth Army's early success, however. As in all battles, the defence was reacting to the first shock and stiffening.[24] During the first fortnight of the battle a hasty, disorganised defence had to be improvised while reserve divisions were deployed to the Somme front.[25] If the British army had not been so badly mauled a large-scale local collapse of the German defence might have ensued: the evidence of other fronts, however, indicates that this would not have proved decisive and that Joffre's long battle was inevitable.

The counterattack was underway and would be sustained as long as German forces remained to be fought and beaten. Falkenhayn immediately halted offensive operations at Verdun. He appreciated that Germany was now facing her worst strategic fear, an encircling alliance attacking on all fronts. Falkenhayn gained a breathing space as a result of the inauspicious start to the British offensive on the Somme, although his own future was now in doubt. He would be relieved of his command at the end of August, ostensibly because he had failed to prevent Rumania from joining the Allies. Hindenburg would replace him, advised by Erich Ludendorff, his chief of staff who assumed the new and all-encompassing

---

*A soldier's female pen friend. Such correspondence was promoted by the high command for the purpose of sustaining frontline morale.

role of first quartermaster-general. Ludendorff's title reflected the sort of war it had become, one in which reserves and resources were the mainstays of strategy: in the new post he would direct the home front as well as Germany's forces. Hindenburg was a popular general: Prussian, patrician, ascetic, unflappable, with a strong sense of duty to kaiser and fatherland and a record of service that dated back to the 1866 war with Austria. Ludendorff was a highly competent military manager. Intelligent, hardworking and with an excellent grasp of the technicalities of making war, he had had a successful General Staff career before the war, when he had risen to be director of operations. His professional talents, unfortunately, were tempered by a tendency to irascibility and panic. Hindenburg and Ludendorff had come together to grip the situation in East Prussia in August 1914 and had made a name for themselves by smashing the Russian Second Army at Tannenberg. They worked well as a command team, and their armies swept all before them in Poland during 1915. Binding saw signs in Hindenburg of the sort of military talent that the high command generally seemed to lack.[26] But a better field commander was not the answer in a war into which nations and empires were locked and in which military operations were deadlocked. 'While he may be their best man,' Sandhurst judged, 'he is not a magician, and he cannot stave off the results economic, as well as the constant all-round steady and inevitable pressure exercised by the Allies.'[27] Binding could certainly see that the writing was on the wall: 'If Hindenburg doesn't have a brainwave we shall gradually come to the conclusion that we are not going to be able to win this War. We shall probably be able to go on holding off the enemy for a long time, but instead of beating him we shall come to be satisfied . . . if he doesn't beat us. The odds against us are too immense.'[28]

Hindenburg and Ludendorff's appointments reflected the way Germany was moving as the war turned against her, and their inheritance was poisonous. With the general Allied offensive the Allies had gained the strategic initiative, and the choices facing the new duumvirate were unpalatable: offence or defence; fight on land or at sea; try to make war more vigorously, or seek peace? Their first visit to the western front showed them a different sort of war, one in which the German army was suffering rather than sweeping the enemy before it. The home front seemed unable to meet the army's needs, but attempts at deeper mobilisation would only show that the German war effort was already running near full capacity. The navy was hamstrung in taking the war to Great Britain by American protests. The phlegmatic field marshal offered a beleaguered Germany some hope. A military dictatorship suited a nation in a state of siege, and thereafter the kaiser faded into the background as the army strengthened its grip on the people. In the second half of the war Germany's effort would be intensified, as far as was still possible, and there would be many more thrashing blows against the encircling alliance, but they would prove no more decisive than Falkenhayn's. The belief that powerful enemies could be annihilated persisted against the evidence, the fundamental flaw in German military strategy thereafter.

Rumania's entry into the war in September suggested that carrion were gathering round the dying Central powers. The alliance did not expire under the constricting pressure of the general Allied offensive, but thereafter it was administered increasingly desperate, unpalatable and ineffective remedies. The workaholic Ludendorff soon emerged as the driving force of the partnership but Hindenburg's significance as military strategist and national figurehead should not be discounted. Beyond containing the pressure on all fronts, the new directors of German strategy would have to mobilise Germany more deeply, a difficult task by this stage of the conflict. A further round of more intense war production, the 'Hindenburg Programme', was initiated – it would be serviced by extended labour conscription legislated by December's Patriotic Auxiliary Service Law. Austria-Hungary was reaching the limit of her resources, however, and Germany was having to divert more and more manpower, money and raw materials to her southern neighbour: the bitter jibe that Germany was now 'shackled to a corpse' was not far off the mark by the end of the year.

First and foremost in summer and autumn 1916 Germany needed to parry the steady, powerful blows raining down on her and her allies from all sides. Troops and guns were railed from Verdun to the Somme and back, then from West to East to meet the ongoing Russian and new Rumanian threats. The key principle of the general Allied offensive, concentration and coordination of effort on all fronts, was now working. That it did not break Germany in 1916, however, was the consequence of two deficiencies. The concentration and coordination could have been better still, and the Allies' material advantage, while obvious and significant, was not yet enough to decide the war. As events on the eastern front unfolded during summer and autumn it became clear that Russia did not have the military strength or will to intensify pressure on Germany, while Rumanian entry on the Allied side, a diplomatic coup that was presented as the potentially decisive factor in the general Allied offensive, turned out to be the final manifestation of the overoptimistic 1915-style of making war.

In the West, on the Somme and at Verdun, the German army would bleed copiously under concentrated Allied gunfire – *Trommelfeur* ('drum fire') that smashed trenches and mutilated men – more so than in any previous battle, but not yet at a rate that would prove mortal. Operations on the Somme settled into a pattern after the first assault. Weather allowing, every few days Fayolle's or Rawlinson's army would launch a heavy attack supported by many guns that moved the front line forward. To the north and the south General Hubert Gough's British Reserve Army and General Joseph Micheler's French Tenth Army conducted less powerful supporting flanking operations. After each set-piece attack there was a process of consolidation, which involved fighting off German counterattacks and straightening the line before the next push. The same was going on at Verdun, where the Second Army kept up an active defence to prevent men and guns from moving to the Somme. This type of war was effective, but to many unsatisfactory. It conformed to its architect's expectations. 'Kitchener it seems thought our staying power and superiority would be asserting themselves in summer 1917!!!' Sandhurst noted of a conversation with Lord Crewe. The lord president of the council in Asquith's cabinet: 'All this Somme business had been planned carefully of course and that we had not only realised anticipations, but had done more. Meanwhile, we keep creeping on.'[29] But creeping was not enough for many, especially as while the army was creeping casualties seemed to be surging. Churchill for one, restless on the backbenches, mounted a sustained criticism of the lengthening casualty lists and the apparent lack of progress in the war.[30] The Somme offensive was one of the positive 'tendencies' that he had alluded to in his resignation speech only months before, but that insight now seemed to have clouded.

In the South, things continued much the same as Italians and Austrians grappled breast to breast along the River Isonzo once more. The Italians' sixth Isonzo offensive finally opened on 6 August. Because the *Strafexpedition* had obliged Cadorna to divert reserves to protect the Italian army's flank, preparations for the Isonzo battle had slowed and Cadorna's ambitions had been scaled down. Nevertheless, the attack proved more effective than those mounted in 1915. Boroević's defending forces had also been thinned to sustain the northern battle and then to confront the Russian breakthrough, while the Italians had many more guns and shells than in 1915. In a few days the Austrian positions on San Michele, Sabotino and Podgora – rocky heights in front of the river against which earlier Italian offensives had smashed themselves – were overwhelmed. With no operational reserves to oppose the Italian advance, within three days the Isonzo had been crossed on a twenty-kilometre front and Gorizia beyond it had been occupied. The Italians were at last recovering 'unredeemed' territory (if only some five kilometres of it), and church bells were rung. The Italian army now faced the challenge of conducting a prolonged offensive battle like those being waged at Verdun and on the Somme: 'The Italians had shifted their problems several kilometres eastwards. The challenge ahead was all too familiar: attacking uphill against well-built positions defended to the death by battle-hardened troops.' Boroević simply withdrew the remains of his forces to the next line of even higher hills where they entrenched to await the next Italian offensive.[31]

Joffre's expectation that the German army would be engaged directly on the eastern front was not coming to pass. Evert's army group had finally attacked north of the Pripet Marshes on 2 July, intensifying the pressure as the Somme offensive opened. However, his methods were not as sophisticated as Brusilov's. Another attack in which the artillery failed to clear the infantry's passage properly, and the infantry were launched in deep waves against a narrow sector of the enemy front in the hope of forcing a breach, only led to heavy casualties. The back-and-forth fight between the Russian and German Tenth Armies lasted a week, wasted a vast number of precious Russian shells and cost eighty thousand men for no appreciable gains. The Germans and Austrians suffered only sixteen thousand casualties, and while the defence was hard pressed, no reserve divisions were drawn away from the south.[32] It meant that when Brusilov's northern armies moved forward again after 4 July they would meet a strong defence and make no spectacular gains like those in June. Thus the pattern was set for Russian operations over the summer: a heavy slogging fight between Russia's masses and a fairly solid Austrian defence stiffened 'like stays in a corset' by German reserve formations doled out sparingly by Falkenhayn, who by then had taken effective control of the Austrian front in Galicia as well.[33]

By August the Allied armies were engaged and everywhere making progress: on 20 August the forces at Salonika also attacked. To that extent Joffre's general Allied offensive was functioning and had gripped the enemy's armies. It was not yet clear if this was a death grip or merely a restraining one, because on all fronts the same pattern of operations had repeated itself. Initial tactical success (which varied in scale but was essentially due to concentrating artillery fire against forward defences) had lapsed into struggling through rearward defences held by the fresh reserves that Falkenhayn had deployed against tiring assault troops. Yet Germany was clearly struggling to meet all the threats at once. During the campaign Falkenhayn and Ludendorff had to create thirty-three new divisions, either by splitting existing formations or raising new ones from scratch. Two-thirds of these went to reinforce the western front. Even then, by the beginning of August the OHL had only one division left in its strategic reserve.[34] The truth was that when hard pressed fresh troops could no longer be moved from West to East or back in a crisis. Divisions that did go from West to East had generally already been fought out and went to hold a quieter sector of the front to free a fresh one to fight elsewhere. Such troops as could be redeployed came from Macedonia or quieter sectors of the eastern or western fronts. Evert's relative inaction, plus the limited number of Allied heavy guns and a growing lack of munitions in the west as shells were fired away in their millions, confined offensive operations to small sectors of the front and greatly assisted Germany's strategic defence. Nevertheless, by August Falkenhayn was stripping German troops from the Salonika front and had even asked Turkey to deploy an army corps to Galicia. In the war of reserves, by late summer the Central powers' were all but exhausted. Their armies' defensive fighting power was far from broken, but the situation was growing uncertain. 'The army which has been formed here has now been completely split up into separate shreds and used to patch the endless front,' Binding, who had been posted as a staff officer to one of the newly raised divisions in the East, noted despairingly.[35] Frontline formations would have to defend positions longer, taking heavier casualties, since there were fewer men to replace them. Come September, therefore, the general offensive would intensify, as Joffre strove to squeeze the life out of the enemy that he now had in a stranglehold. Would German reserves last out, and could enemy morale hold?

As THE GENERAL ALLIED OFFENSIVE GROUND ON, JOFFRE FOUND A NEW CARD to play, hopefully a trump. Rumania – an old-standing ally of Germany (since 1883) – had declined to commit herself during 1915's diplomatic bartering. The situation in the East in 1915 had not given her any hope that intervention would be beneficial. Instead she renewed her alliance with Germany, pending developments (although the treaty was never ratified by Rumania's parliament, a sign of her tergiversation). By August it seemed that the Central powers were on the verge of defeat in the East and the time was right to intervene. A hastily negotiated treaty arranged that Rumania would declare war on Austria-Hungary by 28 August. Her army would make a land grab at Hungary's expense, on the heels of Russia's victorious armies. In return, Rumania was promised money, munitions and the support of a Russian army corps. But the real asset was Rumania's 623,000-man army – 23 extra divisions were committed against an enemy that had no strategic flexibility.[36] All should go well if the general Allied offensive could be renewed in force at the same time.

It could not. By 27 August, the day on which Rumania declared war, Brusilov's offensive had spent much of its force. In July and August a western-front style slogging battle had developed as his armies tried to press on after capturing Lutsk. The Guards Army attacked Kovel seventeen times between 1 August and 16 September, with huge losses.[37] These attacks showed little of the operational skill of the earlier phases of the offensive and enjoyed only a fraction of the success. Now physical obstacles held up the Russian advance: the Pripet Marshes to the north and the foothills of the Carpathian Mountains to the west. Russian battalions could be sucked into these and devastated by artillery fire.[38] Falkenhayn had enough warning of Rumania's entry to scrape together forces and make preparations to contain the new threat, and in the recently sacked chief of staff Hindenburg and Ludendorff found a commander capable of conducting a campaign that broke Rumania's armies by the end of the year. Rather than tip the numerical balance in an attritional war, the Rumanians' military ineptitude merely allowed German commanders to do what they did best, surround and annihilate inexperienced and underequipped enemy forces. First the Rumanians were surprised on 1 September by a strike from the south, across the River Danube and along the Black Sea coast, by a German-led Bulgarian-Turkish army. Rumanian diplomats had miscalculated that Bulgaria would remain neutral in a war with Austria, overlooking the treacherous defeat she had inflicted on Bulgaria in the Second Balkan War which it had come time to revenge. In the second half of September Falkenhayn's newly formed Ninth Army struck from the west. The Rumanians' overconfident invasion of Hungarian Transylvania was checked and repulsed. Thereafter, the pincers closed on the increasingly dispirited Rumanian forces. Rumania's capital, Bucharest, fell on 6 December, and the remains of the shattered army withdrew eastwards to link up with the Russians. The campaign ended in a decisive Central powers' victory, but for a time things had been chaotic and the outcome touch and go. 'Our positions are constantly being changed,' Binding complained, adding:

> Refugees suddenly appear and disappear, nobody knows where from or where to; troops are constantly being borrowed, to be thrown in suddenly at a weak spot in the front; the changes in command, with their comings and goings, are past all understanding . . . Every moment brings fresh surprises into view which appear to be without meaning and without advantage for anybody. So for the ordinary mortal it is difficult to find any explanation of the masked face of events.[39]

Fortuitously, Allied support for the Rumanians had been shambolic. A planned supporting offensive from Salonika in mid-August was thwarted by a preemptive Bulgarian advance. Thereafter a struggle continued along the Struma River valley until the winter. The Allies' forces sapped forward slowly, but their objective, Monastir, was never reached. The Salonika front was under-resourced as guns and munitions were fully committed to the western front offensive, and so offensives there posed no great threat.

Contemptuous of their inept allies, supporting Russian forces had resorted to looting and atrocities in Rumania rather than giving effective military assistance. France could only send a military mission, led by Joffre's former head of operations, General Henri Berthelot, but there was little that could be done to save the situation by the time it arrived.[40] Russia by then had abandoned her offensive: all reserves were needed on the southern end of her front, which had suddenly become three hundred kilometres longer.

The Italians also renewed their offensive beyond the Isonzo, in three more battles during September, October and November. On the Carso Plateau Cadorna's better-equipped and more numerous forces swapped casualties with Boroević's hard-pressed defenders under a heavy metal rain of shells from both sides. The Italians made limited and costly progress against strong, deep field fortifications and a more flexible counterattack based Austrian defence. These offensives pushed the front a few kilometres eastwards, but the Austrians held on until the winter. Cadorna too held on, although criticism of his conduct of the war was mounting.[41]

THE RUMANIAN DEBACLE WAS A FINAL INSTANCE OF HOW NOT TO FIGHT A modern war. Meanwhile, on the Somme, Foch was demonstrating how it could be done. In September the Somme battle took on a new cadence. During that month Foch threw the four armies that he managed one after the other against the enemy's crumbling defences in a series of coordinated, repeated and heavy blows designed to accelerate the destruction of the German army in the West. The front line pushed forwards steadily, and any counterattacks were smashed by concentrated Allied artillery fire. By the end of the month the German army seemed to be nearing its breaking point. But then worsening weather waterlogged the shell-churned ground and slowed the tempo at which the Anglo-French armies could operate. During October and November such intensive pressure could not be sustained: by then Allied logistics were failing and their own reserves of manpower and munitions were severely depleted. The offensive which had promised so much ultimately degenerated into *grignotage*. In deteriorating winter conditions during its final weeks a disjointed series of smaller-scale battles for key positions worked on the enemy's morale but no longer threatened to exhaust German manpower reserves.[42]

During the Somme offensive, Foch demonstrated that a properly managed battle, even if prolonged, would not be unduly costly. However, as Foch had expected before the Somme offensive began, even with their current advantage over Germany the Allies did not yet have enough war material to decide the war once and for all.[43] It also turned out that the organisational and logistical systems required for sustaining such drawn-out military operations were not yet effective. Delivering the daily requirements of multimillion-man armies, even in the relatively confined space of northern France and Belgium where there was a well-developed communications infrastructure, always proved a strain, and supplying them in 1916's lengthy battles ultimately overwhelmed the transport system. In 1914 railways had moved men and guns behind the solidifying front and the men had then marched into battle along roads. During 1915 railways were just about able to sustain the day-to-day needs of entrenched armies. Since the home front was still mobilising, 1915's battles, while requiring increasingly large amounts of war material, had still essentially been manpower-intensive. Moreover, they had been relatively short, ceasing after a few days or weeks as shell supplies dwindled. The logistics systems of 1915 could not cope with the sustained *Materialschlacht* that began in 1916.[44] These prolonged, repetitive battles required more guns to be deployed and supplied regularly with more and heavier shells, as well as elaborate casualty-evacuation arrangements. In 1916 each division in the field required one-and-a-quarter trainloads of stores per day* when merely holding the line. During an offensive a division needed four trainloads per day, all of which had to be unloaded and transported forwards from fixed railheads, placing huge demands on transport and labour resources. Motor vehicles took up some of the strain from the horse-drawn wagons that had predominated in 1914. The French army became the most reliant on motor transport as the war went on. It started the war with 164 cars and lorries, but by its end there were 98,000 motor vehicles in service. Along the *voie sacrée* supplying Verdun, at the height of the battle trucks passed along a single road at five-second intervals. At the peak of the Somme offensive trucks passed along the Amiens-Proyart road at four-second intervals.[46] The strain on logistics was further exacerbated once an offensive was underway by the need to shift more stores across shell-shattered ground with no functioning rail infrastructure. Bad weather often brought everything to a muddy halt when roads became impassable.[47]

---

*These are British figures for 1916 on the western front. Requirements varied army to army and front to front, and inevitably increased as the war became more material intensive.

The modern logistical systems that emerged in response required the same sort of professional managerial methods on the battlefront as had been utilised on the home front. By September 1916, the British army's logistics were reaching their breaking point, and on Lloyd George's recommendation Haig turned to railway manger Eric Geddes to reorganise the lines of communication. Geddes inaugurated a front-line supply system based on narrow-gauge light railways (something the French had initiated during 1915) that enabled bulky loads to be distributed directly to gun positions.[48] Without such a bridge between the national railway systems that moved men and materials strategically and the field armies, operations on the scale undertaken from late 1916 would not have been possible. The enemy had been doing the same: the advancing German army laid its first sixty-centimetre-gauge railways in August 1914 to support the siege of Liège.[49] A light-rail network spread behind the static front during 1915 and 1916. This was an example of dynamic change on one side of the line being countered by parallel developments on the other, binding the two sides into a cycle of measure and countermeasure that confirmed a battlefield stalemate, even as the opposing war machines were modernising and engaging more and more ferociously.

AFTER THE SOMME OFFENSIVE BEGAN THE TABLES WERE TURNED AT VERDUN. Nivelle's Second Army mounted a steady, attritional counterattack against the eastern heights, while the defence was being stripped of resources to feed the avaricious struggle on the Somme. On 13 September 1916 Poincaré presided at a ceremony in the citadel of Verdun to honour the heroic defence and to mark the fact that the fortress had been held. Yet the battle was not over. When fighting two battles, Joffre had to apportion resources between them carefully: while the attack was being pressed on the Somme, the commanders at Verdun had to do the best they could with what their forces had in hand.[50] Once the Somme battle started to wind down, however, Joffre could respond to Pétain and Nivelle's desire for a major counterattack. Verdun ended with two striking successes: the recapture of the symbolic Douaumont and Vaux forts in late autumn, and their disengagement with another two-kilometre advance in December. The Second Army's tactics were now quite commonplace for the French army: they were, Fayolle noted dismissively, exactly the same as those he had been using on the Somme for months.[51]

Foch's and Nivelle's battles had overmastered the German army just as the Russians and Italians had the Austro-Hungarians. In that respect the general Allied offensive represented great progress compared with

1915's ill-coordinated and diffuse operations. Murray had cautioned as he recommend Joffre's strategy to the British cabinet:

> There are no certainties in war, and it cannot be guaranteed that the course recommended would succeed, but the General Staff feel convinced that there is no alternative worth adopting, and that the prospects of success, and perhaps decisive success, for such an offensive are good if all the Allies agree on it, prepare for it without delay and to the utmost of their several and collective abilities, and carry it through whole-heartedly and with the utmost vigour. By so much as any of the Allies falls short of developing his full power of preparation and execution, by so much will be the chance of success be reduced.[52]

Certainly all of the Allies had fallen short of the expectations with which they had begun the year. British ministers' indecision; Haig's delay in preparation and bad planning; the New Army's inexperience; French panic and anxiety over the army's staying power; Russia's reluctance to engage Germany directly; Italy's relative military weakness; Rumania's folly; war industries incompletely mobilised everywhere: these elements were the grit in the Allied war machine that ensured that at the end of 1916 the war remained stalemated. They suggested that Allied unity and the concentration of effort still had some way to go.

Although the general Allied offensive had failed, it turned the fortunes of war in the Allies' favour. Cadorna's battles had 'brought the Italians within sight of the goal of attritional warfare: exhausting the enemy to the point of collapse'.[53] Haig was able to end his despatch on the Somme offensive with the confident claim that, although 'the enemy's power has not yet been broken, nor is it yet possible to form an estimate of the time the war may last before the objects for which the Allies are fighting have been attained . . . the Somme battle has placed beyond doubt the ability of the Allies to gain those objects'.[54] Joffre was confident that renewing the general Allied offensive in early 1917 would bring his strategy to a successful denouement. 'Germany was our principal enemy and . . . her defeat would immediately bring about the dissolution of the coalition opposed to us,' he informed the Allies' military leaders. With a superiority of 2,200 battalions over the enemy, the time had come 'for destroying the enemy's defensive capacity having paralysed his offensive power'. 'Slow and indefinite attrition' was no longer enough. In the coming campaign the enemy should be dealt 'decisive blows at particularly sensitive points'. In 1917, 1916's effective strategic principle, 'attack together and on all our fronts', should be pursued against a weakened enemy with renewed vigour to a decision.[55] His military colleagues agreed. His political masters did not.

ALTHOUGH IT HAD BEEN A FAR TOUGHER YEAR THAN 1915, NEITHER SIDE was exhausted by the end of 1916. Yet all belligerents were starting to tire: casualty lists were lengthening, finances and resource were coming under strain now that mobilisation was complete and political and popular will was wavering. Although peace was starting to be talked about seriously, when, if and how it could be made remained unclear, since the stakes were becoming higher. Casualties remained high in 1916, a year of managed and sustained attrition. Battles were lengthy and apparently indecisive: only in Galicia (where they were always more flexible) had the front lines moved more than few miles, although in practice Brusilov's offensive was also a four-month attritional fight like those at Verdun, on the Somme and along the Isonzo. But, as those such as Asquith who understood the nature of attrition protested on occasion, lines on the map (particularly if it was large in scale) misrepresented the military outcome of the general Allied offensive. It eviscerated the Austrian army and plunged the German army into an acute manpower crisis, and greatly undermined its morale. Binding, who only arrived on the Somme as the winter war of observation began, was horrified by the shattered battlefield over which men had struggled: 'The earth here has been churned up again and again to its very depths. Dead men and animals, arms and equipment, are tossed about in the mud and slime, splashed up on high, pounded down into the earth again, again thrown up and torn into pieces until they are things without form or shape.' It was a miserable environment in which to spend a bitter winter contemplating the folly of the war and wallowing in 'the gloomiest reflections' on what 1917 might bring.[56]

The 'year of attrition' had cost the Allied armies heavily too, but they were fighting the war much more effectively by its end. The balance of attrition was shifting in their favour as technology was applied to the battlefield in a grinding *Materialschlacht*. War had become 'constantly repeated destruction, constant putting forth of effort, development of power and means, employment of masses of men and material, constant physical and mental strain'.[57] Such methods were breaking bodies and traumatising minds on both sides. 'It is not dying that is the demoralising thing,' one Italian lieutenant who fought on the Carso remembered. 'It is dying so uselessly, for nothing.' His commanders were the obvious men to blame.[58] The bigger strategic picture was of course hard to discern from the trenches, and many more men had died during a year of intensified attrition. Italian losses had accumulated over the spring and summer. In the huge battles in the East casualties on both sides were again enormous. Some 2,000,000 Russian casualties were offset against at least 777,000 Austrians killed, wounded or taken prisoner on the eastern front. Such losses could not be redressed with replacements and most Austrian units fought severely under strength in the second half of the year.[59] Germany suffered 1,400,000 irreplaceable casualties on both fronts during 1916. On the Somme between 400,000 and 680,000 men were killed, wounded or captured (estimates are still disputed). There the British and French lost 419,000 and 203,000 respectively.[62] Rumania, coming late and ill-prepared to the fray, lost 310,000 men, half her army, for nothing.[61]

It would have been of little comfort to soldiers that their generals now understood better how to conduct operations. It certainly was no sop to political leaders. Although objectives were being better matched to tactical capabilities, the 'scientific' operational method was too slow, and as yet the scale on which offensives could be resourced was insufficient to defeat the enemy.[62] Foch recognised that '[we are] not just fighting a battle like we did in Champagne or on the Somme, but organising an offensive system against the enemy's defensive system'. For better initial results mobile mechanical means – the tank and armoured car, 'the cavalry of the future' – had to be incorporated into offensive 'combined arms' tactics. Also, he adduced that 'the means had to be found to repeat [such attacks] at several points along the front, and to switch back to the first once the others had been checked'.[63] 'We must attack everywhere. But to attack we must have an offensive armament, which we do not yet have . . . It is therefore production that determines the progress of the offensive, and hence of the war.'[64]

This was a mechanistic approach to making war, imposing on it a slow, grinding attritional rhythm. It was at least a realistic one in the middle of the war and would produce results in time. As Foch had anticipated before he attacked on the Somme, the German army could now be taken on and beaten within its defensive system, with cumulative attrition taking its toll. On the Somme ninety-five and a half German divisions were drawn in and fought out (some more than once). The Allies committed ninety-six divisions of their own, forty-four French and fifty-two British, but for shorter tours of duty than the Germans. If the pace of attrition was not intense enough to break the German army once and for all, *Materialschlacht* of such intensity was a new and deeply damaging experience for it. Positions could no longer be held; local counterattacks would generally be defeated, and larger-scale counteroffensives would be crushed by the weight of Allied artillery fire, which in effect determined the course and outcome of the battle. Although winter came before a decision could be forced, this offensive had tested and proved tactical methods that worked on the entrenched battlefield.

As the war machines ground on during 1916, gradually warfare changed, and the war turned decisively. The Allies secured a clear, if hard to exploit, advantage from the year's fighting: perhaps, however, this was belied by the lengthy casualty lists on both sides. Lieutenant-General Sir Henry Wilson could starkly lay out the balance of achievement: 'A year of indecisive fighting. Verdun, Somme, Greece and Rumania all indecisive, both sides claiming victory . . . on the whole victory inclining to us, and the final decision brought nearer.'[65] The Rumanian campaign demonstrated that German operational skill still allowed the occupation of countries – they would take their biggest prize, Russia, by 1918, if not by main force – but she and her allies had no effective military answer to attrition, and strategically the Central powers had been forced on to the defensive. Skilful defensive tactics, which adapted as the Allies' blows became stronger, enabled them to absorb the shocks delivered on the Somme, at Verdun, along the River Isonzo and at Salonika, in Galicia and Bukovina. But building more and more lines of defence was only a temporary palliative for the cost in lives that were becoming irreplaceable. From 1917, therefore, the war was to be a somewhat different contest. The German army would still thrash to try to break the Allied grip, using operational skill in an effort to offset the attritional grindstone. But thereafter Germany was losing the land and home front wars and her strategic expedients became increasingly desperate, maritime and diplomatic, as a post-Somme manpower crisis gripped and her material disadvantages increased. If the Allies' political leaders had shared the confidence of their field commanders and sustained the pressure on Germany, the war might have ended in 1917. But they did not. 'Two Sommes at once', Wilson's formula for victory in 1917, was not a strategic panacea that the incoming British prime minister, Lloyd George, wanted to acknowledge.[66]

Lloyd George, who as secretary of state for war after Kitchener's death in June was responsible for finding the manpower to sustain the offensive, was genuinely concerned that the British army seemed much less effective on the battlefield than Fayolle's Frenchmen.[67] Indeed to some extent he had been mentally preparing himself for such an eventuality since the start of 1915, when he had warned against throwing away Britain's 'superb' volunteer army in what he feared might prove 'futile enterprises'.[68] Lloyd George never accepted that a mass army is raised to die for its country as well as to fight for it. As it was, in 1916 the professional cadres of the British regular army were too thinly spread to lead a newly raised citizen army that had expanded tenfold in less than two years, particularly since it had to learn new methods of warfare quickly. It meant that the Somme offensive would be a battle school. After its disastrous start the battle progressed increasingly well as fighting sense was inculcated into the raw troops and their keen but untested young officers. Almost all the British and imperial divisions on the western front were engaged at least once, and after a process of adaptation British tactics started to deliver results. It took a while for success to become consistent, and Haig's operational ambitions remained unrealistic. (The Somme finally demonstrated the sterility of the idea of breaking through into open country. When the German line was broken in mid-September at Bouchavesnes and Flers, the breaches were closed before fresh troops could get forward to exploit them. In positional warfare's battle of reserves, the advantage remained with the defender.)[69] Haig's army commanders, Rawlinson and Gough, learned how to mount increasingly effective set-piece attacks. Their subordinates, leading army corps, divisions and brigades, started to mould their formations into efficient fighting units that could be relied on to take on and defeat the enemy. Come September, in the Battles of Flers-Courcelette and Morval, Rawlinson's army was able to break in to the German positions almost as effectively as Fayolle's: Gough's army did the same at Thiepval, and on the Ancre in November.[70]

Being able to beat the enemy on the battlefield, however, was not enough for the impatient and ambitious Lloyd George. Towards the end of the Somme offensive he restated his oft-voiced critique of attritional strategy. Even after the general Allied offensive the enemy 'had in his occupation more territory than ever before, and he still had some four million of reserves . . . How then, Mr Lloyd George asked [the War Cabinet], is the war to be brought to an end?'[71] This is a note of despair, rather than a recognition that potentially another four million Germans and their allies had to be engaged and beaten to end the war. These four million Germans were not the prewar trained reserves that had worried him in December 1914 and had been worn down thereafter. Now an empire in desperate straits was mustering raw young and old levies: 'Germany's last hope' in the opinion of one forlorn civilian who watched them parade for the front.[72] The prospect of Germany being able to replace these men if a general attritional offensive was renewed in good time was slim.

In a lengthy critique of strategy prepared in anticipation of an Allied political conference that met on 15 November (on the same day Joffre was deciding 1917's strategy with the Allies' military leaders), Lloyd George set out all the problems of fighting a war of attrition, although he remained fanciful in his solutions. Attrition certainly did not yet seem to be wearing out German reserves at a rate at which they could not be replaced.[73] Defeating Germany's lesser allies, as the war minister advocated, was not however going to alter the central fact, as Wilson and other generals recognized, that 'the only thing worth talking about is killing Boches . . . If we beat the Boches, all else follows'.[74] After all, by this point in the war the Central powers had occupied Belgium, Serbia, much of Rumania, Russian Poland and parts of France without defeating their armies or forcing them or their allies to the peace table. Why would the defeat and occupation of Bulgaria or Turkey, or even of Austria, bring Germany to terms? Although it obsessed amateur strategists, the occupation of territory was not going to decide the war per se. It could, however, influence the balance of resources. In Rumania, for example, blockaded Germany had won large stores of grain, timber and livestock, and control of huge oil reserves that would see them through a potentially difficult winter.[75] 'The consequences of this may be far-reaching, and will help to prolong matters,' Sandhurst feared.[76]

At the end of 1916 Lloyd George and others were growing unhappy and pessimistic because the reality of attrition was apparent after the Battles of the Somme and Verdun and because there was no end in sight:

> What is our policy? Has anyone mapped out a road to victory? . . . I have only heard of one. People talk of hammering, and of a war of attrition. The success of hammering depends entirely upon whether you are making a greater impression on the barrier or the hammer. The success of a war of attrition depends upon the time it takes, and who can last out the longest.[77]

In that he was correct, but he was impatient and unrealistic about what was possible in a war with mass mobilisation on both sides. In agitating against the conduct of the war to date he had started to call for a 'knockout blow' to be delivered. Such rhetoric went down well in the press and parliament, even though all the evidence of 1915 and 1916 indicated that this was simply not possible.

Robertson, directly challenging Lloyd George, persisted in advocating a 'total' war approach, a policy of all or nothing, rather than a 'limited' war approach predicated on winning battles for political ends or to secure a favourable peace. 'We cannot hope for a conclusion in our favour unless and until we make a full and appropriate use of all our resources,' he represented. As well as a more united and coordinated alliance, he believed that the war effort had to be intensified: 'Have a full day's work from every man and woman. Make all possible use of foreign labour. Check present waste and extravagance in national life. Become as self-supporting as possible. Clearly explain to the nation the grave nature of the task in front of us.'[78]

Allied strategy in 1917 would once again be compromised by competing ideas of warfare and marked by a bitter struggle between soldiers and civilians over the right way to fight the war. At the end of 1916 Joffre was removed from his command and a new military quick fix championed by the victor of Verdun, Nivelle, was backed in place of slow, steady attrition. In Britain Asquith fell from power and his successor Lloyd George engaged his military advisors in battle directly over how the war should be conducted. These were unfortunate political developments, for by now the Entente's military commanders had mastered the new science of war and were starting to wear down the enemy at a more acceptable cost to their own forces.

1916 WAS THE CENTRAL, CRUCIAL YEAR OF THE WAR, WHEN STRATEGY AND policy came together on all fronts – the one in which the war machines engaged and the struggle really commenced. Yet what it offered was not a quick, decisive victory but the inexorable overmastering of one side by the other. The Allies approached the process with growing confidence; the Central powers with trepidation. The strategic theme of 1915 had been the containment of the growing yet diffuse Allied threat by the Central powers with localised yet indecisive successes on all land fronts. In 1916 Allied armies gripped the enemy on all these fronts, held on and endeavoured to grind down their fighting capacity. This was Joffre's plan, conceived haltingly during 1915 but only executed from the middle of 1916. It was a slow-working strategy that had its own flaws and failures. The enemy's actions were the biggest hindrance to the working of the Allied war machine, which while not yet at full capacity was nonetheless much better equipped and increasingly effective. Three further problems hampered Joffre. He had to manage the coalition in order to keep Allied effort focused on the central strategic objective. Offensive military operations had to be designed appropriately so that the unavoidable, and inevitably heavy, losses to the Allied armies would be proportionate. Political and popular support for the general Allied offensive, the people's 'big push', had to be engaged and sustained. 'The great human harvest that would transform the face of Europe' was now underway, *L'Image de la guerre* had informed its readership in July, adding: 'The Allies' vigorous offensive, its methodical preparation, the calm and sangfroid of its leaders, together indicate that at this moment they are in control of the enormous war machines that they have forged slowly, meticulously out of necessity.' In the field it would not be a quick battle but one of sustained pressure on the enemy as they withdrew on preprepared reserve positions.[79] When the 'big push' failed to produce a decision, on the home front an increasingly rancorous struggle over strategy would develop at the same time as the people's willingness to see it through started to come into question.

These problems meant that Germany and her allies would not be broken in 1916. Yet by the end of that year Germany's own forces were in disarray, her principal ally was growing desperate, their peoples were war weary and the options were limited. The fortunes of war seemed to have turned decisively in the Allies' favour. Their armies could fight the war to a conclusion, if only the home front held out. The two sides were now in a death grip, and whichever broke first would suffer complete collapse.

# ELEVEN

# ALLIED HOPES

W HEN THE ALLIES' POLITICAL AND MILITARY LEADERS GATHERED IN
Rome in January 1917 to settle the strategy for their next campaign, Lloyd George was determined to make his mark: 'There
is a very dangerous tendency becoming apparent for the War Cabinet to
direct military operations,' Robertson noted ruefully.[1] The Allies'
prospects seemed bright after Joffre's general Allied offensive had intensified the pressure on the German army and brought Austria to the edge
of defeat. Their war economies were functioning well now, and there
were plans to take up such slack as still existed by arming the Italian and
Russian armies and mobilising imperial resources more fully in 1917. But
the Allies themselves had been tested by the strains of 1916's intensive,
costly campaign. To some extent it seemed to have brought them closer
together: the gathering in Rome was the largest and best-prepared Allied
summit to date. But it also brought long-standing internal divisions to a
head, particularly those between soldiers and civilians. Joffre's intention
to reengage his general Allied offensive strategy in order to complete the
attritional strangulation of the Central powers in the coming spring had
been endorsed at another Allied military council at Chantilly on 15 November 1916. Briand and the Allies' political leaders meeting concur-
rently in Paris had other ideas. Lloyd George in particular had railed
against the generals' costly offensive strategy (with Asquith's somewhat
reluctant backing).[2] Briand was now inclined to rein in the power of his
principal strategic advisor, to ensure his own political survival as much
as anything. Lloyd George's opinions did not sway Briand in Paris, but
by the time they met again in Rome, Lloyd George had risen and Joffre
had fallen. The British prime minister arrived in Rome intending to push
for an offensive on the Italian front supported by British and French

heavy artillery and divisions loaned from the western front. But the sort of backhanded diplomacy that he favoured – he tried to win over Italian political and military leaders before springing his plan on the French and Russian delegates without warning after the conference opened – won him no plaudits. It was another plan that ignored military reality. He tried to persuade Cadorna that with more artillery he could force his way through to the Istrian Peninsula and occupy Trieste (overlooking the inconvenient fact that if not attacked elsewhere at the same time the Central powers would simply move reserves southwards), with the usual fanciful projection of being able to push on Vienna.[3] It required a deeper advance than any the Italians had yet managed, and even had it won a clear territorial prize in Trieste, it would have been a mere pinprick on the flank of the vast Habsburg Empire. Having talked to Robertson too, Cadorna was unenthusiastic. Not surprisingly, the impractical plan was referred to the Allied chiefs of staff for further consideration, a diplomatic way of rejecting it.[4]

While Lloyd George liked to present himself as Britain's (and therefore the Allies') new hope, France countered the maverick British prime minister with a new military hope of their own, Robert Nivelle, who had replaced Joffre in command of the French army. Nivelle, who had been promoted owing to his successes at the end of the Battle of Verdun, had a bold plan to defeat the enemy quickly. His plan revived the two-pronged assault on the flanks of the German salient in France that Joffre had attempted in September 1915 – one a holding attack by the British in front of Arras, the other an attempt by the French to break through along the River Aisne front – but now using the offensive methods developed in 1916. 'It means for us in a short future, when a general offensive will be carried out on a sufficiently broad front, the absolute certainty of a decisive victory,' one French officer confidently announced.[5] But the victor of Verdun offered false hope. Still, he offered just the sort of hope that Allied politicians were grasping for after two years of attrition, and with no end in sight. The War Cabinet had already accepted the plan in principle before Lloyd George on his own initiative tried to steer Allied strategy along personal lines in Rome. The prime minister was to return to London, chastened if not dissuaded that he understood strategy better than the generals, having endorsed Nivelle's plan.

The other issues on the agenda – Salonika and Greece – took up most of the conference. Lloyd George dug his heels in against sending further British troops to Salonika. In this at least he agreed with Robertson, but the rationale was that the shipping situation, that was to become increasingly difficult during 1917, did not allow it. Greece, the last

Balkan neutral, had become an embarrassment. Divided by now between pro-Allied and pro-German factions, Venizelos now led an interventionist movement while King Constantine stood out for neutrality: on the agenda was whether the king should be deposed in favour of his pro-Allied son, high-handed diplomacy of a new sort for the Allies.

The Allies began 1917 by thrashing out differences over strategy and policy similar to those that had marked the last two campaigns. Despite this superficial resemblance, they were in a much stronger position than in previous years, although deliberations over military strategy and delays in implementing the agreed plan would compromise the chance of success as before. Joffre had emphasised the need to strike again powerfully and quickly, not allowing Germany any opportunity to recover and refill the ranks. That looked unlikely come January 1917. As statesmen deliberated and soldiers prepared, the military advantages won by the general Allied offensive were slowly slipping away, replaced once more by the strategic fallacy of the decisive knockout blow. As the plan unfolded, old issues would have to be addressed and new ones engaged. Russia was still arming, against the backdrop of an increasingly troubled political situation as tsarism tottered towards its downfall. The Italian army was still held up in the Julian Alps. Britain and France had to coordinate their military action on the western front: there was obvious tension between Nivelle and Haig. And Germany, while battered, was far from beaten, and would set the Allies new strategic challenges.

As the new campaigning season opened, Hindenburg and Ludendorff dug in the remains of their army in strong defensive positions in the West, went on the defensive in the East and looked to the navy to decide the war. The German army faced the prospect of another year of attrition with foreboding as the manpower situation was growing critical. 'Now practically anyone who can manage to creep on all fours is being called back,' Evelyn, Princess Blücher* noted, after one officer who had been at home on sick leave for the past year-and-a-half was ordered to report for duty.[6] By deploying the 1918 class early, combing out rear areas and reclassifying recovering wounded and men previously judged unfit for service, more soldiers could be found to sustain the defence, though it was unclear for how long. This revision of strategy suggested that as things stood the German army could not win the land war, but the problems that the resumption of unrestricted submarine warfare would induce on the maritime front suggested that the Allies were still some way from winning it themselves.

---

*The English wife of a German aristocrat who saw out the war in Berlin.

\* \* \*

Nivelle's offensive offered some prospect of a major military victory in the West, if it could be launched quickly and in strength and coordinated with Russian and Italian operations. To that extent, one of Joffre's key strategic principles still held sway. The Central powers still appeared to be gripped on all fronts. Over the winter the British army sustained pressure against a demoralised enemy on the Somme front, nibbling away at the German defences with effective localised attacks. The British army had grown in skill and confidence, while the GHQ was busy codifying the lessons of its gruelling baptism of fire into doctrine appropriate for positional warfare. There was every expectation that it would fight much more effectively in the coming campaign. France, meanwhile, was resting and training troops for the coming offensive. Russian armies were engaged in the Carpathians and Bukovina, as far as winter conditions allowed. But this grip was to loosen by the time Nivelle was ready: Russia had let go in the East, Italy was not ready to resume the offensive in February as had been promised and the German army had slipped away in the West.

The tsar received the latest Allied delegations to the inter-Allied armaments summit that met in Petrograd in February 1917 with customary imperial pomp, endeavouring to mask his circumstances. General Wilson, Britain's military representative, could see that the increasing effectiveness of the Russian army at the front contrasted with growing chaos in the rear. His French colleague General de Castelnau, who had inspected the army's lines of communications, doubted that the Russians would be able to take the offensive that spring with any hope of success: he was not impressed by the men who ran the army's logistics, and 'the railways were in a hopeless mess'. Wilson's private conversations suggested that the tsar and his regime were 'heading straight for ruin'. General Vogack, formerly Russia's military attaché in London, confirmed the real situation: 'His chief concern was the internal trouble of the Emperor and Empress, next was the Russian mind which had not yet gone to war, next the total lack of power of organisation.' Tellingly, the businessmen of the Moscow Municipal Munitions Committee were deeply critical of the government's management of the war economy. 'If the poor Emperor would only choose the best man, make him Prime Minister, then go to the Duma and say he would trust himself to the people, he would have the whole of Russia at his feet,' Wilson speculated. But such voluntary experiments in wartime constitutional reform were inimical to the Romanovs. The tsar had postponed the reopening of the Duma in January, calling at the same time for its members to support his ministry in the 'strenuous and unremitting prosecution of the war'.[7] Such rhetoric was becoming increasingly empty. When the Duma reconvened against a backdrop of bread riots in

Petrograd, the liberal opposition took matters into their own hands. The February revolution broke out shortly after the mission's departure, and its plan to set up a British-led commission to oversee Russian munitions production proved stillborn.

The revolution, however, was a hopeful development. After the tsar was forced to abdicate and power became vested in a multiparty Provisional Government pending elections for a constituent assembly that would draw up the new liberal state's constitution, the political embarrassment of being allied to a despot disappeared. Now an alliance of progressive states faced one of militarist autocracies. The Provisional Government determined to honour Russia's Pact of London pledge not to make a separate peace and her agreement to support another Allied general offensive. The need to beat the Central powers remained a rallying cry under the new regime, although the nature of the peace that would follow was now debatable, and whether Russia could muster the forces to win it was uncertain. Certainly the Russian army would be in no position to attack in the spring, although the new regime hoped to be able to mobilise the people to fight on for a just peace. Alexander Kerensky, Socialist Revolutionary* leader and war minister in the Provisional Government, would emerge as its dominant personality. Kerensky fancied himself as a populist war leader in the French-revolutionary mould of Danton or Carnot, and would commit Russia to fight on for a peace without territorial annexations and indemnities that was becoming a rallying cry for the European left.[8] While expanding Russia's forces to their greatest extent in an attempt to build the French-revolutionary style 'nation in arms' that Russia lacked, Kerensky had also sanctioned the 'democratisation' of Russia's forces. This relaxation of military discipline opened up the army to weak collective leadership and also to Lenin's antiwar propaganda. What Russia lost through revolution, perhaps, was the military potency to win that or any other good peace.

AS USUAL THE ALLIES' LONG-STANDING DIFFICULTIES OF COORDINATION AND consensus were exerting friction as a new campaign began. While the Allies were dithering over the timing and nature of the next offensive, Hindenburg and Ludendorff prepared by reorganising their defences. On the land front, the Central powers were struggling. Over the winter manpower had been combed out to furnish reserves for the next campaign. Germany's 1917 class were already at the front, and the 1918 class were now in training. The concomitant release of older soldiers for the Hin-

---

*Russia's agrarian socialist party, rivals of the urban workers' party the Social Democrats.

denburg Programme of manufacturing that was to sustain new material-intensive defensive tactics, however, meant that there was little net increase in military manpower. There was enough manpower to fight on the defensive for another season, although infantry battalion strengths were being cut in favour of the supporting machine-gun and artillery arms. Reserve divisions to meet the expected Anglo-French spring offensive could only be found by shortening the defensive front and strengthening the positions that were being defended. In February and March a strategic retreat to the Siegfried System – the 'Hindenburg Line' as the Allies called it – was ordered. This newly built and very strong defensive system in the centre of the western front comprised several deep positions heavily protected by barbed wire, concrete strongpoints and intermediate defences, sited in such a way that the Allies would be obliged to move their artillery forward to engage each position. Now that the Allies had mastered the linear defensive systems built by the Germans in 1915 they would be set a much more difficult challenge. The retreat freed a strategic reserve of fourteen divisions with which to face-off the Allied offensive and reduced the French army's intended front of attack. For Germany's soldiers, however, the prospect of another grim defensive campaign was dispiriting, the prospects for the war doubtful, the war itself relentless yet abhorrent and its end impossible to foresee. 'Here am I clamouring for inspiration for Germany, of rather for the whole world,' Binding wrote home, adding: 'It is a fact that fine speeches about duty and Fatherland are as worn out as broken-down cab-horses . . . The War is devoid of all grandeur . . . The human soul is absorbed entirely by the struggle against distress and disaster.'[9] Morale, the intangible yet vital human factor against which attrition also worked, was becoming fragile as another year of war began, and in that respect the general Allied offensive had done effective work.

The retreat indicated that Germany's new leaders despaired of winning the war on land now that 1916's campaigns had exposed the growing impotence of Germany and Austria's armies against the Allies' increasing material strength. Instead, in 1917 victory would be sought on the maritime front. It was recognition that the overall situation was difficult, if not yet desperate. Russia and France had been attacked in 1915 and 1916 without defeating them: Hindenburg and Ludendorff concluded that it was now Britain's turn to feel the weight of Germany's blows. Being an island, Britain could not be attacked by the army, but the navy and Germany's air forces could strike back at the enemy that was increasingly seen as the mainstay of the opposing alliance and the principal adversary keeping Germany's other war-weary opponents in the war. Submarines could hit directly at Britain's overseas lifelines and so a resumption of unrestricted submarine warfare was mooted. U-boat attacks would disrupt the flow of war material to the Allied home fronts and potentially starve enemy civilians (to a certain extent this was justified as retribution for Germany's own people's suffering). A submarine counterblockade struck at an adversary's will to victory as well as its war making capacity, suggesting that the solidarity of the home front rather than success or failure on the battlefront could become the strategic centre of gravity of the conflict. Undermining popular morale might prove decisive, or at least force peace negotiations that seemed to be Germany's best hope at this point in the war.

The attack on Britain could be strengthened with air raids. Zeppelin airships had been bombing Britain intermittently since 1915, but now these raids were to be intensified and supplemented by the first ever strategic bomber offensive against London and other British cities, mounted with long-range bombing aircraft that were now based in Belgium. *Gott strafe England* (God strike-down England) was the watchword in Germany by this point in the war, and Germany would make England suffer as much as she could in 1917 in her renewed effort to break the rival coalition. Air raids became a regular, troubling occurrence from March, but they caused more moral outrage than morale collapse once the people of London and the home counties became accustomed to them. After his own London townhouse was damaged, Sandhurst noted defiantly,

> Germans, of course, are trying to make our flesh creep by saying that they are doing everything to make Gothas* so that they may come by the hundred. They want to get us into a state of panic, and they are undoubtedly succeeding in frightening very many; but this will make no difference in the determination of the nation. It will make everyone set their teeth harder and render the hatred of Germans, and everything connected with Germans, more intense than ever.[10]

Air raids distracted attention and resources, particularly of guns and aircraft that were diverted from the western front for air raid defence, but compared to submarine warfare bombing was no real threat to Britain's war making capacity or resolve.

The statisticians of the German naval staff calculated that Allied merchant shipping could be sunk at a rate that would force them to negotiate within five months. Bethmann Hollweg felt the potential gains were not worth the likely diplomatic consequences and acquiesced reluc-

---

*A type of German long-range bomber.

tantly to the OHL's reorientation of strategy. The military now determined Germany's fate, not civilian politicians. Bethmann Hollweg's anxiety was justified because Germany and America were already in a standoff over submarine warfare, and all appreciated that resuming indiscriminate sinkings would make matters worse and might bring America into the war. Up to that point Wilson had been tacking a course through the Entente's high-handed flouting of international maritime law and Germany's aggressive retaliation, not least because he had been campaigning for reelection. Now Germany actually called Wilson's bluff. To a certain extent unrestricted submarine warfare was a response to the facts that since 1915 American finance had been sustaining the Allied war effort and American industry had been supplying munitions for the enemy's attritional battles. Germany's avowed objective being to starve England, her U-boats could best do that by cutting off her supplies from America. Moreover, it was clear that the Allies were winning the propaganda battle in the United States and that the American public's and president's sympathies were not with Germany. In accepting that they would hurt America too, Germany's statesmen reckoned that they could end the war in their favour before America could organise herself to strike back. As Sandhurst rightly judged, 'Germany has now made the gambler's last throw – justified if she wins, but I can't see that this is possible – by practically declaring war on the world.'[11]

Wilson responded to the resumption of unrestricted submarine warfare on 1 February 1917 by breaking off diplomatic relations with Germany, ignoring Bethmann Hollweg's last-minute effort to dissuade him. Another crass diplomatic blunder, the offer of an offensive alliance to Mexico should the United States enter the war, made by the new German foreign minister Arthur Zimmerman in January 1917, ratcheted up tensions. The British, whose intelligence services were adept at intercepting German diplomatic traffic, passed a copy of the 'Zimmerman Telegram' to Wilson in February. The German offer undermined what little trust the liberal statesman still had in German diplomats' good faith, and perhaps more importantly, it gave interventionists an excuse to press the president to declare war. This decided the propaganda battle that the two sides had been waging to sway American public opinion. Initially Wilson adopted a stance of 'armed neutrality' to defend American commercial interests. But the inexorable march of events now that American ships were being sunk was towards intervention. On 2 April Wilson moved a motion in Congress that America enter the war on the Allied side as an 'associated power'.[12]

The German naval statistics office's figures were grossly overoptimistic, but Germany's submariners at least had a fighting chance of making a real impact on the Allies' ability and will to continue the war. U-boat construction had been prioritized since 1915, and by 1917 the navy had more and faster and better armed boats than it had been able to commit to 1915's unrestricted submarine warfare campaign. After two years, their captains and crews were skilled: sinkings had been rising steadily during 1916. Moreover, the Royal Navy's tactics against the submarine threat played into Germany's hands. Aggressive by tradition and inclination, the Admiralty determined that the way to deal with submarines was to hunt them and kill them, and developed tactics and technologies to do so. Antisubmarine nets were spread to protect ships at anchor or to close off harbour entrances and waterways. Q-ships* were commissioned to lay in wait for unsuspecting U-boats: another incentive for submarines to sink vessels with torpedoes without warning. Destroying submerged U-boats was less easy. Depth charges were available, but their use was haphazard. Setting aside the difficulty of destroying it, the real problem was finding a tiny submarine in the vast expanse of the North Sea and Atlantic approaches. Sound-detecting hydrophones that could locate submerged U-boats by listening for their engine noise had only a short range. Aircraft (principally sea planes) would be used extensively as the eyes of the fleet in coastal waters: some even started to fly off primitive aircraft carriers in 1918. But directing surface vessels on to U-boats in a timely manner once spotted was difficult. Such tactics tied up hundreds of small ships in antisubmarine patrols.

SUBMARINES WOULD NOT ALTER THE STRATEGIC BALANCE QUICKLY, AND THEY were no panacea for Germany's problems on land. For the maritime campaign to have any chance of bringing the war to an end, Germany's armies would have to buy time by containing the Allied spring offensive. Joffre had intended to intensify the attrition of the German army as soon as possible in 1917. Nivelle's steady preparations instead gave Hindenburg and Ludendorff time to reorganise their defences. Ominously, they also gave time for the consensus behind his plan to weaken. Nivelle expected to break the German front and defeat the enemy in open warfare. This had not worked in 1915, yet Nivelle's 1917 plan was in essence the same as that for Joffre's Champagne-Artois offensive. The British would attack in strength in front of Arras to engage Germany's operational reserves. Then some days later three French armies would attack on the Aisne front, seize the Chemin des Dames Ridge and push through the German

---

*Merchant ships armed with concealed guns to engage submarines on the surface as they closed for the kill.

defences in the direction of Laon, threatening the railway system that
sustained the German front. Nivelle reasoned that his tactics would
enable a rapid advance through successive German defensive positions
into open country. He then immediately abandoned the central tenet of
France's effective 1916 methods, that the artillery's capabilities should
determine the infantry's tasks. Reasoning, erroneously, that using tanks
to support the infantry (which the French army would do for the first
time) would make the usual heavy bombardment unnecessary, Nivelle
spread the supporting artillery barrage far too thinly. The key lessons of
1915–16 were easily forgotten now that the chimera of quick victory had
reappeared.

Those who understood battle recognised that Nivelle's plan was
fanciful, especially after the Germans' strategic withdrawal. Haig dragged
his feet over preparations since he was in no position to protest, hoping
that wiser councils would prevail or events would force a rethink. The
result was that he was formally subordinated to Nivelle for the offensive
by the terms of February's Calais Agreement, another Lloyd George initiative sprung on Haig and Robertson without warning that further
soured relations between the British prime minister and his military leaders. If anyone could stop the attack, it was France's politicians. Briand,
Nivelle's principal political sponsor, fell from office in mid-March and
was replaced by the conservative republican elder statesman Alexandre
Ribot, who was heading a government of national unity at a time of
growing domestic troubles. His new war minister, Paul Painlevé, a socialist
mathematician who had previously been Briand's minister for public
instruction and inventions, ordered an enquiry into the pending offensive.
Nivelle's subordinate commanders who were to conduct the offensive,
Pétain and Micheler, were not hopeful of success, but with British guns
already firing their preliminary bombardment at Arras it was too late to
call a halt, especially as Nivelle threatened to resign. This might have
brought down yet another ministry and plunged France into political turmoil. As it was, Nivelle's offensive would maintain pressure on the German army, which could not be left free to attack Russia or Italy.[13] It was
allowed to go ahead, not because it might decide the war, but because
France or the alliance might break if it did not.

The offensive demonstrated that both Allied armies could now beat
the German army in its defensive positions, but that the Allies were still
some way from having the strategic vision and material preponderance
needed to win the land war. The British holding attack, the Battle of
Arras, started well. On its northern flank the Vimy Ridge was finally
stormed: its crest was narrow and a deep defensive system could not be
established there. After assimilating the lessons of the Somme, British and

imperial infantry and artillery worked effectively together. In places the infantry was supported by tanks, a new weapon which had made its bat- tlefield debut during the Somme offensive. Above the lines an unprece- dented number of aircraft spotted for the artillery, fought off the enemy's fighter squadrons and supported the ground troops. This new, techno- logical style of military operations – 'combined arms' warfare as it was called – depended on the material and munitions produced on the home front for it success. It allowed German defensive positions to be captured with relative ease. But as the development of the Battle of Arras under- lined, once the defence was alert and reinforced, no amount of material and skill would circumvent a tough fight with an adversary equally well equipped and trained.

The results of the French army's attack one week after the opening of the Battle of Arras fell far short of Nivelle's ambitions. Nivelle intended that sheer weight of numbers would push the French forces through the German defences within forty-eight hours. This turned out to be a recipe for disaster with heavy casualties that harked back to September 1915. In many places the assault troops broke through the German front posi- tion (which was weakly held). They were very skilled at this by now, and this was perhaps the easiest task in a battle. Driving quickly against the next line of defence, however, commanders pushed their troops forwards with inadequate artillery support. Once again the momentum of the attack broke against the second German position where the enemy's reserves and firepower were concentrated. French reserves piled up behind the leading regiments that had been checked and logistical chaos ensued.[14] The inexperienced French tank force, from which so much was expected, gave a poor account of itself in its first battle.[15] The only, and unfortu- nate, outcome of Nivelle's offensive (apart from 134,000 further French casualties) was that it left the French army engaged in prolonged *grigno- tage* along the Chemin des Dames. Although the attack was reasonably militarily effective by the standards of the time, it proved psychologically disastrous, since the army's morale had been raised to a high pitch by the victories of the second half of 1916, only to be dashed in the rain and mud of the spring offensive. The check plunged the French army into a deep morale crisis that temporarily paralysed its offensive capability and brought France closer to defeat than at any time since August 1914.

ALTHOUGH ON THE SURFACE IT APPEARED MUCH THE SAME, THE WAR THAT restarted in May 1917 was subtly different. There would be no knockout blow as many, contrary to the accumulated evidence and experience, had hoped for. Instead, the Allies would have to negotiate their way through a difficult summer in which U-boats preyed on shipping, Russia slipped towards anarchy, France wavered and Italy struggled valiantly but vainly to make progress. America's entry offered future hope, but also further complications. Political actors were different and agendas were changing. France was now weaker and Great Britain stronger; although civil-military relations in London were difficult and strategy remained contested, Lloyd George attempted to assert his leadership at home and among the Allies. Now that Germany placed her hopes on a maritime victory, the naval war had to be prioritized, although the land war could not be ignored. Because maritime supply determined the effectiveness of the land campaigns in France and Turkey, it became a question of how the army could help the navy, and whether the war on land could be decided before the war at sea was lost. It was now clear that there was no way to finish the war quickly – that armies and nations were condemned to slow, grinding attrition. While ending the war was everyone's wish, when and how it would end and on whose terms peace would be negotiated was impossible to predict. The immediate task was to rethink strategy now that America was in the war and Germany had won a reprieve on land. There was still much of the campaigning season left. How to put it to good use while sustaining Allied unity and resolve had to be decided. Fuller mobilisation, more careful military operations, better coordination and steady pressure became the principles by which the Allies would redress their disappointment and prepare for the ultimate trial of strength with the Central powers that would be needed to decide the war.

LLOYD GEORGE MAY HAVE LACKED STRATEGIC COMMON SENSE, BUT HE certainly appreciated how to run a war effort. During 1917, however, he grew increasingly reluctant to use that system against Germany. Lloyd George was growing pessimistic about the likelihood of a decisive end to the war. After the spring offensive failed, he now expected that the war would conclude with an unsatisfactory peace of exhaustion: money would run out before military manpower, or popular will would break before military might. If there was to be a compromise peace, Britain should be in a position where it would be to her advantage, Lloyd George reasoned. Rather than sacrifice more lives in indecisive slogging on the western front, therefore, he argued that military strategy should refocus on Britain's imperial interests in the Near East. In Europe he thought that new populist aspirations, national self-determination and democracy (which chimed with Wilson's idealistic agenda) might be promoted as alternatives to dynastic autocracy in the crumbling empires. Undermining the enemy's home front might prove more cost-effective than trying to decide the land war: as all societies grew war weary there was some sense behind this opportunistic shift. Lloyd George's 'New Eastern' strategy became the guiding principle of the War Cabinet's strategy thereafter.[16] But this was a policy of half-measures and limited rewards because whatever else Lloyd George aimed at, he could never abandon France and Britain's main military commitment on the western front. Moreover Haig and Robertson demurred. They retained their faith in attrition.

An imperially orientated war strategy also reflected the fact that the whole empire was making war. The empire had always been a source of manpower, foodstuffs and agricultural raw materials for the war effort: cotton for uniforms and explosives; jute for sandbags; rubber for vehicle tyres and gas masks; and that overlooked but vital strategic commodity, the tea that fuelled the British soldier on campaign (the enemy soldier had to put up with unpalatable ersatz coffee). As well as raw materials, the empire provided manpower. The forces raised by the Dominions were now fully mobilised (there would be problems keeping the ANZAC and Canadian divisions up to strength thereafter). Nonwhite soldiers, especially those of the Indian Army, had been deployed from 1914, to France, Egypt, Mesopotamia and East Africa. Initially, Indian expeditionary warfare had been badly managed by the viceroy's department in Delhi resulting in early military disasters. As well as the retreat and surrender in Mesopotamia, an Indian Army force landed at Tanga in German East Africa in November 1914 was badly handled by the German native *askari* troops and militia defending the port and was forced to re-embark.

Indian troops and Indian and imperial resources would become the mainstay of the war against Turkey as time went on. A parallel but lesser war of attrition was being waged against a large, populous and difficult to attack Asian land empire: comparisons with Austria-Hungary's situation are obvious. The Turkish war dragged on for a number of reasons, both strategic and political. Extensive, generally arid and with poor internal communications, the Ottoman Empire's landmass was not that vulnerable to Allied military power. The improvised attempt to use sea power to strike at the heart of the Turkish state through the Dardanelles therefore made strategic sense. After that failed, the war against the Ottoman Empire drew in Allied land forces in increasing numbers. From 1916, Turkey was fighting a defensive war on her imperial periphery, while internal problems were increasing. In 1915 a notorious state-sponsored campaign of deportation and terror, in which more than one million people died, was carried out against the supposedly disloyal Armenian Christian population. From mid-1916 the Young Turks faced a British-sponsored Arab revolt.

British operations against the Turks started to replicate the pattern of the resource-intensive extended siege operations being conducted against the Central powers in Europe. Men and resources were deployed for steady, systematic advances into Ottoman territory sustained by appropriate logistics. General Sir Stanley Maude's reorganised Mesopotamian Expeditionary Force reached Baghdad in March 1917. At the end of 1915 Indian troops were redeployed from the western front to defend Egypt. Thereafter they formed the nucleus of the forces that would undertake the most important and effective Allied campaign against the Ottoman Empire, the advance from Egypt to Jerusalem and beyond. In January 1916, after stepping down as CIGS General Murray took command of the forces in Egypt. Murray was the sort of professional, staff-trained soldier who understood that a modern army relied on functioning logistics, appropriate equipment and rigorous training for its effectiveness. Murray spent the summer and autumn of 1916 building the railways, laying the water pipelines and organising the Egyptian labour that would allow his army to advance without risking the sort of disasters others had met in Turkey's deserts.[17] Unfortunately for Murray, his methodical, systematic way of managing military operations did not endear him to Lloyd George, who still sought quick, decisive victories of a sort that attritional warfare could not produce. It would be Murray's successor, General Sir Edmund Allenby, reassigned after commanding the Third Army in the Battle of Arras, who would lead the advance on Jerusalem for which Murray had laid the groundwork. As it progressed, the war against Turkey galvanized the mobilisation of the British Empire in the east, gearing the resources of India and Egypt properly to the allied war machine.[18] As the western and Balkan fronts drew increasingly on domestic resources, there was an increasing 'Indianisation' of Britain's campaigns beyond Europe (and the same was planned for Salonika in 1919).[19] By 1918 the war against Turkey, a central element of Lloyd George's New Eastern strategy, was tying down over two million British and Indian soldiers and the resources needed to sustain them in the field in an inhospitable climate. At least the New Eastern strategy largely utilised imperial manpower and resources rather than drawing excessively on home resources that were needed to sustain Haig's army.

Indeed, the availability of imperial manpower resources allowed the Entente states to keep expanding their war efforts after Germany's had reached its peak. Nonwhite labourers were the next group to be mobilized from the British Empire as the need for manpower intensified. The Cape Coloured Labour Battalion and the South African Native Labour Corps together provided nearly 23,000 workers for service behind the western front. Their recruits from the elite of South African tribal societies proved skilled, speedy workers. A Compulsory Service Act passed in South Africa in March 1917 also raised 100,000 bearers for the long-running campaign in East Africa. The voracious need for labour meant that labour battalions would also be raised in Malta, the West Indies, the Seychelles, Fiji, Mauritius, Egypt, Portugal, Greece, Macedonia, Serbia and from Jewish volunteers and the sons of enemy aliens in Britain.[20] Even neutrals could not escape. A Chinese Labour Corps organised on military lines served behind the French lines from August 1916, and the British from April 1917. In all nearly 140,000 Chinese were recruited, on the sort of indenture terms that had been used to recruit Chinese labourers since the nineteenth century. Five thousand five hundred more served in Mesopotamia.[21]

The increasing demands of war necessitated organising the manpower resources of the French Empire. In the established colony of Algeria and to a lesser extent in French Morocco and other overseas territories the white settler population was subject to the same conscription laws as the metropole: overall 134,000 French citizens were mobilised from overseas, 92,000 of those from Algeria.[22] Indigenous forces were also raised to defend France or her colonies. Colonially raised manpower provided 7 percent of French military manpower, 608,000 men, of whom 449,000 served in France, the others at Gallipoli and Salonika and in ongoing imperial insurrections: small wars did not stop simply because a huge one was being waged, although France had to scale-down counterinsurgency campaigns in its African colonies pending the end of the European war.[23] Labour battalions and transport regiments were also raised from nonsettler colonies such as Tunisia, Madagascar and French Indochina. Workers were also engaged in the colonies (as well as from neutral and Allied countries such as Spain, Greece and Portugal) to work in metropolitan France's war industries, some 140,000 in all, among them the future Vietnamese independence leader Ho Chi Minh.[24]

Proportionately, colonial levies served more in frontline infantry units than in the support and technical branches of the army. Perhaps this was inevitable given that indigenous troops lacked the technical knowledge of Europeans. General Charles Mangin had argued before the war that France's African imperial manpower reserve, *La Force noire* as he called it in an influential treatise, should be developed as a counterweight to Germany's larger population.[25] As the war went on, France raised more and more West African battalions (they were generically identified as 'Senegalese' although they were recruited more widely). The Entente's use of nonwhite troops on the battlefield was one complaint that Germany raised repeatedly, probably because they made formidable soldiers.[26] Some 181,000 West African soldiers were recruited during the war, and such battalions were widely distributed among French divisions by 1918. But increasingly coercive recruitment, leading up to the introduction of conscription in France's West African colonies in November 1917, proved divisive, provoking individual draft avoidance and widespread civil disorder. France's other colonies provided smaller contingents of varying martial value.[27] Moroccans were the best among them, aggressive soldiers who terrified the Germans who encountered them.

In the second phase of mobilisation, from mid-1916, the war became truly global in its reach. European manpower reserves were reaching their limit and so empires were scoured for more workers and soldiers. In French West Africa, for example, the recruitment of large numbers of indigenous troops accelerated in response to the heavy losses of France's earlier campaigns. Non-European labourers and soldiers remained aliens in a white-man's world and war. Africa and Chinese labourers were segregated in camps, denied free contact with the civilian population in France and banned from drinking alcohol. More immediate concerns of immorality and fraternisation with white women masked deeper concerns that participation in the war would give non-Europeans a belief in their equality with the white men who officered the labour battalions.[28] In an imperial war, colonial attitudes about race and rights persisted.[29] While colonial subjects could make a contribution to the war effort, their expectations that they would gain recognition and reward for it did not match those of their white working-class brethren on the domestic home fronts, or even women. Recruiting nonwhite populations for the war effort was merely an adaptation of the existing colonial system to the extreme needs of wartime. When American 'Negro' regiments arrived in France in 1918 they remained segregated from the other units of the American army. With their experience of and trust in African troops, however, the French willingly integrated such troops into their divisions. This was certainly not a war that was going to challenge prevailing perceptions of racial difference and promote equality in the colonies in the same way that it fostered self-determination and social change in Europe.

NIVELLE'S FAILURE FORCED A RETHINK OF MILITARY STRATEGY. ON 4 MAY British and French military leaders meeting in Paris agreed to resume a policy of attrition, pending developments. This their political masters endorsed. Lloyd George seemed temporarily reconciled to an aggressive strategy after April's battles, which had engaged and defeated 36 German reserve divisions and won 45,000 prisoners and 450 guns. 'We must go on hitting and hitting until the German ended, as he always did, by cracking,' he argued to his French colleagues, who now seemed battle shy owing to the French manpower situation.[30] This did not mean passive trench holding, but continuing the battles at Arras and along the Chemin des Dames in the short term and mounting powerful but limited material-intensive offensives over the summer months to further degrade the German army's fighting capacity while Allied strength was built up, 'wearing down and exhausting the enemy's resistance, and if and when this is achieved to exploit it to the fullest extent possible . . . destroying the enemy's divisions . . . with the minimum loss possible'.[31] Pétain's professed policy of 'waiting for the Americans and the tanks' did not imply lassitude in the interim – it testified, however, to the importance of manpower and material in Allied strategy.

As it turned out, the French army was not capable of mounting such operations before August, and the British army had to commence a major operation in Flanders to liberate the Belgian Channel Ports meanwhile. French soldiers' hopes had been dashed by the failure of the Nivelle Offensive, and waves of military protest against engaging in costly attritional battles to no obvious strategic purpose swept through the army from April to June. Its new commander in chief Pétain, who replaced Nivelle in mid-May, would spend the summer restoring morale and reeducating his army in tactical methods that would allow it to fight battles that improved the military position significantly, but with acceptable losses. Pétain's methods drew heavily on the lessons of 1915 and 1916. His battles would be limited in scale and ambition and would employ overwhelming firepower, a technique that became known as 'bite and hold'. When the French army went on the offensive again in mid-August it blasted the Germans off the heights around Verdun with morale-boosting assurance.

The Italians would have benefitted from such methods, as well as some of Pétain's guns. They played their part diligently in the Allied plan by maintaining pressure on the Austrian army, but regrettably Cadorna still insisted on driving his forces onwards against strengthening enemy defences. Two further offensives were launched on the Isonzo front, from mid-May to early June, and mid-August into September. The first, the Tenth Battle of the Isonzo, was badly managed by Second Army commander General Luigi Capello, who on occasion resorted to human-wave attacks against strong Austrian defences. Such costly and outdated methods pushed the enemy back towards Trieste, although the city remained out of reach. Boroević handled the defence well and managed to check and counterattack the Italian Second Army despite his inferior numbers. The largest battle to date cost 157,000 Italian and 75,000 Austrian casualties.[32] Lloyd George still pressed Robertson to release heavy guns for the Italian front to make the Italians' operations more effective, but

Robertson dug in his heels while Haig's army was on the offensive in Flanders. The eleventh battle in August went better, the Italians showing greater drive and skill. The Second Army had more artillery support and finally established itself firmly on the Bainsizza Plateau east of Gorizia. But once again Boroević could withdraw his forces to a rearward defensive line, and the potential breakthrough evaporated. The Italians suffered 166,000 casualties, the Austrians 140,000. But the Austrian army was being used up. Italy could still afford such casualties, which were becoming less disproportionate – Austria could not.[33]

Russia in transition tried her best to honour her commitment to the Allies, but her future contribution to the war was uncertain. 'I do not think that we shall derive any assistance from Russia this year,' Robertson cautioned Foch, who had just become chief of staff in the French war ministry. This presented the Allies with a potential problem. 'The only question seems to be whether Russia can retain the whole or greater part of the enemy divisions now on her front,' Robertson continued, 'and if she cannot whether they are likely to be withdrawn and where employed.'[34] Robertson warned Haig that committees of workers and soldiers appeared to be forming in Russia.[35] Lenin's moment seemed to be coming. Kerensky's determination to pursue the war actively would actually help the Bolsheviks. The Russian army's final offensive in July, to which Kerensky lent his name and Brusilov his skill, ran out of steam quickly. Like Brusilov's previous battle it started very well. The Galician front was shattered once again (by the most powerful bombardment yet fired by the Russians, largely from British and Japanese-made guns) and Russia's armies advanced thirty kilometres. When the enemy inevitably counterattacked, however, the Russian army started to disintegrate. Men deserted en masse, often shooting any officers who tried to stop them.[36] Russia then turned on herself in a typical postrevolutionary struggle for power. In August Kerensky's new commander in chief, General Lavr Kornilov, attempted to suppress Bolshevik-dominated workers', soldiers' and sailors' Soviets that held power in Petrograd. Mistakenly concluding that Kornilov was threatening the Provisional Government with a military coup, Kerensky arrested his commander in chief, losing what little loyalty the army still retained for the new liberal regime. The army was very much in the revolutionaries' pocket by the time a German drive towards the capital catalysed Lenin's supporters to seize power in Petrograd in October in the avowed cause of revolutionary and national defence.[37] The liberal hopes that the February Russian revolution had raised proved ultimately false. Thereafter the Allies had to accommodate themselves to the convulsions of Soviet Russia's painful birth and also confront the domestic enemies that Bolshevism was mobilising. Lenin's bold coup would determine Germany's future too – if she lost the war, or if the Bolsheviks won the civil war that would be ravaging Russia by the middle of 1918.

WITH BRITAIN'S ALLIES IN DIFFICULTIES, THE ATTRITION OF THE GERMAN army would fall disproportionately on Haig's armies in the summer and autumn of 1917. It was the worsening situation on the seas, moreover, that obliged Haig to take the offensive in Flanders. In its first few months, unrestricted submarine warfare proved devastatingly effective. From 369,000 tons in January 1917, merchant ship sinkings peaked at 881,000 tons in April and did not drop below 540,000 tons between February and June.[38] Merchant ships were easier to find than submarines, not least because they would have to make port, and so lurking U-boats could pick them off in the crowded approaches. The fact that merchant ships sailed individually made them even easier prey. The Admiralty seemed to have no effective response. 'The submarine war has become frantic,' Hankey noted on 8 February. 'We seem to be sinking a good many submarines, but they are sinking a terrible lot of ships.'[39] At the end of March Hankey was still 'much worried about the shipping outlook owing to submarines and the inability of the Admiralty to deal with it . . . I am oppressed by the fear that I have always had that, while moderately successful on land, we may yet be beaten at sea'.[40] The navy could not lose the war in an afternoon, but it seemed that they might still lose it in a season. The army might yet relieve the situation with an offensive to recapture the Belgian Channel Ports. 'Can the Army win the war before the Navy loses it?' was the question on many peoples' minds in early 1917.[41]

'I think the country has discovered that we are at war,' Sandhurst noted as foodstuffs became scarcer, 'but it has taken two and a half years really to find it out.'[42] Unrestricted submarine warfare struck directly at Britain for the first time. It also tested the Allies' ability to manage and distribute resources, dependent as this was on shipping capacity. Before 1917, for example, too much of the shipbuilding industry had been employed building new warships; thereafter, merchant ships were prioritized. With the United States turning out standardised ships in increasing numbers by 1918, the situation became less worrying. The threat to shipping was certainly a genuine anxiety, but the response was relatively speedy and effective now that the British war economy was centrally managed. Imports would be restricted and war material prioritized; domestic production, particularly of foodstuffs and bulk commodities such as timber and iron ore that required a lot of tonnage, would increase; a shipping controller, Sir Joseph Maclay, who would balance the shipping needs of the various government departments, was appointed. Maclay was a Glasgow shipowner and one of the 'men of push and go' who Lloyd George increasingly relied on to run the mature war economy. 'The very life of the nation depended on making the best use of our ships', Lloyd George appreciated, and the British people would have to make necessary sacrifices.[44] The import of brewing material, wines and spirits was reduced; but 'on the whole . . . the long-suffering people of this country bore these privations with the same uncomplaining stoicism as they had withstood still greater physical and moral hardships', Hankey believed. There was inevitably some restriction on consumption – public restaurants had to introduce meat-free days for example – but although contingency plans were drawn up food rationing did not have to be introduced until spring 1918. Lloyd George's food controller, Lord Devonport, introduced a scheme of voluntary rationing, setting notional weekly food quotas for people and organisations to observe 'on [their] honour'. But this could be ignored or circumvented. While Sandhurst organised and chaired a committee of London gentlemen's clubs to implement the new regime in their dining rooms and among their staff, he found others who interpreted the recommendations liberally. Lord Derby's 'meat free' dinner for the king consisted of 'soup, fish, chickens and macaroni'.[45]

The antisubmarine strategy also included improved defence of merchant shipping. Until 1917 merchant ships had sailed the world's oceans unarmed and unescorted. As the number of sinkings rose a convoy system, in which merchant vessels would travel in groups escorted by warships, was belatedly adopted. This was forced through against Admiralty objections, principally the belief that there were not enough small ships available to protect merchant shipping. The convoy system obliged U-boats to come to their hunters, rather than these having to seek them out and therefore proved more economical in its use of warships. Since U-boats would now be forced to do battle with convoy escorts before they could sink merchant ships, thereafter sinkings declined while U-boat losses increased. Signals intelligence, the interception of U-boat radio communications, allowed convoys to be diverted away from lurking submarines. Although merchant vessels continued to be sunk until the end of the war – especially those not sailing in convoy, which accounted for 85 percent of sinkings in early 1918 – shipping losses from mid-1917 were manageable, in the last quarter falling by half from their spring peak.[46] Germany probably never had enough U-boats to sink Allied shipping at a rate that would have changed the outcome of the war. Only 41 U-boats were on station at any one time, out of 121 in commission. Prewar calculations suggested that 222 would be required to wage an effective campaign of attrition against enemy commerce.[47] Unrestricted submarine warfare slowed the Allied war machines and obliged civilians to tighten their belts one more notch, but it could not bring the Allied war effort to a grinding halt. On the downside for Germany, it stimulated Allied resolve to defeat German barbarity and added America to Germany's growing list of enemies.

The United States was a major belligerent, with diplomatic clout, enormous economic output and great military potential. America's entry and the bold, moralistic declarations of her president were naturally received with great popular excitement. It was Americans' duty to 'add their authority and their power to the authority and force of other nations to guarantee peace and justice throughout the world', Wilson had pronounced in January 1917.[48] As the leader of an 'associated power', Wilson would pursue his supplementary agenda by diplomatic means among his allies and towards his enemies even as he was applying that power. Moreover, Wilson's self-avowed mission to secure a moral, balanced peace meant that political complications came with the new liberal hope. Although his new allies appreciated American industry and money, ships and men, they resented the counterpoint between Allied war aims and Wilsonian peacemaking. In practice, since American finance and industry had been geared to the Allies' war effort already, and raising a multimillion-man American Expeditionary Force to intervene in the land war would take many months, the United States' active belligerence would not make much difference to the Allies' ability to make war in the short term. It would be a year or more before Wilson's ideals and America's intervention might shift the war irreversibly into new channels.

FOR THE REST OF 1917 ALLIED STRATEGY WOULD REMAIN ATTRITIONAL. Field forces would continue to wear down the enemy's armies, while blockade would sustain pressure on the Central powers' home fronts. From 1917 the blockade was working effectively enough, although until an Allied Blockade Committee was set up in December (and absorbed into the Allied Supreme War Council in March 1918), there was no single administrative body charged with managing the economic campaign. American entry helped tighten the economic stranglehold, although goods were still getting through to Germany. By 1917 the value of Germany's import trade had fallen to only 19 percent of that of 1913, conducted mainly through European neutrals. Switzerland, Norway, Sweden and Denmark were all exporting more to Germany than they had been in 1913. On the other hand, Germany's largest pre-war trading partner among the neutrals, the Netherlands, now exported only 22 percent of the goods to Germany that she had before the war. This drop more than cancelled out the increase from the other neutrals.[49] The Central powers were not reduced to starvation, but a gnawing hunger conditioned the final two years of the war, working insidiously on the resilience of civilians and soldiers who survived on short rations of monotonous, poor-quality foodstuffs.

With the situation on the maritime front still precarious as summer came, the land front had yet to be reengaged. Attrition had been agreed on in principle in May, but what this would amount to in practice had to be decided once the spring offensives ended. There was a case to be made, as championed by Churchill from the backbenches, for 'active defensive . . . so as to economize French and British lives', before the arrival of 'the American millions' would allow a decisive offensive in 1918.[50] This 'wait and strengthen' strategy had its advocates: Pétain subscribed to it too (although he believed in a very active and aggressive defence in the interim), while Foch engaged with the task of equipping the French and American forces amply for the 1918 campaign. It also had its risks. It renounced initiative to the enemy and, as Lord Esher warned Haig, Churchill's strategy 'fails to grasp the meaning to France, to England, to Europe, of a postponement of effort – through the long summer that was crammed full of artificial expectations – and a still longer winter'.[51]

Lloyd George was certainly sympathetic to biding time until American strength made itself felt – attrition to him now meant holding the Germans in France while engaging surplus resources elsewhere in search of more tangible 'victories': heavy guns in Italy or divisions in Palestine. Dependent as he was on the support of Unionist members of parliament and the Northcliffe press that both backed Haig and Robertson, Lloyd George could not act decisively against his military advisers (although he did bring Churchill back into the political fold, appointing him minister of munitions in July despite the misgivings of many Unionists). When in the summer he convened a politico-military War Policy Committee to review strategic alternatives, the generals and admirals prevailed. The long-standing objective of recapturing the Belgian Channel Ports, made urgent by the ongoing U-boat campaign, was to be pursued in a sustained offensive. This operation proffered a tangible and strategically important territorial objective and the prospect of a clear military victory, which might appease the restless prime minister. Yet Haig was explicit that to win these prizes would entail further attrition in order to destroy Germany's remaining strategic reserves.[52] 'Germany is within 4 to 6 months of a date at which she will be unable to maintain the strength of her units in the field', GHQ intelligence had calculated (an overoptimistic assessment Robertson thought), while 'there is a marked and unmistakable fall in the morale of the German troops'. Haig believed, therefore, that he could force 'peace on our terms before the end of the year'.[53] This was, however, conditional on 'adequate *drafts and guns*' from home.[54] Disquietingly, Lloyd George was now indicating that, owing to domestic production needs and incipient labour unrest, *'the time had now arrived when we must face the fact that we could not expect to get any large number of men in the future but only scraps'*.[55] Haig was determined to persist with attrition, despite the political will and the physical and human resources starting to wither. Lloyd George countered that the Allies did not have sufficient superiority in manpower to secure victory in the West before 1918. Thwarted, he continued to push his idea that guns should be sent to Italy in the hope of defeating Austria in the interim, even while Haig's armies were on the offensive.[56]

In the Third Battle of Ypres, the only prolonged offensive with strategic ambitions during the second half of 1917, old problems reappeared. Haig aimed to capture the high ground around the Ypres Salient and push on to capture the Belgian Channel Ports (these submarine and destroyer bases had been a thorn in Britain's side since 1915). The plan was ambitious and to some extent sophisticated: a break out along the coast and an amphibious landing with tanks was planned for its later stages. It also began very well, with the storming of the Messines Ridge on 8 June, aided by the explosion of huge underground mines. The blast shook the windows of the prime minister's country house 140 miles away in Surrey.[57] It also shook the 7,300 German prisoners who fell into British hands. Yet the delay while Haig argued his case for pressing on to a reluctant prime minister allowed the enemy time to strengthen the defensive positions in front of the Passchendaele Ridge. By the time Gough's Fifth Army attacked on 31 July it faced a familiar push forwards through deep, well-organised entrenchments and strongpoints, masterminded by the German army's defensive expert, General Fritz von Lossberg. Although the successive stages of the offensive were better executed than those of 1916's Somme offensive – especially the start of the attack and the sequence of battles conducted by General Herbert Plumer's Second Army on the Gheluvelt Plateau from mid-September to early October – poor logistics, command and control weaknesses and the inevitable autumn mud combined to slow and clog the military machine. The battle ended in a punch-drunk standoff. Although the dogged defenders could slow but not halt the Allied advance, by the time the Canadian Corps established itself on the heights above Ypres at the notorious village of Passchendaele the Second Army had all but fought itself out. But the German army was also reeling from the ordeal. 'The troops are being used up at a disquieting rate,' Binding noted as his division took its turn in the battle. 'Everybody is best pleased if his spell is over as soon as possible. General von Lossberg . . . has not got an unlimited supply of divisions; not many people seem to realise that . . . How little spirit and determination remains, not to speak of such a quality as dash.'[58] There was no end in sight, and as his division returned to the line he opined,

> Nobody can possibly calculate what he or we have got to face . . . You have only got to consider what three years of war did for Russia . . . Even though the effects will not be quite the same with us, they are bound to tend in the same direction, namely, of demoralisation and disintegration . . . The odds against us are too big . . . three times as many guns and five times as much ammunition against us.[59]

After a few days under the English guns 'many of the men can hardly speak. You see wild eyes gazing out of faces which are no longer human . . . One cannot say that the moral is low or weak. The regiments simply show a sort of staggering and faltering, as people do who have made unheard of efforts.'[60]

Once again the campaigning season proved too short and Allied resources and coordination insufficient to decide the war in 1917. Haig's offensive had started too late, and while hard pressed the German army did not break. To some extent, with French, Russians and Italians under pressure the Third Battle of Ypres was an alliance battle, even though it was largely conducted by British arms, 'and in addition heavy losses were inflicted upon the German armies' once again.[61] French support had been intermittent (a French army had participated in the battle, covering the northern flank of the British advance) while Russia's and Italy's summer efforts were tangential to the task of wearing down the German forces. The offensive was fought with better weapons and sounder tactics, based on those developed in 1915 and 1916. But since the defence had also adapted, attrition's fundamental principle, that military success was measured in terms of enemy soldiers put out of action, still held good. The Third Battle of Ypres claimed 271,000 British and 217,000 German casualties: 73 German divisions had been engaged by 57 Allied. Attrition was still working steadily but surely. At the end of the year German battalion strength was reduced once more, from 750 to 700 men.[62] This was the trend in all armies, with weaponry being substituted for manpower. In the summer French battalions had been reduced in size from 1,000 to 800 men, with a machine-gun company replacing one of the four infantry companies.[63] Armies were adapting and methods improving, as the year's last battles would demonstrate.

*　*　*

HALF-AN-HOUR BEFORE FIRST LIGHT ON 23 OCTOBER 1917 THE ASSAULT troops from eight French divisions left their trenches below the crest of the Chemin des Dames Ridge under the cover of thick fog and formed up in no man's land, before advancing on the German lines behind a slowly creeping barrage. A curtain of artillery fire blanketed the German positions in front of them. Machine-gun bullets streamed overhead and heavy shells and gas shells searched out the enemy's defensive strong-points and gun positions. The infantry attack caught the surviving German defenders, who by this point had been subjected to six days of intensive bombardment, in their shelters. The first wave of infantry drove forwards towards deeper objectives, while the second wave 'mopped up' the survivors who had not been wise enough to raise their hands in surrender with grenades, revolvers and bayonets. Schneider and St Chamond tanks, slow and cumbersome but powerful, moved forwards, engaging enemy positions missed by the barrage with 75mm guns and machine guns. These tanks protected the infantry from counterattacks as they dug in around the shattered remains of Fort de la Malmaison that sat atop the Chemin des Dames Ridge, and that gave this now forgotten but remarkable battle its name. It was above all a victory for the artillery. 'What a terrain! It's frightful – everything is devastated, we stumble into huge craters, German corpses everywhere blown to pieces. Others overcome by gas dying. It's dreadful, but superb,' one French infantryman boasted.[64] By the afternoon all objectives had been taken. There had been little fight left in the enemy on the shell-swept plateau, and most survivors were led, demoralised and exhausted, from the dugouts and quarries in which they had cowered during the French firestorm. Twelve thousand prisoners, 200 guns and 720 machine guns were taken, and the enemy suffered another 38,000 killed, wounded or missing. The French themselves suffered 14,000 casualties: even the best planned and executed offensive was not without its human cost, but on this occasion this was less than one-third of the enemy's. Over the next few days the French followed up their striking penetration into the enemy's positions before the Germans could reinforce, advancing off the western end of the ridge into the valley of the River Ailette beyond.[65] The German line atop the Chemin des Dames Ridge was now untenable, since it could be enfiladed from the lost ground. In early November Ludendorff gave up the whole of the ridge that his troops had been contesting tooth and nail with the French since General Nivelle's failed attempt to take it in April, which had been held by the German army since the retreat from the Marne in September 1914. This was the decisive outcome of the Battle of Malmaison, 'the perfect offensive'.[66]

Malmaison was the last of a series of set-piece offensives that blasted the Germany army off much of the high ground that it had occu-

pied along the western front since 1914. The Vimy Ridge had finally
fallen to the British in April, Messines Ridge in June and the Passchendaele Ridge in October. 'Perfect' though it might have appeared in the
catalogue of First World War offensives, the Battle of Malmaison demonstrated both the principles and the enduring difficulties of fighting on an
entrenched, industrialised battlefield. In 1917's third cycle of warfare the
scale and speed of operations had increased to such an extent that armies
could start to pursue strategic ambitions once again. Armies were now
war machines themselves: tanks, aircraft, telegraphic communications,
novel munitions and small arms had been integrated into methods of
'combined arms' warfare utilised by all. 'The infantry takes the ground,
clears it, occupies it, organises it and keeps hold of it,' Pétain's 2 January
1918 infantry instruction explained. 'The artillery destroys or neutralises
. . . The close cooperation between the infantry and the artillery is of fundamental importance.'[67] Other weapons could be integrated as required
into this basic tactical doctrine.

The 1917 western front campaign ended with a surprise, for both
sides, which proved how far warfare had come in three years. In the late-
November Battle of Cambrai six British infantry divisions supported by
concentrated artillery fire and several hundred tanks broke into a weakly
defended section of the Hindenburg Line. The attack was a hybrid of the
now well established artillery-infantry methods of positional warfare – a
surprise and devastating artillery bombardment relying on new predic-
tive-fire techniques accompanied the advance of the infantry and tanks –
with both innovation and outmoded thinking. Despite their use en masse
for the first time, tanks were not the potentially war-winning invention,
Forester's screwdriver, that Churchill and others later made them out to
be.[68] Slow and mechanically unreliable as they were, tanks were merely
a useful supporting weapon for the infantry. Cavalry were still expected
to exploit the break-in and gallop to Cambrai. Tanks' future potential
was glimpsed on the plains south of Cambrai, but their vulnerability to
antitank fire was evident. At Flesquières in the centre of the battlefield
German gunners effectively halted the British tank advance, turning Cambrai into yet another back-and-forth attritional fight. The Germans
brought up fresh reserves and launched a smashing counterattack on the
southern flank of the British penetration, using a hurricane bombardment
to support a rapid advance by well-armed and highly trained specialist
infantry, so-called 'storm troops', capable of overcoming the isolated
pockets of enemy resistance missed by the artillery barrage. Now that
un-silenced machine guns could no longer be relied on to halt an infantry
advance in its tracks, battle had regained a certain degree of dynamism
and decisiveness. In this tanks would play their part. Even before Cam-

brai the Allies had put them into mass production for the faster-paced mechanised campaign contemplated for 1918 and 1919.

AT THE END OF A YEAR IN WHICH DIFFICULTIES MOUNTED FOR THE ALLIES these localised battlefield successes were a small positive outcome: they pointed the way to greater success in 1918. The year had begun with a liberal revolution in Russia and the tsar's dethronement. While this offered some hope for a more vigorous popular war effort in the East, it brought considerable uncertainty concerning Russia's military engagement and ultimate political destiny. The resumption of unrestricted submarine warfare in the spring heralded a hard year for the home front and deeper economic mobilisation. Yet it brought the United States and other neutrals into the war, strengthening the Allies' grip on their enemies' economic lifelines. By the autumn, the submarine threat had been mastered with the introduction of a convoy system and American troops, the Allies' future hope, were starting to come across the Atlantic. But American effort came with conditions. Wilson was pressing a new diplomatic and domestic agenda just at a time when political unity was fragile and war weariness was growing within the European belligerents' populations. As 1917's land campaign drew to a close, the war appeared no nearer to an outcome, but it had changed its shape and nature profoundly.

Another year of attritional battles had intensified the mechanical butchery of soldiers, while the lines remained more or less where they stood at its start. Casualties remained high in 1917 as strategic ambitions were still grand: the destruction of parts of the enemy's army with large-scale, dynamic offensives such as the Battle of Malmaison, for example. Come the autumn, however, although military ambitions had been scaled back, the land war in France and Belgium seemed to be turning in the Allies' favour. Since 1915 warfare had been remodelled into the high-intensity, material-intensive, fast-paced attritional style that would characterise the twentieth century's wars. The battles that would end the war in 1918 would therefore be fought in a very different fashion to those between 1915 and 1917. Malmaison also suggested a better way to take advantage of the ability that now existed to break into the German defensive system more or less at will. Instead of pushing forwards against an alert, reinforced defence (as Haig's forces had been obliged to do in front of Ypres) in the future the battle should expand sideways. Such lateral exploitation, which Foch had trialled in the later stages of the Somme offensive, offered better prospects for quick yet significant victories than grinding 'deep' battles. Other costs, however, had escalated, and these seemed unaffordable: General Percin, a postwar critic of the French high command's methods, extrapolated from the barrage fired at Malmaison that at that rate of expenditure of munitions it would cost 800 billion francs and use 10 years' worth of world steel production to liberate France![69] Extrapolating from Percin's calculations, if the governing factor of victory was the area of ground recaptured per attack, 1,000 Malmaisons would have been required to clear 1,600,000 million hectares of occupied France. But if the measure was the number of German troops put out of action, perhaps 80 such battles would suffice to destroy the German army and end the war: fewer in practice since morale and military capability collapses long before the whole army is annihilated.

The lesson that Joffre had learned by 1916 – 'we incline towards *disorganising their forces, weakening them, wearing them out. Once this wearing out* has been achieved, the liberation of the invaded territory will follow inevitably' – was not appreciated by Nivelle, who reverted to trying to use mass to break through the German defences, Lloyd George's wishful 'knockout blow'.[70] This only served to knock his own army out temporarily. This reverse began a year of difficulties for the Allies, whose early hopes became increasingly empty. While changes and anxieties at home and at sea troubled the coherence and effectiveness of Allied war making, in the land war Haig and Robertson, Pétain, Cadorna and Brusilov stuck to the task of destroying the enemy's armies that Joffre had set as best they could. As they did so the wider political situation was deteriorating. The year's final surprise, the Bolshevik coup d'état in Russia, suggested that 1918 might be even more fraught. Haig had privately qualified his expectation of ultimate Allied victory with the proviso that the Russians had to remain in the field.[71] Come November, it looked as if Russia was on her way out, now that Lenin, an opportunist, had seized his moment in history.

It was a year for opportunists. One had nearly wrecked France, and another was doing his best to undermine Britain's army. Robertson's postwar perspective on strategy in 1917, which had lacked focus, was straight to the point and perceptive: 'There had never been any difficulty in saying what would be a good thing to do. The difficulty lay in being able to do it.'[72] This was the pithy epitaph of amateur strategy, which always hindered rather than facilitated the proper working of attrition. Although in December Allenby's Anglo-Indian forces captured Jerusalem from the Turks, an early Christmas present that ended the year on a triumphant note, it was a largely symbolic one. This capped Lloyd George's preoccupation with the war in the Middle East and vindicated his strategic 'vision' while having no great impact on the actual war situation. But the people needed victories – Lloyd George had been saying as much since 1915 – particularly at the end of such a year. Church bells had rung out in English shires after the success at Cambrai, not so much to signify any major change in the war, but merely that a grim year had ended on a positive note.

Raising a Victory War Loan in Britain in January 1917, just as Lloyd George and Briand met in Rome to plot the Central powers' final downfall, had as Sandhurst anticipated proved overoptimistic.[73] Military errors, political mistakes and naval anxieties had proved that the war was far from over, although attrition had continued to do its steady work throughout. By the end of the year, despite occasional crumbs of comfort, the situation seemed little better than in January. 'Lloyd George has been Prime Minister for a year. The point of the intrigue which led to his upsetting Asquith was to hustle and finish the war – where are we now?' Sandhurst reflected bitterly come December, adding:

> The position is worse than ever – in my view critical in the extreme – Russia good for nothing, or worse, and consequently hordes of Germans and Austrians let loose to crowd by sheer weight of numbers all along our lines and our attack turned into defence of a very difficult nature . . . in the lines the greatest determination will be required to hold on.[74]

If there was one major positive from the year, it was that the Allies had come closer together. The conference in Italy at the start of the year had initiated a trend towards allied military, political and economic unity that culminated, at another summit at Rapallo in Italy in November, with the establishment of a formal Allied coordinating authority, the Supreme War Council.

Moreover, after another year of attrition and blockade the Central powers were in a bad way. The Anglo-French armies in the West could now fight and win big battles, but they could not yet bring the war to an end with sustained attrition, the default strategy on land. Although Germany's armies had not been beaten in West, they had been degraded further, although with the collapse of the eastern front the Austrian forces had a year of relative calm in which to recuperate. This allowed the Central powers to inflict a serious defeat on the Italians in the Battle of Caporetto at the end of the year, but as with other Allies before her, it was not mortal, and she was to recover. At sea the intensified U-boat war continued but without decisive impact. With the second revolution in Russia, Germany was presented with a diplomatic opportunity to knock one major enemy out of the war at last, an unexpected and vital lifeline. While their armies had held on for another year, the cracks which had opened on the Central powers' home fronts during 1916 were much wider and deeper. There was war weariness everywhere, and the military and political situations appeared uncertain. In the next campaign, Germany would be gambling desperately again, that her army could end the war before her people ended it for them.

During the war's most difficult year, the home fronts had become a battleground in response to the events, positive and negative, that unfolded on the other fronts. Having expanded the war to its full extent, diplomacy had shifted into new channels. Peace had become the divisive domestic issue, rather than war making. 'There is no need for panic', Lloyd George's end-of-year injunction to the nation, provoked inevitable scepticism: certainly there was still much more to be done.[75] Many thought that one thing that should be done was to get rid of the British prime minister: it was that sort of year.[76] During it Briand and many other political leaders, notably the tsar, had lost their places. A fair few senior generals had gone with them, most recently Cadorna: Haig appeared to be hanging on by his fingertips, although Foch, now installed as chief of staff in Paris, had got a better grip. But as the war entered a new year the Allied home fronts were remobilised and committed to seeing the war out, come what may. The Central powers, on the other hand, were increasingly riven with domestic controversy over why the war was continuing and what sort of peace should result, catalysed by the social hardships caused by intensifying Allied blockade. It remained to be seen whether the Central powers' armies could force a decision before their peoples' will to victory shattered. The hardships and sacrifices of war, and the elusiveness of peace, would crystallise the alternatives in 1917: 'war, nothing but war', or war against war.

# TWELVE

# THE WILL TO VICTORY

P RESIDENT WILSON ADDRESSED THE VOTERS OF SHADOW LAWN, NEW Jersey, on 4 November 1916. It was his final speech before polling day and the incumbent was seeking reelection. Although he had been elected in peacetime, Wilson's first term had been dominated by war: Americans were caught up in 'the great drift of humanity which is to determine the politics of every country in the world'. Wilson felt that if any man could, he might channel that drift. America's 'purpose is justice and love of humanity', he represented: up to that point he had worked hard to press reconciliation between the belligerents while upholding Americans' rights in Europe's war.[1] Wilson would be reelected on the basis of his previous ability to keep his nation out of that war and professed intention to bring it to a settlement. With that mandate he redoubled his efforts to bring the belligerents to the peace table. Yet within five months America too was at war: rhetoric was no great weapon against submarines.

America went to war with an agenda for peace, which chimed with everyone's mood in 1917. Wilson, an idealistic political science professor who had turned to politics with the hope of doing good, had tried already to act as honest broker between the two sides. On reelection he asked, fruitlessly, for the belligerents to state their war aims as the basis of a negotiated peace. The initiative only showed how far the belligerents were from compromising. Although Germany responded, William II judged that Germany was offering terms from a position of strength and could oblige the Allies to accept overbearing terms. The kaiser's hubristic peace terms and the public anger they provoked made Allied reciprocation unlikely. Undeterred, in January 1917 Wilson made a formal offer to mediate between the belligerents, perhaps in a desperate bid to put off American intervention. In truth, the 'peace without victory' that Wilson proffered was already almost impossible at that turning point in the fortunes of war, when the general Allied offensive had been successful, if not decisive. The two alliances were too enmeshed in the conflict to come willingly to terms, and in both deeper mobilisation was underway.

But a spirit of negotiated peace was abroad in early 1917. As well as Wilson, Pope Benedict XV would offer to mediate, socialists were preparing to meet in Stockholm to discuss how to end the war and Austria-Hungary's new emperor Karl showed, independently of the kaiser, an inclination to negotiate. This meant that the objectives of the war on the diplomatic front would shift from winning new allies to promoting war aims. The aims would be to rally public opinion while undermining cohesion on the enemies' home fronts that were growing fragile as war weariness took hold.

Although Wilson's formula did not strike a chord with imperialistic war leaders on either side, who felt that a compromise peace was a prescription for another war sooner or later, moving war aims on to the international agenda would strengthen the Allies' diplomatic advantage. Wilson's rhetoric was addressed to the peoples of Europe, the seed corn of his new nation, among whom it had greater resonance. He set himself against 'the existence of autocratic Governments backed by organised force which is controlled wholly by their will, not by the will of their people', the representatives of an old world that had lost legitimacy through acts perpetrated in the name of Mars, and a category that at one remove the Allied governments also fitted into.[2] Wilson was promoting an agenda of nationalities' rights, citizens' democratic freedoms and peaceful international cooperation as an alternative to that of Europe's warmongers bent on conquest. In that at least Wilson had something in common with that other denouncer of the war, Lenin. Both wished to make the world 'safe for democracy' (while conceiving it, and the means to secure it, rather differently).[3] A different ideal, a peace without territorial annexations or financial indemnities, was being promoted by the international socialist movement and was seized upon by the leaders of social democracy, notably Kerensky who became leader of Russia's Provisional Government in July 1917. Although imperial war had barely got into its stride by 1916, it was increasingly threatening to morph into class war.

Entering 1917, war leaders on both sides realised that the war had changed its nature, that its objectives were shifting and that its end was hard to envisage. By its third year it had become a struggle for survival with an uncertain future staked on victory – or at least a negotiated peace with advantage as seemed increasingly probable – and with the consequences of defeat too appalling to contemplate. Popular support for the war, solid if questioning through its first two years, was becoming increasingly conditional as casualty lists and food queues lengthened. Military strategy still had to be pursued, but now against a background of incipient domestic crisis. A commitment to winning the war was the one thing that might hold fractious nations and alliances together, but what exactly that war was being won for now determined the domestic political agenda. In the interminable bread queues war-weary civilians started to ask openly whether the sacrifices they made were worth it, and even what they were being made for. The press was full of news of peace initiatives, and wartime censorship could not stifle discussion of war aims. Soldiers at the front, those who might pay the ultimate sacrifice, were restless. Why keep fighting this hellish war in this brutish way? Their leaders would have to acknowledge their concerns and respond. A struggle to sustain domestic unity in pursuit of justifiable war aims defined this mid-war crisis on the home front. Nourishing the 'will to victory' would mean further adaptation to the tyranny of war.

As EARLY AS MID-SEPTEMBER 1914, AS ONE BRITISH SOLDIER NOTED, 'There seems to be a unanimous feeling that nobody would mind how soon this war came to a close'.[4] Then Germany was checked, but not beaten, establishing the essential quandary that nobody thereafter could predict when and how the war would actually end. Soldier and civilian alike became disheartened by 'this daily drudgery, without any vision of an end to it all'.[5] That was the root cause of war weariness and the longing for peace that went with it. Present throughout the war, war weariness reached epidemic proportions during 1917 now that peace was mooted. With the exception of Russia war weariness did not bring down governments or break states, but it obliged statesmen to look anew at their war, at the people's role in it and at the way they managed it. A process or 'remobilisation' was underway, designed to realign popular will with national goals.[6] This would strengthen unity and resolve in the Allied nations, whose home fronts consolidated behind a new, inclusive political and social agenda, to which military activity could be geared. Perhaps, as Corday had speculated after the February Russian revolution and America's entry into the war, 'the triumph of democracy [was] the real aim of the war henceforth'.[7] Democracy, and its nationalist counterpart self-determination, would only prove divisive in the autocracies whose militarist leaders held the people to their pursuit of victory at all costs.

By 1916, Asquith's consensus-building peacetime style of government seemed ill-suited to wartime. Yet in a war in which national unity and resilience were key elements of strategy a war leader's ability to build and sustain consensus at a time of rapid social change and political, diplomatic and military disappointments should not be discounted.[8] Britain could easily have become divided against itself as the war went on had Asquith not steered the nation into political coalition, built a solid consensus behind the legitimacy of the war, and promoted participation in the war effort. His style of mobilisation for Britain's first mass war ensured that during its difficult later years cracks in the wartime consensus were narrow and dissenters were isolated and muted relative to the nation's resolute will to victory. Lloyd George's ascent to the premiership, divisive as it was – the British Liberal Party never recovered from the split it provoked – nevertheless indicated that a society so mobilised and increasingly democratised needed a different sort of leader, a populist rather than a patrician, to steer it towards an uncertain end at some indeterminate time in the future.

It seems paradoxical that in 1916 and 1917 belligerents on both sides promoted new leaders more deeply committed to fighting the war on to victory, while seeming increasingly unsure of how to achieve victory (or even if it was achievable). Contrastingly, on the German side these were military leaders, on the Allied civilian statesmen. Whoever was now in charge – the promotion of soldiers or civilians did not give either carte blanche to direct strategy, so civil-military rivalries carried on – at the beginning of 1917 no one could anticipate how long the war would continue. As the traumatic year unfolded everyone began to fear how damaged societies would be once it finished: Russia's convulsive upheaval furnished a very real example that everywhere provoked a terrified, morbid fascination and widespread expectations of imitation. These events, which were a product of particular Russian circumstances and had been brewing since 1905's partial revolution and probably much longer, took few by surprise. 'Revolution is now inevitable,' Putilov had warned Paléologue during 1915's difficult summer, adding:

> A revolution can be a great benefit to a nation if it can reconstruct after having destroyed . . . But with us revolution can only be destructive because the educated class is only a tiny minority, without organisation, political experience, or contact with the masses . . . No doubt it will be the bourgeois . . . who give the signal for the revolution, thinking that they're saving Russia. But from the bourgeois revolution we shall at once descend to the working class revolution and soon after to the peasant revolution. And then will begin the most frightful anarchy, interminable anarchy.[9]

Putilov was percipient. Lenin would seize his opportunity, assisted by Ludendorff, who saw a chance to further destabilise one shaky enemy and transported the Bolshevik leader and his acolytes from Switzerland to Russia in a sealed train – perhaps the most fateful cargo of the war, even of the century.

On his return to Russia Lenin was just one activist among many, although an increasingly effective one. In the soapbox politics that followed the revolution, as ideologues competed for followers and votes in the first democratic elections that had been promised by the Provisional Government, Lenin could find and hold an audience at his 'pitch' on the banks of the River Neva. Farson, who witnessed this skilled orator rousing the masses, recollected

> a short dumpy figure, with an enormous dome of a head, high cheekbones giving a sinister contemptuousness to his Tartar eyes. The great Lenin . . . was not that "great" to any but a few people then. He was just this undersized new agitator in an old double-breasted blue suit, his hands in his pockets, speaking with an entire absence of that hysterical arm-waving that so characterised all his fellow countrymen.[10]

But Lenin was shrewd. His inflammatory speeches condemned the war of which Russians had grown weary. He denounced the capitalists and diplomats who had started it and who, in the guise of Russia's new Provisional Government, wished to continue it, to honour Russia's commitments to her allies in pursuit of redundant patriotic goals. Engaging with the atavistic desires of ordinary Russians, he presented an alternative path. 'Peace, bread and land' was the simple slogan that rallied workers and peasants to the Bolsheviks: these became the issues around which Russian politics would revolve during the tumultuous summer of 1917. As well as an ideal, Lenin also had a method – 'the most widespread propaganda of this view in the army on active service must be organised' – that was to undermine the fighting spirit of Russia's war-weary army more effectively than Germany's military effort ever could.[11] Ludendorff's gamble would pay off: unlike Serbia and Rumania, internal implosion, not external military force, brought mighty Russia down.

The Bolshevik coup in Petrograd that toppled the Provisional Government took place shortly before the elections for Russia's constituent assembly that would draw up liberal Russia's constitution were due. In seizing power by armed force in the pursuit of peace Lenin, who was no democrat, suggested an alternative to the debating chambers and meeting halls in which liberals and social democrats talked about peace while pursuing war more intently. Even the fierce patriot Binding now despaired that,

The word "peace" had fallen into disrepute, as though it had become marked with some filthy blight or mould. The forces that the nations are bringing into play are gigantic, amazing, almost uncanny, but the sight of them rouses no enthusiasm. They excite feelings of disgust rather than admiration . . . no nation appears really greater than another.[12]

Whether the rest of Europe now faced the same future as Russia, either as consequence of defeat or because victory was impossible, had yet to be determined. During the year, however, French soldiers, British workers, German parliamentarians and Habsburg minorities would all test their societies' wartime resilience. All would pass the test, for now.

'THEY ARE FED UP WITH GETTING THEMSELVES KILLED, WITH NO IMPORTANT success, no decision,' Fayolle had noted of France's infantry during the Somme offensive.[13] There had been a small-scale mutiny among troops of the Colonial Army in July 1916 that had alarmed Joffre. He issued orders that the troops should be encouraged that the victory would come, eventually if not that year.[14] Nivelle's offensive turned what had been occasional localised indiscipline among battle-weary troops – 'It is only during rest periods that discontent breaks out, and not under fire, when they are drunk with the conceit of courage,' one commentator noted – into a crisis for the French army.[15] The failure of Nivelle's 'final' decisive offensive combined with a return to punishing *grignotage* along the Chemin des Dames Ridge provoked a series of mutinies during which soldiers behind the lines refused to go to the front and negotiated for the redress of long-standing military grievances such as lack of leave and poor rations.[16] Almost half the divisions in the French army were affected. Given the fashion in spring and summer 1917 for rousing workers' anthems and red flags, a patina of 'revolution' stained what was essentially a soldiers' work-to-rule. Pétain addressed the *poilus*' material concerns, at the same time introducing a more open command style. These reforms, capped by the successful offensives at Verdun and Malmaison, restored the army's esprit de corps. In an army in which 'all the life force of the nation was concentrated, held together by a willingly accepted military discipline' the parameters of command authority and soldierly obedience could be periodically renegotiated by collective action.[17] This was part and parcel of the working of the republican system founded as it was on its citizens' commitment to duty and consent to sacrifice in the national cause.[18] Inevitably when such actions occurred they were momentarily alarming (especially given recent events in Russia and France's own well-established revolutionary traditions), but a democratic nation at war had no need of the sort of culture shift required in an autocracy to sustain the popular will to victory. If the mutinous soldiers called for peace, then so did everyone else. It was an abstract yearning, not a realistic expectation since their war was far from won: after three years of sacrifice the *poilus* would certainly never accept peace at any price.

The French army's mutinies were one manifestation of the general war weariness that gripped Europe during 1917. The mood of civilians was volatile everywhere, galvanized by economic hardships and expressed in strikes and food riots and occasional pro-peace demonstrations. Wartime privations were only to be expected, and indeed had become accepted (and could to a certain degree be redressed by price controls and the careful management of supplies). Why the war was still going on and what exactly it was being fought for were starting to become issues, however. Over a difficult summer, this would test the spirit of consent and resilience on the home front too.

The French home front was capricious. Towards the end of March the author Anatole France asserted, 'This is not an opportune moment for advocating pacifism', even if many, France's wife included, were sympathetic to the pope's recent appeal for peace. After further German atrocities against French civilians and the very earth of France as they withdrew to the Hindenburg Line, and with the 'final offensive' pending – Nivelle's intentions were common knowledge in Paris (and therefore at the OHL too) – France's spirit might endure a little while longer. Yet with zeppelins terrorizing them by night, and food and coal in short supply, Parisians were restless. The wave of patriotism that had crested with the late victories at Verdun was breaking; in France what happened in Paris would determine what happened in the provinces. Politics were increasingly volatile, ministers came and went and the *union sacrée* was shaky. Divided among itself, Briand's government had just fallen, but Ribot's new ministry offered little encouragement. As the incoming war minister Painlevé himself proclaimed, the future was uncertain: 'To secure peace within three months, we must declare that the war will last eighteen months.' All could agree that the liberation of France was a sine qua non of peace with Germany, but beyond this war aims were negotiable (even the return of Alsace and Lorraine).[19] In truth, they were indeterminable, and the new government was no more forthcoming than the last. 'In his statement to the Chamber . . . Ribot promised the abolition of the political Censorship,' Corday noted. '"And suppose we discuss war aims?" put in a Socialist. "We should not allow that!" Ribot sharply exclaimed. A democracy not allowed to discus the aim it is pursuing!' Corday had hit the nail on the head. While the war was making France a true democracy, war leadership remained in the hands of 'the elements which govern the masses . . . the privileged classes'.[20] At least Painlevé was a radical socialist and committed to the war. France was haltingly recognising the nature of the war she was fighting and who exactly was fighting it for her.

Workers' protests that began in Paris in January spread to many provincial towns as bread prices rose. Some strikers waved the French tricolour to indicate their loyalty, but others marched under a red flag. Workers could at least be bought off with wage rises.[21] Ribot's government survived until September, very wary of the potential infection of the volatile public mood by Bolshevism which it was assumed, largely erroneously, lay behind civilian and military disturbances: France had enough left-wing traditions of her own, and had no need to import Russia's! In September a whole print run of *L'Illustration* was seized as it intended to show an incident during the Battle of Riga in which deserting Russian soldiers had been forced back at gunpoint to the front lines by their officers. In fact the patriotic periodical was intending to illustrate the 'terrible consequences of internationalist theories for the life of states', but with military mutinies fresh in the government's mind such images were just too provocative.[22]

Essentially France's military and civilian demonstrations were protests against the consequences of the war, not the justice of the cause or the need to press on to victory. Eventually France would find a populist war leader to channel such a mood, radical journalist and elder statesman Georges Clemenceau. After Ribot's government fell, Painlevé headed his own short-lived ministry, which lasted two months. It was now impossible to form a ministry that excluded the parliamentary scourge on wartime administrations and Poincaré bowed reluctantly to the inevitable. Could a seventy-six-year-old patriot, who had in his youth seen Germany occupy *la patrie*, rally Frenchmen and women for the final, decisive battles with Germany? In fact, by the time he came to power the French had more or less rallied themselves.[23]

An old Japanese proverb had been circulating in Paris during the spring: 'Victory goes to the side which can hold on a quarter of an hour longer.'[24] France did hold on through 1917, yet in a war that had become a test of endurance, for Clemenceau it was the side that *believed* it could hold on a quarter of an hour longer that would triumph.[25] He embodied France's new will to victory. Although in his inaugural parliamentary speech he promised his people 'war, nothing but war', they were now conditioned to it.[26] Clemenceau was to express and manage the popular will to victory in his forceful leadership, which some went so far as to label a 'dictatorship'. If so, it was a dictatorship on the classical Roman model, one founded on consent: the acceptance of a leader who would command the nation at a time of acute national danger. Clemenceau was not shy of using the stick alongside the carrot. In summer 1918 he put the former minister of the interior Jean Malvy (who in September 1914 had temporarily closed Clemenceau's newspaper *L'Homme libre*) on trial for treason. Malvy was acquitted but exiled for five years for the lesser charge of failing to suppress defeatist publications. In France at least a good political scandal had always served as a helpful distraction from the public's other concerns: the enemy at the gates of Paris on this occasion.[27]

Clemenceau could rely on the commitment of France's citizens and soldiers to defeating the enemy in order to justify and avenge their sacrifice, come what may. He also had the good sense to replace the placemen who had rotated the wartime ministries between them with technical experts of the sort that Lloyd George had brought in to run Britain's war effort. France would be more determined and more efficient as she faced Germany's final offensives in 1918. In Foch, the generalissimo the Allies turned to at their moment of acutest crisis, he found a soldier who agreed with him and who believed in himself and was also 'the one man among the allies capable of handling armies that numbered millions'.[28]

The British home front had its own problems, although the army remained steadfast through its many 1917 battles. Labour militancy, which had periodically troubled the war effort as the more radical trade unions sought to exploit the war for political and social gain, peaked in spring and summer 1917. As usual, the Clyde was the centre of strike action and workers demonstrations, but these spread to munitions factories and other industries in London, Wales and the Midlands. The strikers' varied grievances were social and economic rather than political: shortages of housing in towns which had filled with workers serving the expanding war industries; the rising cost of food and other goods; further government dilution of labour in skilled industries; and tightening controls over labour mobility as a new centralised manpower policy inaugurated by February's Man Power Act, which removed most remaining exemptions from military service, started to function.

The government responded with specific concessions and more general palliatives as the propaganda machine refocused from winning over neutrals to sustaining peoples and allies. A commission was appointed to enquire into the causes of working-class unrest during the summer, and many social consequences of the war were properly investigated and legislated for the first time. Although such measures were not on the scale of the Second World War's Beveridge Report which laid the foundations for Britain's post-1945 National Health Service and welfare state, government attention turned to the new world that would be built after victory. A minister of reconstruction was appointed in July, and in January 1918 Lloyd George chose a meeting of labour leaders as the venue for his first formal pronouncement of Britain's war aims.[29] In August an all-party National War Aims Committee was created, which organised public meetings to promote a positive message of what the war was about and to explain to civilians the reasons why the empire had to fight on to a victorious outcome.[30] In 1918 the Ministry of Munitions' Aircraft Production Department began a programme of shop-floor talks and publications in aircraft factories, relating the actions of the machines they had built 'to give the worker some appreciation of the importance of his personal contribution towards winning the war'. Weekly pay envelopes were adorned with small pictures of the aircraft in action.[31] The nation was now girded for the longer struggle, as long as it would take, as Wilkinson acknowledged: 'Should we not be wiser to assume a long lasting war and to work patiently, than to act hastily in the belief that victory is near at hand?' he asked his Oxford University audience in October.[32] That strategic error could be left to the enemy.

Collectively, such measures calmed social protest on the home front, although they could never eliminate dissent. Although discordant voices persisted, these could be heard without upsetting the wider resolution behind the war, even if they were not heeded. When in October former Unionist Foreign Secretary Lord Lansdowne published an open letter in the *Daily Telegraph* calling on the government to formulate a programme of war aims that would initiate a negotiated peace, it provoked much debate but little action.[33] But the letter acknowledged a bitter irony, as guards officer Victor Cazalet pointed out:

> What people don't realise . . . is that the ordinary Tommy and junior officer has no idea at all why we are fighting and no ultimate aim or achievement is put before him. He has nothing to look forward to except Death. If lucky a wound. He knows that if he survives one battle he is due for the next . . . All we want is a definite statement of our peace terms . . . of course we go on until we get them – until then we must naturally not loosen our hold. Forgive this . . . but people don't seem to realise the extraordinary extent of feeling both among men and officers here, and if they don't soon do something they must expect them to welcome letters like Lord L's . . . Of course we shall win the war – no one doubts that – but whether we shall win by "fighting" – no one quite believes that now – and the talk of "knock out blows" etc. simply infuriates the soldier here.[34]

The difficult mood at home and in the trenches did provoke Lloyd George into stating formally British war aims for the first time, although to some extent this was a diplomatic as well as a domestic political manoeuvre, since Wilson was about to pronounce his famous 'Fourteen Points' and America's allies felt the need to match their own agendas against such high-minded yet hard to realise ideals. Thereafter, the political dividing line in Britain was over whether peace should be negotiated on some or other terms, or the war should be seen out to the bitter end.

While British workers were militant and the French were wavering in the pursuit of victory and volatile during 1917, the peoples of the Central powers were dividing against themselves. Wilson was offering them new choices, while their own leaders appeared anxious and seemed to be losing control.

Germany's soldiers were also growing war weary. Although there was no concentrated mutinous movement in Germany's forces, there were sporadic outbreaks of indiscipline in units behind the western front in the spring and summer of 1917. In the High Seas Fleet, at anchor and restless, there was a full-scale mutiny in August.[35] Ludendorff was worried enough about his troops' morale to introduce a systematic reeducation programme, dubbed 'patriotic instruction', to reinforce the reasons why Germany was at war and had to fight on to victory.[36] 'Dreams of peace prolong the war,' Ludendorff opined in empty platitudes, 'and so does discontent. Unity at home makes us strong; everything else is weakening.'[37]

Consisting of right-wing indoctrination that refused to address questions of constitutional reforms or limited war aims, patriotic instruction did not chime with the mood of an army that had become part of the 'nation in arms' that its patrician leaders had been so fearful of before 1914.[38] The officers charged with enthusing the hard-pressed troops felt listless like their grumbling men, even those such as Binding who remained steadfast in the high command's cause. 'We, on the other hand, are polite enough to talk about duty,' he noted, 'which is what we substitute nowadays for the beautiful idea of keenness and enthusiasm, just as turnip-mash has to do instead of raspberry-jelly.'[39] Developments in the war suggested that Germany's cause was ultimately lost. 'I am scared,' Binding admitted to himself as the British offensive resumed at Ypres. 'For the first time in this war I have doubts whether we will be able to hold out against the odds.'[40] The despondent spirit of the home front (where the Hindenburg Programme to deepen German mobilisation and substitute war material for declining manpower was proving counterproductive, merely speeding wartime inflation and exacerbating shortages of manpower, coal and transport) threatened to undermine efforts to raise morale at the front: 'Ludendorff's memorandum reminds me of what I once wrote, that wars are won or lost by letters from home,' Binding noted perceptively.[41]

The plan for the navy to win the war before the army lost it smacked of desperation, not decision, and further divided an already sundering nation. 'We all know and feel that Germany is playing her last card,' Princess Blücher noted.

> The resolution for sharpening up the submarine war was received silently by the . . . Reichstag. The middle-class Chauvinists and the Pan-Germans hail it as an infallible step to a final victory; whilst the pessimists and wise men who are discontented with the war assert that God has struck the German nation with blindness before utterly ruining it.[42]

In a misguided attempt to repair Germany's fracturing domestic consensus, Bethmann Hollweg allowed the press to discuss war aims openly for the first time.[43] The substance of a peace agreeable to all shades of public opinion proved intractable. In July the democratic majority parties in the Reichstag combined together to force through a 'peace resolution', representing that Germany should immediately negotiate a democratic socialist peace without territorial annexations and financial indemnities. The resolution made no impact on the military leadership's commitment to a total victory, except perhaps to strengthen their resolve to reign in defeatists on the home front, but it indicated that the *Burgfrieden* was at an end. Exasperated at the failure of his efforts to maintain some sort of home-front unity, Bethmann Hollweg had already stepped down, to be replaced as chancellor by the wheat controller Georg Michaelis, a subservient military placeman plucked from the civilian bureaucracy. He was soon removed from office after failing to block the democratic parties' resolution to democratise the Prussian franchise.[44]

The peace resolution indicated the sort of peace many Germans now wanted. There was no expectation that peace would result, since the nation's fate was in others' hands: the contest between their own military leadership and the Allies would determine it. It was clear that the left was starting to assert itself, and its values were thought provoking. 'At the beginning of the war my colleagues in the metal firm kept aloof from me since it was known that I was against the war,' Sender recollected, 'but with each passing year a greater number became friendly. Finally many of them came to me to discuss the political situation. They had begun to feel that things were going wrong in the German ruling circles.'[45] They were not yet ready to accept Sender's antiwar message wholeheartedly, but they were more questioning of the purpose and practice of the war. Although the popular will to victory remained solid, battle lines were being drawn up on the home front, and it was around the nature of victory and peace that differences were crystallising. This 'peace by reconciliation' Ludendorff later noted 'was swallowed most eagerly by those who feared the effect of victory on their political aspirations,' and this was a sentiment he was unable or unwilling to heed. Germany was not defeatist: the right-wing press after all had rejected all suggestions of a negotiated 'socialist' peace.[46] Ludendorff worked to tap that sentiment through the organisation of a German Fatherland Party, a conservative mass movement intended to challenge the democrats' hold over the Reichstag that prefigured the mass movements of the interwar years. Headed by Tirpitz and committed 'not to a weak surrender at home and abroad, but to a German resoluteness and an unshakeable belief in victory,' it attracted the support of big business and the middle classes, who had invested heavily in war bonds and victory.[47] The democrats responded by founding the People's League for Freedom and Fatherland, committed to political reform and a moderate peace.[48] While fighting the world war to its denouement, Germany was also organising for her next war, which would be fought over the shape of the nation following victory or defeat.

Austria-Hungary's domestic problems had different roots and were even more fractious and intractable than Germany's. They were also catalysed by increasing hardship on the home front and an unrepresentative political system. Nationality issues dominated politics in the Habsburg Empire: on the one hand rivalries between the Dual Monarchy's dominant nationalities, the Austrian Germans and the Hungarian Magyars; on the other tensions over the rights of subject minorities. In urban areas there was also a rising current of socialism to muddy the political waters further: in October 1916 reactionary Austrian Prime Minister Count Karl Stürgkh, who had arbitrarily prorogued the Reichsrat (Austria's parliament) in March 1914 and ruled thereafter by emergency decree, had been assassinated by the son of the leader of Austria's socialist party.[49] In 1914 all nationalities had pledged loyalty to the crown and marched off to war (with the hope of postwar rewards for their allegiance). After three years of war nationality issues were starting to undermine military morale, not least because Germans and Magyars dominated the officer corps and subjected their soldiers to racial slurs that undermined discipline and respect. Disloyalty and apathy, always endemic, were chronic in the army, which thankfully had a relatively quiet year compared with previous campaigns. By then, Boroević was dividing his divisions into more reliable German and Magyar 'storm troop' units and line-holding formations of other nationalities.[50]

Imperial domestic politics increasingly revolved around whether, and how, self-determination could be accommodated in the postwar empire, an issue amplified by Wilson's peace agenda (despite America not being formally at war with Austria-Hungary until December 1917). By 1917 the ambitions of Poles, Czechs, Slavs and others were becoming entrenched on the home front: a restored independent Poland, an autonomous Czech and Slovak region and a Habsburg-sponsored south-Slav 'Yugoslavia' were all mooted. Tensions were exacerbated by the fact that wartime political restrictions and censorship limited opportunities to discuss such matters. When in May the Reichsrat was recalled for the first time since the outbreak of war and censorship was relaxed, Czechs, Slavs and others agitated for their demands in the parliament. On the streets outside food riots were taking place. In Hungary reactionary Prime Minister Count István Tisza had held nationalist and socialist ambitions in check until forced from office over the issue of voting reform by the modernising Emperor Karl in May. His successor, Sándor Wekerle, led a Magyar rearguard action against the forces of nationality and democratisation in the Diät (Hungary's parliament) until the empire was defeated. The Hungarians, who produced much of the empire's agricultural surplus, were at least not going so hungry, although their relative comfort had set them against the Austrians.[51] While the empire had had a relatively easy year on the battlefield in 1917 (which was crowned with a major victory in Italy), debates at home over who and what the war was being fought for and what shape the postwar empire should assume promised a very different future for the peoples of Central and Eastern Europe, whatever the outcome of the conflict.

THERE WAS CRISIS ACROSS EUROPE'S BELLIGERENT NATIONS IN 1917, followed by more or less successful remobilisation that geared societies up for the final phase of the struggle. For different reasons perhaps than at the start, the will to victory remained strong: combatants, civilian participants and spectators on the home front remained determined to see their war through to its end. How long this would take, and how much more death and destruction forcing victory would require, none could predict – the very indeterminacy of the war by this point was one of its most troubling features. One of Corday's military correspondents at the front, Colonel Boutteaux, summed up the dilemma succinctly: 'Everybody declares the necessity of continuing, without knowing how or how long. But everybody wants peace and would like to discuss it, even if it were only at Stockholm.'[52] Lloyd George for one had started to believe that the war could not be forced to a final decision, or at least not without unacceptable human and social cost, while others on the margins were starting to call for an immediate compromise peace as a better alternative to pursuing the war to a conclusion.

What was becoming certain by 1917, however, was that the end state would be very different from the beginning. Moreover, the longer the war went on, the more difficult and problematic a negotiated peace became. The will to war of 1914 has been overestimated, but the will to victory has been underplayed. Motivations for continuing the war were evolving with the war itself, although one thing remained constant in a war of attrition: the consequences of not seeing it through were potentially far worse than the effects of fighting on.

Antiwar voices remained muted or could be silenced in most places, although the spirit of 1918 and afterwards would be different to that of earlier years. While the liberal versus authoritarianism imperialist war over issues of national sovereignty, cultural identity, territorial desiderata and 'right versus might' went on, a new ideological battleground on which a war would be waged for the people's future had been laid out during 1917. This was due only partly to Wilson and his liberal democratic agenda. Democratic socialism – and, rather more worryingly for many, Lenin's Bolsehvism – had also enthused popular imagination. Everywhere struggles over national self-determination and class had been engaged. Democracy now challenged dynasticism, and Utopians championing a proletarian dictatorship presumed to usurp both. Bolshevism was not yet a strong enough force to bring the war to a convulsive halt, but revolutionary socialists stood ready to pick over the carcass when attrition had finally wasted the European body politic. Such ideals and causes would determine that a civil war would follow once the old war was over – one that would dictate the course of the rest of the twentieth century.

What kept the old war going meanwhile was something different: a spirit of vengeance, the need to demonstrate that the costs and sacrifices to date had not been in vain and that a better, more peaceful world awaited the victor. What defeat offered the vanquished was becoming obvious – Russia's progressive collapse into anarchy gave a clear example – and that in itself drove the war onwards into its most intense and potentially cataclysmic phase, a final struggle for survival. While peace was on everyone's minds by 1917, it was simply not possible. The war would end in victory or defeat, the former problematic, the latter disastrous.

While societies shook and settled, the war went on. The intensive warfare now being waged on land and at sea offered the prospect of an eventual military decision as long as an alliance held together, ranks were kept full and war machines continued to function. Which side would triumph was becoming more obvious. Foch and Haig were confident that they now had the method, manpower and material superiority to force victory sooner or later. With mobilisation complete, the trench lines, which had started to flex during 1917, would prove malleable enough for national will and military skill to be tested to a decision in 1918.

Among the Central powers military exit strategies from a war that they could never win became more fanciful, as their home fronts and armies started to buckle under the strain. By the end of the year Ludendorff was aware that time was running out for Germany and her shaky allies. His own army was suffering acutely. 'The troops had borne the continued defensive with extreme difficulty,' he admitted after the war, adding: 'Skulkers were already numerous . . . Against the weight of the enemy's material the troops no longer displayed their old stubbornness; they thought with horror of fresh defensive battles and hoped for the war of movement.'[53] German strategy had always been predicated on knocking out her enemies one by one. Italy's precipitate retreat and Russia's final collapse over the winter of 1917–18 offered a slim hope that now the real enemies in the West, which had always held a manpower and material advantage there, were vulnerable. If not, Germany's and Austria's fates were sealed, and their imperial futures bleak.

# THIRTEEN

# GERMANY'S LAST CARDS

ARLY IN THE MORNING ON 27 OCTOBER 1917 CADORNA ISSUED AN order that was to save his army but seal his own dismissal. The Isonzo armies were to retire fifty kilometres westwards, behind the River Tagliamento, abandoning all the land the Italian army had fought so hard for two and a half years to conquer and more besides. For the first time Italian soil would be surrendered without a fight. The military situation had changed suddenly and drastically. Three days earlier German and Austro-Hungarian forces had smashed in General Capello's Second Army's front between Flitsch and Tolmein, infiltrating along the valleys between the mountain strongpoints of the Italian defence and seizing the river crossing at Caporetto on the upper Isonzo. The Second Army appeared to have collapsed rapidly and with sparse resistance and now there was a danger that the Third Army holding the front to the south would be outflanked and destroyed. Once again the Allies faced a localised military crisis, similar to those at Gorlice-Tarnów, Verdun and in Rumania, and Cadorna was dealing calmly with it, if too calmly for many who felt that Italy was likely to collapse if she gave up her northeastern province of Friuli. For there were many now who were questioning why Italy had gone to war in the first place. On the day the enemy attacked socialist members of parliament had endeavoured to initiate a public enquiry into secret foreign funding for interventionist newspapers in 1914–15. After news of the attack arrived the next day Boselli's government was toppled by an overwhelming vote of no confidence.[1] Whether this was just the cut and thrust of factional Italian politics at work or whether it denoted a sea change in Italy's attitude to the war remained to be seen. Not all socialists opposed the war, and many backed liberal nationalist

Vittorio Orlando's new government of national resistance. That depended, however, on whether Italy's soldiers would fight on.

The reasons why the Central powers' offensive had proved so devastating in its first phase were unexceptional. Accustomed to being on the offensive (the Eleventh Battle of the Isonzo had ended little more than a month earlier), Capello had made the sort of defensive errors that other armies had generally eliminated. His front lines were packed with troops and his army's field defences were weak. His reserves were poorly placed. But the military mistakes were not Capello's alone. Cadorna had been wilfully blind to the possibility of an enemy offensive against a previously quiet sector of the front, even when faced with accumulating intelligence suggesting that another *Strafexpedition* was being prepared. Cadorna felt that the Austrians, whose forces had been further worn down during the summer, no longer had the stamina for the fight, and certainly not the resources to take the offensive. Yet Emperor Karl's response to the continued bloodletting was to try to break the demoralising cycle of attrition and defeat with a victory. Ludendorff, who felt that the Austrians would not stand another Italian offensive, concurred and agreed to send German divisions and heavy guns from the quiescent eastern front to support an Austrian attack.[2] German troops brought with them German offensive methods, which added tactical finesse to the attack. A paralysing surprise bombardment, widespread use of gas (which was relatively unfamiliar on the Italian front) and rapid infiltration by storm troops combined to overwhelm the Italians' front positions within forty-eight hours.[3]

It was not simply the military facts of the defeat that mattered now: after all, most armies had had their front lines overwhelmed at some point during the last three years. By November 1917 the complexion of the war had altered, the staying power of armies and nations was starting to be questioned and the Central powers were testing the Italians' will to victory properly for the first time. This had been strong in May 1915 when, with flags flying and civilians cheering, Italy's smartly uniformed regiments had marched off to drive the hated Austrians from 'Italy' once and for all. As the war approached its third winter the troops were bedraggled, Italy's people sullen, and both socialist and patriotic critics of the mismanaged war effort were finding their voices. Soldiers disarming their officers and singing the 'Internationale' and other revolutionary songs as they retired from Caporetto was a sign that their mood was volatile and also that the summer's events in Russia had struck a chord in a dispirited army feeling oppressed by its leaders and uncertain in its purpose. News of Lenin's Bolshevik coup arrived during the retreat, giving the Italian military crisis a wider resonance on the Allies' home fronts. But as in the other Allied nations, a year of military disappointments, home front difficulties and political upheavals would not undermine the Italians' will to victory to the extent that revolution was in the air.

Much of the dissent in Italian political circles had been directed against Cadorna and his conduct of the war: even those who believed in the national cause (Orlando among them) were unwilling to remain quiet while Italians died in large numbers, and the commander in chief had been killing Italians at a faster rate than he seemed to be killing Austrians for too long. That was the nature of the war, and it required a different approach and better motivation than Italians had yet mustered. Although Cadorna probably had a better understanding of the cruel nature of modern war than is realised, he certainly had a poor conception of the sort of army that was required to fight it. Rigorous old-style discipline maintained authority in Cadorna's army, something that ill-suited a citizen army engaged in a patriotic war. Cadorna executed more men and dismissed more senior officers than any other Allied commander in chief.[4] His response to the defeat at Caporetto was true to form. He chose to blame Capello specifically, and his troops and their commanders more generally, for the disaster and resorted to punitive retribution – shooting stragglers and summarily executing senior officers who had lost control of their units in a misguided attempt to put some backbone into his demoralised troops.[5]

What really happened after Caporetto was a collective loss of willpower. Officers had no control over their units, men no desire to throw their lives away needlessly: defending units melted away; regiments surrendered en masse without a fight; reinforcements refused to engage the enemy. The Second Army ceased to exist as a fighting formation, losing 686,000 men and 3,000 guns. But only 6 percent of the Second Army's losses, 42,000 killed or wounded, were as a consequence of enemy action. Two hundred and ninety-four thousand men surrendered, and more shockingly 350,000, over half the army, dissolved in rout, many throwing away their arms then milling around in the rear or heading for home.[6] Orlando hesitated over dismissing his hated commander in chief until his allies forced his hand.[7] In Cadorna's place the relatively unknown Lieutenant-General Armando Diaz, 'an exceptional administrator and skilful mediator', took in hand the task of restoring the Italian army's fighting spirit. 'You are ordering me to fight with a broken sword,' he told the king, confirming: 'Very well, we shall fight all the same.'[8] After all, by the end of 1917 all the swords, and the hands that wielded them, were damaged.

On the surface, Caporetto appeared to be a very dangerous military crisis, although its striking success took the Germans by surprise more than the Allies, and Ludendorff failed to exploit the defeat of the Second

Army vigorously enough to precipitate a general Italian collapse. This had not been his objective – the campaign was intended to support Germany's principal ally, whose resolve was flagging, as much as to defeat another enemy. Ludendorff doubted that the Central powers had the reserves to sustain the sort of battle that would be needed to destroy Italy's armies once and for all, and it was too late in the campaigning season to expect to do so. They certainly did not have the resources to conquer and occupy much of Italy if, as seemed likely on the pattern of the other states Germany had beaten, Italy would not sue for a separate peace.[9] For their part, Italy's allies would not let her fall. Experience had shown that despite the military and naval grip that held them, the Central powers retained the strength and strategic flexibility to pick off weaker states. Italy was hardy in the weak military class of Belgium, Serbia or Rumania, so although a crisis, Caporetto was not a disaster. The Allies had learned from earlier years to be ready to meet any individual threat collectively. This time there would be no hasty and chaotic improvisation. In the spring Foch had toured the Italian front and concerted plans to reinforce it with French and British divisions in the event of a powerful Central powers' offensive there. Eleven divisions, commanded by the competent western front commanders Plumer and Fayolle, were despatched to Italy in late October and early November, although by the time these started to arrive the crisis was abating. Cadorna had ordered a second retreat to the line of the River Piave where his troops would hold. Only one French division arrived in time to reinforce the Third Army, which unlike the Second Army had retreated in good order from the Isonzo front. A final push by the now exhausted and overstretched Austrian and German forces was checked on this new defensive line. Once again, once fresh reserves were deployed in strength a short-term crisis lapsed into yet another positional stalemate.

As well as despatching reinforcements, Allied leaders responded to the crisis with alacrity. Lloyd George and Painlevé, with their chiefs of staff Robertson and Foch in attendance, met their Italian colleagues at Rapallo from 5–7 November to review the situation in Italy and the Allies' management of the war more generally. This momentous summit finally set up a Supreme War Council (SWC) for managing Allied strategy, composed of permanent Allied political and military representatives advised by a joint Allied military staff, which would sit at Versailles in France. The precise details of how the new strategic coordination body would operate had still to be worked out and would prove contentious. However, the fact that Foch, the most experienced Allied general when it came to conducting coalition military operations, was effectively French military representative boded well for future military cooperation.

The establishment of the SWC formalized the trend towards closer Allied cooperation which had been developing since 1915. A united front was a vital element in a successful strategy of attrition, contributing to efficiency, military effectiveness and resilience. Events at the end of 1917, a year of great strain for both alliances, indicated that both sides had taken this on board, and that the Allies had accepted and applied this principle far better than the Central powers. France and Britain were ready and willing to come to Italy's assistance in her hour of need, and the Caporetto crisis, although worrying, actually brought the Allies closer together. Disagreements would inevitably still arise, but now a managerial forum in which these might be aired and resolved existed. Unity and cooperation among their enemies was less assured. Divisive political battles were underway in both Germany and the Habsburg Empire. Ludendorff, meanwhile, had lost faith in the reliability of Austrian troops fighting without German leadership and collaboration, a development that had not escaped the attention of Allied intelligence officers.[10]

'THE WORLD IS CRYING OUT JUST AS BUSILY FOR PEACE AS IT IS ARMING ITSELF to carry on the War,' Binding noted as a new year dawned. But now there was a note of guarded optimism in his judgement:

> Both sides are no doubt genuine in their outcry. We should find it most extraordinary of all to except ourselves, since we are longing not only for peace but also for the great victory in the West. Yes, no peace in the East at any price without victory in the West. There is nobody with sound sense who does not catch himself thinking that. If our military situation were worse we should think otherwise, but people talk now of Calais, Amiens, and Paris as they did in the first months of the war, and at the same time they speak of peace as of a fact which will happen as surely as the beginning of spring.[11]

The elimination of Russia and Rumania in the spring would give Germany opportunities in 1918, both to take on the Anglo-French armies on more equal terms and to relieve the hardships on her own home front. Ludendorff for one expected as much, although his review of the strategic situation at the end of 1917 was far from comforting and to a great extent the conclusions that he drew from it were unrealistic. Once again his armies had hit one of Germany's enemies hard, but this seemed only to have brought them all closer together. The navy's promise to bring Britain to the negotiating table with unrestricted submarine warfare had not been honoured. If anyone wanted to negotiate, it was Germany's democrats, obliging Ludendorff to muster resources to hold the home front. By now industrial unrest, which had grown steadily through 1917, was taking on the trappings of Bolshevism, with workers' councils forming to push overtly political rather than purely economic demands. In that respect, Ludendorff's one real gain from 1917, the internal collapse of Russia, threatened to rebound on Germany unless the war could be ended quickly. An antiwar faction, tired of the impotency of their social democratic parliamentary colleagues, had split from the SPD in April 1917 and formed an Independent German Social Democratic Party advocating an immediate end to the war, around which such agitation coalesced. Its extreme wing, the Spartacus League, was even advocating revolution. At the end of January 1918 one million industrial workers went on strike across Germany: a comparable general strike had paralysed Vienna a few days before.[12] Troops were sent in to restore order and strike leaders were conscripted into the army. The January strikes set the pattern of events on the Central powers' home fronts during 1918, a year in which the number of days lost through strikes steadily increased, while military authority was more harshly applied.

If Ludendorff had a strategic objective it was the same as Falkenhayn's, to split the enemy alliance – physically in this case – and to suggest to Germany's battered adversaries that fighting on was not worth it. Like earlier strategic gambles, this was a desperate undertaking. While hoping to break the individual and collective Allied will to victory, Ludendorff had given up the thought of forcing a peace of mutual exhaustion in favour of pushing for all-out victory and enforcing a victor's peace. The Treaty of Brest-Litovsk that the desperate Bolsheviks were to sign with the Central powers in March 1918 invigorated the German right's imperialist agenda of conquest. By its terms Russia's Baltic provinces, the Ukraine and Finland gained independence as potential client states of Germany. Russian Poland was already effectively incorporated into the Reich. Nothing else would justify the sacrifices Germans had made or hold the home front together after the privations of a long war. Germany 'must triumph or go under', Ludendorff informed Crown Prince Rupprecht of Bavaria, the army group commander who was to initiate the spring offensive, a perspective with which the kaiser agreed.[13] Ludendorff was fanciful to think that the temporary advantage that peace with Russia would bring in spring 1918 would be enough to win a decisive military victory before American strength started to count. Binding was more realistic:

> Not a single bottle of wine was drunk to celebrate [the Russian peace] . . . the most important event which has happened to us since the outbreak of the war. But we have no joy-peals left in us; people seem to

have left them behind with some other part of their being. And then, now come the Americans.[14]

But in early 1918 that was the best and last hope that Germany retained.

The collapse of the eastern front promised short-term relief of the Central powers' acute manpower problems. Veteran divisions were now available for use on the other fronts. Peace with Russia and Rumania also allowed the repatriation of prisoners of war, a large number in Austria's case. Ludendorff calculated that he could force one more campaign out of his battle-hardened yet war-weary soldiers, their morale boosted by the hope that this would be their last, and it would end in victory on all fronts. Binding was not so sure: 'I don't believe any of it. We shall never have peace with England and America so long as they do not need to make it, and they do not need to yet.'[15]

At the same time, peace with Russia raised new commitments. Although Germany seemed now to be achieving some of her nationalist leadership's expansionist war aims, policing vast new territories in Eastern Europe, organising their resources and shipping them westwards would take time and effort. This would absorb manpower to the extent that while the contest in the West went on 1,500,000 men remained under arms in Eastern Europe performing security and labour duties (and because there was not enough food to feed them in the West). The East was far from quiescent. By the early summer of 1918 the eastern front was springing back into life as 'White' Russian nationalists, and even some 'Red' patriots, repudiated the Bolsheviks' humiliating peace and set about raising a new army to fight German occupiers and their Soviet puppets together. From July civil war in the East would absorb more and more of the OHL's attention as their new empire showed itself to be a liability rather than an asset.

This overt manifestation of German imperialism in the East only reinforced the Allies' sense of the justice of their cause while accentuating the menace posed by German militarism. Old-style imperialists, left-wing supporters of peace with or without annexations and indemnities and liberal anti-imperialists could all agree that Germany's new empire in Eastern Europe was inimical to their values and interests. Furthermore, on the evidence of the Peace of Brest-Litovsk, a punitive peace awaited Germany's defeated enemies – on the evidence of Lloyd George, Clemenceau and Wilson's recent war aims speeches, a democratic one that guaranteed long-term international security would be a fair reward for Allied sacrifices. Before that was possible, however, the German army remained to be beaten. Moreover, for Allied troops a German army aggressively on the offensive, pillaging more of France as they came on, was now a genuine danger rather than the abstract threat it presented when on the defensive.[16]

Nor was their erstwhile Russian ally forgotten. The Bolshevik regime might have been recognised by its German creators in order to negotiate a legitimate peace treaty, but that diplomatic sleight of hand ignored the reality of incipient civil war in Russia and the successor states of the Romanov Empire. In this conflict the Allies would take sides too, as rebuilding an eastern front, which had always been central to the Entente's diplomatic and military grand strategy, became increasingly important for the wider strategy of the war, especially to the British. While Foch took on the Germans, the SWC was managing the mature coalition war effort and operations in other theatres. The Allies refused to recognize the Bolshevik regime diplomatically, not least because Lenin had repudiated tsarist debts to Russia's former allies and exposed the annexationist terms of the Allies' secret treaties made with the tsarist regime in the early years of the war. Lloyd George and his new CIGS, General Wilson, in particular devoted a lot of attention to organising support for the emerging White forces commanded by former imperial generals in the hope of reviving the eastern front and tying down German forces there. New partners emerged from the melting pot of nationalist aspirations that post-imperial Russia had become. One element of Lloyd George's 'New Eastern' strategy that all the Allies could agree on (if for different reasons) was support for state-building in Eastern Europe. A Czech Legion formed from former Austrian prisoners of war was recruited and armed in Russia and a Polish national army was raised and equipped in France with a view to shipping it to the East. Small Allied expeditions were despatched to north, south and east Russia to support anti-Bolshevik White Russian movements.[17] This was sensible strategy in a global war, using relatively limited resources to keep the enemy stretched (and to protect wider Allied interests) on all fronts. The new eastern front may have proved of great strategic significance if the war had continued into 1919. 'To revitalise Russia in some form' was therefore vital, Wilson acknowledged in June: 'Without this the future of the British empire will be seriously menaced and we shall ultimately have to fight at the gravest disadvantage.'[18] The main strategic fear was that Russia's collapse had opened the way for a German advance on the Middle East and India through the Caucasus should the war be prolonged into 1919 and beyond as they expected.[19] This defensive precaution anticipated an inconclusive outcome to the war, which many still expected to end in a negotiated peace of exhaustion. This was manifest pessimism, but such fears about the East would distract the prime minister sufficiently to enable Haig to get on with the job of beating the enemy in the West relatively undisturbed. As it turned out, Foch ended the war before the SWC's ambitions (and Britain's imperial defence plans) could reach fruition, although in an uncertain postwar world their usefulness would be tested.

Thus the stakes in 1918 were raised on both sides, just as the fighting reached its highest pitch. Ludendorff's decision to stake all on winning a decisive military victory meant that in 1918 the war refocused once more in France and Flanders, on to the land front. The western front campaign became a fight to the finish, a year of attack and counterattack, orchestrated by Ludendorff but ultimately controlled and determined by Foch's superior military intellect. The rest of the war would carry on and the other fronts would still matter. The wars against Turkey and Bulgaria could not be suspended, although they were largely conducted as holding actions while the adversaries lined up their guns and their armies to slug it out in the 'decisive theatre', as Robertson, Haig and Joffre had always expected. At sea the rhythm of submarines sinking merchantmen and destroyers chasing submarines wore on, but the Allied blockade was tightening, while the Central powers' counterblockade failed to grip. Hunger and political agitation persisted on the home fronts (much more so on those of the Central powers), countered by campaigns of patriotic education and pronouncements on war aims. The tit-for-tat diplomatic battle for international leverage, to promote unity and to split the enemy coalition, remained part of strategy.[20] But now that Germany offered large-scale battle to her main enemies in the western theatre for the first time since 1914 the immediate problem of fighting the enemy removed the luxury of speculative strategic alternatives to engaging available resources in the principal theatre. This was a desperate gamble – Germany's adversaries were ready to meet her blow for blow, in a back-and-forth contest that would ultimately be decided by Allied superiority in material, manpower, maritime control and military skill. The war had come a long way since 1914, but the destruction of the enemy's fighting capacity remained the decisive objective.

The strategic assessments drawn up by the SWC's joint Allied staff over the winter were realistic. It was clear that the defeat of Russia presented Ludendorff with a brief window of opportunity in which to engage the Anglo-French armies with some prospect of success, although whether Germany would attack or strengthen her defensive front and hope to hold out for another year or more remained to be seen. Counting up the numbers on each side once more, Allied statisticians rightly concluded that for the first time Germany would start the year with a numerical advantage in the West. By this point in the war Germany's home depots were more or less empty apart from the un-deployed men of the 1919 class that had been called up during 1917, reclassified rear-area soldiers and 'reformed' wounded, but veteran divisions from the East would become available in the spring.[21]

The Allied armies' ranks were also thinning, in particular the British army's for the first time. Whether this was Haig's fault due to the profligate use of men in his offensives or Lloyd George's for starving the army of manpower to deter Haig's attritional propensities became a matter of heated political debate once Germany attacked. This was the latest round in the bitter civil-military disagreements that had divided Britain's wartime leadership. Lloyd George had recently removed Robertson as CIGS after they fell out over the organisation of the SWC's military staff. The former War Office director of military operations, Major-General Sir Frederick Maurice, who was also sacked, inaugurated the crisis with a letter to *The Times* in early May accusing the prime minister of starving the army of men at a time of military crisis. Lloyd George defended himself adroitly if disingenuously in the House and things settled down. The real truth, however, was that the fully mobilised war economy would need more manpower than in previous years to produce the war material needed by a large mechanised army. This would inevitably be at the expense of military manpower. Conscription had now extended about as far as it could in Britain, with the age of conscription recently raised to 50 by another Man Power Act. Although extending conscription to Ireland remained a possibility, it was considered politically unwise while Ireland remained (like so many places by 1918) 'sullen and in many respects restless'.[22] The aircraft industry employed 174,000 male and female workers by the end of 1917, nearly three times as many as in August 1916. That number would double before the end of the war: one of Sandhurst's parlour maids would be among them.[23] The number of female employees had increased tenfold during the same period.[24] As the year went on British divisions were going to have to be broken up to balance the manpower needs of the military and manufacturing, especially if – as was expected – the war continued into 1919 or 1920.[25] British army strength had peaked towards the end of 1917, but Britain was now reaching the limit of her reserves, the point at which Germany had found herself at the end of 1916. Infantry battalions were under-strength following the 1917 campaign and Haig was in the process of restructuring British infantry divisions by reducing the number of battalions in each from 12 to 9, just as Germany and France had done previously. Unfortunately this large-scale structural reorganisation undermined the esprit de corps that British divisions had developed on the battlefield between 1915 and 1917, just when they had to meet the renewed and vigorous German threat. Dominion divisions, which retained the old 12-battalion structure, proved better able to sustain the demands of intensive battle and won themselves a reputation as elite formations during the final campaign. Despite the rigours of the 1918 campaign Haig managed to maintain the British army's division strength more or less, but only by incorporating category 'B' men into the ranks on occasion.[26] On the Allied side, there was some substance to Foch's aphorism 'the French were exhausted, the Americans were disappointing, and the British were invincible'.[27] The reality was that all armies were on their last legs come 1918, with the exception of the slowly growing and green American army and the small Belgian army (which had actually doubled in size after its divisions were restructured over the winter).

The SWC with its inter-Allied military staff effectively presided over by Foch finally established a mechanism for systematic strategic assessment and planning, cross-alliance resource coordination and management. Its careful investigation of the complete strategic and resource picture over the winter naturally highlighted manpower shortages and other supply problems. Now, however, through its system of subcommittees (controlling sea and land transportation, food supply, munitions, coal and steel, finance and other common supply and logistical matters, tobacco included) those commodities and processes that the mature war effort depended on could be managed to sustain armies in the field as well as to maintain home front living standards.[28] In the longer term, the Allied position was judged to be secure. American manpower and the increased production of war material were expected to redress the temporary imbalance of early 1918 and allow the Allies to resume the offensive, although it was anticipated that the war would continue into 1919. In the meantime plans were concerted by Haig and Pétain to reinforce the British or French sector of the front with reserves from the other according to necessity: the setting up of an Allied 'general reserve' that pooled divisions from all armies under Foch's control proved a step too far politically.[29] But, as Foch emphasised, the Allies would counterattack when the time was right, mounting 'a *combined offensive with decisive objectives*, the moment the wearing-down process, or any other favourable circumstance arising in the general situation, offers the hope of success'.[30] When the enemy attacked the Allies responded by reinforcing with as many divisions as they could from Britain, Egypt and Italy – four British, four French and even two Italian divisions strengthened the western front between April and June – and speeding up the flow of American troops to Europe.

LUDENDORFF'S ARMIES STRUCK THE FIRST BLOW IN THE FINAL BATTLE ON 21 March 1918. A stunning tactical surprise caused short-term panic yet again, but the Allies were flexible and resilient and 'Operation Michael', as the offensive was code-named, was not an operational success. A hur-

ricane bombardment by previously concealed guns caught the British
Fifth Army by surprise south of the River Somme. Storm troops advancing rapidly under the cover of fog overwhelmed thinly held frontline
defences and pushed on into open country. As in Poland in 1915, Rumania in 1916 and Italy in 1917, temporarily knocking one army out of the
Allied line of battle would not prove decisive. Foch, who was quickly
appointed Allied supreme commander, had reserves enough to contain
armed tide sweeping towards the strategic rail junction at Amiens. The
Fifth Army's retirement was not a rout like that of the Italian Second
Army at Caporetto. Improvised centres of resistance established in the
Fifth Army's rear areas exacted a heavy toll from the advancing Germans
as the British troops withdrew in good order behind and beyond the
River Somme. This slowed the momentum of the attack, buying time for
Haig to march reserves southwards and Pétain to rail them westwards.
The British Third Army to the north and the French Third Army to the south
held firm, forming the hinges of the doors that Foch closed in the Ger-
mans' path. By the end of March a new defensive line was consolidating
on the ridges east of Amiens. Fayolle, who had been given command of
the French forces plugging the gap – two armies formed into a new
Reserve Army Group – appreciated that the prospects of containing the
German penetration increased day by day:

> The Boche is strong, but not very intelligent. He has made a crude
> error. Having opened the breach between the Oise and the Somme, on
> a 60-kilometre front, he has tried to turn its flanks. To the south he
> has been held between Noyon and Montdidier . . . Not much happen-
> ing in the centre, where the wave has spent itself near the latter town.
> We have been given the time to concert our riposte.

As he predicted, the battle would be over by Easter. Come Easter Mon-
day, 'We are saved. Now the situation is fine.'[31]
    Ludendorff seemed not to understand the principles of attritional
battle, or of modern military operations. When asked what the objective
of the spring offensive was, Ludendorff brashly claimed that it was
enough to punch a hole and that the rest would follow.[32] The day-by-day
development of the Michael offensive suggested that he had reverted to
the 'breakthrough' mentality of 1915. Perhaps this was an unfortunate
legacy of Germany's success in the East in that year: such a method had
worked against thinly held lines backed by inadequate railway logistics,
but was inappropriate against the western front's well-manned deep
defences sustained by mobile operational reserves and extensive railway
networks. Fortuitously Ludendorff's blow in March 1918 had fallen

against the most thinly held sector of the Allied front in which new deep defences were incomplete, exaggerating the effect of his offensive tactics. Thereafter Ludendorff seemed to be questing for some weak point whose exploitation would turn another typically efficient German tactical success into something more decisive. The focus of his first offensive, and of Ludendorff's spring campaign as a whole, shifted according to circumstances and events, often on a daily basis, a manifestation of Ludendorff's 'stunning strategic and political ineptitude'.[33] Foch anticipated that the enemy's attack would lack operational coherence: 'It will be combined as a function of *space* and *time*; that is to say it will be directed upon different portions of the Anglo-French front, perhaps of the Italian front, at various intervals of time.'[34] The Allies would still have to fend off powerful flailing blows, even if the OHL had a weak conception that destroying enemy reserves was the basis of a military victory. Nevertheless, due to its scale and the early shock Operation Michael cost the Allies heavily: 255,000 casualties, including 90,000 prisoners. It was to cost Ludendorff's armies dearly too: 240,000 irreplaceable men.[35]

Ludendorff would attack again. But the first signs that his troops were feeling the strain were appearing. Resources were scarce, and after German troops broke into the British defences the reality of the two sides' war efforts was manifest. Advancing in Operation Michael, Binding had come across huge Allied supply dumps.

> There are new guns of the latest type, masses of gun-parts, valuable brass fittings, cables, electro-motors, axles, wheels, gun-carriages, and everything you can think of, standing about in such colossal quantities that one runs amazed and staring from one to the other just as if it were an exhibition . . . One sees . . . a pyramid of iron nails of every sort (while with us a packet of nails is a rarity, to be indented for in writing in the most elaborate way) . . . I got the impression that the English made everything out of rubber or brass, because these were the two materials which we had not seen for the longest time.[36]

The abundance of Allied war material contrasted starkly with the difficulty Binding encountered finding horses for his division, which went into action 200 short: these were promised to him once the spring offensive was underway, hopefully to be captured in the advance no doubt.[37]

Prospects of victory and of forcing a peace favourable to Germany, which many still saw as a fair reward for Germany's trials and sacrifices, would sustain the German soldiery during the spring offensives, even if they were by now 'no more than the positive expression of war weariness'.[38] Binding for one reflected as he looked on the death and destruction of what was by previous western front standards a very successful offensive:

> Undoubtedly if the statesmen and politicians of all countries . . . could have taken part in this progress through the desert and stopped here for a while in this most recent devastation, if they could bear the privations in the dirt and blood and have to sit tight under constant fire from in front and above, none of them would be against peace. Any peace would be good enough for them. But as it is they sit at their conference tables and regard it almost as a scandal that the armies cannot succeed in advancing on all the fronts together.[39]

Operation Michael had cost Binding's own division dearly: it was reduced to a fighting strength of only six hundred by the end of the battle, having been badly mauled by fresh French reinforcements.[40] The subsequent blows struck by Ludendorff's armies were to lengthen the casualty lists with equally indecisive results, and all the while a wilier adversary was awaiting the opportunity to counterattack.

Until midsummer the initiative lay with Germany. After the initial drive towards Amiens had been contained Ludendorff's armies repeated his 'smash-and-grab' strategy four times without managing to seize any vital strategic objective or break the will of any of Germany's adversaries expect perhaps the Portuguese, whose army corps bore the brunt of the second German attack across the River Lys on 9 April 1918 and melted away in confusion. In this offensive, code-named 'Operation Georgette', the German Sixth Army pushed towards another strategic railway junction southwest of Ypres at Hazebrouck, although the momentum of the advance was again contained by British and French reinforcements before Allied communications could be compromised. Ludendorff was finding it more difficult than he had expected to break 'the present unity front of the Entente'.[41] This had actually been strengthened by the appointment of Foch as Allied generalissimo as now for the first time Allied reserve divisions could be employed along the whole front at the behest of a single directing mind. French divisions had helped to halt Ludendorff's two thrusts against the British front, while American divisions had taken over quieter sectors of the line to liberate French reserve units.[42]

The German spring offensive was accompanied by an escalation of the air and sea campaigns against the Allies' home fronts. The bombing of Paris and London was intensified, and to this was added a new, outrageous terror: long-range guns that bombarded Paris and Amiens after the German army advanced. Although casualties and physical destruction were limited, there was renewed panic, and civilians left the threatened cities in large numbers. Even well away from the danger area, the constant threat of aerial bombardment produced sustained anxiety – in Bruce Cummings's case, that the print works that was producing the first edition of his published diary would be bombed.[43] Now, however, the Allies could strike back in kind. In the summer newly formed British and French independent air forces flying new types of bombing aircraft started to raid German industrial cities.

Ludendorff would attack for the third time on the Aisne front, where the line was held more thinly. Manpower reserves were starting to dwindle, morale was starting to decline and although ample munitions remained, sufficient guns were only available to support one operation at a time. There would be a delay, therefore, as the heavy artillery moved to a less well-defended sector of the front. On 27 May the 'Blücher-Yorck' offensive struck against the French army. Three million shells carried the assaulting infantry through the Allied defences on the first day, after which it became a matter of pursing Allied rearguards southwards until a new defensive line could be formed.[44] The Chemin des Dames Ridge was retaken and another huge salient was punched into the Allied front before the momentum of the advance was contained two weeks later. By that point the Seventh Army had reached the River Marne, which German troops had not seen since early September 1914. But it had been a deceptive and rather lucky victory. The initial attack had overwhelmed understrength, resting British and French divisions that had been badly handled in earlier battles, while the French army commander, General Denis Duchêne, had concentrated his troops in the front lines where they were most vulnerable to the new German offensive techniques rather than trying to hold his defensive front in depth as French doctrine now prescribed. Not surprisingly, Pétain relieved him of his command and his actions were subject to a court of enquiry.[45]

This was the most spectacular success seen on the western front to date, but it would not end the struggle. Although the 16 divisions in Duchêne's Sixth Army had been shattered, once again defeating one army did not mean defeating them all. Foch would find reserves to throw into the battle (with the parsimony he had learned at Ypres in 1914), as each day the momentum of the advance slowed and more fresh Allied divisions (including whole American divisions used in the battle line for the first time) deployed to contain and to counterattack the enemy penetration. Less steady than Foch, who by this time had all Allied reserves in hand and distributed them to meet any eventuality, Ludendorff again overplayed his hand.[46] He ordered further advances through an apparently open door, allowing losses to accumulate until it was again shut in his face, rather than halting once the initial objectives of the advance had been taken, consolidating and striking at his off-balance enemy else-where. It had been another costly battle both for sides, with 105,000 German and 127,000 Allied casualties inflicted in a little over a week: offensives of this scale and nature greatly intensified the rate of attrition for all armies.[47] Yet at the battle's end, although his armies appeared to be menacing Paris, all Ludendorff had to show for his latest advance was an extended and vulnerable salient thrust into Allied territory.

Ludendorff continued to press the Allied armies through June, but with diminishing returns. A fourth German blow between the recently created Somme and Marne salients, code-named 'Operation Gneisenau', struck General Georges Humbert's Third Army astride the River Matz on 9 June, aiming to break through and cross the River Oise. But after the usual early German success the French easily brought the advance to a halt. Ludendorff could no longer muster the number of men and guns he had for previous battles so attacker and defender were more evenly matched – 8 German storm troops divisions supported by 2,276 guns and 16 second-line divisions engaged 15 French divisions supported by 1,058 guns and 165 tanks – while the French army had learned quickly how to counter German offensive tactics.[48] The German blow again over-whelmed the French forward defences, but the Third Army was able to conduct an orderly retreat. Reinforced, it turned and held the Germans, while a hastily improvised counterattack directed by the aggressive General Charles Mangin 48 hours into the offensive knocked the enemy off balance. The next day, 12 June, an attempt to push forward on the western flank of the Marne salient was also contained, largely by French artillery fire. The losses were 25,000 German and 35,000 French: the tide of battle was starting to turn.[49]

Belatedly, Austrian forces had also resumed the offensive on the Italian front. Ludendorff had expected General Arthur Arz von Straussen-burg, Conrad's successor as chief of staff, to take the offensive against the apparently beaten Italians at an early point. It was indicative of the shaky relationships between the allies that Arz's armies did not attack until 13 June. Relations between Germany and Austria-Hungary had worsened after their joint victory on the southern front in autumn 1917. Thereafter Germany had progressively withdrawn her divisions from the Italian front to strengthen the western front offensive. Details of the peace feelers Emperor Karl had offered to the Allies in spring 1917 had recently been published by the French in an attempt to undermine the enemy coalition. The kaiser responded by strengthening Germany's hold over her ally. Karl was obliged to sign a closer treaty of alliance in May that effectively tied the Habsburg Empire economically to Germany and bound the German and Habsburg armies more closely together through the creation of a single high command and the standardization of arms and uniforms.[50] This did not stop Karl from sending out further peace feelers, but none were acceptable to his enemies. Austria was now obliged to fight to the death or glory with Germany.

Still, after the defeat of Russia there were many among the Austrian high command who shared Ludendorff's view that the Allied armies were so weakened that they could be dealt a knockout blow. Arz and his two army group commanders, Conrad and Boroević, had been planning to renew the offensive all along the Italian front, and Emperor Karl was persuaded to agree, not least because it might placate the Germans. Since peace with Russia and Rumania had liberated guns and experienced divisions for operations elsewhere, for the first time Austria would have numerical parity on the Italian front: sixty divisions faced fifty-six Italian, three British and two French. Twenty-one divisions came west during the spring, their ranks filled up with over half a million repatriated prisoners of war, although this manpower boost was somewhat offset by the Bolshevik ideas these men brought with them, as insubordination and mutiny became common in the army. More usefully, Arz had taken advantage of the spring lull to train his forces in the new offensive tactics that were proving so successful on the western front.[51] But the support they might expect from the home front was uncertain. In January, war weariness had inspired a general strike. There were calls, in obvious imitation of the Bolsheviks, for 'peace, justice and bread'. Troops were needed to keep order on the streets, reducing the army's frontline strength. The navy, cooped up in its harbours in the Adriatic, mutinied in February.[52] Armaments and munitions production was slumping owing to the growing impact of the Allied blockade, coupled with continuing strikes in the munitions industries.

Although Austria's forces had received a boost, their Italian opponents were no longer the army they had smashed so easily in November 1917. Diaz proved a much more professional commander in chief than Cadorna. His promotion after Caporetto was earned through proving himself as a capable division and army corps commander. His first actions in command, echoing Pétain's, were designed to improve the ordinary soldiers' conditions of service. He also introduced systematic monitoring of their morale, part of a wider national pro-war propaganda drive by the so-called 'P service', 'a model of integrated information management' that engaged Italian writers in 'a fervour of moral renewal'.[53] His armies too were developing apace, trained in material-intensive tactics by the British and French troops that had come to their aid, and were now more fully equipped by Allied and Italian industry, the latter now expanded by Italy's own 'architect of victory', armaments minister General Alfredo Dallolio.[54]

The Italian army now had the support of 7,000 guns and 676 aircraft and sufficient lorry transport to move reserves rapidly to any threatened point. The army had also been rebuilt, with 25 divisions being reconstituted from the stragglers of 1917's rout. The manpower situation was delicate, however, with only two annual contingents (including one of 18-year-olds called up in February), around half a million men, to replace losses.[55]

While awaiting the resumption of battle, Italy and her allies were simultaneously engaged in another offensive, distributing pro-nationality propaganda among Habsburg troops and encouraging self-determinist movements in a sustained campaign to undermine their cohesion and resolve. More practically, Italy added a Czech Legion of fourteen thousand Habsburg prisoners of war to the army's order of battle. The people's mood remained delicate, with a wave of industrial strikes during the spring and summer and peasant unrest in the south, although like those in 1917 these were largely clashes over economic issues rather than expressions of war weariness. Italy was clearly endeavouring to democratise her war effort under Orlando's more enlightened leadership. Like his French counterpart Clemenceau, he presented Italians with the stark choice between fighting on or the humiliation and chaos of defeat. Now that Friuli and part of the Veneto were occupied, an unpopular war of conquest could be neatly metamorphosed into a war of national defence and liberation, and a robust, aggressive patriotism sprung up, expressed through the appearance of populist organisations such as the Anti-German League. Italy had belatedly become a fully mobilised state like its Allies, with a new series of war orders boosting the industrialisation of the northern regions. By the end of the war Italy had one hundred thousand people working in an aeronautical industry that had not existed in 1915.[57] It seemed that 1917's troubles had been redressed and a fight to the finish was in the offing on the southern front too. But Italy's underlying social and political divisions persisted: a simmering domestic conflict over the modernisation of Italy remained to be fought out once the international war was over.

The determination of the two sides would to be tested in mid-June. A two-pronged Austrian attack against the wings of the Italian front would attempt to repeat the success of October 1917. Conrad's army group mounted a preliminary attack to take the contested Tonale Pass at the western extremity of the front on 13 June. This attack was contained by Italian artillery and machine-gun fire before it made much progress. Success was mixed in the main attack on 15 June. On the Asiago Plateau Conrad's forces broke into the Italian defences but were contained by the end of the day. Despite a shortage of munitions only allowing a relatively weak bombardment, Boroević's attack across the River Piave enjoyed more success in its early stages, but this was because the Italians had adopted 'elastic' defensive tactics. Having contained the northern threat Diaz deployed his reserves southwards against the Austrians' bridgeheads, checking the momentum of their advance. With supply proving difficult and under pressure from Italian counterattacks supported by powerful artillery fire the Austrian commanders chose to retire behind the river. Nine days of fighting cost the Austrians 118,000 casualties and the Allies 85,000. By the offensive's end the lines were more or less where they were beforehand. The Austrian threat, such as it was, had been contained, although despite the fact that captured prisoners revealed a state of deep demoralisation after the offensive failed, Diaz was reluctant to follow up aggressively. Stalemate seemed to have resumed on the southern front.[59]

By the end of June 1918 Austria seemed fatigued if not quite finished. In the offensive the troops' morale had been strong, believing that they might end the war, although they were physically dishevelled and their bellies were empty.[60] It was now up to her ally to win the war, but she remained obliged to support Germany, which was also running short of men. The upshot of the defeat on the River Piave was that Austria would now be pressed to send divisions to support Ludendorff's armies on the western front, where the battle continued to rage, and where as summer passed into autumn it was clear that the land war was reaching a climax. Although the Austrian army's ranks were fuller than they had been for some years, the willingness of the men to battle on was questionable. Thereafter they held their lines, watching events unfold in France: during the summer and early autumn fighting on the Italian front settled into localised *grignotage*.

Come the summer, Ludendorff's own troops were starting to show signs of the strain of continual battle.[61] But their commander persevered. He planned further strikes along the western front, against Reims, in Flanders and then against Amiens and Paris – more flailing, ill-coordinated blows that he hoped might capture some strategic prize and break the Allies' will.[62] He was wildly overoptimistic when he dubbed what was to be his final attack the *Friedensturm*, or 'peace storm'. His troops were tiring and resources were hard to obtain. Binding was concerned because the oat supply had run out and his division's draught horses were now living on turnips too. The Allies it was rumoured had 4,500,000 horses and ample fodder, while his army had only 1,500,000. In the coming offensive his division would have to leave one-quarter of its guns behind since there were no horses to pull them. 'All the same, everybody hopes for the best. I should do so too if I did not see these flaws in the reckoning. Three gun batteries (though counted as four), reduced ammunition quotas, and horses without oats in their bellies to haul these guns.'[63]

Come the summer of 1918, the Allied blockade was finally having a noticeable impact on Germany's ability to make war.

Ludendorff attempted to exploit the push to the River Marne by pinching out the city of Reims on the new salient's right flank – an important rail junction and frontline cathedral city whose loss would impact badly on French national morale – and found the defence better prepared. Although in the 'Marneschütz-Reims' offensive from 15–17 July German troops crossed the Marne west of Reims, the attack in the Champagne sector east of the city was contained by a more elastic defence in depth. General Henri Gouraud's matter-of-fact order of the day made it explicit that German forces would be destroyed: 'Every soldier must have only one thought – to kill them, and to keep on killing them, until they have had enough.'[64] Binding, who was acting as a liaison officer during the offensive, 'lived through the most disheartening day of the whole war'. On a scorching summer's day, his troops were attacking across a chalky wasteland that had last been fought over in 1915.

> No shade, no paths, not even roads; just crumbling white streaks on a flat plain. Across this wind rusty snakes of barbed wire. Into this the French deliberately lured us. They put up no resistance in front; they had neither infantry nor artillery in this forward battle-zone . . . Our guns bombarded empty trenches; our gas-shells gassed empty artillery positions; only in little hidden folds of the ground, sparsely distributed, lay machine-gun posts, like lice in the seams and folds of a garment, to give the attacking force a warm reception.
>
> After uninterrupted fighting from five o'clock in the morning until the night, smothered all the time with carefully directed fire, we only succeed in advancing about three kilometres . . . In the whole area in which we were kept confined by the enemy's fire and our own helplessness neither man nor beast had anything to eat or drink . . . We did not see a single dead Frenchman, let alone a captured gun or machine-gun, and we had suffered heavy losses . . . Since our experiences of 16 July I know we are finished.[65]

He was right. With the Germans preoccupied to the east, Foch had prepared a surprise that he would unleash against the western flank of the Marne salient, finally reversing the fortunes of battle.

All Germany's early 1918 offensives began with a striking tactical success. They demonstrated how armies had adapted to fighting on the fortified battlefield. As well as the development and manufacture en masse of specialist munitions such as high-explosive, gas and incendiary shells and the variety of modern weapons that fired them, the science of ballistics had advanced astonishingly. Gunners could now fire 'blind', accurately predicting where their shells would fall. Overwhelming firepower could now facilitate forward movement, briefly at least. Instead of lengthy artillery preparations that aimed to destroy defensive positions before an assault, which were the defining characteristic of mid-war offensives, in 1918 local surprise could be achieved (in most cases) through carefully concealed preparations followed by a short 'hurricane' bombardment that temporarily paralysed the defence. Offensives kicked off the moment artillery laid down a curtain of fire that rolled forwards with infantry following closely behind it. When the barrage's effectiveness relied on careful observation of the fall of shells, battles had been drawn-out affairs, fought over shell-shattered landscapes. Now they were shorter, would take place in more open country, but would peter out within a week or two once the shocking effect of the artillery's early firepower was spent. The internal combustion engine added some dynamism, but essentially battles still took place at slower than walking pace. It was a tactical system that worked – the Allied armies had developed equivalent 'combined arms' methods by the end of 1917 – but it could be countered if the defence was organised in depth to absorb the momentum of the initial advance, as Gouraud's Fourth Army demonstrated east of Reims, and the Italians on the River Piave. Even when the potent first assault knocked the enemy off balance, it only bought a short period of time, generally a few days, before he reinforced and organised a defence or counterattack. However powerful, offensives had their own built-in inertia. Advancing away from railheads against thickening defence lines would inevitably slow and then halt each German advance once the tyranny of logistics combined with the exhaustion of men and the attrition of reserves.[66] Once beyond its railheads the German army had only thirty thousand lorries at its disposal (with limited fuel and iron-rimmed wheels as oil and rubber were interdicted by the Allied blockade), compared with one hundred thousand on the Allied side.[67] Therefore the plan of attack envisaged capturing the narrow-gauge railways behind the British front and putting them rapidly back into service to sustain offensive momentum.[68] 'One cannot go on victoriously for ever without ammunition or any sort of reinforcements,' Binding opined.[69] In that respect, 1918's battles were exactly the same as those earlier in the war.

Foch understood perfectly well that 'the waves will diminish' as an attack's energy dissipated and that therefore while there were moments of alarm, there was no need to panic.[70] Ludendorff's series of operations differed from those that Foch would direct against him in the second phase of the 1918 campaign because they lacked system and purpose. Germany's earlier victories suggested that her army might eliminate enemies one by one: yet such an 'annihilation strategy' had little chance against the more powerful Allied nations, especially now that their armies were fighting as a single coordinated force. In themselves battles were insufficient to bring the war to an end: the capture of a local objective or the defeat of one or more of the enemy's armies along a front was never significant strategically. Yet while not conceived as attritional offensives per se, the scale and intensity of these spring battles contributed significantly to the attrition of both sides' forces. Foch knew that the attrition of Germany's army would determine the outcome of the war and appreciated how to pursue this long-standing objective to its denouement. Ludendorff had tested and tired his enemies over four months but had not come close to defeating them. Over a similar period Foch would break his.

# FOURTEEN

# VICTORY ON
# ALL FRONTS

A T FIRST LIGHT ON 18 JULY 1918, 2,133 ALLIED GUNS SWEPT THE German defences west of Soissons with a sudden hurricane of fire. Simultaneously, nine infantry divisions advanced behind a curtain of high-explosive and shrapnel shells, in the usual procession of companies and battalions, through and beyond the German trenches. To all appearances it was just another barrage, the cacophony and firestorm that heralded one more battle. Foch knew otherwise: he was beginning his long-prepared destruction of the German army. For the Germans who were engaged in their own offensive, the Allied counterattack came as a complete surprise. The western flank of the overextended Marne salient that the Germans had punched into the French line in May was weak. The carefully planned attack by Mangin's Tenth Army aimed to recapture the railway junction at Soissons, which had fallen on 28 May. It was a truly Allied offensive. British, French and also three American infantry divisions, taking part in their first major offensive, were all under Mangin's command. A modern, mechanised army was on the move. The assault troops were supported by 493 tanks, including light Renault FT17s, a new model fast enough to keep up with the rapid pace of the infantry advance that had become the norm in 1918; 1,143 aircraft buzzed overhead, supporting the advancing infantry by strafing retreating enemy columns and bombing more distant targets.[1] Mangin's troops did well, and by mid-morning they were through the thinly fortified crust of the German defences and engaging scratch positions at close quarters in open country. As was always the case the advance started to slow on the second day, but by then the attack had achieved its objective. The attack had the momentum to reach the enemy's gun-line, the ultimate goal of offensive operations, and 20,000 prisoners had been captured as well as 518 guns, 300 trench mortars and 3,000 machine guns.[2] It was now realistic for Mangin to aim for Soissons, which fell on 2 August, while it had not been so for Falkenhayn to target Verdun or for Haig to target Bapaume in 1916. Around the perimeter of the Marne salient French, British, American and even a few Italian divisions were joining the counteroffensive as Foch ordered the four armies surrounding it to destroy the enemy's forces trapped south of the Rivers Aisne and Vesle.[3] Under concerted pressure, and with communications threatened on both flanks, Ludendorff had no option but to evacuate the salient and organise a new defensive line along the River Vesle.[4] After months of intensive battle Allied troops were tired and they could not stop the Germans from slipping out of the net that Foch had tried to close around them. But the tide of battle had clearly turned.

In the Second Battle of the Marne 52 Allied infantry divisions supported by 3,679 guns, tanks, aircraft and cavalry engaged along an 80-mile front. On both sides casualties were heavy: 133,000 Allied and 168,000 German, including 27,000 prisoners. Ludendorff's strategic reserve had been reduced by 20 divisions, and those divisions that remained were largely fought out: the first phase of the sequence of Malmaison-sized battles needed to destroy the German army had been engaged successfully. French intelligence calculated that there were now only 543,000 German replacements available including 300,000 men of the 1920 class (a contingent that France was not due to call up until October).[5] Although it was not yet apparent, the Second Battle of the Marne was significant because it marked the start of the final defeat of the German army. Foch had developed an appropriate attritional operational method that was to make the difference between the two sides in their most intensive campaign to date.

'The newspapers emphasise our entry into the fifth year of war,' Corday noted. 'They all preach resignation and sacrifice, with all the attitude and phraseology of religion. They all promise victory, but naturally without defining it.' The turning of the German tide sweeping into France so emphatically renewed faith in ultimate victory, and in a proper victory. 'No compromise peace; we must crush them!' former minister Puech declared.[6] The final battles would engage two weakened and punch-drunk opponents in a fight to the finish. Manpower problems were growing acute on both sides. The German army's temporary advantage in manpower reserves that reinforcement from the East had brought had been worn away during the spring offensive. Reserves, such as they were, were now very thin. The next annual contingent of young men would not be available until the autumn. Such men as could be found meanwhile were physically weak or potentially unreliable: old men, re-categorized sick and wounded, released prisoners of war from the East tainted with Bolshevism, pressed home-front strikers and criminals were processed through Germany's depots.[7] Troops from the eastern front, who had either fraternised with the Russians or been indoctrinated by the Bolsheviks while prisoners of war, did not share their western front comrades' commitment to victory. Indeed many, perhaps as many as half a million, of the '*Schlactvieh* (animals for slaughter) for Flanders' as they styled themselves simply melted away as their troop trains passed through Germany. Those who reached the western front spread their defeatist message among their comrades, particularly behind the lines where they had the time and the inclination to listen. The ranks were further thinned by the Spanish flu epidemic. It afflicted all armies, but the ill-nourished German soldiers had weaker resistance to it than Allied troops. 'Six hours of shivering, a temperature of 102 [degrees], then hours of perspiration till I was so weak that I could not move a limb without help, and all my nerves were in commotion': Binding was laid low in August and never returned to his unit.[8] He was not there to witness the progressive breakdown of authority on the German army's lines of communication as Foch's armies pressed on. Although the summer's intensive battles suggested that the field army still had plenty of fight in it, behind the lines deserters proliferated, and 'straggling' – pretending sickness (easy with the flu epidemic in full flood), delaying a return to the front and other evasion strategies – became widespread as war-weary troops awaited the end of a war that seemed to be on its last gasp. But collective outbreaks of 'pro-Republican' agitation and refusal to fight do not seem to have been widespread before October, when it was realised that the war was lost.[9]

To meet the German offensive with fresh manpower, the age of field service for British conscripts had to be lowered from nineteen to eighteen and a half. But the French army's losses remained within statistical forecasts, and there were always the Americans to call upon if the front could hold. Some 3,700,000 Americans were by now under arms, in anticipation of building a 100-division army. 'Doughboys' were now arriving at a great rate after the SWC had negotiated an accelerated deployment of American manpower in response to the German attacks (not without some difficulty).[10] By July 1918, 25 formed divisions were in France (although 10 of these were still training and 2 were depot divisions).[11] The American Expeditionary Force would largely be equipped from British and French stocks, saving time and scarce shipping capacity in mobilising American strength. Despite its commander in chief, General John Pershing, pressing for the formation of a separate American army for political reasons, from late April American divisions started to take part in the fighting piecemeal, closely supported by seasoned Allied formations. Although they were still raw formations they were powerful, with twice the infantry strength of other Allied divisions. More had taken over quieter sections of the line to free veteran French and British units for battle. Together, these shifts in the manpower balance restored parity between Allied and Central powers' forces in the West by July. Pétain stressed to Pershing that as well as manpower and material, morale would count in the outcome of the war.[12] Although they remained greenhorns for the rest of the campaign, the very presence of American troops in the fighting line in large numbers was a real boost for Allied morale and dispiriting for their enemies. 'The steady arrival of American reinforcement must be particularly valuable for the enemy,' Hindenburg later suggested. 'Even if these reinforcements were not yet up to the level of modern requirements in a purely military sense, mere numerical superiority had a far greater effect at this stage when our units had suffered so heavily.'[13]

On 4 August Ludendorff issued an order of the day to his weary troops, commending their efforts during the spring offensive, but announcing that the army was resuming defensive warfare. His hollow promise that an Allied offensive 'will only speed the attrition of [their] forces' fooled no one and dashed German soldiers' hopes of forcing a quick end to the war.[14] 'One feels that the year from which for the first time one seriously hoped for a decision, because there was no holding out any longer, has been simply thrown away,' Binding lamented.[15] 'At home they are impotent . . . [and] there is endless self-delusion,' he recognised, so under the thrall of the army leadership the war would continue. Ludendorff's armies would still have to be vanquished before he accepted that Germany had failed in its endeavour. The enemy was not yet short of reserves: French intelligence calculated after their reverse in the Second battle of the Marne that there were still thirty-nine fresh and twenty-eight reforming German reserve divisions to be engaged and defeated.[16] These were losing their relish for the fight. With his own division at rest Binding had time to reflect. Even such an ardent patriot was reaching the limit of physical and mental endurance.

> One keeps on repeating that there is no sense in using oneself up. One repeats, too, that one is not here to go on being used up in this never-ending folly . . . I have no more to do with the theory that one is bound to go on sharing in the folly of the human race because one belongs to it . . . Here is the stupidest war of position starting afresh. It is necessary because it is forced upon us, and from the military point of view it may

yet prove justified; in the end it may lead to something which can be called peace. But I am not convinced that it is reasonable for me personally, and therefore I feel it is unreasonable for me to go on.[17]

The German army that Foch would engage in the second phase of 1918's campaign was certainly not as formidable as that which the Allies had faced hitherto.

Foch had the manpower, resources and method to bring this shaky leviathan down, not with a knockout blow, but by pummelling his weary adversary into submission. 'Hit here and hit there . . . hitting and kicking without cease so as to give the enemy no time to recover. It turned out to be a dramatic forecast of his method which the great soldier was soon to employ and which ended in compete victory for the Allies,' Lloyd George acknowledged after witnessing Foch demonstrate his method animatedly with flailing fists and feet to the British foreign secretary.[18] The actual plan would take shape as events dictated, as was Foch's way. Now, however, a counteroffensive could be mounted with some hope of success, and the attrition of the early months of the year could be completed, perhaps before 1918 was out, or if not in 1919. On 7 August Foch issued an order of the day to the French army: 'Four years of effort aided by our faithful Allies, four years of trial stoically accepted, commence to bear their fruit . . . Today I say to you: Tenacity, Boldness and Victory must be yours.'[19] This was nothing new: all previous offensives had been prefaced with stirring exhortations to the troops. Unlike Joffre and Nivelle, however, Foch understood how to destroy the enemy's army once and for all. This was not a call for tenacity and boldness for one fight, for a single offensive: it was a plea for his troops to see out the final long, intense sequence of battles that, once engaged, he intended would go on until one side or the other broke. Since the end of 1916 he had been planning to fight a decisive attritional battle of reserves. Now that time had come, and according to his calculations his armies would win it easily.

Foch was a rare thing: a soldier who Lloyd George was prepared to acknowledge as a 'genius'.[20] Largely forgotten nowadays, Foch was the one soldier who really engaged with, understood and resolved the problems of waging attritional warfare. Since 1914 he had put his theoretical knowledge into practice at the various levels of command, always reflecting on and learning from his experience. This wide understanding of command and his familiarity with coordinating Allied operations made him the obvious choice for supreme commander. His conduct of the defensive battle from March to July gave his political masters and military subordinates confidence in his ability to wage a war of reserves with skill and sufficient parsimony. He shuttled divisions along the front from sector to sector, army to army, in a process of *roulement* (rotation) that ensured that each German thrust was contained, while all the Allied armies grew accustomed to working side by side under the careful direction of their generalissimo. When it came to counterattacking, Foch understood, it was important that he had all Allied forces under his control. '*Tout le monde à la bataille!*' (everyone into the battle!) was one of his frequent exclamations. They would all be needed in the sophisticated attritional offensive that he had been gestating.

Come 1918, it was possible to pursue the cumulative attrition of the enemy's fighting power with hope of success. At the end of the Somme offensive Foch had noted that the Anglo-French forces had engaged and defeated 120 enemy divisions in four and a half months, but that the slow tempo of the battle and the power of the defensive had allowed the enemy to repair the damage. He reasoned that if the same could be done in weeks, if 120 German divisions were reduced to half their strength and put out of action for several weeks, it would mean the whole German army in the West had been beaten. To do so, he concluded, required 'army-sized actions geared towards consistent tactical and strategic objectives, complete agreement and reciprocal loyalty' as well as a large space in which to operate.[21] Foch's *bataille générale* (general battle) would engage the German army from August 1918 and not let it go, eroding its manpower, material and morale. A sequence of offensives, each one within the capabilities of a single army's fighting power and logistics, would be engaged at a pace that would exhaust Germany's ability to sustain battle once and for all. Ludendorff's attacks had drawn his armies out of the deep, solid defences of the Hindenburg Line, beyond their strategic railway system and into vulnerable salients. This gave Foch an operational advantage that he could exploit – Mangin's Tenth Army smashed in the flank of the biggest of these salients on 18 July – and made the reinforcement of Ludendorff's frontline armies problematic during the first stage of Foch's counteroffensive. The specific instructions Foch issued to Allied army commanders set geographical objectives for each component attack during the *bataille générale* – a dominant ridge, a railway junction, an enemy defence line to be occupied – yet cumulatively this series of battles had a specific strategic objective: 'To embarrass the enemy in the utilising of his reserves and not allow him sufficient time to fill up his units.'[22] Three or four powerful concerted attacks would get through the enemy's fixed defences, after which his reserves could be engaged in hastily constructed positions. How long they could resist would depend on the quantity of their reserves.[23]

Foch's planning and decision making was founded in careful calculation of the balance of the two sides' resources: in practice, he was still pursuing the plan for active defence followed by counterattack that he had presented to the SWC in January.[24] By July, for the first time that year, the Allies had superiority in fresh reserves, enhanced by a great material advantage in tanks, aircraft and guns. In contrast the enemy, Foch assured the Allied commanders in chief, had been forced to take 'urgent measures . . . in order to meet the crisis in the supply of men for the month of May [and] a new crisis is now asserting itself'.[25] By the middle of 1918 the German army was desperate for reserves and suffering from the cumulative impact of three years of Allied attrition and its own spring offensives. The OHL's statisticians had calculated at the start of the year that if wastage continued at the usual rate, the German army would run out of replacements except reformed wounded soldiers by August, and during the intensive battles of the spring the rate of attrition had actually increased.[26] Foch would therefore take on an army that could no longer adequately refill its ranks, which perhaps made Foch's task easier than he anticipated. Once battle was engaged there would be insufficient time for resting and reconstituting fought-out divisions, so that Germany's already flagging forces would finally be exhausted before the year was out. Foch would accept the reciprocal wearing down of his own forces' fighting strength, secure in the knowledge that a steady supply of new American divisions and thousands of tanks, aircraft and guns would be available to support them if the French and British armies could not complete his grand design that year. Concomitantly the enemy's morale, the other objective of attrition, which reports from prisoners indicated was already shaky, would be broken.[27]

Foch's counteroffensive, 'the Hundred Days' Offensive' as it is known, had three phases. The first, which lasted through August and September, was designed to free Allied forces' communications and to position them to take on the enemy in a sustained final battle. Phase two, which Foch determined to launch in late 1918 rather than hold over until 1919, engaged the enemy's whole army in a huge battle along the western front, evicting them from their line of fixed defences. Phase three, one of the most intense phases of fighting of the whole war, drove the remains of the German army out of most of occupied France and part of Belgium, sustaining military pressure while armistice terms were negotiated. All along men were killed and captured, equipment and supplies were taken and already shaky morale was degraded. All this was now possible because the Allied armies could mount offensive operations that would carry them to the enemy's gun-lines and beyond in rapid succession.

Foch was asking a lot of his subordinates and their troops. When he called the Allied commanders in chief to a conference on 24 July and presented his plan, initially they demurred. Pétain and Haig represented that their troops were too exhausted after the spring battles to resume the offensive, while Pershing had yet to form the American army that he intended to command in the field. Nevertheless, after twenty-four hours reflection they all agreed, given Foch's assurance that he would regulate the pace of the counteroffensive 'according to the success obtained as we went along'.[28] Albert I, king of the Belgians, who until then had commanded an army that did little more than hold a quiet sector of the line (and defend the last corner of unoccupied Belgium), assented to taking the offensive after the first phase of Foch's operation proved successful. In September a new Allied army group with orders 'to exploit the weakening and attrition of the enemy' was formed, which would undertake the liberation of Belgium. It was nominally commanded by the king, but in practice directed by General Jean-Marie Degoutte, its French chief of staff appointed by Foch.[29]

It remained to be seen how many set-piece army-scale battles like that fought at Malmaison would still be needed to break the German army. Foch had 17 Allied armies at his disposal with which to fight them: 10 French, 5 British, 2 American and the Belgian army. Each would have to fight several battles and sustain pressure on the enemy between them, although Ludendorff's spring battles had already achieved some of the necessary attrition. The burden of fighting fell disproportionately on the formations in the Allied centre, the British Third and Fourth and the French First and Third Armies, that mounted the first phase of the operation against the Somme salient that had been created by Operation Michael. The British Third Army, one of the most heavily engaged, mounted 10 set-piece attacks against defensive positions, carried out improvised attacks on temporary defences on 17 days and pursued retreating Germans for 15 days between 21 August and the armistice. During that period it advanced 60 miles, captured 67,000 prisoners (out of 100,000 casualties inflicted) and 800 guns, and lost between 115,000 and 120,000 casualties itself.[30]

Foch's counteroffensive began on 8 August with an Anglo-French offensive to disengage the railway junction at Amiens, carried out by Rawlinson's Fourth and General Marie-Eugene Debeney's First French Armies. Today the Battle of Amiens is remembered as a triumph for the Australian and Canadian forces that on 8 August advanced rapidly with artillery, tank and air support, shattering the German defences south of the River Somme. Subsequently the battle expanded southwards as the French First and Third Armies advanced 20 kilometres to capture Montdidier by 11 August.[31] The Allies inflicted 75,000 casualties, including nearly 30,000 prisoners, and captured over 450 guns, suffering 44,000 casualties themselves.[32] For Binding, whose division was ordered back to the front, the writing was on the wall.

I shudder to think of going through the Somme wilderness for the fourth time. It will be the same all over again, but without any confidence. Our troops will be thinner and worse; for days the horses have not had a grain of oats; the men are being given barley-bread which will not rise in the oven, and we have taken some knocks. Against us we shall have thousands of tanks, tens of thousands of airmen, hundreds of thousands of hearty young men, behind whom there will be an American army which may number a million.[33]

The night before he had dreamed that ordinary people had hung the kaiser, and he did not seem disappointed.[34] It was a time for regicide: rumours were abroad that the Bolsheviks had just executed the tsar and all his family.[35]

At this rate only twenty battles would be needed to complete the destruction of the German army. Set-piece offensives thereafter were rarely as spectacular or successful. The pursuit of the enemy to his pre-March defences continued through August and September. Operations developed a certain pattern. The enemy would be driven out of a fixed defensive position. He would then conduct a fighting retreat to the next defensive position, against which a new set-piece attack would be organised. Haig's Fourth and Third Armies, with Debeney's First, were in the van, with the British First and the French Third and Tenth Armies supporting their flanks. They advanced at a steady but not spectacular pace: the British Third Army advanced 15 miles in 18 days between 21 August and 7 September (including recrossing the devastated Somme battlefield of 1916) before pausing to regroup and bring its heavy guns forward. Its next obstacle was the much more solid Hindenburg Line. All the while the German army was disintegrating: 51,576 casualties, including 33,827 prisoners, were inflicted during the Third Army's advance.[36] Farther to the east the American First and French Second Armies pinched out the St Mihiel salient east of Verdun in mid-September. Although somewhat tangential to Foch's desired axis of advance, this long-anticipated operation did at least give Pershing's now-constituted American army some much-needed experience in conducting a large-scale offensive and added 13,250 prisoners and 460 guns to the Allied haul.[37]

Now that his *bataille générale* was progressing well, Foch had to make an important and potentially war-ending decision. Was his offensive going well enough, were his own armies strong and fresh enough and were the enemies' armies weakening enough for there to be a real chance that they could be defeated before the year was out? Certainly his armies were operating dynamically and usually achieving their objectives, more or less. Ludendorff on the other hand was increasingly disheartened. After the Battles of Amiens and Montdidier he had informed the government that the army could no longer win the war and that a diplomatic resolution should be sought. Then he remained hopeful that the army could hold a 'winter line' behind the old Somme battlefield while the diplomats conducted negotiations. But Haig's armies stormed that line at the start of September, obliging withdrawal to the Hindenburg Line, Germany's last fully engineered line of defence.[38] The Allied troops' morale was on the rise from the moment that they turned back the enemy in the Second Battle of the Marne even though their ranks were thinning like the Germans' (if not as fast).[39] Being successfully on the offensive and the fact that American manpower was starting to engage were real boosts to troops that had exhausted themselves in defensive warfare. But the troops were growing tired and would have to be carefully husbanded as the campaign went on. The ever-cautious Pétain had warned Foch during the Marne counterattack that French soldiers 'certainly have excellent morale, but fatigue is high. We are at the limit of our efforts'.[40]

Once again Foch's tiring central armies would have the main task to break the deep central section of the Hindenburg Line. But Foch had yet to engage all his forces: two more British, one American, four French armies and the Belgian army were poised to attack elsewhere along the front. Ludendorff would be so engaged that he could not find the reserves to reinforce when the main blow struck. German forces were being degraded – divisions were now being broken up to find reinforcements for others, and French intelligence estimated that the enemy only had twenty fresh reserve divisions available by this point – and signs were increasing that their morale was declining.[41] Formed units were surrendering en masse, although that was in part because Allied operations were fast enough to cut them off before they could retire.[42] The soldiers thus captured were exhibiting all the signs of war weariness and reporting a severe morale crisis among their comrades. Foch was not a man to hesitate in such circumstances: he would always choose the boldest course. The decision to '[organise] immediately a general battle of the Allied Armies' was taken at the end of August.[43] Through the autumn the armies under Foch's direction would push the German forces back slowly, steadily, continually, in what he later described as 'a series of well-ordered actions, [bringing] all the Allied resources into play as rapidly as possible, so as to prevent the enemy from recovering before we could effect his definite destruction'.[44]

The climax came at the end of September. On 26 September the second phase of the general offensive, a concerted sequence of battles all along the western front 'from the Meuse to the North Sea with the objective of fixing and using up reserves', began.[45] The American First Army attacked in the Meuse-Argonne sector, west of Verdun, supported by the French Second Army to the east and the French Fourth Army in Champagne to the west. The next day the battle shifted elsewhere, when the British First and Third Armies struck at the northern end of the Hindenburg Line towards Cambrai. On 28 September the new Flanders Army Group, comprising the Belgian, British Second and later French Sixth Armies, started the Fifth Battle of Ypres by attacking north and south of the Ypres Salient. On 29 September the British Fourth and French First Armies struck the final blow in the centre, against the strongest sector of the Hindenburg Line. Ludendorff had no reserves with which to resist: on 30 September he informed his army group commanders that the OHL no longer had reserve divisions to draw on and that they must do the best they could with the troops under their own command.[46] Foch had won the battle of reserves. Ludendorff had lost his nerve along with his army. He informed the kaiser on 3 October that an armistice must be sought.

By the time the kaiser asked the Allies for an armistice and a peace negotiated on the basis of Woodrow Wilson's 'Fourteen Points' on 4 October most of the Hindenburg Line defensive system was in Allied hands. The remnants of the German army had no choice thereafter but to conduct a fighting retreat while politicians and diplomats settled Germany's fate. It would not be Ludendorff's army much longer. As part of a belated 'democratic' political reshuffle in Germany he would be replaced, on the grounds of nervous collapse, on 29 October. The final phase of the campaign – Haig's long-anticipated exploitation phase – entailed pursuing the retreating Germans across France and Belgium during the time it took to negotiate an armistice, to sustain pressure and to prevent the enemy from resting and recovering.[47] In these weeks, if the German defence threatened to solidify along a river or canal line or other natural obstacle, a quickly organised set-piece attack could restore the momentum of the advance.[48] On the whole, however, these were mobile operations, with mixed forces of infantry, horse-drawn field artillery and cavalry supported by aircraft and on occasion tanks and armoured cars, snapping at the heels of the scurrying Germans. Such operations cleared territory at a far faster rate than previously, with much ground being given up voluntarily when Allied flanking attacks made it untenable, but battle remained linear. Foch's armies never broke the German front, but they pushed it back at a steady pace degrading their adversary all the time: less than a mile a day averaged over the period from 8 August to 11 November. In their turn, in their pursuit of the German army across France and Belgium the Allied armies soon outstripped their supply lines. However, a more dispersed front-wide linear offensive did allow pauses to reorganise the logistic system, extend rail lines and bring up reserves and supplies. Although the number of shells fired in an offensive had increased vastly since 1916, the railway and road systems, if stretched more than ever before, could cope. Yet the armistice was timely, since the Allied armies would need to pause to sort out their supply lines eventually.[49]

Elements of the German army would still fight hard during this final phase, some of the hardest fighting of the war: military traditions, and the engrained practices of four years of war, do not disappear overnight, and tenacious machine-gun armed rear guards exacted a steady toll of their pursuers. If nothing else, the army had to buy time for the plenipotentiaries to negotiate armistice terms and also to show that there was still some fight left in Germany should the Allies seek harsh terms, as Lloyd George, Clemenceau and Wilson inevitably did.[50] But the fact that surrenders were increasing and men were being led by their officers into captivity once it became known that an armistice was under negotiation and that the war would be over soon suggested that the German army in the West was exhausted and demoralised by November.[51] But Allied troops were tiring too. Back with the Guards Division after being gassed during the spring fighting, Oliver Lyttelton noted how tired his comrades had become. Even though the enemy was clearly also tiring, he feared the annual cycle of attrition might yet be reengaged.

> Strategically the Boche is in a little easier condition . . . for the moment there are no dangerous salients for him. He will escape individual disaster but cumulatively he is hammered terribly. Every day we take 4–6,000 prisoners on the 200-mile battle front. That cannot go on for ever, though I think it will last longer than people think. His new class, 400,000 men about, are not yet engaged I believe, but I don't know.[52]

But his men were exultant in their pursuit: 'We all have the feeling of men let out of prison into the open.'[53]

When the armistice came three weeks later, however, there was a great sense of anticlimax:

> I had expected riotous excitement, but the reaction of everyone, officers and men, seemed the same – flat depression . . . By the afternoon we were already bored . . . We had lost our profession, in which we had been immersed for five years . . . we had already begun to wonder what awaited us in peace-time.[54]

FOCH'S ATTRITIONAL *BATAILLE GÉNÉRALE* HAD ACHIEVED ITS OBJECTIVE OF breaking the fighting power of the German army once and for all. French military intelligence calculated that there were only two fresh German reserve divisions capable of being sent into battle behind the western front on 11 November, the day the armistice came into force. Since the Allied counteroffensive had begun Ludendorff had had to break up twenty-three divisions to find reserves for the rest of his army. During that period it had lost 385,500 prisoners and 6,615 guns on top of the killed or wounded casualties that, with the breakdown of its administrative systems, the army was no longer able to collate, but which probably reached a similar number.[55] By November 1918 Foch's offensive had completed the work of attrition, which in 1918 developed at a pace, and with a cumulative effect, more substantial than that of earlier years. The scale and tempo of the *bataille générale* that Foch had conceptualised and that the modern semi-mechanised armies under his control were now able to fight proved too much for an exhausted, demoralised, manpower- and material-deficient enemy. This was more than 'a strategy of opportunity'.[56] Foch the thinker was pursuing a plan based on his military experiences since 1914 and grounded in careful calculations of what was necessary to decide the war.[57] While the individual engagements that defeated the German army were planned and synchronised according to operational developments week by week, overall the *bataille générale* was governed by the strategic goal which the Allied commanders had set at the end of 1915 – 'the destruction of the German and Austrian armies'. Foch the leader was able to inspire the Allied forces to victory. 'It was a victory of intelligence and willpower,' General Maxime Weygand, the chief of staff who had been at Foch's side since 1914, attested. 'And also of the offensive spirit with which, never tiring himself, he had reanimated the armies, never letting them forget, even during the days of a murderous defensive, that their final duty was to attack.'[58]

Now that the German army was being bled white and could no longer shore up the southern and Balkan fronts, her allies were also vulnerable. While Germany's forces were collapsing in the West, simultaneously her allies were dropping one by one. Foch subscribed to the principle of concerted Allied military action that had been followed since 1915, and pressed during the summer months for supplementary offensives in Italy against Austria and at Salonika against the Bulgarians. Although Foch directed the armies in the West, he had also assumed authority to coordinate with the Italian front where British and French divisions remained deployed. Diaz stalled, asking Foch for tanks and gas shells, then trucks and extra divisions. Come October, however, he could see that the tide of the war was finally washing in the Allies' favour and that Italy should seek to win her own war by breaking the Habsburg armies once and for all.[59] Italy's autumn offensive, when it came on 24

October, was on a scale and had an impact far greater than anything Italy's armies had managed in earlier years. But the grandiloquently titled 'Vittorio Veneto' offensive – 'the victory in the Veneto' – fell on an army that had already decided to be defeated and Diaz's armies did not have to fight too hard. An overwhelming preparatory bombardment had escalated the rate of desertion from the highly demoralised Habsburg army, and once the Austrian front had been broken advancing Italian troops were more likely to encounter white flags than machine guns. The fact that five hundred thousand enemy prisoners were taken in ten days, while only thirty thousand battle casualties were inflicted, was proof that the fight had gone out of the Austrians.[60] An armistice came into force on 4 November. Austria-Hungary's war was over. The Habsburg Empire was also at an end: it would dissolve into its component nationalities over the ensuing weeks.

At Salonika General Louis Franchet d'Espèrey, in command since June, had been preparing to strike at Bulgaria's weary divisions. The Allied counteroffensive in France had drawn off most of their supporting German battalions, and they were heavily outnumbered, by 670,000 to 170,000 men. On 15 September, a cosmopolitan French-British-Serbian-Greek-Italian army crossed the Vardar River and drove northwards, their enemy all but collapsing.[61] The Bulgarians signed an armistice that came into force on 30 September, before German divisions could reinforce them: although the stiffening that these divisions could provide was questionable by this point. Fearing the Allies could now advance unhindered into Austria and Rumania just as the western front was collapsing, Ludendorff and Hindenburg deemed it time to ask for an immediate armistice. Their own army would be broken before Franchet d'Espèrey's forces could make much more progress.[62]

The Turkish fronts remained a sideshow to European operations, effectively run by the government of India by this point, but here too offensive operations intensified. Allenby's forces resumed their offensive in Palestine from mid-September, and in cooperation with Arab nationalist irregulars reached Damascus by early October. The British army in Mesopotamia was advancing too, and captured the oil fields at Mosul by early November. Turkey's strategic position worsened when the defeat of Bulgaria isolated her from Germany and left her capital, Constantinople, threatened by Franchet d'Espèrey's advance. This threat, rather than the Allied advances in the Levant and Mesopotamia, brought the Turkish government down, and its replacement asked for an armistice, which was signed on 30 October.[63] The defeats of Bulgaria and Germany forced Turkey to seek terms. The small wars that simmered on the edges of the former Ottoman Empire until a revised peace treaty was signed with

Kemal Atatürk's nationalists in 1923 indicated that Lloyd George's 'New Eastern' strategy had fermented postwar imperial problems in the Middle East while having little impact on the outcome of the war in Europe.

The Central powers did not exactly collapse like a house of cards: that would suggest they were mutually supporting. During 1918 the Entente alliance grew together and got stronger when faced first with adversity and later with opportunity, while their adversaries split. Although their enemies' surrenders coincided, they were all defeated separately, and tellingly, each negotiated for an armistice independently. Successes on the other fronts did not determine the outcome of the battle in the West, or have much impact on the cohesion of an alliance which existed in name only by this point. For some time Germany's allies had been unwilling participants in Hindenburg and Ludendorff's deluded quest for decisive victory while no longer sharing their convictions. Victory over Russia and Rumania offered all the members of that alliance some reward for their sacrifice, although imperial conquests no longer reflected the desires of a great section of their populations. By summer 1918 they were not really fighting a joint war anymore and stayed together only because none of them could secure separate peace terms. Germany had effectively abandoned them to concentrate what remained of her military strength on the western front before any of them were engaged and defeated by Allied forces. Once Germany had been beaten, her allies would not have fought on. Ludendorff could be expected to struggle on whatever happened in the East and the South. Ludendorff might use Bulgaria's defeat as an excuse to press the kaiser to seek an armistice for Germany, establishing a pervading myth that Germany was obliged to capitulate following the collapse of her allies. But Ludendorff was fully aware that the Allied offensive was sweeping his armies from France and Belgium and destroying their fighting capacity while Germany's conservative military dictatorship was imploding.

THERE IS A VIEW THAT THE EARLY MONTHS OF 1918 DETERMINED THE WAR'S outcome – that by mounting costly but indecisive offensives Ludendorff exhausted the already tiring, hungry and inadequately supplied German army to a point that the Allies could turn the tables and reap the rewards of their enemy's own folly.[64] In this judgement based on the shifting balance of resources, the arrival of Americans in large numbers weighs heavily, as much for its moral effect as for its military impact, which was limited. Certainly the heavy losses sustained in Germany's offensives added significantly to the cumulative attrition of previous years. But the Allied armies suffered severely too: overall, 1918 was the greatest year of attrition for both sides since 1914, with attack and counterattack stretching both sides ever more thinly. Superficially, the moves and counter-termoves of 1918's final decisive western front campaign suggested that positional warfare was at an end and that operational manoeuvre had returned to warfare and would prove decisive. But the underlying deter-minant of the shifting fortunes and the outcome of the campaign was the availability and attrition of reserves, not the ground captured by armies. The Allies would have had a much harder task to defeat the enemy in 1918 had the German army remained on the defensive throughout the year. Indeed the plans taking shape by mid-1918 for a material-intensive 'decisive' campaign in 1919 suggest that Allied leaders appreciated that fact. However, this judgement negates the impact of Foch's prepared and coordinated counteroffensive on the German army's ability to fight on. Explanations of the German army's defeat in terms of its own internal breakdown go only so far, and the thwarted nationalists' postwar attempt to blame Germany's overall defeat on a collapse of the will to victory on the home front rings hollow. Ludendorff's forces were battered by July 1918, but they were not beaten and far from broken, as the strength of their frontline soldiers' resistance from August to November, even while their support services were imploding, demonstrates. It would not be a 'stab in the back' that finally toppled German militarism and the army that manifested it, but many thousands of bayonets in the front. When it was obvious that the war was lost Ludendorff and the kaiser would try to spread the burden of responsibility around 'defeatists' at home through a belated attempt at democratisation that might save their own skins and hopefully secure easier peace terms from the Allies. Such hubris did not alter the fact that by then the army had lost the land war, something that would have to happen for the war to end.

The fact that this occurred simultaneously on all the Central pow-ers' hard-pressed land fronts indicates that the Allies had won the war on the other four fronts too. Their navies held and kept the seas against Germany's submarines throughout the war, enforcing an ever tighter attritional blockade that starved enemy populations and by 1918 had severely degraded the Central powers' ability to manufacture war mate-rial. Their diplomats expanded the coalition while undermining the cohesion of the Central powers. By 1918 the Central powers were only held together by Germany's refusal to let them break apart, at least until their separate military defeats allowed each an honourable way out. This indicated that the Allies' united front was also stronger and strengthened as the war went on, as its attritional nature became apparent and Ger-many's ability to strike powerful blows against individual members of the coalition demonstrated the need to pull together. In the SWC the

Allies created a sophisticated modern administrative mechanism for political, economic and military coordination that would serve as a model for future coalition wars and peacetime international collaborative organisations.* Their home fronts were also more solid. Although all home fronts experienced unrest in various forms as the war dragged on, liberal democratic institutions were flexible enough to respond to the intensifying economic and social challenges of modern war, while Allied war leaders were able to offer their peoples just rewards for participating in the war effort. This allowed the people's will to victory and soldiers' commitment to the cause to adapt and remain broadly solid despite the short-term fluctuations in the fortunes of war.[66] It also meant that war mobilisation could be more intense, sustained and productive.

Neither the Royal Navy nor the American army won the war, although they made it unwinnable for the Central powers, the former by keeping the seas for the Allies, the latter by ensuring that Germany could never triumph in the manpower struggle. As it turned out, the vast majority of America's millions were never needed in the fight, which by 1918 the French and British armies, and to a certain extent the Italian army, could conduct effectively and with purpose. The victory on land was achieved by the three armies that had engaged with and fought the attritional war from 1915, and with increasing skill, determination and results from 1916. They wore out the German and Austro-Hungarian armies, to a great extent on account of the munitions produced on home fronts. In that respect this was the people's victory, one in which British, French, Italian and American workers and citizens in uniform, led by determined soldiers and statesmen, fought and won the world's first war of attrition against equally resolute adversaries.

---

*It should come as no surprise that Jean Monnet, the founding father of the European Community, served as a junior functionary in the SWC and other inter-Allied coordinating bodies.

# 'THE GREAT WAR
# FOR CIVILIZATION'?

A S 1916'S GENERAL ALLIED OFFENSIVE GOT UNDERWAY CORDAY
noted, 'An officer posted to Paris on special duty portrays Joffre
. . . as a tired man, who declares over and over again, in a gruff
tone muffled by his moustache, "We must kill as many of them as possible . . . kill Boches . . . kill Boches."' To a middle-aged civil servant on
the home front whose son was at the front and potentially a victim of
Joffre's strategy this was 'a really puerile attitude, which wilfully over-
looks the immense reserves of German manpower'.[1] The logic of attrition
was hard to grasp for a nonmilitary, casualty-conscious, essentially paci-
fistic observer – it still is. The military mind better appreciated the necessity for a strategy of attrition. Far from puerile, it suggested strategic
thinking attuned to the era of mass mobilisation, although inevitably it
was odious to those who analysed war on moral, not practical, criteria.
Joffre's strategy was developed in full awareness of the vast reserves of
German manpower, the centre of gravity of his, France's and the Allies'
war of attrition against the invader. This obliged Joffre to kill Boches and
to accept losses in his turn.

Joffre and the other soldiers who dominated the first half of the
war determined on and set in train the war of attrition. Falkenhayn's
strategy was founded on wearing out his enemies' military strength and
commitment to the war to such a point that they would come to the negotiating table. A peace of exhaustion was considered Germany's best
hope once the war had stalemated. If she exhausted her enemies more
than herself, Germany might even emerge with some advantage, and the
war might thereby be justified to patriots on the home front. But even to
achieve this modest victory Germany would have to maximise manpower

and material mobilisation in the face of a superior, hostile coalition determined to squeeze the lifeblood out of her with aggressive siege warfare and blockade. Even in these straitened circumstances there were many (on both sides) who overestimated Germany's power and still believed that the Central powers had the strength to inflict a crushing defeat on their enemies, principal among them Hindenburg and Ludendorff, the military duumvirate who would inherit Falkenhayn's responsibilities. In pursuing this goal, they would stake Germany's political future on an impossible victory.

In raising Britain's new armies, Kitchener had grasped the nature of the conflict straight away, recognising that the last fresh reserves would be the decisive factor in a long attritional war. Britain's military forces were raised to take their proper share in the struggle: 'to play a part worthy of England' as well as 'to impose terms in consonance with our interests' at any peace conference, he informed Repington in the only press interview he ever gave.[2] He was wont thereafter to declare when asked how long he thought the war would last that the real war would only begin after two years, when attrition would start in earnest. Despite 1915's horrendous casualty rates, by the time Britain's armies were ready and her allies were more fully mobilised, battlefield attrition had barely started.

The land war really began in 1916, when Joffre, Kitchener and Falkenhayn engaged their expanded mass armies on the western front in a prolonged fight for superiority. In the East and in Italy the Russians, Austrians and Italians were doing the same. After false starts in 1915, the four supporting fronts were also engaged. Diplomats had expanded alliances through 1915, sailors had engaged competing naval blockades and statesmen had begun to draw their peoples behind the war effort and to work more closely with allies and neutrals to coordinate strategy and military operations and to fund the war. Above all, the home fronts were reaching a state of wartime mobilisation that allowed the armies' voracious consumption of war material to be satisfied thereafter.

Above all attrition was Joffre's military strategy, although Kitchener shared his grasp of what was necessary while disagreeing with Joffre over what was practicable. Although neither man saw their strategy through to victory, they found reliable executants in Foch and Haig: attrition was the guiding principle of their military policy. Perhaps they did not execute it as well as they might have. More accurately, it took time and experience for them to learn how to implement it properly. Yet from early 1915 they were reequipping, retraining and reconceptualising warfare to make destroying Germany's vast reserves practicable within four years. Even while they were doing so, many doubted that this was possible.

Did the war end with the exhaustion of nations rather than the victories of armies as Churchill had forewarned in December 1914?[3] In 1918 there were clear victories of the armies of one side over those of the other. The decisive outcomes to the land campaigns in France and in Italy, at Salonika and in the Middle East were built on earlier victories that had exhausted Germany and her allies steadily and tired the Allies themselves greatly. This collective land war would be the decisive front, and breaking the Imperial German Army would be its crowning act, although victory in the field depended on success on the other four fronts. The Allies had endured and secured victories on each by the time the final land battle was engaged in 1918. Their navies controlled the seas and were squeezing the life out of the enemy's home fronts, while merchant shipping kept their own increasingly collaborative war effort running. Their peoples had out produced the Central powers. Form 1917 their societies has remobilised to pursue democratising and moral political, social and international aims. Their diplomats had constantly expanded the coalition against Germany and managed neutral states' engagement with the war largely to the Allies' benefit. By the second half of the war the Allies worked effectively together to improve the efficiency of their war effort through new, centralising institutions, the joint Allied command and the Supreme War Council, while Germany only held her coalition together on sufferance.

Lloyd George had feared in December 1914 that the enemy possessed 'an enthusiasm and a spirit, according to every testimony, which cannot be worn down by a two or three years' siege of German armies entrenched in enemy territory'.[4] That in effect turned out to be exactly how the war was conducted and decided (although much energy which could have been devoted to the task was dissipated by Lloyd George and other pessimists during the process of attrition). Whether the popular will to victory could be sustained while they did this became an issue by 1916. It could be, but doing so entailed deep-seated social and political shifts towards democratisation and the recognition of the citizen's role and rights in a mobilised state. France managed to adapt her system of military discipline from one founded on passive obedience to harsh military authority – with execution by firing squad the ultimate sanction – towards participatory individual consent founded on a republican 'social contract' of mutual duty and responsibility between soldiers and their commanders as the war progressed, for example.[5]

The human costs and psychological consequences of mass war temporarily broke the popular will to repeat such a military trauma, in Britain and France at least, even if it was to revive when a new German menace emerged. Perhaps that was a paradoxical consequence of a 'democratic' victory. In Germany, Italy and Russia, states that did not achieve their war aims, defeat or disappointment necessitated remaking the state in a totalitarian form. These new states took wartime organisation as their model and geared up for continuous war, against internal class or racial enemies in peacetime, and looming external threats. This was a misguided attempt to unite their societies in a sort of community 'war effort' that they had not been able to manufacture or sustain between 1914 and 1918.

IN A WAR OF ATTRITION THE CONTROL OF TERRITORY, IF NOT IRRELEVANT, was much less significant than reserves and resources. Lord Esher lamented the misjudgement of strategic progress in the summer of 1916 by ministers who counted up losses while examining small-scale maps.[6] The German army could drive the Russians from Poland in 1915 without significantly altering the balance of the war in their favour. Conversely, they could hold a more or less static line in France and Belgium from 1915–18 while gradually surrendering their early tactical and material advantages over the Allied armies facing them. When Côte 304 was recaptured by the French army in August 1917 Corday lamented, 'This struggle over Verdun is a perfect proof of the hideous futility of war in itself. For, after eighteen months of fighting, the two opposing armies are back exactly where they began. It is just as if they had never fought at all – except that there are now two hundred thousand corpses on that small plot of earth.'[7] It was those corpses, the inevitable and terrible price of attrition, that were proof that they certainly had fought.

'The trenches form a vast furrow in which seethe two million men. What will be the Harvest?' Corday asked himself when stalemate set in.[8] By 1918 that harvest had risen to 9,408,615 men killed. In all 71,500,000 men were mobilised, of which 53 percent became casualties of some kind. Twenty-one million men were wounded, and more than 7,500,000 were recorded as missing or prisoners of war. Many of the others remained psychologically scarred. In absolute numbers, Germany suffered heaviest of all the great powers. In pursuing Joffre's attritional strategy the Allied armies had to kill 2,037,000 Germans and 1,100,000 Habsburg Empire soldiers and wound and capture more than 11,000,000 more before 'the destruction of the German and Austrian armies' was complete. France sacrificed 1,375,000 men to do so, the British Empire 908,371, Russia around 1,800,000, Italy 578,000 and America 114,000. Nearly 17,000,000 Allied wounded, missing or prisoners, 7,500,000 of them Russians, were also incurred for victory. In absolute numbers the Allies suffered more casualties than the Central powers, although proportionately they came off better in the war of attrition, with 46 percent of the men they mobilised becoming casualties as opposed to 63 percent on the other side. The burden of loss fell disproportionately and depended largely on how long an army was fighting. France came off worst, with 78 percent of those mobilised becoming casualties, then Austria-Hungary with 77 percent. Germany lost 56 percent of the men she mobilised, while Italy and the British Empire lost 38 and 36 percent respectively. Russia lost 59 percent, and Turkey 48 percent, with the smaller states suffering losses between Bulgaria's 67 percent and Greece's 14 percent. American only lost 8 percent of the men she mobilised, although a rather higher percentage of those who actually saw action in France. Such stark statistics have to be treated with caution: lies, confusion and errors in summation all skewed the figures, as well as the fact that a man might be recorded as wounded (perhaps more than once), return to action and then become a prisoner or be killed, or be released from captivity at some stage in the war and then be wounded or killed. The figures for men killed are therefore the clearest statistics on which to judge the effects of attrition. Roughly 12 percent of those mobilised were killed: 17.5 percent in France, 15 percent in Germany, 12 percent in Austria-Hungary, 11 percent in Russia and 10 percent in Italy and the British Empire, but only 2.5 percent in the United States.[9] In addition, many millions of civilians suffered the direct or indirect consequences of war: famine, disease, displacement and death.

This was a high price to pay for victory and an even higher one for defeat. Thereafter the survivors and their descendants have had to live with 'the weight of the dead on the living'.[10] Societies entered a cycle of protracted mourning and ongoing commemoration that shows no sign of abating as the war's centenaries pass. Nevertheless, it should be recognised that for early twentieth-century societies this sacrifice was not considered too high a price to pay to resolve a conflict over deeply felt and divisive issues – be they patriotic, imperialistic, political, social or economic – fuelled by atavistic hatreds that lurked beneath modernising mass society's veneer of civilization. Europeans had always settled their differences, temporarily at least, with wars, and for statesmen in 1914 the parameters of international diplomacy were no different.[11]

It turned out that the parameters of war were very different, something with which statesmen were to struggle and which citizens would come to regret. Attrition, the strategy that both sides were forced to adopt after stalemate set it, while militarily essential in a war in which millions of men fought over deeply felt ideas to the bitter end, was always morally questionable. Achieving victory over the Central powers involved a reciprocal sacrifice of Allied troops which has weighed heavily on their descendants, to such a degree eventually that it became their own leaders, incompetent commanders or belligerent politicians who slaughtered them, not the enemy's soldiers who actually manned the machine guns and artillery pieces that killed and maimed men in huge, repetitive battles. This harsh truth opened a gulf between civilian sensibilities and military realties that still divides opinion on the conduct of the First World War. Post-war, this conflict over the necessity for and conduct of attrition boiled down, in Great Britain in particular, into a standoff between statesmen and soldiers. The former accused their military leaders of narrow-mindedness and inhumanity, while the latter condemned their political masters for amateurishness and wishful thinking. In truth, all were engaged in the same war and must share responsibility for its conduct and consequences.

Although heavily implicated in the pursuit of attrition himself, Lloyd George could still represent afterwards that 'a war of attrition was substituted for a war of intelligence'.[12] By the time he did he had many sympathetic readers. Along with Corday, Forrester and other moral critics of attrition the former prime minister became the conscience of the war generation. By the time they were publishing in the 1930s disillusionment with the war had set in – hopes for postwar peace and democracy founded on wartime corporatist principles, collective international security and the reintegration of states into a prosperous global economy were receding, and another, greater conflagration loomed. No wonder then that the sacrifice of 1914–18 was questioned. The Great War's soldiers became its victims – of a new sort of impersonalised killing, orchestrated and managed by the state and predicated on the duty of all to serve, and if need be to die for it, a phenomenon which rising totalitarianism was to take to an extreme. It needs to be acknowledged that these soldiers were not victims of those who directed them but of a determination that most of them shared to secure victory by destroying the fighting capacity of their adversary. Dutiful soldiers, civilians who manufactured shells and guns and invested in war loans to pay for them and those who consumed newspapers' bellicose war rhetoric and wrote daily to their menfolk at the front were all complicit in the bloodletting. The statesmen and soldiers who managed it, meanwhile, strove to master the unprecedented tasks of mass mobilisation, war production and military action that confronted capitalist empires at war.

The generals who managed and fought costly attritional battles remain society's scapegoats, their reputations tarnished by political animals shocked at the true nature and consequences of modern warfare. Lloyd George's provocative *War Memoirs* set out the case for the prosecution of Haig and Robertson in particular and British military leadership more generally. 'I saw how the incredible heroism of the common man was being squandered to repair the incompetence of the trained inexpert (for they were actually trained not to be expert in mastering the actualities of modern war),' he asserted in answer to his critics. The generals' inadequacies were manifested 'in the production of equipment, in transport, in tackling the submarine menace, in the narrow, selfish and unimaginative strategy and in the ghastly butchery of a succession of vain and insane offensives'.[13] Condemnatory adjectives aside, these are the essential components of a war of attrition – economic organisation, supply and large costly battles – the type of war that had crystallized in 1915 and was thereafter waged by Britain's political and military leaders. Such a war was already underway between Britain's allies and enemies. There were false starts everywhere, but the belligerents soon attuned to the nature of the conflict in which they were embroiled. In a war of national survival, in which effective mobilisation of men, manufacturing and shipping determined success or failure, home fronts sustained armies and navies, mass armies had to be broken in battle and popular will to victory had to be engaged and sustained, the sort of leadership Lloyd George accused his generals of would mean defeat. The fortunes of Russia, and ultimately of Germany and Austria-Hungary, proved that.

In condemning his own warriors, Lloyd George was some twenty years later also mounting a critique of modern war as another approached – of 'not only the horrid and squalid aspects of war but its muddles; its futilities; its chanciness; its precariousness; its wastefulness of the lives, the treasure and the virtues of mankind'.[14] His war had not, as he had hoped, ended wars, and that may explain his bitterness and disappointment. Lloyd George was a fine war leader, attuned to the needs of the time. With others – Asquith, Churchill, Clemenceau, Diaz, Foch, Haig, Jellicoe, Joffre, Kitchener, Pétain, Orlando, Wilson – he faced up to the demands of a war of attrition and brought his country and his allies successfully through their greatest challenge. He was certainly no strategist. Yet he was a bumptious and vindictive man who wrung his hands throughout the conflict and nursed deep resentments at his powerlessness in the face of militarism unleashed by both sides. Perhaps his tendentious criticism might best be confined to the dustbin of history. It did not dupe the warriors themselves. Watching the BBC's groundbreaking fiftieth-anniversary documentary series The Great War, whose script drew heavily on Lloyd George's writings, Lyttelton

had many times to exclaim, 'No, it wasn't like that.' We, by which I mean both officers and men, did not feel so doom-laden, so utterly disenchanted. We thought we were fighting in a worthy cause and had no idea that our efforts would one day appear . . . as merely absurd. No one who has not experienced it can know the heart-beat of a battalion, or its discipline and corporate spirit, and how they sustain the individual man, and how the whole greatly exceeds the sum of its parts.[15]

The warlike mood of the war generation has become diluted down the years, such that it is now hard to understand the reasoning and motivation of those who went to war and fought on to the end, through horror, trauma and loss, or indeed why those who stayed at home sustained them in their fight. For Lyttelton and the rest, their individual motivations – to do one's bit, to defend one's home, to help one's friends – meshed with a collective societal mood, no doubt founded in prewar lessons and values, but mediated very greatly by the events and experiences of the war itself. The war's early traumas – enemy atrocities, civilian suffering and vicious mass battles – paradoxically engaged with these core values, and its course sustained them. Only its consequences fractured them.

THE GREAT WAR'S END, WHEN IT CAME, WAS UNEXPECTED AND UNCON-trolled: perhaps uncontrollable, since world war had escaped the parameters of conflict as its practitioners and participants understood them. Conventionally the war ended with the armistices in autumn 1918. Peace of sorts in Europe and the Middle East took until 1923 to sign and settle. The victors, wishfully rather than confidently perhaps, dubbed it the 'The Great War for Civilization', the inscription common to the Allied nations' victory medals. Such intense barbarity was not a good advertisement for, nor could it be a precursor to, civilization: we can fully see the irony in this postscript at the war's centenaries. In 1918 there was the potential for it to be a democratic victory, and for promoting values that in time would come to determine Europe and the world's future.

The war did confirm the virtue of peace. Not as an outcome of war that set the parameters for the next one – although in this instance that certainly occurred in the flawed peace treaties drawn up at the Paris Peace Conference – but as an abstract concept. From 1917 peace had become the objective of the war, alongside justification of the sacrifice, but revenging the dead, survival and issues of state and imperial power, societal change and political reward remained mixed in. The war had become more complex and more divisive as mass mobilisation transformed a war between states to a war between peoples. While America's liberal president admirably wished to change the world for the better, he failed to appreciate how difficult it was to change the world. His better world was not considered so by many. The conflict crystallised in time into a war between democracy and autocracy, but this was merely the drawing up of new battle lines for the twentieth century's wars. Both democracies and autocracies could raise and equip mass armies and had the resources to fight long and bloody wars. But a stronger, unifying belief in the cause existed on the Allied side, alongside a collective public acceptance of duty and sacrifice and, heartfelt clashes over specifics notwithstanding, a genuine civil-military compact.[16] Such democratic advantages built resilience and allowed victory in this war, as long as the physical power required to break autocracies' military machines could be harnessed and the intellectual will to undermine the militarism that sustained the German leadership and replace it with something more humane persisted. This impetus for change came not just from without, but also from within the restive autocracies. The sacrifice in the First World War gave these values a chance in a remade world. Come 1918 international relations and internal relationships were both starting to reform, although a century later the principles of Wilson's new diplomacy are still bedding in, and social democracy's eventual success remains fragile. These would still have to be fought for, as Germans found.

Many of Germany's defeated soldiers at least hoped there would be a victory for democracy. Marching into Germany under the terms of the armistice they invaded a different country, familiar yet alien – one that was verdant, orderly, undamaged by the passage of armies and at war with itself. The kaiser had tried far too late to acknowledge the impact of war on social relations within Germany by establishing a constitutional monarchy before seeking peace terms. Ludendorff's bitter judgement, that it was the defeatist elements on the home front that had brought Germany down, and that they should 'clean up the mess for which they are responsible', suggested, however, that conservative attitudes in Germany would die hard.[17] Most combat veterans only wished to return home and resume their civilian lives as best they could, but the political rivalries that had been brewing behind the front would force them to take sides. Nevertheless, the military were to become players, and the outcome of the war a battleground, in interwar German politics.[18] There would be war on the streets in the short term. The kaiser had gone, abdicating and fleeing to the Netherlands after he lost the confidence of the army's leaders.[19] Political power now rested nominally with the SPD's moderate social democratic leaders, who had gained all they wanted but were threatened by the revolutionary left who saw an opportunity to imitate Lenin and seize power on behalf of the workers. The navy had mutinied and workers', soldiers' and sailors' councils on the Bolshevik model were springing up, so in order to hang on to power the social democrats would make a fateful compromise with the army, big business and moderate trade unionists, creating a temporarily stable but doomed democracy, the Weimar Republic. Wartime corporatist structures became the model for postwar politics and social relations, but Germany's revolution was incomplete.[20] 'A curious revolution,' Binding had thought as he lay in his hospital bed listening to the chants of workers marching in the street beyond his window. 'What surprises me, in spite of the constant talk of violent convulsions, is its superficiality.' After the workers' councils had had their moment, he expected a stronger government to step in and he was proved correct.[21] This shaky compromise between democrats and what remained of the wartime military-industrial complex, in which political modernisation was not accompanied by genuine social change, left Germany vulnerable to a drift to the antidemocratic political extremes. International Communism (as Bolshevism redefined itself in 1919) and a new hybrid 'totalitarian' philosophy of nationalist right and patriotic left, National Socialism, would contest Germany's and Europe's future with liberal democracy. Germany's imperialist survivors waited in the wings. Ludendorff was to march alongside Adolf Hitler, the emerging populist leader, in a failed right-wing putsch in 1923. Thereafter, belatedly recognizing that popular determination as much as military capability underpinned a successful war effort, he set about formulating a military philosophy by which Germany might organise her home front properly to do better in the next world war.[22] President Hindenburg was to preside over the dismantling of German democracy in the early 1930s, opening the way for Hitler to try to do so. Tightening the state's grip through promoting a now racially defined 'community' rather than expressing the will of all the people would have even more disastrous consequences for Europe and the world than the war of which he was a disillusioned veteran.

Germany was just one of the battlegrounds of the war after the war, a civil war in which nationalistic ex-soldiers and militant workers took sides over the future of Europe and its nation states. Immediately afterwards it appeared that the war had been a triumph for liberalism and democracy. Yet the peacemakers who met in Paris to determine Europe's fate still held true to many of their prewar imperialist assumptions and capitalist values: if states had changed, statesmen had not. It was not to be a peace without annexations and indemnities, although there came into being in the new League of Nations an international forum with the potential, although hardly the power, to keep the peace through collective security. As the fate of the Weimar Republic showed, peace on the home front was to be compromised by a deep postwar economic slump that meant that political reforms were not buttressed with social improvements. Fatefully, the reach of the peacemakers extended only tenuously into Eastern Europe where legacy conflicts over national self-determination, dis-

puted borders and political ideologies persisted. It was to be a French-
trained Polish army that stopped the spread of Communism westwards on
the River Vistula in the autumn of 1920, not the statesmanship of Lloyd
George or Wilson. Armies remained more potent than ideals in the troubled postwar world, whose territorial and ideological clashes lumbered Europe with simmering resentments and a political vacuum along its eastern
frontier where liberal Poland separated Nazi Germany and Stalin's Soviet
Union. Here a new ideological conflict, threaded through with unfinished
business from 1914–18, would resume in 1939, and a second, more disastrous war of attrition would play out between 1941 and 1945.

Europe was not to be safe for democracy until 1945. Even then it
would not be secure, with Eastern Europe in the grip of Soviet Communism and the continent divided into two armed camps. Thereafter Western Europe flourished for forty years under a social democratic
consensus, although it relied on American protection and remained
armed for self-defence until the collapse of the Communist Eastern Bloc
after 1989. The issues of the First World War, and the practices of
wartime mobilisation, were to determine Europe's destiny for the rest of
the century. He would not live to see any of this, but Cummings was dismayed by the consequences of a war that he had watched, appalled and
aghast, while wishing that he might participate in it himself. 'Some spec-
ulators have talked wildly about the prospect of modern civilisation, in
default of a League of Nations, becoming extinct . . . Civilization in its
present form is ours to hold and to keep in perpetuity, for better, for
worse.' Worse was to come, now that war had shattered the societies that
fought it. 'We are now entered on the kingless republican era. The next
struggle, in some ways more bitter and more protracted than this, will
be between capital and labour. After that, the millennium . . .'[23]

During this war, which would burn hot and cold for the next seventy years, societies would inculcate the principles and practices of the
First World War. For all the talk of a 'war to end wars', warfare remained
a legitimate means to promote or defend the interests of the state and
these were now bound up with the ideologies that emerged militant from
the Great War. In the ensuing decades men of the war generation would
rise to lead states and strive to impose their beliefs in domestic and international politics, and violence had been legitimised as the means to do
so. The war had brutalised a generation and soldiers returning to civilian
life saw no incongruity in imposing the methods and values of the
trenches on their shattered societies. This was felt most profoundly in
German politics, where Nazi thugs adapted the communitarian values
and militarist structures of army life into the foundation on which they
attempted to build a united racial community, the pure alternative to the

apparently fractured Germany that had lost the war.[24] The lessons some Germans had learned from the war were anti-democratic, and the menace of militarism was far from extirpated. 'The spirit of German militarism, as Prussia first developed it, is every whit as monarchical as it is aristocratic and democratic,' Germany's leading military writer Lieutenant-General Baron von Freytag Loringhoven wrote as the nation approached its 1918 Gotterdammerung:

> It would cease to be Germany and the mighty expression of German imperial military power and military efficiency if it were to change. If our enemies, to whom with God's help our militarism will bring defeat, abuse it, we know that we must preserve it, for to us it means victory and the future of Germany.[25]

On this residue of pre-1914 values – and abetted by the remnants of imperial Germany, the army in particular – the Nazis could establish a new Third Reich. They were determined to excise the residual weaknesses in the German body politic and to test that spirit once more to destruction. The Nazis were not alone in wishing to fight once more for the undecided causes of 1914–1918. In the 1920s Benito Mussolini's Italian fascists redirected disappointed Italy's politics into stridently nationalistic channels in anticipation of founding a second Roman empire. Communists everywhere, but in the Soviet Union in particular, were organised to fight the class struggle against the proletariat's enemies, while Lenin's successor Josef Stalin turned the fury of militant Communism against his own people.

Since the bloodthirsty values of wartime remained abroad, the worthy attempts of liberal democratic peacemakers would come to nothing. The beneficiaries of the post-war peace settlement found that victory rested on shallow foundations, and that their newborn civilization had to be defended. Although a spirit of pacifism prevailed in the 1920s and early 1930s, a period in which societies plunged into deep mourning for their wartime fallen, when a new menace to world peace emerged their citizens could be rallied once more to fight against militarist totalitarianism. In 1916 when his battalion attacked on the Somme, Lyttelton had thought it neither incongruous nor insensitive to write to his mother of his first face-to-face meeting with the German enemy: 'Then we killed. I have only a blurred image of slaughter. I saw about ten Germans writing like trout in a creel at the bottom of a shell-hole and our fellows firing at them from the hip. One or two red bayonets.'[26] Lyttelton and many others had gone to France to kill Germans, with the blessing of his mother and the encouragement of his country, and when the time came to kill them again there was some disappointment but little compunction. Following

his father's example, Lyttelton's eldest son strove despite the residual effects of childhood polio to join the fighting services.[27] Nor was it only
the defeated and disappointed states that were organised for refighting
industrialised war should the need arise.[28] First World War models of
state–private enterprise collaboration and professional secondment to
government were utilised. In the Second World War Lyttelton would serve
as minister of war production in Churchill's cabinet. In that role he pro-
cured the munitions with which to engage and defeat Germany and her
allies. As the war approached he had been seconded from his City career
to manage Britain's purchases of strategic metals.[29]

Foch's prediction that the Versailles peace settlement with pseudo-
democratic Germany would serve only as an armistice for twenty years
proved remarkably accurate. Britain and her former allies would have reason and means to kill Germans once more in September 1939. In all nations but Soviet Russia, where after German invasion there was no choice
but to engage in all-out war, the reciprocal sacrifice that this entailed was
conditioned by First World War experience. Before the war Neville Chamberlain's British government was reluctant to commit a large army to the
continent for a second time – 'no more Sommes' was one injunction heard
in the corridors of power. As it turned out a second BEF would go to
France in 1939, and the mass conscript army that Britain raised once again
would no doubt have followed it there had not the German army rapidly
smashed the French army in summer 1940: the nation that had made the
greatest blood sacrifice between 1914 and 1918 seemed enfeebled and
proved unable to repeat its defiance. With the fall of France Britain was
spared a repeat of the entrenched bloodletting of 1914–1918, but Britain
would not be spared the trials and traumas of another long attritional
war. Blockade and submarine counter-blockade once gain determined the
course and outcome of the maritime war. To this was added the new
scourge of aerial bombardment now that the home front was a legitimate
military target. In retaliating in kind against Germany it was the airmen
who served in Britain's Bomber Command who were to fight the most
costly attritional campaign of Britain's Second World War. Yet where
British forces did find themselves engaged on the battlefield in static campaigns, against successive German defensive positions in the Italian Peninsula and among the hedgerows of Normandy, fighting had all the
characteristics of trench warfare and casualty rates were equivalent to and
frequently exceeded those in the worst battle of the First World War.[30]

Once again this was a war that was decided by a combination of
American industrial might and the willingness of one allied nation to engage and defeat the powerful German army in a prolonged attritional
campaign. Soviet Russia had no choice once Hitler let loose his armies in

summer 1941. Between 1941 and 1945 the Red Army contained and then counterattacked Germany and her allies and then pressed on to Berlin to complete the final humbling of German militarism. Between them Hitler and Stalin unleashed upon Eastern Europe a war that took its exemplar from the First World War. In its scale of destruction and barbarity, however, it exceeded all previous human experience and escaped all humanitarian constraints. Refugees, deportations, slave labour, famine, genocide and Holocaust amplified the extensive physical destruction and huge casualties of battle itself – 8,688,000 Soviet military deaths, and more than 2,000,000 German battle fatalities on the eastern front.[31]

The victory over Nazism was won by incongruous allies. The united front of the Second World War was born out of of strategic necessity rather than ideological affinity (much like the Franco-Russia alliance of the previous war). The Cold War between liberal democracy and communism that ensued after their shared victory was only to be expected. Since the spectre of nuclear holocaust was ever present, hot war was wisely avoided and conflict between capitalism and communism was waged by proxy in small wars of decolonisation or on the diplomatic front. This confrontation had its phases of attrition, notably for America in Vietnam and the Soviet Union in Afghanistan. These superpower humiliations broke credibility and public confidence rather than armies or nations but were decisive campaigns nonetheless. The Cold War dragged on until the obsolescence of communism, born out of 1917's traumas but increasingly irrelevant as the prosperous twentieth century drew to an end, became manifest. It had lasted just about as long as the war generation had. Thereafter only superannuated war veterans remained to remind us of the horror and futility of the trenches, which following a new shift in the parameters of war and diplomacy seemed quaint, a black and white war rather than the colourful backdrop to confrontational world affairs. These men too are now gone.

Looking back from our vantage point a century later their war seems remote, irrational and perhaps now unknowable. To dismiss it as futile as many do is however a regrettable failure of understanding. We will continue to mark the veterans' passing, to seek out their stories, to mourn our societies' losses, to honour their contemporaries' sacrifice and to lament and commemorate the sacrifices and slaughters that their generation unleashed on the world. We will do so as long as we still live in their flawed civilization.

# NOTES

PROLOGUE: SIEZING THE HINDENBURG LINE

1.    Captain Alban Bacon, *The Wanderings of a Temporary Warrior: A Territorial Officer's Narrative of Service (and Sport) in Three Continents* (London: H., F. & G. Witherby, 1922), pp. 191–2.

2. Private Edward Williamson, quoted in Peter Hart, *1918: A Very British Victory* (London: Weidenfeld and Nicholson, 2008), p. 444.

3. Lieutenant Richard Dixon, quoted in ibid., p. 424.

4. Haig Diary, 10 September 1918, in Gary Sheffield and John Bourne (eds.), *Douglas Haig: War Diaries and Letters, 1914–1918* (London: Weidenfeld & Nicholson, 2005), p. 458.

5. Robin Prior and Trevor Wilson, *Command on the Western Front: The Military Career of Sir Henry Rawlinson, 1914–1918* (Oxford: Blackwell Ltd, 1992), p. 366.

6. Letter, 27 August 1918, quoted in Bernd Ulrich and Benjamin Ziemann (eds.), *German Soldiers in the Great War: Letters and Eyewitness Accounts*, trans. Christine Brocks (Barnsley: Pen & Sword, 2010), p. 177.

INTRODUCTION: 'THE WAR IS EVERYTHING'

1. Cummings diary, 31 July 1916, in W. N. P. Barbellion [Bruce Cummings], *Journal of a Disappointed Man* (London: Chatto & Windus, 1919), p. 243.

2. Cummings Diary, 17 December 1915, ibid., p. 226.

3. J. B. Priestley, *English Journey* (Ilkely: Great Northern Books, 2009 edition of the 1934 original), p. 158.

4. Quoted in Winston S. Churchill, *The World Crisis 1911–1918* (London: Odhams Press Ltd, 2 vols., 1938 edition), ii, pp. 915–16.

5. Carter Malkasian, *A History of Modern Wars of Attrition* (Westport, CT: Praeger, 2002), p. 1.

CHAPTER 1: READY AND WILLING

1. 21 July 1914, *The Memoirs of Raymond Poincaré, 1913–14*, trans. Sir George Arthur (London: William Heinemann, 1928), pp. 168–69.

2. 22 and 23 July 1914, ibid., pp. 177–79.

3. J. F. V. Keiger, *Raymond Poincaré* (Cambridge: Cambridge University Press, 1997), pp. 165–69.

4. Poincaré diary note, 27 July 1914, quoted in ibid., p. 170.

5. John Lowe, *The Great Powers, Imperialism and the German Problem, 1865–1925* (Abingdon: Routledge, 1994).

6. 'War in Eighteen Months, 1912', diary of Admiral Georg von Müller, 8 December 1912, in John Röhl (ed.), *From Bismarck to Hitler: The Problem of Continuity in German History* (London: Longman, 1970), pp. 68–69.

7. Ibid.

8. Keiger, op. cit., pp. 14–16.

9. John Keiger, 'Raymond Poincaré', in David Bell, Douglas Johnson and Peter Morris (eds.), *A Biographical Dictionary of French Political Leaders Since 1870* (Hemel Hempstead: Harvester Wheatsheaf, 1990), pp. 342–45.

10. Keiger, *Poincaré*, p. 157.

11. Steven Beller, *Francis Joseph* (London: Longman, 1996), p. 228.

12. Quoted, ibid., p. 80.

13. Quoted, ibid., p. 189.

14. Ibid, p. 195.

15. Ibid., pp. 194–98.

16. Quoted in Holger Herwig, *The First World War: Germany and Austria-Hungary, 1914–1918* (London: Arnold, 1997), p. 11.

17. Quoted in Beller, op. cit., p. 157.

18. 'Kaiser Wilhlem II: A Suitable Case for Treatment?' in John Röhl, *The Kaiser and His Court: Wilhelm II and the Government of Germany* (Cambridge: Cambridge University Press, 1994), pp. 9–27, 10.

19, Arno J. Mayer, *The Persistence of the Old Regime: Europe to the Great War* (Beckenham: Croom Helm, 1966).

20 V. R. Berghahn, *Modern Germany: Society, Economy and Politics in the Twentieth Century* (Cambridge: Cambridge University Press, 1987), pp. 31–36.

22. Well explained in Lowe, op. cit.

22. David Stevenson, *Armaments and the Coming of War: Europe 1904–1915* (Oxford: Oxford University Press, 1996), pp. 18–26.

23. Quoted in Williamson Murray, MacGregor Knox and Alvin Bernstein (eds.), *The Making of Strategy: Rulers, States, and War* (Cambridge: Cambridge University Press, 1994), p. 260.

24. Stevenson, op. cit., pp. 301–21 passim.

25. Guy Pedroncini, 'L'armée française et la Grande Guerre', in André Corvisier (ed.), *Histoire Militaire de la France, vol. 3: 1871–1940* (Paris: Quadrige, 1997), p. 164.

26. Jules Maurin, "Sous le drapeau', ibid., pp. 99–118, 100.

27. Mark Osborne Humphries and John Maker (eds.), *Germany's Western Front: Translations from the German Official History of the Great War, vol. II* (Waterloo, Ontario: Wilfred Laurier University Press, 2010), p. 31, n. 15.

28. Statistics of population and military strength inevitably vary. Here, unless otherwise stated, they are taken from Paul Kennedy, *The Rise and Fall of the Great Powers: Economic Change and Military Conflict from 1500 to 2000* (New York: Random House, 1987).

29. Quoted in Bruce Menning, 'Mukden to Tannenberg: Defeat to Defeat, 1905–1914', in Frederick W. Kagan and Robin Higham (eds.), *The Military History of Tsarist Russia* (Basingstoke: Palgrave, 2002), pp. 201–25, 215; Stevenson, op. cit., pp. 35–36.

30. Herwig, op. cit., p. 13.

31. Stevenson, op. cit., pp. 30–32.

32. Quoted in Michael Neiberg, *Dance of the Furies: Europe and the Outbreak of World War I* (Cambridge MA: The Belknap Press, 2011), p. 56.

33. Ibid., p. 102.

34. Ibid., pp. 111–14.

35. See for example Jan Rüger, *The Great Naval Game: Britain and Germany in the Age of Empire* (Cambridge: Cambridge University Press, 2009).

36. Eugen Weber, *The Nationalist Revival in France, 1905–1914* (Berkeley, CA: University of California Press, 1998); Keiger, op. cit.

37. Eugen Weber, *Peasants into Frenchmen: Modernization of Rural France, 1870–1914* (London: Chatto and Windus, 1977).

38. Journal 8–13 August 1914, in Edouard Cœurdevey, *Carnets de guerre, 1914–1918: un témoin lucide* (Paris: Plon, 2008), pp. 25–27.

39. Quoted in Lawrence Sondhaus, *World War One: The Global Revolution* (Cambridge: Cambridge University Press, 2011), p. 87.

40. Michel Corday, *The Paris Front: An Unpublished Diary, 1914–1918* (London: Victor Gollancz Ltd, 1933), p. 8.

41. 8 September 1914, Mildred Aldrich, *A Hilltop on the Marne* (London: Constable & Co., 1915), pp. 158–59.

CHAPTER 2: INTO BATTLE

1. Aldrich, *A Hilltop on the Marne*, pp. 125–26.

2. Ibid., p. 127.

3. Ibid., pp. 127–28.

4. Ibid., p. 152.

5. Ibid., pp. 144–45.

6. Ibid., pp. 145–46.

7. Robert Foley, *German Strategy and the Path to Verdun: Erich von Falkenhayn and the Development of Attrition, 1870–1916* (Cambridge: Cambridge University Press, 2005), p. 73.

8. Asquith to Sylvia Henley, 2 June 1915, Bodleian Library, Oxford, Ms Eng. Lett. c 542/1, ff. 43–48.

9. Spenser Wilkinson, *War and Policy* (London: Constable & Co, 1910), p. 6.

10 Foley, op. cit., pp. 14–81 passim.

11. 'The Army Demands a Preventive War, 1914', by Gottlieb von Jagow, quoted in Röhl, *From Bismarck to Hitler*, p. 70.

12. Stevenson, *Armaments*, pp. 323–24.

13. Berghahn, *Modern Germany*, pp. 29–37 passim.

14. Von Moltke to his wife, 29 January 1905, quoted in Foley, op. cit., p. 73.

15. 'The Army Demands a Preventive War, 1914', quoted in Röhl, op. cit, p. 71.

16. Quoted in Herwig, *The First World War: Germany and Austria-Hungary*, p. 48.

17. Martin van Creveld, *Technology and War: From 200 B.C. to the Present* (New York: The Free Press, 1991).

18. Herwig, op. cit., p. 19.

19. Ibid., p. 51

20. Ibid., p. 110.

21. Quoted in ibid., p. 95.

22. Ibid., pp. 111–12.

23. Ibid., pp. 94–95.

24. Sondhaus, *World War One*, pp. 88–89.

25. Quoted in John Seely, *Adventure* (London: William Heinemann Ltd, 1930), p. 150.

26. Friedrich von Bernhardi, *Germany and the Next War*, quoted in Röhl, op. cit., p. 66.

27. Paul Halpern, *The Naval War in the Mediterranean, 1914–1918* (London: Allen & Unwin, 1987), pp. 3–7.

28. Nicholas A. Lambert, *Planning Armageddon: British Economic Warfare and the First World War* (Cambridge MA: Harvard University Press, 2012), pp. 238–41.

29. Ivan Bloch, *Is War Now Impossible? Being an Abridgment of 'The War of the Future in its Technical, Economic and Political Relations'* (London: Grant Richards, 1898).

30. Lambert, op. cit., p. 30.

31. Quoted in ibid., p. 2.

32. Ibid., pp. 111–16.

33. David Lloyd George, *War Memoirs of David Lloyd George* (London: Odhams Press, 2 vols., 1938 edition), i, pp. 6–9.

34. Asquith to Venetia Stanley, 17 August 1914, in Michael Brock and Eleanor Brock (eds.), *H. H. Asquith Letters to Venetia Stanley* (Oxford: Oxford University Press, 1982), p. 171.

35. Lambert, op. cit., passim.

36. Quoted in David French, *British Economic and Strategic Planning, 1905–1915* (London: Allen & Unwin, 1982), p. 170.

37. David French, *British War Aims and Strategy, 1914–1916* (London: Allen & Unwin, 1986), p. 15.

38. Quoted in Eric Osborne, *Britain's Economic Blockade of Germany, 1914–1919* (London: Frank Cass, 2004), p. 16.

39. Richard Hough, *The Great War at Sea, 1914–1918* (Oxford: Oxford University Press, 1983), pp. 61–62.

40. 'War in Eighteen Months, 1912', diary of Admiral Georg von Müller, 8 December 1912, quoted in Röhl, op. cit., p. 66.

41. Hough, op. cit., p. 63.

42. Quoted in ibid., p. 64.

43. Asquith to Venetia Stanley, 6 August 1914, in Brock and Brock (eds.), op. cit., p. 158.

44. Paul Halpern, *A Naval History of World War One* (London: University College London Press, 1994), p. 27.

45. Lambert, op. cit., pp. 222, 261–62 and 296–98.

46. Asquith to Venetia Stanley, 30 December 1914, in Brock and Brock (eds.), op. cit., pp. 34–36.

47. David Stevenson, *Cataclysm: The First World War as Political Tragedy* (New York: Basic Books, 2004), p. 202.

48. Memorandum by Selborne for Asquith, 6 August 1915, Selborne Papers, Bodleian Library, Oxford, box 80, ff. 36–39.

49. Neiberg, *Dance of The Furies*, pp. 180–215 passim.

50. MacGregor Knox and Williamson Murray, 'Thinking about Revolutions in Warfare', in MacGregor Knox and Williamson Murray (eds.), *The Dynamics of Military Revolution, 1300–2050* (Cambridge: Cambridge University Press, 2001), pp. 1–14, 10.

51. Fayolle diary, 4 February 1915, in Henri Contamine (ed.), *Maréchal Fayolle: Cahiers secrets de la grande guerre* (Paris: Plon, 1964), p. 82.

CHAPTER 3: STALEMATE

1. Rudyard Kipling, *The Irish Guards in the Great War: the First Battalion* (Staplehurst: Spellmount, 1997 edition), p. 66.

2. Quoted in Ian Beckett, *Ypres: The First Battle, 1914* (London: Pearson Education, 2004), p. 73.

3. Quoted in Kipling, op. cit., pp. 59–60.

4. Ibid., p. 53.

5. Ibid., p. 66.

6. Douglas Porch, *The March to the Marne: The French Army, 1871–1914* (Cambridge: Cambridge University Press, 1981), pp. 213–45 passim.

7. Major-General Sir George Aston, *The Biography of the Late Marshal Foch* (London: Hutchinson & Co., 1930), p. 118.

8. Joseph Monteilhet, *Les Institutions militaires de la France* (Paris: Alcan, 1926), p. 262.

9. Beckett, op. cit., pp. 76–83.

10. Ibid., pp. 189–96.

11. Marshal Ferdinand Foch, *The Memoirs of Marshal Foch*, trans. Colonel T. Bentley Mott (London: William Heinemann, 1931), p. 132.

12. Kipling, op. cit., p. 67.

13. 'End of October 1914', Rudolf Binding, *A Fatalist at War*, trans. Ian Morrow (London: George Allen & Unwin, 1929), pp. 20–21.

14. 10 November 1914, ibid., p. 24.

15. 16 January 1915, ibid., p. 48.

16. Foch, op. cit. pp. 183–84.

17. Seely, *Adventure*, p. 150.

18. Asquith to Venetia Stanley, 5 August 1914, in Brock and Brock (eds.), *Letters to Venetia Stanley*, p. 157.

19. Major-General Sir Charles Callwell, *Experiences of a Dug-out, 1914–1918* (London: Constable & Co., 1920), pp. 108–109.

20. Callwell to Wilson, 2 January 1915, cited in David French, 'The Meaning of Attrition', *The English Historical Review* 103 (1988), pp. 385–405, 390; Callwell, op. cit., p. 108.

21. French, ibid.

22. Callwell, op. cit., p. 391.

23. Balfour to Hankey, 2 January 1915, in ibid. *Winston S. Churchill, 1914–16, vol. III: Companion, part 2: May 1915–December 1916* (London: William Heinemann Ltd, 1972), pp. 363–64.

24. Churchill to Asquith, 29 December 1914, in Martin Gilbert (ed.), pp. 343–45.

25. Churchill to Kitchener, 23 December 1914 (two letters), in ibid., pp. 327–31, 332.

26. Churchill to Asquith, 31 December 1914, in ibid., pp. 347–49.

27. Asquith to Venetia Stanley, 30 December 1914, in Brock and Brock (eds.), op. cit., pp. 345–6.

28. Memorandum by Hankey, 28 December 1914, in Gilbert, op. cit., pp. 337–43.

29. Balfour to Hankey, 2 January 1915, op. cit.

30. Lloyd George, 'Suggestions as to the Military Position', 1 January 1915, reproduced in Lloyd George, *War Memoirs*, i, pp. 219–26.

31. Ibid.

32. David French, *British Strategy and War Aims, 1914–1916* (London: Allen & Unwin, 1986), p. 73.

33. Asquith to Venetia Stanley, 24 January 1915, in Brock and Brock (eds.), op. cit., pp. 393–94.

34. Fisher to Churchill, 3 January 1915, in Gilbert, op. cit., pp. 367–68.

35. Marshal Joseph Joffre, *The Memoirs of Marshal Joffre*, trans. T. Bentley Mott (London: Geoffrey Bles, 2 vols., 1932), ii, pp. 327–403 passim.

36. Ibid., p. 327.

37. French to Kitchener, 28 December 1914, Kitchener (Creedy) papers, The National Archives, Kew (TNA), WO 159/2/60.

38. David Stevenson, *The First World War and International Politics* (Oxford: Oxford University Press, 1988), p. 110.

39. Memorandum by Churchill, 31 December 1914, in Gilbert, op. cit., pp. 347–49.

40. 'A Comparison of the Belligerent Forces', 6 January 1915, by Callwell, War Council and successors: Photographic Copies of Minutes and Papers, TNA, CAB 42: CAB 42/1/10.

41. William Philpott, 'Kitchener and the 29th Division: A Study in Anglo-French Strategic Relations, 1914–1915, *The Journal of Strategic Studies,* 16 (1993), pp. 375–407; Keith Neilson, 'Kitchener: A Reputation Refurbished?', *Canadian Journal of History* 15 (1995), pp. 207–27.

42. Lord Esher journal, 13 August 1914, Esher Papers, Churchill Archives Centre, Cambridge (ESHR), ESHR 2/13.

43. Quoted in French, 'The Meaning of Attrition', p. 392.

44. French to Kitchener, 28 December 1914, op. cit.

45. Notes of a conversation between Count Charles de Broqueville (the Belgian Prime Minister) and Kitchener, 16 February 1915, de Broqueville papers, Archives Générales du Royaume, Brussels, file 391.

46. French, 'Meaning of Attrition', pp. 394–95.

47. Secretary's notes of a War Cabinet, 14 May 1915, quoted in French, *British Strategy and War Aims*, p. 103.

48. Notes of a conversation between de Broqueville and Kitchener, op. cit.

49. Philpott, op. cit., pp. 386–96.

50. Lloyd George, 'Suggestions as to the Military Position', op. cit., p. 222–23.

51. Diary entry, 22 April 1915, in Viscount Sandhurst, *From Day to Day, 1914–15* (London: Edward Arnold, 1928), p. 182.

52. David Stevenson, op. cit., pp. 47–58.

53. Quoted in R. J. B. Bosworth, *Italy, The Least of the Great Powers: Italian Foreign Policy before the First World War* (Cambridge: Cambridge University Press, 1979), p. 10.

54. Quoted in Mark Thompson, *The White War: Life and Death on the Italian Front, 1915–1919* (London: Faber and Faber, 2008), p. 244.

55. Stevenson, op. cit., pp. 52–55.

56. Asquith to Venetia Stanley, 27 December 1914, in Brock and Brock (eds.), op. cit., p. 341.

57. Balfour to Hankey, 2 January 1915, in Gilbert, op. cit., pp. 363–64.

58. Asquith to Venetia Stanley, 7 and 8 February 1915, in Brock and Brock (eds.), op. cit., pp. 418–19.

59. Balfour to Hankey, op. cit.

60. Hamit Bozarslan, 'The Ottoman Empire', in John Horne (ed.), *A Companion to World War I* (Chichester: Wiley-Blackwell, 2010), pp. 494–507, 494–99.

61. Bozarslan, op. cit., pp. 495–96.

62. Edward Erickson, *Ordered to Die: A History of the Ottoman Army in the First World War* (Westport, CT: Greenwood Press, 2001), pp. 7–11.

63. George Cassar, *The French and the Dardanelles: A Study of Failure in the Conduct of War* (London: Allen & Unwin, 1971), p. 43.

64. Ibid., pp. 94–95.

65. Fisher to Churchill, 3 January 1915, in Gilbert, op. cit., pp. 367–68.

66. Cassar, op. cit., p. 73.

67. Ibid., pp. 73–4, 77–8.

68. Hamilton Diary, 15 March 1915, in General Sir Ian Hamilton, *Gallipoli Diary* (London: Edward Arnold, 2 vols., 1920), i, p. 9.

69. Cassar, op. cit., p. 93.

70. Hamilton to Churchill, 26 May 1915, in Martin Gilbert (ed.), *Winston S. Churchill, 1914–16, vol. III: Companion, part 2: May 1915–December 1916* (London: William Heinemann Ltd, 1972), p. 952.

71. Cassar, op. cit., p. 237; Field Marshal Lord Carver, *The Turkish Front, 1914–1918: The Campaigns at Gallipoli, in Mesopotamia and in Palestine* (London: Sidgwick & Jackson, 2003), p. 101.

72. Quoted in John North, *Gallipoli: The Fading Vision* (London: Faber & Faber 1936), pp. 121–22.

73. Quoted ibid.

74. Tim Travers, *Gallipoli 1915* (Stroud: Tempus, 2001), pp. 123–36.

75. Ibid., pp. 143–60.

76. Diary, 6–8 August 1915, in Joseph Murray, *Gallipoli As I Saw It* (London: William Kimber, 1968), pp. 108–109.

77. Lloyd George, *War Memoirs*, i, p. 226.

78. Churchill, *The World Crisis*, i, p. 461.

79. Memorandum by Churchill, 31 December 1914, op. cit.

80. 15 March 1915, Binding, op. cit., p. 53.

81. Memorandum by Selborne for Asquith, 6 August 1915, Shelborne Papers, box 80, ff. 36–39.

82. Ibid.

## CHAPTER 4: A PEOPLE'S WAR

1. 'What a War of Attrition Means', by A British Army Officer, *The Vivid War Weekly*, 6 February 1915.

2. Bethmann Hollweg, Reichstag speech, 2 December 1914, in *Seven War Speeches by the German Chancellor, 1914–16* (Zurich: Art. Institut Orell Füssli, 1916), p. 13, 22.

3. 'What a War of Attrition Means', op. cit.

4. John Horne, 'Public Opinion and Politics', in Horne (ed.), *A Companion to World War I*, pp. 279–94, 279.

5. John McEwen (ed.), *The Riddell Diaries, 1908–23* (London: The Athlone Press, 1986); John Grigg, *Lloyd George: War Leader, 1916–1918* (London: Allen Lane, 2002), p. 220.

6. Neiberg, *Dance of the Furies*, p. 154.

7. Horne, op. cit., p. 281.

8. Neiberg, op. cit., p. 167.

9. Jean-Jacques Becker, *The Great War and the French People* (Oxford: Berg, 1985), pp. 48–49.

10. Alain to Halévy, 25 November 1914, quoted in ibid., p. 43.

11. Both advertised in *The Vivid War Weekly*, 6 February 1915.

12. 13 May 1917, Corday, *A Paris Diary*, p. 251.

13. Leonard Smith, 'France', in Horne, *Companion to World War I*, pp. 418–31, 424.

14. Quoted in Allen Douglas, *War, Memory, and the Politics of Humor: The Canard Enchaîné and World War I* (Berkeley, CA: University of California Press, 2002), pp. 21–22.

15. Neiberg, op. cit., p. 182.

16. 'The Power of Aircraft', by A British Army Officer, *The Vivid War Weekly*, 6 February 1915.

17. 18 May 1915, Mildred Aldrich, *On the Edge of the War Zone: From the Battle of the Marne to the Entrance of the Stars and Stripes* (London: Constable & Co., 1918), p. 92.

18. 'What a War of Attrition Means', op. cit.

19. H. W. Wilson and J. A. Hammerton (eds.), *The Great War: The Standard History of the All-Europe Conflict* (London: The Amalgamated Press, 1916), vol. 7.

20. Joëlle Beurier, 'Information, Censorship or Propaganda? The Illustrated French Press in the First World War', in Heather Jones, Jennifer O'Brien and Christoph Schmidt-Supprian (eds.), *Untold War: New Perspectives in First World War Studies* (Leiden: Brill, 2008), pp. 293–324; Pierre Sorlin, 'Film and the War', in Horne, *Companion to World War I*, pp. 353–67.

21. 'What a War of Attrition Means', op. cit.

22. Hew Strachan, 'The Morale of the German Army, 1917–18', in Hugh Cecil and Peter Liddle (eds.), *Facing Armageddon: The First World War Experienced* (London: Leo Cooper, 1996), pp. 383–98, 392–93.

23. Neiberg, op. cit., pp. 150–52.

24. *The Times*, 5 August 1914.

25. Alexander Watson, *Enduring the Great War: Combat, Morale and Collapse in the German and British Armies, 1914–1918* (Cambridge: Cambridge University Press, 2008), pp. 49–50.

26. Max Hastings, *Catastrophe: Europe Goes to War, 1914* (London: William Collins, 2013), p. 100.

27. Hartmut Pogge von Strandman (ed.), *Walther Rathenau: Industrialist, Banker, Intellectual and Politician, Notes and Diaries, 1907–1922* (Oxford: Clarendon Press, 1985), pp. 183–86.

28. Watson, op. cit., pp. 49–53.

29. Quoted in Neiberg, op. cit., p. 152.

30. 21 October 1914, Binding, *Fatalist at War*, p. 17.

31. Becker, op. cit., p. 46.

32. Quoted in Hastings, op. cit., pp. 192–93.

33. Statement by Robertson, 3 November 1916, Quoted in Lloyd George, *War Memoirs*, p. 540.

34. Quoted in Judith Cook, *Priestley* (London: Bloomsbury, 1997), p. 32.

35. Dulcie Grey, *J. B. Priestley* (Stroud: Sutton Publishing Ltd, 2000), pp. 11–12.

36. Quoted in Max Egremont, *Siegfried Sassoon: A Biography* (London: Picador, 2005), p. 63.

37. Matthew Hollis, *Now All Roads Lead to France: The Last Years of Edward Thomas* (London: Faber & Faber, 2011).

38. Diary, 28 June 1915, Barbellion, *Journal of a Disappointed Man*, p. 206.

39. Oliver Lyttelton, *Viscount Chandos: The Memoirs of Lord Chandos* (London: The Bodley Head, 1962), pp. 31–34.

40. Herwig, *The First World War: Germany and Austria-Hungary*, p. 6.

41. André Corvisier, 'Le Peuple français en guerre', in Corvisier (ed.), *Histoire militaire de la France*, 295–326, 297.

42. Tim Dayton, 'Alan Seeger: Medievalism as an Alternative Ideology', *First World War Studies* 3 (2012), pp. 125–44, 126.

43. Seeger to his mother, 28 September 1914, in Alan Seeger, *Letters and Diary of Alan Seeger* (London: Constable & Co., 1917), p. 3.

44. Seeger to his mother, 17 October 1914, ibid., p. 8.

45. Jean Colin, *France and the Next War*, trans. Major L H. R. Pope-Hennesey (London: Hodder and Stoughton, 1914 edn) pp. 305–6.

46. Neiberg, op. cit., pp. 100–110.

47. Quoted in Hastings, op. cit., p. 96.

48. John Horne, 'Public Opinion and Politics', in Horne (ed.), *A Companion to World War I*, pp. 279–94, 278.

49. Neiberg, op. cit., p. 180.

50. Esher Journal, 9 October 1914, quoted in French, 'Meaning of Attrition', p. 388.

CHAPTER 5: MOBILISING MANPOWER

1. Seeger to his mother, 28 September 1914, in Seeger, *Letters and Diary*, p. 2.

2. Seeger to his mother, 17 October 1914, ibid., pp. 6–7.

3. Ibid.

4. Letter to a friend, 28 June 1916, ibid., p. 204.

5. Letter to the *New York Sun*, 8 December 1914, ibid., p. 30, 33.

6. General Sir Alexander Godley, *Life of an Irish Soldier* (London: John Murray, 1939), p. 224.

7. Seeger to his mother, 23 October 1914, in Seeger, op. cit., p. 12.

8. Seeger to his father, 12 November 1914, ibid., p. 20.

9. Seeger diary, 10 November and 4 December 1914, ibid., pp. 18–20, 22–23.

10. Seeger diary, 22 December 1914, ibid., p. 47.

11. Joffre to army commanders, 10 December 1914, in *Les Armées françaises dans la grande guerre, tome II* (Paris: Imprimerie Nationale, 1931), *annexes vol. 1*, annexe 301.

12. Jules Maurin, 'Les Combatants face à l'épreuve de 1914 à 1918', in Corvisier (ed.), *Histoire militaire de la France*, pp. 257–93, 257–58.

13. Marjorie Farrar, *Principled Pragmatist: The Political Career of Alexander Millerand* (Oxford: Berg, 1991), pp. 162–63.

14. Ibid., pp. 177–78.

15. Ibid., p. 163.

16. Major-General Sir Alfred Knox, *With the Russian Army*, 1914–17 (London: Hutchinson & Co., 2 vols., 1921), ii, p. 412.

17. Quoted in Timothy C. Dowling, 'A Superlative Army: Raising and Sustaining the Imperial Russian Army in the Great War', in Peter Dennis and Jeffrey Grey (eds.), *Raise, Train and Sustain: Delivering Land Combat Power* (Australian Military History Publications, 2010), p. 77.

18. Ibid., pp. 74–79.

19. Ibid., pp. 81–84.

20. Ibid., pp. 85–87.

21. Esher journal, 22 January 1915, in M. V. Brett and O. Brett (eds.), *Journals and Letters of Reginald Viscount Esher, vol. 3: 1910–1915* (London: Ivor Nicholson & Watson, 1938), p. 208; Peter Simkins, *Kitchener's Army: The Raising of the New Armies, 1914–16* (Manchester: Manchester University Press, 1988), pp. 302–303.

22. William Philpott, 'Managing the British Way in Warfare: France and Britain's Continental Commitment, 1904–18', in Keith Neilson and Greg Kennedy (eds.), *The British Way in Warfare: Power and the International System, 1856–1956* (Farnham: Ashgate, 2010), pp. 83–100.

23. 'JB Priestley', in Richard Van Emden and Victor Piuk, *Famous 1914–1918* (Barnsley: Pen and Sword, 2008), pp. 299–311, 304–308.

24. Simkins, op. cit., p. 39.

25. Keith Grieves, *The Politics of Manpower, 1914–18* (Manchester: Manchester University Press, 1988), pp. 8–11.

26. Simkins, op. cit., pp. 40–46.

27. 8 September 1914, in Sandhurst, *From Day to Day, 1914–15*, p. 35.

28. Grieves, op. cit., pp. 9–11.

29. 15 April 1915, Sandhurst, op. cit., p. 175.

30. 12 May 1915, ibid., p. 199.

31. 29 May 1915, ibid., p. 220.

32. Grieves, op. cit., pp. 19–22.

33. Simkins, op. cit., p. 150.

34. Grieves, op. cit., pp. 24–26.

35. Edward M. Spiers, *Haldane: An Army Reformer* (Edinburgh: Edinburgh University Press, 1980), pp. 130–4.

36. Philip Magnus, *Kitchener: Portrait of an Imperialist* (London: John Murray, 1958), pp. 344–45.

37. Robert Aldrich and Christopher Hilliard, 'The French and British Empires', in Horne, *Companion to World War I*, pp. 524–39, 526.

38. William Philpott, *Bloody Victory: The Sacrifice on the Somme and the Making of the Twentieth Century* (London: Little, Brown, 2009), pp. 332–33.

39. David Stevenson, *With Our Backs to the Wall: Victory and Defeat in 1918* (London: Allen Lane, 2011), pp. 261–62.

40. Gerald Feldman, *Army, Industry and Labor in Germany, 1914–1918* (Princeton, NJ: Princeton University Press, 1966), pp. 31–34.

41. Bethmann Hollweg, Reichstag speech, 2 December 1914, in *Seven War Speeches by the German Chancellor*, p. 14.

42. Foley, *German Strategy and the Path to Verdun*, p. 84.

43. Bethmann Hollweg, Reichstag speech, 2 December 1914, op. cit., p. 22.

44. Niall Ferguson, *The Pity of War* (London: Allen Lane, 1998), pp. 93–95.

45. Feldman, op. cit., p. 64.

46. Humphries and Maker (eds.), *Germany's Western Front*, pp. 85–88, 381.

47. Feldman, op. cit., pp. 65–73.

48. Humphries and Maker (eds.), op. cit., pp. 149–51.

49. Herwig, *The First World War: Germany and Austria-Hungary*, pp. 136–37, 139.

50. Ibid., p. 129, 234.

51. Quoted in ibid., p. 137.

52. Ibid., pp. 130–31, 234–35.

53. Ibid., p. 131.

54. 23 June 1915, Sandhurst, op. cit., p. 249.

55. 25 June 1915, Sandhurst, op. cit., p. 250; Gerard De Groot, *Blighty: British Society in the Era of the Great War* (London: Longman, 1996), p. 136.

56. Roger Chickering, *Imperial Germany and the Great War, 1914–1918* (Cambridge: Cambridge University Press, 1998), pp. 114–18.

57. Toni Sender, *The Autobiography of a German Rebel* (London: Routledge, 1940), pp. 53–55.

58. Chickering, op. cit., p. 119.

59. 20 September 1914, Sandhurst, op. cit., p. 50.

60. Feldman, op. cit., p. 3.

61. Colin, *France and the Next War*, p. 299.

62. Ibid., p. 302.

63. Joffre's *bulletin des opérations*, 21 September 1914, quoted in Michael Neiberg, *Fighting the Great War: A Global History* (Cambridge MA: Harvard University Press, 2005), p. 11.

64. 'The Aisne', Alan Seeger.

CHAPTER 6: WAGING WAR

1. Philpott, 'Kitchener and the 29th Division', p. 397.

2. Cabinet minute, 2 July 1915, enclosed with Balfour to Asquith, 2 July 1915, Asquith Papers, Bodleian Library, Oxford, box 14, fol. 77B.

3. Table plan and rough notes of the Calais conference, 6 July 1915, Bodleian Library, Oxford, ms Eng. Lett. C 542/1, ff. 212–16.

4. Philpott, 'Managing the British Way in Warfare', passim.

5. Lloyd George, *War Memoirs*, i, p. 93.

6. Selborne to Countess de Franqueville (his sister), 29 November 1914, Ms Selborne, Adds 8, ff. 73–76.

7. Callwell, *Experiences of a Dug-out*, p. 108.

8. William Philpott, *Anglo-French Relations and Strategy on the Western Front, 1914–18* (Basingstoke: Macmillan Press Ltd., 1996), pp. 72–3.

9. Joffre to Millerand, 15 January 1915, *Cabinet du Ministre, Service historique de la défense, Archives de l'armée de terre* (AAT), Vincennes, 5N132.

10. Foley, *German Strategy and the Path to Verdun*, pp. 105–10.

11. Selborne to Countess de Franqueville, 25 October 1914, Ms Selborne, Adds 8, ff. 55–56.

12. Quoted in Margaret Macmillan, *The War that Ended Peace* (London: Profile Books, 2013), p. 200.

13. Humphries and Maker (eds.), *Germany's Western Front*, p. 128.

14. Ibid., xxxvii, pp. 84–85.

15. Lieutenant-General Sir Henry Rawlinson, 'Notes on the Situation of the Allied Forces in Flanders at the Beginning of 1915', 29 December 1914, Kitchener (Creedy) papers, TNA, WO 159/3/1, sent with Rawlinson to Kitchener, 3 January 1915, Kitchener papers, TNA, PRO 30/57/51/11.

16. Humphries and Maker (eds.), op. cit., pp. 89–105, 84.

17. Ibid., p. 84.

18. Falkenhayn to Conrad, 8 February 1915, cited in ibid., p. 107.

19. Joffre, *Memoirs*, ii, p. 452.

20. 'Tactique', end of 1914, Fonds Weygand, AAT, 1K130/9/6.

21. 19 March 1915, Binding, *Fatalist at War*, p. 55.

22. GQG note 5779, 'Goal and Conditions for a General Offensive Action' (April 1915), discussed in Jonathan Krause, *Early Trench Tactics in the French Army: The Second Battle of Artois, May–June 1915* (Farnham: Ashgate, 2013), pp. 23–31.

23. Jonathan Bailey, 'The First World War and the Birth of Modern Warfare', in Knox and Murray (eds.), *The Dynamics of Military Revolution*, pp. 132–53.

24. Prior and Wilson, *Command on the Western Front*, pp. 44–73 passim.

25. Krause, op. cit., pp. 69–74.

26. Ibid., pp. 75–82.

27. Fayolle diary, 9 June 1915, in Contamine, *Cahiers secrets*, p. 111.

28. Churchill to Asquith, 30 December 1914, in Gilbert, *Churchill: Companion Volume III*, i, pp. 345–47.

29. Ibid.

30. 18 May 1915, Aldrich, *On the Edge of the War Zone*, p. 92.

31. Thompson, *The White War*, pp. 52–58; John Schindler, *Isonzo: The Forgotten Sacrifice of the Great War* (Westport, CT: Praeger, 2001), pp. 13–15.

32. Schindler, op. cit., pp. 15–16.

33. Ibid., pp. 41–60 passim.

34. Thompson, op. cit., p. 149.

35. Schindler, op. cit., p. 92.

36. Quoted in Thompson, op. cit., p. 219.

37. Schindler, op. cit., p. 16, 92.

38. Thompson, op. cit., pp. 154–56.

39. Asquith to Sylvia Henley, 2 June 1915, Bodleian Library Ms Eng. Lett. c 542/1, ff. 43–48.

40. Selborne to Countess de Franqueville, 20 June 1915, Ms Selborne, Adds 8, ff. 157–58.

41. Asquith to Sylvia Henley, op. cit.

42. Kitchener to French, 16 May 1915, War Office: Reports, Memoranda and Papers (O and A Series), TNA, WO 33: WO 33/739/2470.

43. Secretary's notes of a War Cabinet, 14 May 1915, TNA, CAB 42/2/19.

44. Balfour to Kitchener, 6 June 1915, quoted in French, 'Meaning of Attrition', p. 394.

45. Humphries and Maker (eds.), op. cit, p. 220.

46. Ibid., p. 128.

47. Keith Neilson, *Strategy and Supply: The Anglo-Russian Alliance, 1914–17* (London: George Allen & Unwin, 1984), pp. 92–95.

48. Joffre, op. cit., ii, p. 366.

49. Ibid., ii, p. 329.

50. Quoted in ibid., ii, p. 358.

51. Kitchener to Asquith (draft), 17 August 1915, quoted in Neilson, op, cit., p. 96; Asquith to King George V, 20 August 1915, Asquith papers, box 8.

52. Philpott, op. cit., p. 80

53. Minutes of the Dardanelles Committee, 20 August 1915, TNA, CAB 42/3/16.

54. Joffre, op. cit., ii, pp. 359–60.

55. Robert Doughty, *Pyrrhic Victory: French Strategy and Operations in the Great War* (Cambridge MA: The Belknap Press of Harvard University Press, 2005), pp. 184–85.

56. Ibid., pp. 182–83, 187–88.

57. Quoted in Jack Sheldon, *The German Army on the Western Front in 1915* (Barnsley: Pen and Sword, 2012), p. 250.

58. General Noel de Castelnau, 'Rapport d'ensemble sur les opérations offensives de Champagne (Septembre 1915)', 27 October 1915, *Les Armées françaises dans la grande guerre, tome III* (Paris: Imprimerie Nationale, 1926), *annexes vol. 4*, annexe 3019, pp. 92–110.

59. Doughty, op. cit., pp. 190–95; Joffre, op. cit., ii, pp. 361–62.

60. Seeger to his mother, 25 October 1915, Seeger, *Letters and Diary*, pp. 169–70.

61. Prior and Wilson, op, cit., pp. 129–32.

62. Foch to Joffre, 6 November 1915, *Les Armées françaises dans la grande guerre*, III/4, annexe 3056, pp. 206–13, 211.

63 .'An Examination by the General Staff into the Factors Affecting the Choice of a Plan of Campaign; Together with a Recommendation as to the Best Plan to Adopt', by Murray, 16 December 1915, TNA, CAB 42/6/14.

64. 23 August 1915, Binding, op. cit., pp. 72–73.

65. 25 October 1915, ibid., p. 77.

66. 12 December 1915, ibid., p. 84.

67. Selborne, op. cit.

68. Robert Foley, 'What's in a Name? The Development of Strategies of Attrition on the Western Front, 1914–1918', *The Historian* 68 (2006), pp. 722–46, 729–35.

69. Lloyd George, *War Memoirs*, ii, p. 2,038.

70. C. S. Forrester, *The General* (London: Michael Joseph Ltd, 1936), p. 210.

71. Relative rates of loss are analysed statistically in François Cailleteau, *Gagner la grande guerre* (Paris: Economica, 2008), pp. 101–11.

72. Sender, *Autobiography of a German Rebel*, p. 51.

73. Lloyd George, op. cit., i, p. 95.

CHAPTER 7: WAR MACHINES

1. *The Times*, 14 May 1915.

2. 13 April 1915, Sandhurst, *From Day to Day*, 1914–1915, p. 174.

3. Lord Beaverbrook, *Politicians and the War, 1914–1916* (London: Thornton Butterworth, 1928), pp. 92–93.

4. 21 April 1915, Sandhurst, op. cit., p. 179.

5. John Turner, *British Politics and the Great War: Coalition and Conflict, 1915–1918* (New Haven, CT and London: Yale University Press, 1992), pp. 61–62.

6. Beaverbrook, op. cit., p. 95.

7. 'A Holy War', speech by Lloyd George, 28 February 1915, in Frances Stevenson (ed.), *Through Terror to Triumph: Speeches and Pronouncements of the Right Hon. David Lloyd George M.P., Since the Beginning of the War* (London: Hodder and Stoughton, 1915), pp. 75–89, 81.

8. Lord Croft, *My Life of Strife* (London: Hutchinson & Co., 1948), p. 145.

9. Andrew Suttie, *Rewriting the First World War: Lloyd George, Politics and Strategy, 1914–1918* (Basingstoke: Palgrave Macmillan, 2005).

10. 'What a War of Attrition Means', *The Vivid War Weekly*, emphasis in original.

11. Turner, op. cit., p. 56.

12. Cailleteau, *Gagner la grand guerre* , p. 8.

13. 10 June 1915, Sandhurst, op. cit., p. 236.

14. 17–18 March 1916, Sandhurst, *From Day to Day, 1916–1921* (London: Edward Arnold, 1929), pp. 33–34.

15. Guy Hartcup, *The War of Invention: Scientific Development, 1914–1918* (London: Brassey's, 1988).

16. Cailleteau, op. cit, p. 106.

17. Hew Strachan, *The First World War. Vol. 1: To Arms* (Oxford: Oxford University Press, 2001), p. 120.

18. Chickering, *Imperial Germany and the Great War*, p. 35; Major von Redern diary, 12 November 1914, cited in Foley, *German Strategy and the Path to Verdun*, p. 112, n. 15.

19. Chickering, op, cit., pp. 36–40.

20. Sender, *Autobiography of a German Rebel*, pp. 55–56.

21. Ibid., pp. 62–64, 72–74.

22. Strachan, op. cit., p. 1028.

23. Ibid.

24. Rémy Porte, *La Mobilisation industrielle: premier 'front' de la grande guerre?* (Paris : SOTECA Éditions 14–18, 2005).

25. Strachan, op. cit., p. 1062.

26. Ibid., pp. 1052–64; Doughty, *Pyrrhic Victory*, pp. 116–18.

27. Strachan, op. cit., pp. 1060–62.

28. Ibid., p. 1053.

29. Ibid., pp. 1060–64.

30. Paléologue diary, 31 May 1915, in Maurice Paléologue, *An Ambassador's Memoirs*, trans. F. A. Holt (London: Hutchinson & Co, 3 vols., 1923), i, p. 347.

31. Paléologue diary, 2 June 1915, ibid., i, p. 349.

32. Negley Farson, *The Way of a Transgressor* (London: Book Club Edition, 1940), pp. 128–31.

33. Ibid., p. 137.

34. Strachan, op. cit., pp. 1098–99.

35. Menning, 'Mukden to Tannenberg', p. 214; David Jones, 'The Imperial Army in World War I, 1914–1917', in Kagan and Higham (eds.), *The Military History of Tsarist Russia*, pp. 227–48, 236–37.

36. Strachan, op. cit., pp. 1097–1101; Norman Stone, *The Eastern Front* (London: Hodder & Stoughton, 1975), pp. 191–92.

37. Stone, op. cit., pp. 191–92.

38. Neilson, *Strategy and Supply*, ix, p. 9.

39. Gerd Hardach, *History of the World Economy in the Twentieth Century, vol. 2: The First World War, 1914–1918* (Berkeley and Los Angeles: University of California Press, 1977), pp. 145–47.

40. Farson, op. cit., pp. 159–64.

41. Ibid., p. 168.

42. Hardach, op. cit., p. 94.

43. Henry Wilson diary, 24 January and 24 February 1917, in Major-General Charles Callwell (ed.), *Field-Marshal Sir Henry Wilson, His Life and Diaries* (London: Cassell & Co, 2 vols., 1927), i, pp. 312, 321–22.

44. Strachan, op. cit., pp. 1092–93.

45. Hardach, op. cit., p. 94.

46. Porte, op. cit., p. 290.

47. Ibid., pp. 235–39, 250.

48. Kathleen Burk, *Britain, America and the Sinews of War, 1914–1918* (London: George Allen & Unwin, 1985), p. 5.

49. Ibid., pp. 22, 27.

50. Ibid., pp. 5–8.

51. Osborne, *Britain's Economic Blockade of Germany*, p. 137.

52. Ibid., passim.

53. Ibid., p. 168.

54. Farson, op. cit., p. 248; Lambert, *Planning Armageddon*, pp. 398–99.

55. Farson, op. cit., p. 243.

56. Lambert, op. cit., pp. 396–98.

57. Byron Nordstrom, *The History of Sweden* (Westport, CT: The Greenwood Press, 2002), pp. 94–96.

58. Reported in *The Times*, 14 May 1915.

59. Feldman, *Army, Industry and Labor*, pp. 18–30.

60. Leon Trotsky, 'The Zimmerwald Manifesto Against the War', September 1915, reprinted in Leon Trotsky, *An Appeal to the Toiling, Oppressed and Exhausted Peoples of Europe* (London: Penguin Books, n.d.), pp. 1–6.

61. Sender, op. cit., pp. 62–64.

62. Neil Harding, *Leninism* (Basingstoke: Macmillan, 1996), p. 1.

63. Hardach, op. cit., p. 93.

64. Bethmann Hollweg, Reichstag speech, 2 December 1914, in *Seven War Speeches by the German Chancellor*, p. 22.

65. De Groot, *Blighty*, p. 58.

66. Jere C. King, *Generals and Politicians: Conflict between France's High Command, Parliament, and Government, 1914–1918* (Berkeley, CA: California University Press, 1951).

67. Herwig, *The First World War: Germany and Austria-Hungary*, p. 77.

68. Christian Wolmar, *Engines of War: How Wars Were Won and Lost on the Railways* (London: Atlantic Books, 2010), pp. 130–37.

69. De Groot, op. cit., p. 65.

70. Ibid., p. 59.

71. Hardach, op. cit., pp. 79–80.

72. De Groot, op. cit., p. 112–14.

73. Ibid., p. 114.

74. Ibid., p. 83.

75. Hardach, op. cit., p. 151.

76. Ibid., pp. 139–50.

77. Ibid., p. 147.

78. 'A Civilian's Impression of the War', in Lord Northcliffe, *At the War* (London: Hodder & Stoughton, 1916), pp. 35–55.

79. 'The Army Behind the Army', in Northcliffe, op. cit., pp. 11–25.

80. 'A Civilian's Impression of the War', op. cit., p. 40.

81. 19 December 1916, Sandhurst, op. cit., p. 131.

82. Hardach, op. cit., pp. 66–67.

83. Ibid., p. 87.

84 Quoted in ibid., p. 54.

CHAPTER 8: CONTROLLING THE SEAS

1. E. Keble Chatterton, *The Auxiliary Patrol* (London: Sidgwick and Jackson, 1923), p. 172; Wilbur Cross, *Zeppelins of World War I* (London: I. B. Tauris, 1991), pp. 57–58.

2. Captain Herbert Richmond diary, 24 October 1914, quoted in Hough, *The Great War at Sea*, p. 65.

3. Halpern, *Naval History of World War One*, pp. 38–47.

4. 'On the possibility of using our Command of the Sea to influence more drastically the Military Situation on the Continent', memorandum by Fisher (November 1914), in Gilbert, *Churchill Companion III*, i, pp. 284–87.

5. Churchill to Fisher, 22 December 1914, in ibid., i, pp. 325–26.

6. Churchill to Fisher, Sir Arthur Wilson and Vice-Admiral Oliver, 3 January 1915, in ibid., i, pp. 365–66.

7. 'On the possibility of using our Command of the Sea . . .', op. cit.

8. Lambert, *Facing Armageddon*, pp. 417–20.

9. 'On the possibility of using our Command of the Sea . . .', op. cit.

10. Osborne, *Britain's Economic Blockade of Germany*, p. 120.

11. Lord Robert Cecil, House of Commons Speech, 9 March 1916, quoted in ibid., pp. 129–30.

12. Ibid., pp. 128–32.

13. Ibid., p. 125, 135; Stevenson, *Cataclysm*, pp. 203–204.

14. Osborne, op. cit., pp. 125–26.

15. Ibid., p. 141.

16. Herwig, *The First World War: Germany and Austria-Hungary*, p. 287.

17. Halpern, *Naval War in the Mediterranean*, p. 204, 228, 245, 250 and 253.

18. Herwig, op. cit., pp. 186–87.

19. Ibid., p. 287.

20. 3 June 1916, Sandhurst, *From Day to Day, 1916–1921*, pp. 58–59; Sondhaus, *The First World War*, pp. 279–82.

21. Murray, 'An Examination by the General Staff into the Factors Affecting the Choice of a Plan of Campaign', 16 December 1915, TNA, CAB 42/6/14.

22. Quoted in Field Marshal Sir William Robertson, *Soldiers and Statesmen, 1914–1918* (London: Cassell & Co., 2 vols., 1926), i, p. 263, 268.

23. Ross Anderson, *The Forgotten Front: The East African Campaign, 1914–1918* (Stroud: Tempus, 2004), pp. 51–55.

24. Maurice Hankey, *The Supreme Command* (London: Allen & Unwin, 2 vols., 1961), ii, pp. 633–34.

25. Ibid., ii, p. 609

26. Elizabeth Greenhalgh, *Victory through Coalition: Britain and France during the First World War* (Cambridge: Cambridge University Press, 2005), pp. 112–13.

27. Quoted, ibid., pp. 128–30.

28. Herwig, op. cit., p. 285.

29. Ibid., p. 286.

30. Ibid., pp. 285–86.

31. 10 April 1916, Binding, *Fatalist at War*, p. 99.

32. Hankey, op. cit., ii, p. 632.

33. Quoted in Greenhalgh, op. cit., pp. 265–80 passim.

34. Asquith to Venetia Stanley, 31 December 1914, in Brock and Brock (eds.), *Letters to Venetia Stanley*, pp. 348–50.

35. Sender, *Autobiography of a German Rebel*, p. 77.

CHAPTER 9: ATTACK

1. 26 February 1916, Binding, *Fatalist at War*, p. 94.

2. Ibid.

3. 'Le Maréchal Philippe Pétain', in Paul Gaujac, *Les Généraux de la victoire* (Paris: Histoire & Collections, 2007), pp. 46–48.

4. William Van der Kloot, *The Lessons of War: The Experiences of Seven Future Leaders in the First World War* (Stroud: The History Press, 2008), pp. 103–104.

5. 15 March 1915, Binding, op. cit., p. 97.

6. Humphries and Maker (eds.), *Germany's Western Front*, p. 377.

7. Quoted in ibid., p. 372.

8. Foley, *German Strategy and the Path to Verdun*, p. 179.

9. Ibid., pp. 183–87.

10. Malkasian, *A History of Modern Wars of Attrition*, p. 7.

11. Joffre, *Memoirs*, ii, p. 410, n. 1.

12. Humphries and Maker (eds.), op. cit., p. 376.

13. Herwig, *First World War: Germany and Austria-Hungary*, p. 172.

14. Humphries and Maker (eds.), op. cit, p. 376.

15. William Philpott, 'Squaring the Circle: The Coordination of the Entente in the Winter of 1915–16', *English Historical Review* 114 (1999), pp. 875–98.

16. Joffre, op. cit., ii, pp. 410–11.

17. 'Written Statement of the Conference Held at Chantilly, December 6th 1915', TNA, WO 106/1454.

18. 'Plan of Action Proposed by France to the Coalition', ibid., appendix 2.

19. Joffre, op. cit., ii, p. 414.

20. 'Plan of Action', op. cit.

21. Quoted in Churchill, *The World Crisis*, ii, pp. 915–16.

22. Murray, 'An Examination by the General Staff into the Factors Affecting the Choice of a Plan of Campaign', 16 December 1915, TNA, CAB 42/6/14.

23. Note on 'A Paper by the General Staff on the Future Conduct of the War' (16 December 1915), Field Marshal Sir William Robertson Papers, Liddell Hart Centre for Military Archives, King's College London, I/15/10.

24. Hankey, *Supreme Command*, ii, pp. 466–69.

25. Neilson, *Strategy and Supply*, p. 144.

26. Philpott, *Bloody Victory*, p. 83.

27. 5 February 1916, Lieutenant-Colonel Charles à Court Repington, *The First World War, 1914–1918* (London: Constable & Co, 2 vols., 1920), ii, p. 120.

28. 'Haig: Master of the Field', 31 January 1928, in Guy Liardet and Michael Tillotson (eds.), *The Times: Great Military Lives, a Century in Obituaries* (London: Times Books, 2008), pp. 135–45.

29. Haig diary, [5] August 1914, in Sheffield and Bourne (eds.), *Douglas Haig: War Diaries*, p. 54, Haig's emphasis.

30. Tim Travers, *The Killing Ground: The British Army, the Western Front and the Emergence of Modern War, 1900–1918* (London: Unwin Hyman, 1990), p. 86; Haig diary, 18 January 1916, Sheffield and Bourne (eds.), op. cit., p. 178.

31. Philpott, op. cit., pp. 76–81.

32. Joffre, op. cit., ii, p. 413.

33. Thompson, *The White War*, pp. 156–57.

34. Joffre, op. cit., ii, p. 422.

35. Thompson, op. cit., p. 158.

36. Knox diary, 10 and 11 December 1915, in Knox, *With the Russian Army*, i, pp. 362–65.

37. Ibid., i, p. 366.

38. Joffre, op. cit., ii, pp. 419–20.

39. Ibid., ii, pp. 421–22.

40. Neilson, op. cit., p. 145.

41. Jones, 'The Imperial Army in World War I', p. 239.

42. Stone, *The Eastern Front*, pp. 229–32.

43. Seeger to his *marraine*, 4 June 1916, Seeger, *Letters and Diary*, pp. 206–207.

44. Quoted in Hew Strachan, *The First World War: A New Illustrated History* (London: Simon and Schuster, 2003), p. 184.

45. Alastair Horne, *The Price of Glory: Verdun 1916* (London: Penguin, 1993 edition), pp. 161–72.

46. Ibid., pp. 327–28.

47. Foley, op. cit., pp. 192–93.

48. Philpott, op. cit., p. 85.

49. Strachan, op, cit., p. 185.

50. Philpott, op. cit., pp. 103.

51. Fayolle diary, 21 May 1916, in Contamine (ed.), *Cahiers secrets*, p. 161.

52. 'Note sur la situation militaire et les projets militaires de la Coalition', by the GQG, 26 March 1916, *Les Armées françaises dans la grande guerre, tome IV/1* (Paris: Imprimerie Nationale. 1926), *annexes vol. 1*, annexe 1539.

53. Philpott, op. cit., pp. 123–24, 144.

54. Haig diary, 9 June 1916, in Robert Blake (ed.), *The Private Papers of Douglas Haig, 1914–1919* (London: Eyre & Spottiswoode, 1952), p. 149.

55. Foley, op. cit., p. 182.

56. Herwig, op. cit., p. 204.

57. Stone, op. cit., pp. 242–44.

58. Herwig, op. cit., p. 205.

59. Schindler, *Isonzo*, pp. 144–47; Thompson, op. cit., pp. 162–63.

60 Schindler, op. cit., p. 149.

61. Herwig, op. cit., pp. 205–206.

62. Stone, op. cit., p. 245.

63. 19 July 1916, Binding, op. cit., pp. 113–14.

64. 9 August 1916, ibid., p. 116.

CHAPTER 10: COUNTERATTACK

1. Timothy Dowling, *The Brusilov Offensive* (Bloomington, IN: Indiana University Press, 2008), pp. 67–75.

2. Stone, *The Eastern Front*, p. 254.

3. Ibid., p. 233.

4. Ibid., pp. 231, 237–38.

5. Dowling, op. cit., pp. 42–46.

6. Stone, op, cit., p. 235.

7. Ibid., pp. 223–24.

8. Ibid., pp, 244–45.

9. Dowling, op. cit., p. 104.

10. Stone, op. cit., pp. 246–47.

11. Ibid., p. 239, 246.

12. Dowling, op. cit., pp. 90–91.

13. Joffre to Foch, 21 June 1916, *Les Armées françaises dans la grande guerre, tome IV/2* (Paris: Imprimerie Nationale, 1932), *annexes vol. 2*, annexe 1385.

14. War Office: Military Headquarters: Correspondence and Papers, First World War, TNA, WO 158/14/121a, Haig's emphasis.

15. 'Enseignements à tirer de nos dernières attaques', by Foch, 6 December 1915, in Maréchal Foch, *Oeuvres Complètes* (Paris: Economica, 3 vols., 2008), ii, pp. 439–47.

16. Quoted in Général Percin, *Le Massacre de notre infanterie, 1914–1918* (Paris: Albin Michel, 1921), p. 100.

17. Groupe des armées du nord, 'La bataille offensive', 20 April 1916, AAT, 18N148.

18. Philpott, *Bloody Victory*, pp. 145–50, 170–71.

19. Fayolle diary, 21 January 1916, in Contamine (ed.), *Cahiers secrets*, p. 142.

20. Haig diary, 5 April 1916, Sheffield and Bourne (eds.), *Douglas Haig: War Diaries*, p. 184.

21. Philpott, op. cit., pp. 106–11, 117–25.

22. Seeger to his *marraine*, 24 June 1916, Seeger, *Letters and Diary*, p. 211.

23. 'Experience of the German 1st Army in the Somme Battle', 30 January 1917, by Von Below, (trans., General Staff (Intelligence) GHQ, 3rd May 1917).

24. Philpott, op. cit., pp. 222–23.

25. Ibid., pp. 172–243 passim.

26. 2 January 1915, Binding, *Fatalist at War*, p. 44.

27. 5–11 September 1916, Sandhurst, *From Day to Day, 1916–1921*, p. 97.

28. 14 September 1916, ibid., pp. 130–31.

29. 28 September 1916, ibid., p. 103.

30. Philpott, op. cit., pp. 319–20.

31. Thompson, *The White War*, p. 169–77.

32. Dowling, op. cit., pp. 106–108.

33. Ibid., p. 106.

34. Ibid., pp. 166–67.

35. 14 September 1916, Binding, op. cit., p. 130.

36. Dowling, op. cit., pp. 150–53.

37. Ibid., pp. 148–49.

38. Ibid., p. 149, 155.

39. 5 October 1916, Binding, op. cit., p. 134.

40. Herwig, *First World War: Germany and Austria-Hungary*, pp. 218–22.

41. Thompson, op. cit., pp. 217–24.

42. Philpott, op. cit,, pp. 345–428 passim.

43. Ibid., p. 99.

44. Ian Malcolm Brown, *British Logistics on the Western Front, 1914–1919* (Westport CT: Praeger, 1998).

45. Porte, *La Mobilisation industrielle*, p. 303.

46. Philpott, op. cit., p. 389.

47. For example on the Somme. Philpott, op, cit., pp. 386–91.

48. Brown, op. cit., passim; Philpott, op. cit., pp. 390–91.

49. Wolmar, *Engines of War*, pp. 167–68.

50. Philpott, op. cit., pp. 350–51.

51. Fayolle diary, 8 January 1917, in Contamine, (ed.) op. cit., p. 197.

52. Murray, 'An Examination by the General Staff into the Factors Affecting the Choice of a Plan of Campaign',16 December 1915, TNA, CAB 42/6/14.

53. Thompson, op. cit., p. 224.

54. GHQ, 'The Opening of the Wearing-out Battle', 23 December 1916, in John H. Boraston (ed.), *Sir Douglas Haig's Despatches* (London: Dent, 1919), p. 58.

55. Joffre *Memoirs*, ii, pp. 500–502, summarising a memorandum to the Allied commanders in chief, 12 November 1916.

56. 8 January 1917, Binding, op. cit., pp. 141–42.

57. 26 December 1916, ibid., p. 140.

58. Quoted in Thompson, op. cit., p. 225.

59. Dowling, op, cit., pp 167–69.

60. Philpott, op. cit., pp. 600–602.

61. Dowling, op. cit., p. 159.

62. Unsigned and undated memorandum on the results of the Somme offensive, in 'After the Somme: studies', Fonds Weygand, 1K130/3/J.

63. Note by Foch, 24 November 1916, Fonds Weygand, 1K130/9/6.

64. 'End of November 1916', Fonds Weygand, 1K130/9/6.

65. Wilson diary, 31 December 1916, Callwell, *Henry Wilson*, i, p. 306.

66. Wilson diary, [14] November 1916, Callwell, op. cit., i, p. 296.

67. Philpott, op. cit., p. 326.

68. 'Suggestions as to the Military Position', 1 January 1915, Lloyd George, *War Memoirs*, i, p. 220.

69. Philpott, op. cit., pp. 354–56, 367–68.

70. Ibid., pp. 264–66, 359–84 and 414–16 passim.

71. War Cabinet minutes, 3 November 1916, quoted in Lloyd George, op. cit., i, p. 541.

72. Quoted in Philpott, op. cit., p. 279.

73. Memorandum in Lloyd George, op. cit., i, pp. 545–55.

74. Wilson diary, 26 October 1916, Callwell, op. cit., i, p. 296.

75. Herwig, op. cit., p. 222.

76. 17–25 October 1916, Sandhurst, op. cit., p. 110.

77. Memorandum in Lloyd George, op. cit., i, p. 551.

78. War Cabinet memorandum by Robertson, 3 November 1916, quoted in Lloyd George, op. cit., i, p. 541.

79. 'The Somme Offensive', *L'Image de la guerre*, July 1916, in Fonds Foch (Fournier-Foch), AAT, 1K129/2.

### CHAPTER 11: ALLIED HOPES

1. Robertson to Haig, 24 December 1916, in David Woodward (ed.), *The Military Correspondence of Field-Marshal Sir William Robertson, Chief of the Imperial General Staff, December 1915–February 1918* (London: The Bodley Head for the Army Records Society, 1989), pp. 131–32.

2. Lloyd George, *War Memoirs*, i, p. 544.

3. Robertson to Lieutenant-Colonel Clive Wigram, 12 January 1917, Woodward, op. cit., p. 138.

4. John Grigg, *Lloyd George: War Leader, 1916–1918* (London: Allen Lane, 2002), pp. 27–29.

5. 'Lecture by French Officer on Teachings of the War, January 1917', in US military Attaché, London to Chief, War College Division, Washington, DC, 13 March 1917, United States National Archives and Records Division, College Park, Maryland, 8698-66.

6. February 1917, in Evelyn Princess Blücher, *An English Wife in Berlin* (London: Constable, 1920), p. 163.

7. 20 January 1917, quoted in Lord Edward Gleichen (ed.), *Chronology of the*

*Great War, 1914–1918* (London: Greenhill Books, 2000 reissue of 1919–20 original), p. 279.

8. Horne, 'Public Opinion and Politics', p. 290.

9. 15 March 1917, Binding, *Fatalist at War*, p. 151.

10. 8–14 October 1917, Sandhurst, *From Day to Day, 1916–1921*, p. 206.

11. 23 January–4 February 1917, ibid., p. 137.

12. Stevenson, *Cataclysm*, pp. 256–57.

13. Philpott, *Bloody Victory*, pp. 469–71.

14. Doughty, *Pyrrhic Victory*, pp. 350–52.

15. Tim Gale, *The French Army's Tank Force and Armoured Warfare in the Great War: The Artillerie Spéciale* (Farnham: Ashgate, 2013), pp. 33–51.

16. Brock Millman, *Pessimism and British War Policy, 1916–1918* (London: Frank Cass, 2001), passim.

17. Kristian Coates Ulrichsen, *The Logistics and Politics of the British Campaigns in the Middle East, 1914–22* (Basingstoke: Palgrave Macmillan, 2011), pp. 55–61.

18. Ibid., passim.

19. Millman, op. cit., p. 208.

20. John Starling and Ivor Lee, *No Labour, No Battle* (Stroud: Spellmount, 2009), passim.

21. Ibid., pp. 297–301.

22. Aldrich and Hilliard, 'The French and British Empires', p. 526.

23. Corvisier, 'Le Peuple français en guerre', p. 297.

24. Ibid., p. 315.

25. Charles Mangin, *La Force Noire* (Paris: Hachettte, 1910).

26. For example in their 11 January 1917 response to the Allies' rebuff of their 12 December 1916 'Peace Note', Gleichen, op. cit., p. 278.

27. Aldrich and Hilliard, op. cit., pp. 526–27, 531.

28. Starling and Lee, op. cit., pp. 219–36 passim.

29. John Morrow Jr, *The Great War: An Imperial History* (London: Routledge, 2004).

30. Lloyd George, *War Memoirs*, i, pp. 926–27.

31. Statement by Robertson, 4 May 1917, quoted in ibid., i, pp. 925–26.

32. Thompson, *The White War*, pp. 251–54.

33 Ibid., pp. 278–83.

34. Robertson to Foch, 23 May 1917, in Woodward (ed.), op. cit., pp. 188–89.

35. Robertson to Haig, 26 May 1917, summarised in John Terraine, *The Road to Passchendaele: The Flanders Offensive of 1917: A Study in Inevitability* (London: Leo Cooper, 1977), pp. 158–67.

36. Eric Lohr, 'Russia', in Horne, *Companion to World War I*, pp. 479–93, 486–87.

37. Ibid., pp. 489–90.

38. Hankey, *Supreme Command*, ii, p. 639.

39. Hankey diary, 8 February 1917, quoted ibid., ii, p. 645.

40. Hankey diary, 30 March 1917, quoted ibid., ii, p. 648.

41. Fisher, quoted in Hankey diary, 29 April 1917, ibid., ii, p. 650.

42. 1–7 March 1917, Sandhurst, *From Day to Day, 1916–1921*, p. 149.

43. Hankey, op. cit., ii, pp. 641–43.

44. Lloyd George, op. cit., i, p. 641.

45. 23 January–4 February, 6–9 February, 10–11 February 1917, Sandhurst, op. cit., pp. 138–39, 141, 143.

46. Stevenson, *With Our Backs to the Wall*, pp. 311–17.

47. Ian Beckett, *The Great War* (London: Pearson, 2nd edition, 2007), p. 244.

48. 'Proposal of Peace', speech to the Senate, 22 January 1917, in Lloyd Smith (ed.), *War Speeches of Woodrow Wilson* (Girard, KA: Haldeman-Julius Company, 1924), p. 12.

49. Osborne, *Britain's Economic Blockade of Germany*, pp. 168–69.

50. Quoted in Martin Gilbert, *Winston S. Churchill, vol. IV: 1916–1922* (London: Heinemann, 1975), p. 17.

51. Esher to Haig , 30 May 1917, quoted op. cit., p. 22.

52. 'The Present Situation and Future Plans', Haig to the War Cabinet, 1 May 1917, and War Policy Cabinet Committee, 7th meeting, 19 June 1917, in Terraine, op. cit., pp. 83–84, 149.

53. 'Present Situation and Future Plans', Haig to Robertson, 12 June 1917, and Robertson to Haig, telegram and letter, 13 June 1917, quoted in ibid., pp. 135–36.

54. Haig to Robertson, 28 May 1917, quoted in ibid., p. 107, Haig's emphasis.

55. Robertson to Haig, 26 May 1917, quoted in ibid., p. 106, Haig's emphasis.

56. War Policy Cabinet Committee, 10th meeting, 21 June 1917, ibid., p. 149; Lloyd George to Robertson, 26 August 1917, in Woodward (ed.), op. cit., pp. 219.

57. 3–7 June 1917, Sandhurst, op. cit., p. 174.

58. 18 October 1917, Binding, *Fatalist at War*, pp. 188–89.

59. 2 and 7 November 1917, ibid., pp. 191–92.

60. 14 November 1917, ibid., p. 194, Binding's emphasis.

61. Robertson, *Soldiers and Statesmen*, pp. 261–62.

62. Herwig, *First World War: Germany and Austria-Hungary*, p. 332.

63. Doughty, op. cit., p. 368.

64. 24 October 1917, Henri Desagneaeux, *A French Soldier's War Diary, 1914–18* (Morley: The Elmfield Press, 1975), p. 55.

65. William Philpott, 'Malmaison – the "Bite and Hold" Battle', in Matthew Hughes and William Philpott, *The Palgrave Concise Historical Atlas of the First World War* (Basingstoke: Palgrave Macmillan, 2005), p. 37.

66. Cyril Falls, *The First World War* (London: Longmans, 1960), p. 285.

67. Quoted in Percin, *Le Massacre de notre infanterie*, p. 100.

68. Churchill, *World Crisis*, ii, pp. 1219–20.

69. Percin, op. cit., p. 121.

70. GQG pamphlet. '*L'usure adverse*' ('attrition of the opposition'), 30 July 1916, quoted in Percin, op. cit., p. 169, Percin's emphasis.

71. 'Post-war Recollections of Haig as Commander-in-Chief', n.d., ESHR 19/5.

72. Robertson, op. cit., ii, pp. 260–61.

73. 8–14 January 1917, Sandhurst, op. cit., p. 134.

74. 11–14 December 1917, ibid., p. 217.

75. 15–17 December 1917, ibid., p. 217.

76. 11–20 November 1917, ibid., pp. 212–13.

CHAPTER 12: THE WILL TO VICTORY

1. Quoted in Thomas Knock, *To End All Wars: Woodrow Wilson and the Quest for a New World Order* (Oxford: Oxford University Press, 1993), p. 98.

2. Declaration of War Address to Congress, 2 April 1917, ibid., p. 22.

3. Ibid., p. 25.

4. Quoted in Neiberg, *Dance of the Furies*, p. 187.

5. 11 July 1916, Corday, *The Paris Front*, p. 183.

6. John Horne (ed.), *State, Society and Mobilization in Europe during the First World War* (Cambridge: Cambridge University Press, 1997).

7. 18 April 1917, Corday, op. cit., p. 245.

8. George Cassar, *Asquith as War Leader* (London: The Hambledon Press, 1994), pp. 233–36.

9. Paléologue diary, 2 June 1915, in Paléologue, *An Ambassasor's Memoirs*, i, p. 349.

10. Farson, *Way of a Transgressor*, pp. 286–87.

11. 'On the tasks of the Proletariat in the Present Revolution', by Lenin, 7 April 1917, quoted in Robert Daniels (ed.), *A Documentary History of Communism, vol. I: Communism in Russia* (Hanover, NH: University Press of New England, 1984), pp. 55–57.

12. 15 March 1915, Binding, *Fatalist at War*, p. 151.

13. Fayolle diary, 6 August 1916, in Contamine (ed.), *Cahiers secrets*, pp. 171–2.

14. Joffre journal, 14 August 1916, in Guy Pedroncini (ed.), *Journal de Marche de Joffre (1916–1919)* (Vincennes: Service historique de l'armée de terre, 1990), p. 88.

15. 4 July 1916, Corday, op. cit., p. 179.

16. Philpott, *Bloody Victory*, pp. 471–73.

17. Général Léon Godfroy, 'Souvenirs Militaires, 1894–1945' (c1961), p. 2, Papiers Godfroy, AAT, 1K534.

18. Emmanuel Saint-Fuscien, *À vos orders: La relation d'autorité dans l'armée français de la Grand Guerre* (Paris: Éditions EHESS, 2011); Smith, 'France', pp. 424–27.

19. Ibid., p. 428.

20. 1–24 March 1917, Corday, op. cit., pp. 234–39.

21. Smith, op. cit., pp. 427–28.

22. Quoted in Beurier, 'Information, Censorship or Propaganda?', pp. 316–17.

23. Smith, op. cit., p. 428.

24. Corday, op. cit., p. 235.

25. Cited in Horne, 'Public Opinion and Politics', p. 283.

26. Quoted in Jean-Baptiste Duroselle, *La Grande guerre des français, 1914–1918*, (Paris: Perrin, 2002 edition), p. 322.

27. Georges Clemenceau, *Grandeur and Misery of Victory* (London: George Harrap & Co, 1930), pp. 347–51.

28. P. A. Thompson, *Lions Led by Donkeys: Showing How Victory in the Great War Was Achieved by Those Who Made the Fewest Mistakes* (London: T Werner Laurie Ltd, 1927), p. 266.

29. Arthur Marwick, *The Deluge: British Society and the First World War* (Basingstoke: Palgrave Macmillan, 2nd edition, 2006), pp. 243–50.

30. David Monger, *Patriotism and Propaganda: The National War Aims Committee and Civilian Morale* (Liverpool: Liverpool University Press, 2012).

31. H. A. Jones, *The War in the Air: Being the Story of the part played in the Great War by the Royal Air Force, vol. VI* (Oxford: Clarendon Press, 1937), pp. 88–89.

32. Spenser Wilkinson, *Some Neglected Aspects of the War: A Lecture Delivered Before the University of Oxford, October 25, 1917* (Oxford: Oxford University Press, 1917), p. 21.

33. 1–7 December 1917, Sandhurst, *From Day to Day, 1916–1921*, p. 215.

34. Victor Cazalet to Austen Chamberlain, 31 December 1917, quoted in Turner, *British Politics and the Great War*, p. 266.

35. Strachan, 'Morale of the German Army', pp. 386–88, 392–93.

36. General Erich Ludendorf, *My War Memories, 1914–1918* (London: Hutchinson & Co, 2 vols, 1919), ii, pp. 460–62.

37. Quoted in ibid., p. 462.

38. Horne, op. cit., p. 290.

39. 22 July 1917, Binding, *Fatalist at War*, p. 175.

40. 29 July 1917, ibid., p. 177.

41. 8 September 1917, ibid., p. 183; Strachan, op. cit., p. 384.

42. February 1917, in Blücher, *An English Wife*, p. 164.

43. Horne, op. cit., p. 289.

44. Chickering, *Imperial Germany and the Great War*, p. 166.

45. Sender, *Autobiography of a German Rebel*, p. 77.

46. Ludendorff, op. cit., ii, p. 514.

47. Quoted in Laurence Moyer, *Victory Must be Ours: Germany in the Great War, 1914–1918* (London: Leo Cooper, 1995), p. 224.

48. Chickering, op. cit., p. 165.

49. Stevenson, *Cataclysm*, p. 232.

50. Geoffrey Wawro, 'Morale in the Austro-Hungarian Army: The Evidence of Habsburg Army Campaign Reports and Allied Intelligence Officers', in Cecil and Liddle (eds.), *Facing Armageddon*, pp. 399–412, 399–403.

51. Mark Cornwall, 'Austria-Hungary and "Yugoslavia"', in Horne (ed.), *Companion to World War I*, pp. 371–85.

52. 26 August 1917, Corday, op. cit., pp. 272–73.

53. Ludendorff, op. cit., ii, pp. 476–481.

CHAPTER 13: GERMANY'S LAST CARDS

1. Thompson, *The White War*, p. 307, 312.

2. Ibid., p. 295.

3. Mario Morselli, *Caporetto 1917: Victory or Defeat?* (London: Routledge, 2001).

4. John Peaty, 'Capital Courts Martial in the Great War', in Brian Bond et al, *Look to Your Front: Studies in the First World War* (Staplehurst: Spellmount, 1999), pp. 89–104, 97.

5. Thompson, op. cit., p. 319.

6. Ibid., p. 324.

7. Morselli, op, cit., pp. 64–65.

8. Quoted in Thompson, op. cit., p. 323.

9. Thompson, op. cit., p. 296.

10. Wawro, 'Morale in the Austro-Hungarian Army', p. 403.

11. 31 December 1917, Binding, *Fatalist at War*, pp. 200–201.

12. Chickering, *Imperial Germany and the Great War*, pp. 156–60.

13. Quoted in Stevenson, *With our Backs to the Wall*, p. 33.

14. 12 February 1918, Binding, op. cit., p. 201.

15. 31 December 1917, ibid, p. 201.

16. Watson, *Enduring the Great War*, p. 182.

17. Millman, *Pessimism and British War Policy*, pp. 212–25 passim.

18. Quoted in ibid., p. 188.

19. Ibid., pp. 176–95 passim.

20. Stevenson, op. cit.

21. Jack Sheldon, 'The German Manpower Crisis', *The Douglas Haig Fellowship Records* 15 (2011), pp. 35–49, 36–37.

22. 2–9 March 1918, Sandhurst, *From Day to Day, 1916–1921*, p. 235.

23. 11–17 March 1918, ibid., p. 237.

24. Jones, *The War in the Air, vol. VI*, p. 85.

25. Millman, op. cit., pp. 107–108, 200–207.

26. Foch, *Memoirs*, pp. 347–50.

27. Quoted in Lord Chandos, *From Peace to War: A Study in Contrast, 1857–1918* (London: The Bodley Head, 1968), p. 135.

28. Greenhalgh, *Victory through Coalition*, pp. 265–80 passim.

29. Philpott, *Anglo-French Relations and Strategy*, p. 153.

30. Memorandum for the SWC, 1 January 1918, quoted in Foch, op. cit., p. 271, Foch's emphasis.

31. Fayolle diary, 29 March and 1 April 1918, in Contamine (ed.), *Cahiers secrets*, p. 265, 268.

32. David Zabecki, *The German 1918 Offensives: A Case Study in the Operational Level of War* (Abingdon: Routledge, 2006), pp. 28–29.

33. Ibid., p. 312.

34. Memorandum for the SWC, 1 January 1918, quoted in Foch, op cit., p. 270, Foch's emphasis.

35. Zabecki, op. cit., p. 160.

36. 29 March 1918, Binding, op, cit., p. 211.

37. 20 March 1918, ibid., p. 205.

38. Strachan, 'Morale of the German Army', p. 390.

39. 31 March 1918, Binding, op. cit., pp. 213–14.

40. 4 and 9 April 1918, ibid., p. 216, 218.

41. Quoted in Stevenson, op. cit., p. 79.

42. David Trask, *The AEF and Coalition War Making, 1917–1918* (Lawrence, KA: University Press of Kansas, 1993), p. 55.

43. Cummings diary, 1 June 1918, in W. N. P. Barbellion [Bruce Cummings], *Last Diary* (London: Chatto & Windus, 1921), p. 7.

44. Stevenson, op. cit., pp. 78–83.

45. 'Denis Duchêne', in Gaujac, *Les Généraux de la victoire*, i, pp. 36–37.

46. Général Maxime Weygand, *Idéal vécu: Mémoires* (Paris: Flammarion, 1953), pp. 553–54.

47. Zabecki, op. cit., p. 226.

48. Ibid., pp. 238–39.

49. Ibid., pp. 240–43; Stevenson, op. cit., pp. 88–91.

50. Stevenson, op. cit., pp. 98–99.

51. Ibid., pp. 99–101.

52. Thompson, *The White War*, pp. 342–43.

53. Ibid., p. 332.

54. Stevenson, op, cit., pp. 400–401.

55. Thompson, op. cit., pp. 330–32.

56. Ibid., pp. 339–41.

57. Ibid., pp. 332–35.

58. Wawro, op. cit., p. 407.

59. Thompson, op. cit., pp. 344–46; Stevenson, op. cit., pp. 101–105.

60. Thompson, op. cit., p. 343, 347.

61. Watson, op. cit., pp. 196–97.

62. Stevenson, op. cit., pp. 106–107.

63. 29 June 1918, Binding, op. cit., p. 229.

64. Quoted in 21 July 1918, Corday, *The Paris Front*, p. 360.

65. 16 and 19 July 1918, Binding, op. cit., pp. 234–37.

66. David Zabecki, op. cit., p. 151.

67. Ibid., p. 86.

68. Ibid., pp. 130–32.

64. 2 April 1918, Binding, op. cit., p. 324.

70. Quoted in Aston, *The Biography of the Late Marshal Foch*, p. 226.

CHAPTER 14: VICTORY ON ALL FRONTS

1. Michael Neiberg, *The Second Battle of the Marne* (Bloomington, IN: Indiana University Press, 2008), pp 120–27.

2. Ibid., p. 130, 135.

3. Foch, *Memoirs*, p. 364.

4. John Terraine, *To Win a War: 1918, The Year of Victory* (London: Papermac, 1986), pp. 95–99.

5. Neiberg, op. cit., p. 155, 184.

6. August 1918, Corday, *The Paris Front*, p. 364.

7. Watson, *Enduring the Great War*, pp. 187–88.

8. 25 August 1918, Binding, *Fatalist at War*, p. 244.

9. Strachan, 'Morale of the German Army', pp. 390–91; Watson, op. cit., pp. 200–201, 206–10.

10. Trask, *AEF and Coalition War Making*, pp. 62–65.

11. Ibid., pp. 90–91.

12. Strachan, op. cit., p. 385.

13. Quoted in Trask, op. cit., p. 92.

14. Quoted in Philpott, *Bloody Victory*, p. 591.

15. 4 August 1918, Binding, op. cit., p. 240.

16. Philpott, op. cit., p. 518.

17. 4 August 1918, Binding, op. cit, p. 241.

18. Lloyd George, op cit.,*War Memoirs*, ii, p. 1,844.

19. Quoted in Terraine, op. cit., p. 100.

20. Lloyd George, *War Memoirs*, ii, p. 1,688.

21. Untitled memorandum on the offensive battle [spring 1917], in 'Après la Somme: études', Fonds Weygand, 1K130/3/J.

22. Memorandum by Foch for the Allied Commanders in Chief, 24 July 1918, in Foch, op. cit., pp. 425–49.

23. Untitled memorandum on the offensive battle, op. cit.

24. Weygand, *Idéal vécu*, pp. 581, 584–85.

25. Memorandum by Foch op. cit.

26. Sheldon, 'German Manpower Crisis', p. 37.

27. Memorandum by Foch, op. cit.

28. Foch, *Memoirs*, p. 430.

29. Directive by Foch, 9 September 1918, quoted in Weygand, op. cit., p. 605; Foch, op. cit., pp. 470–71.

30. Jonathan Boff, *Winning and Losing on the Western Front: The British Third Army and the Defeat of Germany in 1918* (Cambridge: Cambridge University Press, 2012), pp. 36–37.

31. Philpott, op. cit., pp. 519–27.

32. Stevenson, *With our Backs to the Wall*, pp. 122–23.
33. 12 August 1918, Binding, op. cit., p. 242.
34. Ibid.
35. 26–28 June 1918, Sandhurst, *From Day to Day, 1916–1921*, p. 258.
36. Boff, op. cit., p. 29.
37. Foch, op. cit., pp. 462–67.
38. Trask, op. cit., p. 98; Philpott, op. cit., pp. 527–29.
39. Neiberg, op. cit., p. 159.
40. Quoted in ibid., p. 165.
41. Philpott, op. cit., p. 532.
42. Watson, op. cit., p. 217.
43. Foch to Pershing, 31 August 1918, quoted in Foch, op. cit., pp. 463–64.
44. Foch, op. cit., p. 424.
45. Weygand, op. cit., p. 604.
46. Boff, op. cit., p. 31.
47. Weygand, op. cit., p. 637.
48. Boff, op. cit., pp. 31–35.
49. Brown, *British Logistics*, pp. 196–202.
50. Herwig, *First World War: Germany and Austria-Hungary*, pp. 426–28.
51. Watson, op. cit., pp. 223–30.
52. 22 October 1918, Chandos, *From Peace to War*, p. 194.
53. 13 October 1918, ibid, p. 193.
54. Ibid., pp. 198–99.
55. Philpott, op. cit., p. 532.
56. Citing Basil Liddell Hart, Doughty, *Pyrrhic Victory*, p. 461.
57. Weygand, op. cit., p. 581.
58. Weygand, op. cit., p. 642.
59. Weygand, op. cit., pp. 607–10.
60. Wawro, 'Morale in the Austro-Hungarian Army', p. 409.
61 Weygand, op. cit., pp. 621–22.
62. Doughty, op. cit., pp. 490–91, 501–502.
63. Stevenson, op. cit., pp. 529–30.
64. Herwig, op. cit., p. 433; Tim Travers, *How the War Was Won: Command and Technology in the British Army on the Western Front, 1917–1918* (London: Routledge, 1992), p. 175.
65. Watson, op. cit., pp. 184–231 passim.
66. Cailleteau, *Gagner la grande guerre*, pp. 193–207 passim.

EPILOGUE: 'THE GREAT WAR FOR CIVILIZATION'

1. 11 July 1916, Corday, *The Paris Front*, p. 183.
2. Quoted in French, 'Meaning of Attrtion', p. 388.
4. 'Suggestions as to the Military Position', 1 January 1915, in Lloyd George, *War Memoirs*, i, p. 225.
5. Saint-Fuscien, *À vos orders*; Leonard Smith, *Between Mutiny and Obedience: The Case of the French Fifth Infantry Division during World War I* (Princeton, NJ: Princeton University Press, 1994).
6. Esher journal, 6 August 1916, in M. V. Brett and O. Brett (eds.), *Journals and Letters of Reginald Viscount Esher, vol. 4: 1916–1930* (London: Ivor Nicholson & Watson, 1938), p. 45.

7. 24 August 1917, Corday, op. cit., p. 273.

8. November 1914, ibid., p. 31.

9. Jay Winter, 'Demography', in Horne (ed.), *Companion to Word War 1*, pp. 248–62, 248–51.

10. Stéphane Audoin-Rouzeau and Annette Becker, *1914–1918: Understanding the Great War* (London: Profile Books, 2002), p. 1.

11. Margaret Macmillan, *The War that Ended Peace* (London: Profile Books, 2013).

12. Lloyd George, *War Memoirs*, i, p. 617.

13. 'Foreword to New Edition', David Lloyd George, *War Memoirs* (London: Odhams Press, 2 vols., 1938), i, pp. v–vi.

14. Ibid, p. vi.

15. Chandos, *From Peace to War*, pp. 83–84; *The Great War*, BBC Television, 1964.

16. Cailleteau, *Gagner la grande guerre*, pp. 203–207.

17. Quoted in Herwig, *First World War: Germany and Austria-Hungary*, p. 425.

18. Scott Stephenson, *The Final Battle: Soldiers of the Western Front and the German Revolution of 1918* (Cambridge: Cambridge University Press, 2009).

19. Herwig, op. cit., p. 445.

20. Charles S. Maier, *Recasting Bourgeois Europe: Stabilization in France, Germany and Italy in the Decade after World War I* (Princeton, NJ: Princeton University Press, 1975).

21. 11 November 1918, Binding, *Fatalist at War*, pp. 244–45.

22. Erich Ludendorff, *Der Totale Krieg* (Munich: 1935), trans. A. Rappoport, *The Nation at War* (London: Hutchinson & Co., 1936).

23. 3–26 November 1918, Barbellion, *Last Diary*, pp. 25–27.

24. George L. Mosse, *Fallen Soldiers: Reshaping the Memory of the World Wars* (Oxford: Oxford University Press, 1990).

25. Lieutenant-General Baron von Freytag Loringhoven, *Deductions from the World War* (London: Constable, 1918), p. 142.

26. Lyttelton to his mother, 21 September 1916, Chandos, op. cit., p. 166.

27. Lyttelton, *The Memoirs of Lord Chandos*, pp. 161–62.

28. David Egerton, *Warfare State: Britain, 1920–1970* (Cambridge: Cambridge University Press, 2006).

29. Chandos, op. cit., pp. 148–61.

30. Gary Sheffield, 'The Shadow of the Somme: The Influence of the First World War on British Soldiers' Perceptions and Behaviour in the Second World War', in Paul Addison and Angus Calder (eds.), *Time to Kill: The Soldier's Experience of War in the West, 1939–1945* (London: Pimlico, 1997), pp. 29–39, 35–36.

31. Richard Overy, *Russia's War* (London: Penguin, 1997), p. 288.

# ACKNOWLEDGEMENTS

IN WRITING A BOOK THAT HAS TAKEN TWENTY YEARS OF RESEARCH AND thought the debts owed to family and friends, colleagues, archivists and librarians and students are immense. Groups and individuals have lived with my interest in the First World War (and some would say my unhealthy admiration for Foch) for many years. If I cannot acknowledge all of them individually, nonetheless I thank all those who I have taught, lectured to, listened to or on occasion disagreed with for the stimulation and insight that this has brought. I can justly claim having now written about the whole of the First World War that I still know very little about it. Any errors of fact and interpretation that therefore remain are my own.

First and foremost I must thank Limor who has been by my side while I have been writing this book. Her love and support have been all and more than an author could wish for. I owe her apologies for the way this book has taken over my life for the last two years, and thanks that she has stuck with it and with me, and diverted me from it when needed. I must also thank the Simhony family who have welcomed me as a son. I am so glad that she and they will be by my side for my next book.

My own family have also been supportive and interested over the years and during the writing of this book. My father James, my sisters Mary and Anna, my brothers-in-law Paul and Ben and my niece and nephews, Elena, Tom and Sam have all been welcoming and helpful in ways that I cannot list (but I can thank Anna and Ben for lending me their house in Cambridge). This book is dedicated to my late mother May, who although she did not live to see me write this book would have been very proud that I did.

The students and colleagues who have engaged with me on the subject of the First World War are numerous. My King's College London undergraduates in the course 'The Emergence of Modern War, 1914–1921' and my postgraduates in the courses 'Entente at War' and 'Mind, Body and Spirit in the First World War' may not have been aware of it, but they were the sounding boards for my ideas, and the providers of considerable insight themselves. Among my always engaging research students and colleagues, the members of the First World War Operations Research Group not only stand at the forefront of current research on the military conduct of the First World War, but were also vital helpers since they allowed me to develop and refine key ideas in good company and convivial surroundings. The published work of Jonathan Boff, Jonathan Krause and Tim Gale has directly informed this book, and the insights and judgments of other members of the 'Coal Hole club' have been invaluable on so many occasions which cannot be directly identified and acknowledged. The members of the University of London's Institute of Historical Research's military history research seminar have also provided a thoughtful audience for my developing ideas, as well as good company down the years. The same must be said of the members of the British Commission for Military History, who have given back more than they have taken out of me, their Secretary General. My colleagues in the Department of War Studies have been as ever interested and helpful as my work has progressed. The award of a term of research leave in 2012 was vital for the timely progression of this book, for which I thank my then Head of Department, Professor Mervyn Frost. Dr Simon House and Professor Stephen Badsey read this book in early draft. Both helped me strengthen weaknesses in my argument, and saved me from careless errors of fact and interpretation, for which I am most grateful.

Among my friends, Sophy Kershaw deserves thanks not only for her continued friendship and support, but especially for reading the second draft of the manuscript speedily and with care. Her sharp editorial eye saved me from many errors and her insightful comments greatly improved both the clarity and style of the book. Amy Marshall and her family lent me their home, and I thank them for providing a restful writer's retreat: I hope Steve enjoys the book. Jean-Yves and his team at the Beaujolais have as ever provided a hungry writer with a welcoming estaminet. As always, my many other friends have been supportive and patient and I am sorry if I have been too busy while writing this book to enjoy their company as much as I would have liked. A special thank you should go to the 'Diplomats', who have tried to show me that France might not necessarily have won.

Finally I must thank Dan Crissman and his editorial team at Overlook who have provided the support and guidance needed to bring the book to is finished form, and my agent Charlie Viney whose efforts on my behalf have once again been invaluable at all stages of the process of creating the work.

# INDEX